INDIRECT SUBJECTS

NOLLYWOOD'S
LOCAL ADDRESS

Indirect
Subjects

Matthew H. Brown

DUKE UNIVERSITY PRESS   Durham   2021

Printed in the United States of America on
acid-free paper ∞

Project editor: Annie Lubinsky

Designed by Matt Avery

Typeset in MeropeBasic Regular by
Westchester Publishing Services

Library of Congress Cataloging-in-
Publication Data
Names: Brown, Matthew H., [date] author.
Title: Indirect subjects : Nollywood's local
address / Matthew H. Brown.
Description: Durham : Duke University Press,
2021. | Includes bibliographical references and
index.
Identifiers: LCCN 2020056100 (print) |
LCCN 2020056101 (ebook)
ISBN 9781478013280 (hardcover)
ISBN 9781478014195 (paperback)
ISBN 9781478021506 (ebook)
Subjects: LCSH: Motion pictures—Nigeria—
History. | Motion picture industry—
Nigeria—History. | Mass media and culture—
Nigeria—History. | Mass media—Political
aspects—Nigeria—History. | Mass media
policy—Nigeria. | BISAC: SOCIAL SCIENCE /
Media Studies | PERFORMING ARTS / Film /
History & Criticism
Classification: LCC PN1993.5.N55 B76 2021
(print) | LCC PN1993.5.N55 (ebook) |
DDC 791.4309669—dc23
LC record available at https://lccn.loc
.gov/2020056100
LC ebook record available at https://lccn.loc
.gov/2020056101

Cover art: Stills from *Checkmate* (1991–1994,
Nigeria). Crystal Gold/Moving Movies.

*Duke University Press gratefully acknowledges
the University of Wisconsin-Madison's Office of
the Vice Chancellor for Research and Graduate
Education, which provided funds toward the
publication of this book.*

Contents

Acknowledgments

As is the case for many people in my profession, this book is both the product of and the ticket to my dream job. Therefore, the first thing to acknowledge is the immense privilege that this book represents. To have the opportunity to study a subject for more than a decade, to write many drafts about it, to have many different people read and offer feedback on those drafts (and not just for pleasure but often for the sake of their own jobs) makes me unfathomably fortunate. Do I deserve that fortune? In many ways, no, because part of what allowed me to live on a graduate student's stipend for many years, take long trips to Nigeria (often with my spouse), get taken seriously every time I spoke up, gain access to certain spaces across Africa, and much more derives largely from my Whiteness and my masculinity. It would be a severe oversight to fail to *acknowledge* those privileges here. The reader will have to judge for themselves whether I have put those privileges to work in any useful way. And if I have, well, that is the least I could do. Moreover, I must acknowledge that doing so gains me even greater privilege, which I must admit is one of the reasons I have done the work in the first place.

Although Whiteness and masculinity aid success, they do not, by themselves, constitute the skills and passions that make writing a book possible. Indeed, I had to learn those skills, and even some passions, by apprenticing myself to many people far more accomplished than I — none more so than the late Tejumola Olaniyan, my chief scholarly mentor. Teju was well aware of all the privileges that propelled me in this profession, but he worked very hard to ensure that they were not wasted. I am more deeply indebted to him than I can articulate here, but it suffices to say that I would not have found myself in the position to write this book without his guidance. It is to him that this book is dedicated. And as I acknowledge the role that he played in shaping this book, I must also acknowledge the role that members of his family played in making it possible for him to work so hard and maintain his presence, not just in my life but in the lives of so many other colleagues. Moji, Bola, and Bimpe, *Mo dupe.*

Others to whom I have apprenticed myself, in one way or another—whether they realize it or not—include Moradewun Adejumobi, Karin Barber, Jonathan Haynes, Adeleke Adeeko, Carmela Garritano, Akin Adesokan, Brian Larkin, Keyan Tomaselli, Hyginus Ekwuazi, Akintunde Akinyemi, the late Frank Nwachukwu Ukadike, Ato Quayson, Henry Drewal, Cilas Kemedjio, Juliana Makuchi Nfah-Abbenyi, and Ann Elizabeth Willey. They all have my sincerest appreciation.

This book contains little in the way of ethnography or interviews, but it would not have been possible without my spending time in Nigeria. During many trips, long and short, I made friends and connected with minds that have inspired much of what appears on the following pages. To Abigail and Vincent Ihaenacho, I will never forget our nights of watching Nollywood movies and Mexican *telenovelas*, eating lemon cake, and laughing hysterically. To Joseph Ayodokun and his family, you have kept my research *and* my love of Nigeria constantly moving forward. Tejiri Aweto, "Chairman," you too much, o! Thanks also to Festus Olaoye and his family for many good meals and many hours of yelling at the Africa Magic channel. To the Elebuibon family in Oshogbo, especially Lola: *E ku oro omo. E pele. Ba mi ki gbogbo ebi yin.* And to the Oyebisi family, my first taste of Nigerian TV was in your welcoming home, where I learned that the screen was not something simply to look at but to engage with, something that comes alive when our own voices bounce off it. *E se ganan ni o.*

I also learned about the other side of the screen from many Nigerian professionals who were patient enough to talk to me or, indeed, let me watch them work. Emem Isong, the late Amaka Igwe, Charles Igwe, the late Adebayo Faleti, Tunde Kelani, Clarion Chukwurah, Desmond Elliot, Uche Jombo, Monalisa Chinda, Joseph Benjamin, Nse Ikpe Etim, Bhaira Mcwizu, Uduak Isong Oguamanam, Austin Nwaolie, Temisan Etsede, Emeka Duru, Bode Sowande, Emeka Mba, "Christian Dior," and Adegboyega Arulogun, thank you for your brilliance, time, energy, and indulgence.

This book is also profoundly shaped by my years as a graduate student, during which I was extremely lucky to take classes, work, write, and hang out with people who still inspire me. Many continued thanks to Akinsola Ogundeji, John Stafford Anderson, Carmen McCain, Joseph Chikowero, Florence Ebila, Frances Lukhele, Mary Youssef, Mukoma wa Ngugi, Ben Cross, and Olusegun Soetan. Other scholars I met in those days who still inspire me include Laura T. Murphy, Esther de Bruijn, Kirk

Sides, Matthew Omelsky, Lindsey Green-Simms, and Cajetan Iheka. I also received important financial support for my research during those years in the form of a Fulbright-Hays DDRA fellowship and a grant from the Ebrahim Hussein Foundation. Since grad school, support for this research has been provided by the University of Wisconsin–Madison Office of the Vice Chancellor for Research and Graduate Education with funding from the Wisconsin Alumni Research Foundation.

Indeed, writing this book has depended on the supportive professional environment at UW–Madison, especially in the Department of African Cultural Studies. I am grateful to former and current faculty, including the late Harold Scheub, Aliko Songolo, Jo Ellen Fair, Michael Schatzberg, Ron Radano, Luís Madureira, Dustin Cowell, Katrina Thompson, Nevine El Nossery, Vlad Dima, Sam England, Marissa Moorman, Mustafa Mustafa, John Nimis, Damon Sajnani, Reginold Royston, Jacqueline-Bethel Tchouta Mougoué, and Ainehi Edoro, for making the quotidian chores of running a department feel meaningful and at times even enjoyable.

Many of the conversations that I have tried to weasel my way into with this book are being advanced in books published by Duke University Press. It has been both an honor and a pleasure to work with the staff at Duke, especially my gracious and indefatigable editor, Elizabeth Ault.

Above all, the work that went into this book was possible only because of great support at home. To my parents—Edward, Kathie, Laurie, and Becky—and my sisters, Lesley and Katie, thank you for shaping me. To my father, Edward, thanks especially for fostering critical thinking in our home. And to my mother, Kathie, thanks for instilling in me your love of language, of telling stories, and of conjuring good things in the kitchen. I thought about this book while cooking as much as anywhere else. My partner, Sarah—who has traveled with me throughout Africa and Europe, and who has inhaled as much archival dust as I have—is my primary coconspirator in this endeavor. She has my deepest love and gratitude. And although they did not conspire, as such, my children, Louis and Hazel, certainly found ways to impress themselves upon this project. It is for them that I keep pressing ahead.

Introduction

The title of this book is a prism. By focusing the light of Nigerian screen media on it, three observable wavelengths disperse, illuminating Nollywood—Nigeria's commercial film industry—in different but complementary ways. At one end of the spectrum, *indirect subjects* are ancillary thematic concerns, the subjects of narrative exposition and contemplation that operate at a slight remove from the primary subjects of screen media texts. At the other end of the spectrum, *indirect subjects* are imagined spectators, members of a theoretical public addressed and positioned by certain examples of screen media in certain ways. They are invited by Nollywood and some of its antecedents to participate in the process of subject formation—of being conscious, perceiving agents who are nevertheless subject to a wide range of material and ideological limits on perception—but they are invited to participate indirectly, both as central to and held at arm's length from the political and economic processes that shape the modern world. In the middle of the spectrum is a wavelength more clearly visible to the naked eye. It initiates the method by which this book gains access to the extreme ends of the spectrum and sees Nollywood as part of a larger cultural and historical formation. In film theory terms it is known as *free indirect subjectivity*.

This book is premised on the idea that deeply historicizing and critically theorizing Nollywood and its relationship to key concepts in global political economy require close attention to matters of audiovisual form and style. The introduction to this book is therefore designed to illustrate not only how the formal convention of free indirect subjectivity works in Nigerian screen media but also how it can help us see the whole spectrum of Nollywood's indirect subjects. After drawing attention to the ancillary thematic concerns of two important examples and how those concerns are addressed to imaginary publics, this introduction then develops a vocabulary to render the indirect subjects of Nollywood historically legible. My goal is to establish that Nollywood's way of addressing its public often participates—both critically and uncritically—in a discourse about modernity, and Africa's place in it, that stretches back more than a century and that I call *periliberalism*. To see how the prism works, and why periliberalism helps describe it, let us consider two scenes from Nigerian screen media.

SCENE ONE: *CHECKMATE*

Ada Okereke (Mildred Iweka), a principal character from the early-1990s soap opera *Checkmate*—which ran on Nigeria's state television network for five years—lies in a hospital bed (see figure I.1). Her husband, Nduka (Bimbo Manuel), sits in a chair next to her. He is doubled over with shame and pity, his head resting on Ada's mattress, while she lightly strokes the back of his neck. Nduka's family put her here. They do not approve of his marriage, and while he was at work the previous day, they confronted Ada, who is several months' pregnant. She tried to escape but fell onto her belly. Now, as the camera zooms out to disclose the full tableau—Nduka's penitence, Ada's gesture of solace—a voice-over invites spectators into Ada's subjectivity. "I've got to leave you," she laments.

Ada's lips do not move. Instead, spectators are being offered an opportunity to hear her thoughts, as though her consciousness were telling a story in addition to the one the camera is telling. The image then cuts to a medium shot of Nduka, a flashback, in which he professes his love. Here the camera is positioned just to the left of Ada, capturing some of her hair in the frame. Therefore, the visual perspective of the flashback is not hers but that of a third-person narrator, as if it were inviting spectators to recall this scene. In other words, this memory belongs to the "narrator," not Ada. After Nduka's "I love you," the image cuts back to the hospital, once again showing the couple from a similarly distant, third-person point of view. On the sound track, however, spectators continue to hear Ada's voice, as if inside her head: "I know, but I have to think about myself and the baby too. I don't want to hurt you, but your people are monsters. They are wicked!"

Two more flashbacks then quickly roll by. The first shows members of Nduka's family lashing out at Ada. "What haven't they done to me?" the voice-over continues. The second shows a Christian *Aladura* prophet who is blessing water that Ada will later drink in hopes of becoming pregnant. "What haven't I done to make them happy?" she asks. These two

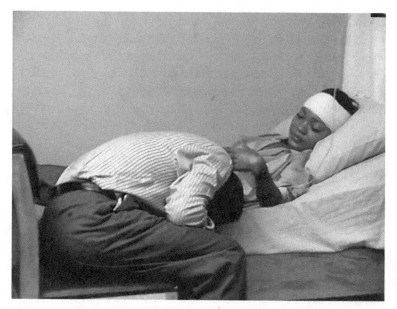

FIGURE I.1. *Checkmate.* Ada consoles Nduka while spectators hear her thoughts.

vignettes, coupled with Ada's words, suggest that her pregnancy, which did not come easily, was pursued as much for the sake of her in-laws as it was for her and her husband. "I have even sought help," she adds, referring to the prophet. "What more can I do?" The image then returns to the hospital—this time offering a close-up of Nduka, still prostrate—as Ada concludes, "I will always love you, my dear. Mom and Anne, they don't understand that I love you too. But I've got to let you go. I've got to let you go. I've got to let you go."

Before the scene ends, spectators are treated to one final flashback. Ada's mother and Ada's best friend, Anne (Ego Boyo, née Nnamani)—the central character of *Checkmate*—are visiting the hospital. Ada has just apprised them of her intention to leave Nduka, but they plead with her to reconsider. "Don't hurt the darling boy," Ada's mother implores. "I mean it. Don't hurt him."

SCENE TWO: *LIVING IN BONDAGE*

Andy Okeke (Kenneth Okonkwo), protagonist of the 1992 film *Living in Bondage* (dir. Chris Obi-Rapu[1]), sits on a large chair in his parlor. The camera zooms in to a close-up of his forehead, and the image dissolves, then cuts to a scene of several bare-chested men, surrounding a red altar, over which looms a tall man cloaked in black. Immediately, one of the bare-chested men—it is Andy—falls to his knees, arms stretched toward the ominous figure, who issues a stern ultimatum in Igbo. Translation: "Andy, if you don't bring your wife at the next meeting, you will die!" This is another flashback. Like Ada's in *Checkmate*, the action here is filmed from a third-person point of view, as though the narrator of the story were inviting spectators to recall this incident.

A knock then interrupts Andy's meditation. The image returns to his parlor, where he rises and walks to the door. His wife, Merit (Nnenna Nwabueze), has just returned from a visit to her family's village. Andy takes Merit's luggage and follows her to their sofa. She is wearing an electric blue head tie, a white blouse, and a green *aso oke* wrapper. Gold jewelry graces her neck and ears. As she takes her seat, she unshoulders a fashionable handbag. Andy then settles in next to her. He wears a fine red-and-gold floral-print tunic. By outward appearances, they occupy the margins of Lagos's post–oil-boom middle class—no thanks to Andy. As established in the famous first scene of the film, he has worked for several companies and has failed at several investment schemes while Merit sustains their household with a steady secretarial job, where she is sexually harassed by her boss. Several times, Andy laments that he cannot perform what he considers his duty as a provider and protector. His latest investment scheme was a total loss, prompting him to confide in a wealthy friend, Paul (Okey Ogunjiofor). In several memorable scenes of revelatory spectacle, Andy comes to learn that Paul's wealth derives from a satanic cult that specializes in human sacrifice. Andy is shocked but is willing to enlist, until the cult members demand his beloved wife. At first, he tries to pass off a prostitute as a surrogate, but as the flashback recalls, his subterfuge is easily uncovered, resulting in the high priest's ultimatum.

But Merit has good news! Her brother and parents have given her ₦50,000 (nearly $3,000 in 1992). She pulls a massive stack of cash from her handbag and passes it to Andy, who examines it and places it on the coffee table. As if enchanted, the camera lingers and then zooms in on the stack. The money temporarily buoys Andy's spirits, and he begins to speculate about starting life afresh, but his eyes fix into a distant stare, and the words of the high priest resound on the sound track once more: "Andy, if you don't bring your wife at the next meeting, you will die!" (See figure I.2.) Like Nduka, Merit cannot hear these words; they ring in Andy's head. He then slouches into the sofa, and Merit worries over the look on his face. Slowly, however, Andy straightens and begins laying the

FIGURE I.2. *Living in Bondage*. Andy hears the voice of the priest in his head.

foundations of a flimsy lie. He tells Merit that a friend has given birth to twins and that he has promised to pay them a visit. Merit claims exhaustion from her travels, but Andy convinces her to change and come with him. After a brief time cut, she emerges in a floral-print outfit matching Andy's tunic (what many Lagosians, using Yoruba terms, would call *aso ebi*, literally "family cloth"). The lie, it seems, was premeditated. Andy wore his aso ebi in anticipation of inviting Merit on this fabricated social call. As they turn to leave, a prescient feeling of uneasiness washes over Merit, and she begs to reschedule the visit, but Andy is adamant. They pass through the door, and unearthly sounds begin to echo on the sound track. The screen fades to black.

*   *   *

Common to both these scenes are brief moments in which two narrative perspectives overlap. The image assumes a detached perspective, as if the story were being told by a third-person narrator. However, the sound track provides fleeting access to a first-person point of view, or "point of audition"—Ada's in *Checkmate* and Andy's in *Living in Bondage*.[2] Essentially, spectators are invited to see with third-person eyes and hear with first-person ears. It is this invitation that constitutes *free indirect subjectivity*, the film-theory equivalent of what literary critics call *free indirect discourse*. In both media, the term designates a situation where otherwise consistent third-person narration momentarily slips into a different narrative voice, often belonging to one of the story's characters. It is not that the character simply speaks, as if quoted; rather, the character's consciousness, voiced or not, seems to take over the telling of the story, often briefly and sometimes inconspicuously. Of course, some trace of the third-person narrator always remains, rendering the character's narration of themselves inevitably *indirect*.

Free indirect subjectivity has been theorized across several periods and schools of thought in film studies and is not, therefore, beholden to any. Pier Paolo Pasolini, inspired by Russian formalists, first proposed free indirect subjectivity in the 1960s, in a series of essays concerned with cinema's growing poetic possibilities. His initial claims for the radical possibilities of indirect narration—to give voice to many subjectivities at once, and not merely through reportage—eventually gave way to what he describes as an anthropological mode of storytelling, in which "the bourgeois class itself, in sum, even in cinema, identifies itself, again, with all humanity, in an irrational interclassism."[3] Two decades later, Gilles Deleuze attempted to rescue free indirect subjectivity by way of postcolonial documentaries in which otherwise marginalized subjects take control of a film's narrative and fully collaborate with a European auteur in the telling of their own story. As Louis Georges Schwartz notes, however, only the choices of the European auteur make it onto the pages of Deleuze's book, seemingly affirming Pasolini's darkest suspicions.[4] As such, I am less interested in the possibility that free indirect subjectivity democratizes screen media narration (indeed, that would affirm a normative, bourgeois, liberal conception of the relation between screen media and society that this book disavows); rather, I treat free indirect subjectivity as an invitation to spectators to participate in the experiences of on-screen characters and therefore know themselves—however vaguely—as subjects, as agents of their own life stories who, like on-screen characters, are simultaneously subjected to many forms of political and economic circumscription. In a summary of Deleuze's thinking, Schwartz writes that this form of indirect identification is what makes cinema "a machine for producing subjectivities."[5] Therefore, moments like the ones from

Checkmate and *Living in Bondage* are indications not of screen media's potential voice so much as their *modes of address*, or the ways in which they imagine, speak to, and—as Karin Barber argues—call forth a theoretical public.[6] The question, we might say, is less about who gets to talk than who is invited to listen, and how.

Let us return to Ada's evaluation of her marriage. She is a confident, *modern* woman who generates a modest income and enjoys a great deal of personal freedom, yet her sense of personhood is refracted through her husband and his inability to shelter their marriage from external forces. Her problems would be solved, *Checkmate* suggests, if Nduka could provide for his family better: if, instead of a humble schoolteacher, unable to fend off his parents, he was a *real man*. Moreover, Ada is willing to inflict further suffering upon herself (while her mother begs her not to hurt "the darling boy") precisely because Nduka's predicament is not of his own making, because his status, the show painstakingly establishes, is the result of structural rather than personal failures. Indeed, Nduka is an ideal companion—loving, hardworking, and devoted—but at the end of the day he does not really stand on his own two feet, socially or financially. Several scenes before the one described here establish that Nduka earns far less than he is capable of earning. Their household thus relies a great deal on Ada's income, while her wealthy parents sometimes offer assistance that Nduka plainly characterizes as emasculating.

Ada's assessment of Nduka's masculinity may be normative, but it is nonetheless unlikely to align with many spectators' socially constructed conceptions of gender and family. In southern Nigeria, extended-family members are not only necessary but often welcome factors in many marriages, whereas women's productivity and financial independence, although they may be dominated by patriarchal discourse, are central features of micro- and macroeconomic life. Most households must pool resources and often do so amicably. Ada's perspective on masculinity is therefore distinct, seemingly derived from a specific, liberal, nineteenth-century ideal of companionate marriage, organized around a male breadwinner. As I will establish in chapter 3, *Checkmate*—which is otherwise primarily concerned with Ada's friend Anne, whose family and business dealings constitute the direct subject of the series—repeatedly returns to questions of Nduka's earning potential, his ability to protect Ada, and his domestic authority. The show rarely resorts to free indirect subjectivity with Anne yet often uses it with Ada, making her perspective a privileged site of spectator identification and the indirect subject of the series. I will also establish in chapter 3 that *Checkmate* is but one example of a

larger pattern that persists in later media and contributes to a recogniz-
able mode of address—that I call the *feminine melodramatic mode*—which
comments on the state of the Nigerian economy by inviting spectators
to identify with women who desire male breadwinners but who live in a
social dispensation that cannot produce them on any measurable scale.
From the subject position imagined by the feminine melodramatic mode,
therefore, women cannot expect to change the Nigerian economy, but
they can at least stand by men upon whom those expectations are then
foisted. Thus, women are indirectly subjected to a liberal ideal that
is focused on men. And if that form of subject positioning is not interchangeable with the lived realities of many southern Nigerian women,
then we must ask why it crops up over and over across the history of
Nigerian screen media. Why are spectators so often invited to identify
with women characters who have some combination of money, a job,
freedom, and access to sex yet fret about landing and keeping a particular
kind of socially and economically independent man? As I explore several
examples, I consider the kinds of political and economic fantasies that are
wrapped up in Nollywood's feminine melodramatic mode.

Living in Bondage, as I will show in chapter 4, responds to Checkmate,
initiating what I call a *masculine melodramatic mode*. The direct subject of
many of the mode's screen media stories tends to be money and its moral
ambiguity, but the examples I trace take up the indirect subject of breadwinning, which, if it is impossible to achieve—if the Nigerian economy
cannot reward the kind of hard work and conjugal devotion exemplified by Nduka, Andy, or several similar characters—then there may be
something evil lurking at the heart of breadwinner ideology. Nollywood
is clearly on to something here. However, that does not mean that Andy
should be rewarded, according to Living in Bondage, for circumventing
hard work and conjugal devotion by turning to the occult. Instead, like
the men at the center of so many subsequent Nollywood films, Andy must
reach rock bottom, must destroy those for whom he would win bread,
in order to win bread and then find salvation for his crimes through an
institution such as the church or the state. Moral rectitude, in this formulation, comes not from bypassing the unjust waiting line for the good life
but from taking one's number, and perhaps one's seat in a pew. It may be
true that life in Nigeria exposes a lie at the heart of modern conceptions
of gender. Masculinity may have always been an unsatisfactory construct
for men, and an unjust construct generally, but liberal masculinity, from
the point of view of Nigerian screen media, seems to be so clearly ideological, so obviously materialist, while being cast as immaterial, that it

must be exploded. Yet exploding it to reveal the ideological rapacity at its core is never the end of the story. In Nollywood men who stumble upon the diabolical nature of modern masculinity retreat into, or are saved by, churches and state institutions: the very ones responsible for spreading breadwinner ideology in the first place. And they do not come as reformers. Instead, they often come as supplicants, apologists for an ideal that instead of being cast aside is qualified and tempered. It is as if, through prayer and time, the liberal construct of the male breadwinner might be purified. As one popular *danfo*, or minibus, inscription proclaims, which any commuter in Lagos might see any day of the week, "God's Time Is the Best."[7]

To wait for a condition by which one's life is already conditioned, in which one not only participates but to which one contributes, yet from which one seems to be excluded is what it means to be—at the other end of our spectrum—an indirect subject. *Checkmate* invites spectators to identify with a woman who chooses to suffer spectacularly in the shadow of her hopes for a modern, companionate, male-breadwinner model of marriage, all the while knowing that Nigeria's economy produces very few people—let alone men—who win enough bread to fit the model. *Living in Bondage* invites spectators to identify with a man who, when he realizes that his wife is the breadwinner in his home, is forced to follow through with a plan to destroy her, yet he never relinquishes faith in the male breadwinner ideal. Why, once again, is that ideal so persistent, given the fact that it is relatively new to and uncommon in Nigeria? And not only the breadwinner ideal. Why do other concepts with specific meanings under liberalism, such as sovereignty and the rule of law, hold sway over other modes of address, such as the Gothic and comic modes I discuss in chapters 5 and 6? Ultimately, Nollywood is too big an industry, too complex and constantly changing, to be described in full or with any kind of finality, but this book nevertheless advances the argument that a significant number of Nollywood video films respond to liberalism—through concepts such as gender, family, and other social hierarchies—by imagining and addressing an audience that is distinctly local and has a distinct experience of the modern world that could be described as simultaneously within and without.

Elaborating on Nollywood's distinct construction of locality, within and without modernity, is a key objective of this book—to which I will return shortly—but equally important is grappling with the relationship between Nigerian state television programs, such as *Checkmate*, and Nollywood video films, such as *Living in Bondage*. By "video films," schol-

ars of African screen media mean feature-length films that, beginning
in the late 1980s, were produced by midlevel entrepreneurs operating in
the informal economic sector and using video technology to release their
stories into the market as hard copies, initially on VHS and later on VCD.[8]
Video filmmaking in Nigeria would not be known as "Nollywood" until
2002,[9] but it very quickly constituted a major revolution in audiovisual
storytelling that over the last three decades has dramatically changed
the media landscape in Africa and made Nigeria one of the world's most
prolific filmmaking nations.[10] Why would these two media forms—state
television and commercial video film—one operating squarely within
Nigeria's formal economic sector, the other produced by informal means
(without state sponsorship, loans, a regulated paper trail, or other forms
of institutional support), imagine and address similar publics in similar
ways? By examining many examples of Nigerian state television and their
relationship to Nollywood, this book argues that despite the divergent
means of production and dissonant political mandates of each form,
they participate in a system of governmentality that has long sustained
liberalism.[11]

To make my case, I will establish that liberal governmentality extends
beyond Nigerian screen media yet is exemplified by them. Indeed, Nigeria's relationship with liberal governmentality long precedes screen
media, stretching all the way back to the pivotal role that Nigeria played in
constituting the global system of trade from which mercantile capitalism
emerged. To quickly retell a well-known story, many parts of Nigeria—
especially in the south of the country, with which this book is primarily
concerned—supplied the material and conceptual resources on which
the modern world is built.[12] Several locations became slave-trading ports
that abetted massive amounts of capital accumulation in the global North.
Many also produced key commodities—such as palm oil, cocoa, cotton,
and crude oil—that were central to both industrialization and the rise of
global mass consumer culture. And of particular concern for this book,
many locations in southern Nigeria have served as a laboratories for juridical innovations that have sustained capitalist enterprise as well as liberal
political philosophy for four centuries. In fact, southern Nigeria played a
decisive role in the resolution of several crises that threatened liberalism
in the late nineteenth and early twentieth centuries, as I will soon explain.
A short time later, between the two world wars, southern Nigeria also
provided the raw material for emerging forms of global cinema culture,
which I describe in chapter 1. Today, having been united with the Colony
and Protectorate of Northern Nigeria, and then becoming a sovereign

nation-state in 1960, the South is part of the most populous country in
Africa with the biggest economy on the continent. It is a place without
which global modernity would not be what it is and without which global
conceptions of Africa would be quite different. Yet when screen media
arrived in Nigeria, they did not represent Nigeria's central position in the
liberal world order. Nor did they represent Nigeria's marginality. Instead,
from colonial cinema through video film, screen media have positioned
themselves between the liberal world order and an imagined public, one
that supposedly understands and desires all the benefits of liberal modernity, that feels entitled to its share, but whose job in sustaining that
version of modernity is to endure without it until, it bears repeating, conditions somehow change. If, in the context of 1950s Cuba, television can
be said to have been "broadcasting modernity," as Yeidy M. Rivero writes,
Nigerian television screens seem to have been *mediating modernity* — that
is, situating themselves between modernity and ordinary people as part
of a larger social process.[13]

   In the remaining pages of this introduction I sketch the conceptual
means by which this book envisions and historicizes that "larger social
process," where Nigeria is both central to and held at arm's length from
the liberal world order. To capture those spatial dimensions while also
trying to avoid unnecessarily cumbersome phrasing, I resort to a neolo-
gism, *periliberalism*, that describes the ideological nature of indirect subjection and its function as a form of global governmentality. Following an
elaboration of periliberalism, I then explore this book's relationship to the
field of Nollywood studies before describing the role that each chapter
plays in supporting my key arguments.

PERILIBERALISM

*The problem, of course, is to uncover the rules, regularities, and reproductive logics that under-
pin our current condition — a condition that is of necessity global, although always global in a
variety of local ways, shapes, and forms.*[14]

— ACHILLE MBEMBE

The story of *Indirect Subjects* begins in the formal colonial period, around
the turn of the twentieth century (see chapter 1). Until then, it was not
necessarily clear, or a foregone conclusion, that societies in Africa would
be held at arm's length from the increasingly global political and economic order that Europeans had been constructing — relying on African
and other non-European resources — since the fifteenth century. Liberal
accomplices of empire, such as John Locke and Edmund Burke in Britain,

as well as Alexis de Tocqueville in France, conceptualized colonialism as a process of economic integration and convergence.[15] They did not deny the fact that colonial conquest was an illiberal enterprise, but they imagined that it was the means to more noble ends. Let us be clear: that was non-sense. Instead of simply trading freely with parties in various locations across the planet, European joint stock companies and, later, imperial states imposed political and military subjection on non-European people in order to extract as much surplus value from them as possible. Thus, the core principles of liberalism—including property rights, individual liberty, open markets, and the need for a juridical infrastructure, such as contract law, capable of ensuring the free deployment of property in open markets—were mendaciously subverted in the sanctimonious process of spreading liberal values. That critique, of course, is not new. It is one of the foundational, if implicit, arguments of postcolonial theory. Even in political theory, as Uday Singh Mehta has written, "when viewed as a his-torical phenomenon, the period of liberal history is unmistakably marked by the systematic and sustained political exclusion of various groups and 'types' of people."[16] However, those exclusions were repressed enough during the first few centuries of the "period of liberal history" that they would return with a vengeance by the turn of the twentieth.

The effects of that return are taken up in several recent interventions in the study of what scholars now call *liberal imperialism* (or *imperial liberalism*).[17] For the purposes of this book the overlapping perspectives of Karuna Mantena and Mahmood Mamdani on the subject of "nativism," as well as the revisionist materialism of Onur Ulas Ince and his use of the term *colonial capitalism*, best illustrate how it came to pass that by the beginning of the twentieth century, instead of converging with Europe, vast regions of the world were decisively and, from the point of view of European investors, productively being held at arm's length from the political and economic body of liberalism. Indeed, the features of what I am calling periliberalism lie where these recent revisionist histories intersect.

In *Alibis of Empire*, Mantena argues that by the time colonial holdings in Africa were formalized at the 1884 Berlin conference, the project of liberal imperialism had come under threat in Britain. In some circles the 1857 Indian rebellion, followed closely by the 1865 Morant Bay rebellion in Jamaica, brought the purpose and efficacy of liberal colonial policy into question. Many wondered why colonial subjects would rebel if they were being integrated into a system of converging global prosperity. And when colonized subjects did rebel, many liberals wondered what methods were appropriate for responding. Should rebellions be put down militarily or politically embraced? John Stuart Mill, a foremost defender of what many imagined were the most egalitarian principles of imperialism—its so-called civilizing mission—pursued vigorous prosecution against the governor of Jamaica, Edward John Eyre, for brutally suppressing the Morant Bay rebellion, although Mill's efforts came to naught. The prevailing sentiment in Parliament as well as the wider society favored the use of illiberal force to protect imperial interests. Meanwhile, several members of Parliament sought a state of exception to use illiberal force in their own backyards, hoping to suppress what was then an increasingly vocal campaign for manhood suffrage. As Mantena writes, they "likened the Hyde Park riots to the events of Morant Bay as evidence of a growing anarchy fanned by liberal sentimentalism." However, those reactionary impulses only fanned the flames of liberal imperialism. Mantena's core argument is that the liberal project was saved by a conservative idea, *indirect rule*, revealing an uncanny symbiosis between liberal and conservative thought.[18] To get there, she focuses on Henry Maine, the historian who in 1862 was appointed as legal member of council to the viceroy's cabinet in India and who, in the course of his work, would generate the principles upon which the British version of indirect rule was built.

Maine's ideas are the subject of Mantena's history of liberal politics, but they are also the subject of Mamdani's work on the long-term political implications of colonial administration in Africa. The key concept in both cases is "nativism," the ideological distinction between and even promotion of incommensurable differences between regional cultures, even races. As Maine theorized it, European culture, from Roman times on, was built on a foundation of laws that rationalized people's understanding of community and morality. Meanwhile, "oriental" societies, according to Maine's diagnosis, clung to ancient regimes of "custom" that mystified social relations and principles of moral conduct. Maine's conclusion—that non-European societies may be complex and even fascinating but also ill-equipped for liberal jurisprudence—warranted, to his thinking, the isolation, close study, and protection of "native" cultures. They may have been slated for eventual liberalization, but the process was to be carried out slowly and deliberately to avoid fracturing ancient social bonds and thereby contributing to political upheaval. Moving too fast would only lead to results like those in Jamaica. In order to manage the growing conceptual space between the metropole and "natives," Maine called for collaboration with local political elites in the colonies. He assumed that those who understood local society best—such as the African chiefs and emirs who would become the so-called native authorities under indirect rule—could mediate between the dynamism of law and the static tendencies of custom. Maine's ideas influenced several colonial policy innovations across the British Empire but achieved their fullest expression in Africa. Mantena describes Maine's theoretical moves as "alibis of Empire," which she argues "made possible the deferral and disavowal of moral and political responsibility for imperial domination."[19]

Maine's alibis were taken up by Fredrick Lugard, who experimented with their application in Nigeria—first in the North, then in the South. However, Mamdani has long argued that the version of indirect rule with which Lugard is widely associated was already at work to some degree in other parts of British Africa. Indeed, what Lugard implemented was a more formal variation of the practice that was already well on its way to becoming apartheid in South Africa. Rather than forcibly alter native forms of social organization, the architects of apartheid and indirect rule concluded that colonial governments should define a geography within which native society could flourish and *allow* it to abide by its own legal and political authority, which, of course, merely quarantined native society from the commercial and political processes that otherwise shaped colonial life, especially in urban centers and ports. This conceptual and material segregation resulted in the bifurcation of what Mamdani refers to "citizens" of empire and its "subjects."[20] Moreover, Mamdani argues that the economic, legal, and geographic inequalities inherent to indirect rule continue to be "reproduced through the dialectic of state reform and popular resistance" in contemporary Africa.[21] Much of that popular resistance now occupies urban centers, so the division is no longer neatly urban versus rural. The former subjects of empire have become citizens of postcolonial nation-states; nevertheless, they remain—to a large extent—subjects, though indirectly, of the liberal world order that was constructed on and eventually supplanted empire.

More recently, Mamdani has also taken up Maine's body of work by way of returning to the theoretical roots of indirect rule, noting that in addition to setting limits on the degree to which colonial subjects could access the liberal world system, "The prerogative to define the boundary, the substance and the authority of the 'customary,' gave vast scope to the powers of the occupying authority."[22] Besides creating spaces outside of the liberal world order, therefore, indirect rule enlarged and enhanced the hegemonic power of liberalism. And it was this increased power, along with the disavowal of moral questions raised by intellectuals such as Mill, that not only resolved—or at the very least papered over—the crisis of liberal imperialism but also made the liberal project stronger than ever. Indeed, it became fashionable among British liberals to celebrate, as a form of reverence for authenticity, the removal of Africans from the very modernity built on their backs (which I further illustrate in chapter 1 by exploring the creation, exhibition, reception, and distribution of film in and from Nigeria during the early twentieth century). However, the attempted removal of Africans from modernity saved liberalism in more than political and conceptual terms; indirect rule also reinvested in the material processes by which liberal capitalism had emerged and long sustained itself.

The idea that colonial rule was driven primarily by the logic of capital accumulation is, like the idea that liberalism is inherently exclusionary, not at all new. Indeed, for Marxist political economists the so-called imperial turn in studies of liberal political philosophy must seem more than a little belated. Lenin defined imperialism as the "highest stage of capitalism," in which the foundations of the liberal world system were financed by the political and material domination of colonies.[23] Frantz Fanon wrote in *The Wretched of the Earth* that the polished emblems and executors of liberal jurisprudence—colonial flags and police—are just the grimy signifiers of violent expropriation.[24] And Walter Rodney argued that through colonialism, Europe not only profited from but also painstakingly "underdeveloped" Africa.[25] Indeed, centuries of liberal claims to have spread democracy and human rights may be easily interpreted as nothing more than good old-fashioned bourgeois false consciousness. More recently, however, where some theorists of liberalism are willing to admit only that its rise was unfortunately accompanied by colonial violence, Ince makes a compelling case for colonial violence as the economic and philosophical bedrock of liberalism, a form of "primitive accumulation," which in Marx's original formulation is less the highest stage of capitalism than its larval stage. As Ince phrases it, primitive accumulation is "a frontier phenomenon that arises at the interface of accumulative and nonaccumulative logics of social reproduction and consists in the assimilation or subordinate articulation of the latter to the former through the deployment of extraeconomic and extralegal force."[26] Key here is the idea that capital makes use of "extraeconomic" political and social logic—in addition to brute force—to define and enclose zones free from capital accumulation, all for the purposes of either imminent or eventual expropriation. Ince's formulation aptly describes the Scottish land enclosures on which Marx based his theory of primitive accumulation, but it also describes many later processes, including what Ince straightforwardly describes as "colonial capitalism."[27] Colonies, according to this perspective, functioned for European liberals as spaces where crucial political, legal, and economic experimentation could be undertaken. However, they were not uniformly horizontal spaces; indeed, they were economically topographical, with mining and port cities occupying the highest elevations, as it were, while the native authority jurisdictions of indirect rule came to define low points on the economic map: the areas below global liberal sea level. Therefore, zones subject to indirect rule were not beyond capitalism, nor were they straightforwardly exploited for their wealth in rubber, cotton, gold, copper, labor, and so on (although of course they were). They were included in liberalism by being excluded from many forms of direct capital investment and sometimes from direct exploitation while being subjected to all manner of bureaucratic vivisection. For Ince, then, capitalism is like the so-called immortal jellyfish, regularly returning to its larval stage throughout its life, living off places where its logic and modes of production are necessarily absent. Timothy Brennan has likewise argued that primitive accumulation is not only ongoing under contemporary capitalism but also serves an "image-function" in the liberal world, making modern life seem coherent by contrasting it to postcolonial chaos as well as whetting the appetites of investors by offering them a "smorgasbord of locally varied legal options" where liberal values need not apply.[28] Throughout the story of the modern world, therefore, spaces of violent illiberalism have, rather than call it into question or suggest its limitations, arisen within and fortified the liberal world order.

The term *periliberalism* may therefore seem unnecessary, even redundant, for states of exclusion from the core functions and benefits of liberalism have always been central features of the liberal philosophical framework. In fact, liberalism seems to desperately need and therefore actively reproduce its outside, conceptually and materially, in order to endure. But recognizing that fact does not tell us anything more about what the outside looks or feels like. Screen media can help, although—and this is *very* important—not because they depict or represent that outside; rather, they participate in the constitution of inside and out. Technically, they are not beyond the liberal world order, but they can make it seem as if inside and outside are distinct, that certain forms of wealth or governance are *out there* while certain reactions to it belong *in here*. For example, in the colonial and early independence periods—which I explore further in chapters 1 and 2—state-sponsored screen media participated in what historian Fredrick Cooper has called the "gatekeeper state," the colonial, then independent government that was positioned at the threshold between global political economic networks and African citizens. However, what ultimately defines a gatekeeper state, Cooper insists, is not "effective control of the gate" as much as "the intensity of struggle over it, which has had varying outcomes." In Nigeria oil has made the state what Cooper describes as a "caricature of itself."[29] The federal government has invested oil revenues in cultural projects such as its television network, which has become the most comprehensive in Africa, while marshaling those investments to position itself as the bearer of development or the gatekeeper between some form of modernity, which is not yet widely available to many of its citizens and their local aspirations.[30] However, there is no obvious reason why commercial video filmmakers, who came on the scene in the 1990s, would assume a similar position relative to their audience unless they too were struggling, in one way or another, over control of the gate. In that sense the "state" in state television should be considered in Gramscian terms, not exactly as a dominant power in postcolonial Africa and not a *"thing* to be seized" but an "arena of social contestations," to borrow Stuart Hall's phrasing.[31] It is an essential site of struggle for the meaning of modern sovereignty. The remaining chapters of this book explore why and how Nollywood, which emerged during a period of structural adjustment in Nigeria and thus without direct state oversight, would imagine and address its spectators in ways similar to the state's modes of address: as indirect subjects queuing at the gates of modernity. But first, just a few notes on etymology and semantics.

Periliberalism is not simply about being peripheral to the liberal world order; it is about being fundamentally and indispensably constitutive of the liberal world order precisely by being held at arm's length from it. My use of the term draws on a long history of liberal exclusions and self-consciously invokes a "world systems" approach to the study of global inequality, recalling such concepts as capitalist "core" and underdeveloped "periphery."[32] However, my intention is to augment the work of economic historians and political philosophers by closely attending to the formal dimensions of relatively recent cultural developments. Meanwhile, the term *periliberalism* also self-consciously invokes the concept of neoliberalism, although I hope to maintain some ambivalence about whether economic policies that supposedly reinvigorate liberal logic in the global North, with increasingly global pretensions, create substantially new experiences of liberalism in the global South. In terms of southern Nigerian screen media, we might ask whether the current liberal moment looks and feels very different from previous ones. Indeed, what periliberalism does share with certain uses of the term *neoliberalism*, especially those inspired by Michel Foucault, is an emphasis on subjectivity.[33] My aim is not so much to describe a world system as to describe a particular subjective construction of it: Nollywood's local address.

The subjectivity that I am proposing as "periliberal" is also very different from the subject position with which neoliberalism is often associated. In much of the scholarly literature, subjects of neoliberalism are described as selves invited to appraise their economic status, to accept that they have quantifiable value and therefore should calculate the return on any investment they might make with or in their own personhood, whether in time, effort, affect, or assets.[34] Their fate is tied to the rise and fall of the value of those investments, which is determined in the market. However, periliberalism describes a context in which subjects are invited to regard themselves not as sites of fungible value as much as placeholders for value. They are not—and this is key—imagined to be worthless; they may be filled with value at any time, thereby bringing value to the society, the nation, or even the empire, depending on when, where, and how one is looking. The value of the periliberal subject is therefore tied to the value of the local context, as if the subject's ability to achieve full personhood depends on whether the nation or local community can meet certain political and economic benchmarks, and vice versa. Regardless, both the local community and its members are imagined, in screen media if not other systems of address, to be sites of indeterminate, potential value precisely because they are not themselves recognized as investors or investments in the larger global market where primary value is determined. Put simply, periliberal subjects constitute zones of primitive accumulation that amplify the value of subjects who already do live and labor under liberalism proper. It is the possibility of becoming a site of liberal value, of becoming what Wendy Brown calls a "speck of capital," that may elevate current specks to positions of asymptotic desire.[35] And it is within this context that Nollywood's spectator-subjects are invited by free indirect subjectivity to tentatively identify with characters who desire certain dividends of modernity while simultaneously acknowledging that those dividends cannot yet be realized because of both the current state of the nation and, supposedly, the current state of themselves. Brown's assessment suggests that those of us who do live under conditions of fully established neoliberalism ought to find our status revolting. Yet the very notion that such a tainted status might constitute someone else's desire can short-circuit revolt—in every sense of the word. Neoliberalism thus thrives on periliberalism, although it remains worthwhile to distinguish one from the other.

My description of these political and economic logics, of the screen media aesthetics that intersect with them, and the power they all have to imagine, position, and address subjects may seem to deny the agency of those subjects. But that would be too simplistic a way of understanding both subjection and agency. To begin with, my title, *Indirect Subjects*, may suggest but is not interchangeable with the grammatical concept of an *indirect object*. Whereas indirect objects receive the action of a subject at a slight remove, indirect subjects are the actors of their own utterances. They make their world, but it would be disingenuous to deny that they do so—as James Ferguson argues—in the *shadow* of processes that otherwise organize social life on Earth.[36] If one of the central arguments of this book is that the liberal world *needs* indirect subjects, then those subjects do indeed make the world as we know it; they are just rarely imagined to be doing so directly. More importantly, my analysis of Nigerian television and video films frames screen media as the constitutive, porous barriers between subjects and objects, as the verbs—the action words—that render different noun phrases, different *things*, grammatical or meaningful. Nollywood tends to imagine its spectators as indirect subjects partly because of history and partly as a way of making history, of finding a place for and participating in the reproduction of certain logics and relationships that keep the global economic and social system running. I therefore maintain awareness not only of spectator agency but also of the agency practiced by people in the Nigerian film industry, the people who make the sounds and images I attend to in this book and who thus make the world I observe. Regardless, there is also a sense in which agency does not really matter at all.

My understanding of agency follows from the work of philosophers such as Foucault, Pierre Bourdieu, and Judith Butler; as such, it also diverges from some of the work done under the banner of African studies.[37] As Lynn M. Thomas has recently argued, African studies suffers from a widespread tendency she calls "agency as argument," the idea that Africanist research may be validated by the degree to which its overarching goal is to assert the agency of the human subjects whom it studies. For Thomas, agency is not an argument, but a fundamental assumption— along with structure—to which questions of *"form, scale, and scope"* may be posed as part of a more extensive and probing research agenda.[38] After all, human life is full of choices, small and large, made every minute of every day that constantly produce and reproduce the world. The social structures that those choices create both constrain and enable further choosing. Therefore, agency is mundane, a way to describe everyday world making, not necessarily "human creativity and resilience," as some would have it.[39] In fact, if only those choices that register as creativity or resilience are considered acts of agency, then agency becomes too privileged a category, too exclusive a domain, to be methodologically useful. It ends up looking a lot like liberal, Enlightenment conceptions of individual choice and instrumentality, which therefore obscures from view the agency of billions of people across history who participate in social life but in ways that may be complicit, socially distributed, or otherwise not easily identified according to instrumental metrics. Moreover, if agency is happening all the time, everywhere—if it is ubiquitous—then structure constitutes an especially explanatory site of analysis. Structure is the result of agency, but it also gives agency its form and makes it legible. In order to understand "indirect subjects," therefore, this book is principally concerned with articulating the structural conditions within which those subjects are imagined and to which they may contribute. Indeed, if the engine that drives the story of this book comprises the choices that Nigerian screen media professionals have made as they have produced content, it is within and against structural conditions—which they have not chosen—that video film and television experts have participated in making a world that critics and scholars can acknowledge, contemplate, scrutinize, and enjoy. The agency of Nigerian screen media professionals as well as spectators is therefore assumed: to do otherwise, to draw special attention to it or *return* it to them, as if that were possible, would be condescending. Instead, the *"form, scale, and scope"* of their agency, and the conditions that structure it, require further elaboration.

Finally, my repeated use of the phrase "arm's length," as I trace the contours of periliberalism, is meant to convey something *visceral* about the structural conditions underlying Nollywood's local address. "Arm's length" captures the closeness, mutual coconstitution, and embodiment of an otherwise abstract description of an equally abstract global order of things. I want to suggest that the shoulder of the periliberal world is held in the grip of the liberal world's (invisible) hand, although it is not embraced.[40] The two seem to be locked in this configuration. One cannot abandon the other. And for both, there may be a perverse kind of comfort in the grip. Nevertheless, the relationship is one of bodily and intimate violence. It manifests in subjective and affective categories such as Blackness and Whiteness—which, although they are abstract, or not biological, not essential but indeed contingent and historical—do real work, both damaging and productive, on real bodies every day. In fact, racialized thinking is not simply inscribed upon bodies, although it is; the social construction of race is deeply embedded in them, manifesting in intimate quotidian as well as sometimes spectacular experiences of the self, the other, and the material world. The arm in "arm's length" is thus a separator and a link. The two bodies it spans may be nominally equal in their humanity, yet the separator link produces difference and inequality; indeed, it is a form of *in*humanity. And because the arm belongs to the liberal world, it is there that inhumanity lies. The separator link, we might say, is quite simply *power* in its quintessentially modern form. Can the periliberal world escape its grip? Must it cut off the liberal world's arm, in some way either discursive or material? Must it find some new way to finally, fully decolonize? Meanwhile, does the liberal world order understand what it is doing? Does it understand how it has found itself in this posture? And in considering the ways that it might bring this destructive relationship to an end, is it ready to acknowledge that it may have missed its chance for an embrace, that it must instead let go? Perhaps the embrace can come later. But if it turns out that it really is too late, even to let go, if the liberal world has been holding on for so long that some kind of *rigor habitus* has set in, indeed, if liberalism cannot imagine itself without its stifling grip on the periliberal world, then there may be no other choice — if justice is any kind of virtue — than cutting off its own arm. If that seems unlikely to happen anytime soon, then in the meantime, as the periliberal world searches for answers and perhaps a sharp knife, we can more closely consider the arm, the separator link, the gate between the two. Thus, while exploring the many brilliant and world-making choices that Nigerian screen media producers have made over several decades, this book nevertheless considers the ways in which Nollywood and its antecedents may have participated in the performance of the separator link. That claim, of course, is not the last word on Nollywood or the only way to think about the industry, but the study of Nollywood does need new ways to think about video films, the world they imagine, and the ideological processes that bind them to one another.

NOLLYWOOD STUDIES: FORMATIONS AND FORMS

This is not the first book to acknowledge that Nigerian video films imagine modernity from a local perspective, which in turn may be different from perspectives generated in the wider liberal world. Moradewun Adejunmobi draws a contrast between the video films that built Nollywood and several newer films that depart in various ways from the original model: "Many Old Nollywood films cater to the visual pleasure of desired access to modernity by exhibiting its supposed bounty — grand homes, stylish clothing, and expensive cars—as obtained frequently through vice and debauchery. They also link the acquisition of these 'spoils' of modernity to egregious violations within the moral economy that call for appropriate penalties and the ultimate forfeiture of the 'spoils.'"[41] This kind of profound insight has rarely been pursued further, whether by scholars interested in the formal dimensions of video films or scholars examining the films' ideological ontology. In the case of Ghana, Carmela Garritano provides a generative conceptual model in which she elaborates on video films' "global desires" or "expressions of global membership." She writes that Ghanaian movies "issue strong moral condemnations of greed and the immoral attainment of wealth and yet position the spectator as a consumer, one who gazes on and desires the movie's extravagant commodity displays."[42] Meanwhile, Adejunmobi contrasts the overt morality of early video films with the aesthetics of "New Nollywood" films—which are made possible by new forms of financing, production, and distribution—in which characteristically moral modes of address may be giving way to themes of ethical ambivalence corresponding to neoliberalism's flat view of the world, in which inequality is supposedly incidental rather than inherent to the diffusion of liberal economic policy. But what accounts for the profoundly moralizing tone of early video films in the first place? And is it true that video films are "highly critical of materialism and capitalistic values," as Garritano argues? Or does criticizing materialism—when material resources are not widely available—perhaps affirm the "capitalistic values" that have organized social relations in Ghana and Nigeria in the modern era?[43] It may in fact be necessary, from the point of view of African video films, to cast materialism as immoral precisely because its pursuit is not often possible.

Such questions call for renewed attention to the ideological functions of screen media in West Africa. Brian Larkin has established a strong foundation, aptly describing the philosophy of video films as an "aesthetics of outrage" in which the "architecture of insecurity" or "widespread feelings of vulnerability" are "dramatized" in "melodramatic terms," but he also argues that "Nigerian films represent the waning of state-based visual media (from mobile film units to television dramas) and their ideologies of progress and uplift."[44] Certainly, Nollywood has eclipsed "state-based visual media" in Nigeria, Ghana, and across the African continent, but the contrast between the two may not be all that stark. State-based media, we will see, can also be profoundly moralizing, indeed profoundly given to vulnerability, outrage, and melodrama. Likewise, video films may engage in their own projects of calculated, mediated uplift. Therefore, a key objective of this book is to revisit one long-standing argument in Nollywood studies concerning the relation between the spheres of formal and informal screen media production.

In 1997 Jonathan Haynes inaugurated the academic study of Nigerian videos by publishing in Nigeria an edited collection of essays by several leading film and literary critics. Some of the authors in that volume seem to have felt compelled to draw a contrast between video films and celluloid African cinema. After all, what we might call *big-screen* African cinema has traditionally been so invested in anticolonial nationalism that many of its examples serve as proxies for the study of nation building and postcolonial statecraft. On the other hand, Nigerian video films have very different interests, more akin to certain forms of popular culture such as music and traveling theater. Videos therefore seem to have opened up space in African film and media studies to contemplate modes other than the macropolitical and power relations other than the governmental. As Haynes wrote at the time, "The radically different basis of Nigerian videos thus makes them . . . a singularly convenient subject for theoretical orientations that want to look past or around the African state."[45] In Larkin's contribution to the same volume, he argued that Nigerian video films created a new public sphere, a "cultural and political space . . . outside of the control of the state and corporations."[46]

In the meantime, however, Nigerian video filmmaking was widely recognized as the "child of television."[47] Nollywood's products, after all, were designed for viewing on television screens. More importantly, many pioneers of video filmmaking had deep professional relationships with the state television network, the Nigerian Television Authority (NTA). Some were salaried employees, whereas others had worked on independent productions broadcast by the NTA. (I review the work of many such individuals in this book.) Therefore, to call Nollywood the child of television is to say that Nigeria's formal screen media brought informal screen media into existence and raised them with varying degrees of attention. Though acknowledged by many observers, that relationship has attracted little sustained research, in part because of a lack of resources available to do so. State television productions, even those only a few decades old, are very difficult to obtain. This book is the result of a prolonged effort to scrape together enough examples to make proper comparisons, contributing to a unique though still admittedly meager archive. But there are many holes in my account, which call both for further research and plenty of speculation.

If state television and video films share some genetic material, the key difference between formal and informal media in Nigeria, as John C. McCall points out, concerns bureaucratic documentation and regulation. There is a paper trail at the NTA and associated government agencies, though often difficult to access, but no comparable forms of documentation exist with respect to the first two decades of video film production: "The video industry is a network of scattered informal economic activities and interactions held back from capitalization because the system depends on informal practices to produce and distribute its products."[48] Similarly, Alexander Bud describes the ways in which the Nigerian state has tried, and mostly failed, to establish formal means of documenting and regulating video film production and distribution.[49] And although practices are rapidly changing, with formal capitalization beginning to take hold in New Nollywood, the initial emergence of Nigerian video films had a great deal to do with commercial activity undertaken outside formal systems of authorization and accumulation.[50] As McCall puts it, "While the 'of and for the masses' quality of Nollywood's mode-of-production is extremely important, it is also the video industry's greatest obstacle."[51] Many scholars and journalists thus celebrate the grassroots origins of Nollywood, but we must be willing to acknowledge that those roots grew in soil neglected by the global economy and yet may still have been fertilized by it. My approach to comparing state television productions and video films, especially those produced in the 1990s and early 2000s, proceeds in large part from the kinds of distinctions between formal and informal, state and commercial, made by Haynes, Larkin, McCall, and Bud, but it takes seriously the idea that, as with children and their parents, Nollywood may have been shaped by state media more than it realizes.

Indirect Subjects pursues that possibility, however, not by way of industry analysis as much as through attention to matters of form and style. If state and commercial screen media modes of production are organized differently yet several individuals have worked across both, we might ask whether they have produced similar work in each sector. My primary interests lie in the formal and stylistic features of that work, the way that both television and video film address their audiences and what that might say about the politics of culture in Nigeria. I am therefore not so much invested in filling gaps in the historical record concerning Nigerian television and Nollywood, although this book does do so in places. Rather, I am chiefly interested in *critique*, the idea that scholarship can invest in and even promote the significance of a form of cultural expression not so much by uncovering all the "facts" about it but by repeatedly returning to the representations it produces. Only by (re)reading primary texts as well as (re)reading criticism do we contribute to generating a language capable of dealing with the importance and complexity of cultural expressions. So this book takes up several television programs and a few video films that have rarely, if ever, been written about before, but it also deals with several video films that have been written about extensively. My goal is to offer new terms and meanings to the critical lexicon associated with Nollywood. And to those ends, I have woven into my analysis, wherever possible, films that have received serious attention elsewhere, although I try to push the analysis of those films further and in new directions.

In my attempt, therefore, to contribute to Nollywood Studies, *Indirect Subjects* applies a formal mode of critique to audiovisual texts in order to explore several continuities, changes, and ruptures in the history of Nigerian screen media aesthetics. Undoubtedly, many important patterns and paradigms are overlooked. To wit, this book is largely silent on celluloid film production in Nigeria during the independence period. That too is about a lack of resources (I do not have access to any of those very rare films) but also because of active and acknowledged forms of neglect baked into my epistemological priorities. Nollywood video films have generally been full-length features, so they have generally invited comparisons with other feature films. This book shifts emphasis from the form of the cinematic feature to the medium and social positioning of television, with which Nollywood may have a more important historical relationship. Additionally, it is the social position of television that invites a comparison to colonial cinema, which is the subject of chapter 1. In the remaining pages of this introduction I further describe the structure and methods of the book, highlighting particular conjunctures and points of comparison while also indicating my other epistemological priorities and possible blind spots.

THE STRUCTURE OF THE BOOK

The research for this book essentially started with Nollywood and worked backward through time to state television and then to colonial cinema, yet the argument is laid out in chronological order. The first two chapters form part 1 of the book, together reconstructing the history of state-mediated motion pictures in Nigeria from colonial cinema up through television and into the early 1990s. The next four chapters form part 2, which oscillates between some of the most important and memorable of both the NTA's television serials and Nollywood's video films. The early 1990s form a kind of conjuncture—where television meets video film—around which the book is built.

Chapter 1 begins with one of the earliest documented instances of film production in Nigeria: an "expedition" undertaken by two brothers from London. The footage they *captured* would eventually play a key role in the history of global cinema, leading to the emergence of a documentary film movement in Britain and to the codification of guiding principles for film exhibition in Africa. However, the primary site of exhibition for that early footage was not in Africa but at the 1924 Empire Exhibition in Wembley. Several reviews of the exhibition as well as the films shown there—films that were created by editing and titling the raw footage from Nigeria—reveal key links among indirect rule, the medium of film, and the ascendance of a new political philosophy that celebrated, as a triumph of liberalism, the increasingly illiberal conditions prevailing in Africa.

Chapter 2 traces the related philosophical innovations that accompanied the growth of television broadcasting in postcolonial Nigeria. The key figure whose theoretical and artistic production I follow is Segun Olusola, a pioneer of radio and television who worked in various levels of government and who created Nigeria's longest-running television serial, *The Village Headmaster*. His numerous speeches and essays paint a picture of state television's conception of itself as a gatekeeper between global liberalism and the developing nation. By the 1980s, following the collapse of Nigeria's oil boom and the hollowing out of the state by structural adjustment, it seems all that was left was the relation to liberalism. Close readings of *The Village Headmaster* suggest that free indirect subjectivity was at work early in Nigerian screen media history, addressing spectators as subjects of but also sympathizers with the unwavering developmental gatekeeper state.

Chapter 3, which kicks off part 2 of the book, plays a pivotal role in the story of *Indirect Subjects*. A revolution in Nigerian television programming began in the mid-1980s, when the NTA started purchasing content from independent producers (as well as bulk distributors of Latin American content). Local public-private collaboration initiated a shift in aesthetic practices, although the mediated orientation of the developmental state to its subjects remained distinctly hierarchical. Several Nigerian soap operas, *Checkmate* (1991–1995) in particular, were at the center of that shift. They were widely popular, as suggested by newspaper reviews, and treated their spectators as sophisticated cosmopolitans, although soap operas still imagined an audience in need of developmental assistance. *Checkmate*'s key innovation, which was replicated by several subsequent Nollywood films (including early Nollywood hits made by *Checkmate*'s creator, Amaka Igwe), was its indirect focus on the ideal of the male breadwinner, a man whom women are imagined to desire and who therefore serves as the standard by which masculinity itself is measured. I refer to this formal complex as a feminine melodramatic mode of address. However, an assemblage of historical sources fleshes out the argument already signaled in this introduction that the male breadwinner ideal, while cropping up repeatedly in screen media, has featured very little in the lives of Nigerian spectators. In addition to being the measure of a man, the breadwinner ideal seems to be a fantasy by which access to a liberal form of life can also be measured.

One of the key arguments of the book is that although plenty of Nollywood's signature films carried forward the modalities of state television, others reacted forcefully, often negatively. In chapter 4 I examine this dynamic by revisiting *Living in Bondage* and several films that extend its modal operations. As I have already indicated, *Living in Bondage*—which is the subject of many great examples of Nollywood studies scholarship— characterizes what I am calling a masculine melodramatic mode of address that makes use of occult images and themes in order to respond to the feminine modalities of soap operas and related video films. Films that reuse the central story structure from *Living in Bondage*, in motif-like fashion, suggest that if the breadwinner ideal is the measure of a man, then it simultaneously represents the regulation and standardization of masculinity in ways that individual men may find troubling, to say the least. My reading, which draws on many other scholars' readings but is novel in several ways, is accentuated by close attention to the actors and key characters from state television soap operas who became iconic occult figures in Nollywood films. My approach suggests that something sinister was lurking under the surface of state television narratives that Nollywood was able to exhume. If the feminine melodramatic mode tends to address a public waiting for liberal conditions to arrive, the masculine melodramatic mode suggests that any attempt to hasten their arrival may be diabolical.

Whereas Nollywood's "occult" video films display patently gothic characteristics, I argue in chapter 5 that Nollywood's ubiquitous epic genre is characterized by a more distinctly gothic mode of address. The term *epic* is reserved in Nollywood for films set in versions of the precolonial past that are, very often, fantastically imagined. The ruins of that imagined past are designed to haunt contemporary popular culture. Of particular interest is the figure of the *igwe*, or Igbo king, who features in virtually all Nollywood epics but who is a minor player in the historical record. Drawing on the NTA's adaptation of Chinua Achebe's novel *Things Fall Apart*—a thirteen-episode miniseries that first aired in 1986—I demonstrate that Nollywood invests the image of a strong-willed, prominent man with fantasies of sovereign power. Those fantasies appear in Nollywood epics, such as *Igodo: Land of the Living Dead* (1999), which have received some attention from scholars but have rarely been the subject of close, extended critique. My readings suggest that if the nation cannot directly participate in the liberal world order, Nollywood epics have recourse to an invented past where sovereignty from outside influences may have been chaotic but was nevertheless enjoyed.

The first three chapters of part 2 draw on moments of free indirect subjectivity that are relatively straightforward: the image or the sound momentarily entering the dual perspectives of narrator and character. However, Nigerian comedies offer examples of something very different. In chapter 6 I examine *Basi and Company*, one of the most successful situation comedies in NTA history (1986–1990), which made use of a mirror, placed strategically in one of the principal sets, to provide a secondary perspective on the action of the show. One of the writers for *Basi and Company* (and sometimes an actor in the series), Nkem Owoh, went on to become Nollywood's premier comic icon. Conspiratorial mirrors also feature in some of his most beloved and successful films, including *Osuofia in London* (2003) and *The Master* (2004), which have both been studied extensively. All three primary texts tackle the issue of official corruption but in remarkably different ways. I argue that although *Basi and Company* invites its spectator-subjects to regulate their own collaborative roles in political corruption and remain skeptical of their own desires—perfectly in line with periliberal thinking—Nollywood comedies seem to revel in turning the tables, accusing the liberal world order of greedily preying upon and actively denying modernity to people who not only desire it but without whom it would never have been possible in the first place. Therefore, the comic mode of address is the most critical of periliberal subjectivity. Nollywood comedies may be addressed to indirect subjects, but indirect subjection does not necessarily rule out critical engagement with the spatial configurations of modernity.

Indeed, Nollywood's remarkable sincerity about the morality of modernity is itself a kind of criticism. Although it is overstating the case to characterize Nollywood as a clean break from statist postcolonial ambitions, it is equally overstating the case to say that Nollywood fully reproduces state governmentality. Rather, linking Nollywood's modes of address to those of the (gatekeeper) state suggests that Nollywood contributes to a form of social organization that makes it possible to endure periliberalism. In the end, it is not necessarily incumbent upon Nollywood—as it might be incumbent upon the state—to resist the liberal world order or ease Nigeria into it; rather, the liberal world order itself needs fundamental reformation—if not outright overthrow—so that its most illiberal features, especially its tendency toward indirect subjection, no longer serve as its ongoing justification and raison d'être. Reading and rereading Nollywood reiterates just how unjust liberalism continues to be.

Part I

1 Subjects of Indirect Rule

NIGERIA, CINEMA, AND LIBERAL EMPIRE

In 1922 brothers Norman and Vincent Greville, two well-established film consultants based in London, traveled through the Colony and Protectorate of Nigeria exposing hundreds of feet of celluloid film to various forms of daily life, industry, and social pageantry. Two years prior, the Grevilles had premiered a film in London about the Gold Coast colony (today Ghana), which they titled *The White Man's Grave*. It had not gone over very well. Several reviewers, showcasing their liberal bona fides, described the film as patronizing. Among their specific criticisms was the fact that it showed very few Africans, and when it did, they were usually climbing trees.[1] So for their second trip to West Africa, the Grevilles enlisted the help of a Nigeria expert, one J. Withers Gill, the former resident minister of Zaria.

In preparation for the trip, Gill wrote to the colonial secretary, Winston Churchill, asking for a meeting to discuss the expedition and methods to ensure a proper outcome. As "someone with expert knowledge," Gill recommended in his letter, he would be able to guide the Grevilles to "scenes and incidents which will illustrate the romance and colour of Native life, an [sic] well as depict the industrial developments which have followed upon modern progress."[2] By the 1920s, it had become not only genteel but also a matter of colonial policy to harmonize metropolitan interest in "native life" with the mission of "modern progress." In fact, Gill was party to the development of that policy, having served in Zaria under the governorship of Fredrick Lugard, the chief architect of indirect rule in Africa. New developments in imperial ideology, it seems, were closely aligned with emerging liberal tastes in colonial cinema.

Lugard famously described the tension between metropolitan interests in native life, on one hand, and the material development of colonies, on the other, as a "dual mandate," writing that "the civilised nations have at last recognized that while on the one hand the abounding wealth of the tropical regions of the earth must be developed and used for the benefit of mankind, on the other hand an obligation rests on the controlling Power not only to safeguard the material rights of the natives, but to promote their moral and educational progress."[3] However, Lugard did not advocate for, say, admitting a massive wave of literate Africans, of whom there were already thousands, to British universities in order to promote educational progress; instead, he developed a version of indirect rule as the practical means by which tropical wealth could be exploited while simultaneously safeguarding, if not rights per se, native institutions. Yet his fealty to those institutions was not his alone but was inspired by the comparative jurisprudence of his elder statesman, Henry Maine. Both men rejected the long-standing liberal program of wholesale social reformation in the colonies. Moreover, Lugard's implementation of Maine's ideas came at a critical moment for the British Empire. Following the First World War, global imperialism appeared to be quixotic—chivalrous, in the minds of many British policy makers, but impractical. In London, liberal political and economic orthodoxy was also being called into question, although transnational liberal projects were on the rise elsewhere, particularly in North America. If the United Kingdom was going to *carry on*, then its leaders needed a way to reconcile their increasingly protectionist instincts with growing global interest in a liberal world order, not to mention the demands of running a vast empire. Film would play a critical role in the way the process played out, and Lugard would praise it for doing so.

This chapter begins with a brief description of the context to which indirect rule responded and then moves on to chart the life of the film footage captured by the Greville brothers in Nigeria. Edited into several short films, their footage would become a key showpiece at the 1924 British Empire Exhibition as well as a forebearer of the British documentary film movement. After the exhibition gates closed, the Greville footage would also intersect with and illuminate the growth of commercial film exhibition in colonial Africa. Finally, the Greville footage eventually played a pivotal role in the emergence of "colonial cinema," the British initiative to carefully plan the production, curation, and—most importantly—exhibition of short films all across the African continent, from the biggest cities to the most remote villages. In conjunction with Lugard's "dual mandate," colonial cinema would assume a developmentalist orientation to its spectator-subjects that would have a direct influence on the ascent of state television in postcolonial anglophone countries, particularly Nigeria. What the story of the Greville brothers' footage indicates is an aesthetic link among developmentalism, indirect rule, and the salvation of liberalism.

THE DUAL MANDATE

Liberal ideals and imperial ambitions were always coeval, as discussed in the introduction to this book. Nevertheless, the term *liberal world order* has never described a sort of blanket, covering the globe, but rather a constellation of ideas, political actors, and policies separated by time and plenty of geography, though with extensive global influence. Indeed, few liberal thinkers, from the seventeenth century to the twentieth, assumed that their ideas applied to every single person and every inch of the map. However, that came into question with the "scramble for Africa" in the late nineteenth century, when most of the borders that still define contemporary maps of the continent were drawn. Before then, many indigenous African states participated in the global constellation of liberal capitalism primarily through asymmetric and exploitative trade, some of which—particularly the transatlantic slave trade—weakened African states in ways that were compoundingly favorable to European merchants. Therefore, selectively applied liberalism was quite profitable to colonists. So why alter that arrangement? Some scholars suggest that by the mid-nineteenth century, African commodity prices rose high enough to incentivize gaining political control over their production.[4] Others suggest that a sense of status sent certain European nations looking for colonies where others had already claimed territory.[5] Regardless of the underlying reasons, however, the formal colonization of the continent— in which thousands of miles of enforceable borders were drawn and legal jurisdiction was spread over vast expanses of land—was not cheap. Some Europeans, especially those given to religious evangelism, welcomed formal colonial rule enthusiastically, but many others felt browbeaten into the position of "trustees." In London, politicians quarreled fiercely with one another about how best to deal with Britain's new possessions. The scholarship on this period is vast, and it includes many narratives of vocal, public disagreement among government offices, among liberal thinkers, and even among agents of merchant and finance capital.[6] How extensive should the administrative staff on the ground be? How much money should be invested in colonial infrastructure? Should "natives" enjoy the same rights as settlers? These and other questions were hotly debated.

Indirect rule was forged in the furnace of the trusteeship debate. The doctrine's basic outlines involve establishing an official distinction between, on the one hand, modern, urban, Western legal and political institutions and, on the other, indigenous or "native" institutions. In Britain's African colonies, these sets of institutions were designed to operate in parallel. One set, governed by civil law, was staffed primarily by British personnel as well as a few Western-educated Africans and non-African immigrants, and it mirrored institutions that operated in the imperial metropole. The other set of institutions, constituting the so-called "native authority" and governed by "customary law," was staffed primarily by Africans and managed by indigenous authoritarian superintendents. Native authorities had no universal ideal form; rather, they differed from each linguistic and geographical context to the next—giving rise to the concept of "tribes."[7] Some of the "headmen," "chiefs," or "emirs" who emerged to rule each so-called tribe may have already commanded local institutions, but many others were promoted to or installed in offices that the British invented to manage otherwise decentralized communities. In any case, most native authorities acquired powers never before seen in African social organization. At the pleasure of the British empire, they collected taxes, adjudicated legal disputes, and recruited labor for colonial industry and transnational warfare, all without having to establish or maintain much in the way of local political legitimacy.

The doctrine of indirect rule is therefore often erroneously conceptualized as having been prosaically pragmatic, less a political philosophy than an efficient use of finite resources. By casting native authorities as mediators between the colonial government and its subjects, indirect rule seems to have made it possible for a relatively small number of British officials to manage a geometrically expanding empire. But indirect rule was, as I have already indicated, deeply theoretical. Karuna Mantena argues that the idea of safeguarding native society emerged from and resolved a simmering "crisis of liberal imperialism," sparked by the anticolonial rebellions and internal policy debates briefly discussed in the introduction to this book.[8] Whereas liberals were at pains to reconcile military domination with democratic governance, conservatives such as James Fitzjames Stephen seized upon the rebellions to call the entire idea of self-government into question, and not only in the colonies. In fact, British conservatives had been looking for just these kinds of reasons to reproach liberal values regarding mass enfranchisement. Suddenly, liberal ideology was no longer the kind of political consensus it once was, and it seemed as though authoritarianism and aristocracy would make a dramatic comeback. Ironically, the eventual salvation of liberalism would depend on ideas generated by the conservative resurgence.

Henry Maine's ideas, in particular, made it possible for liberalism to evolve by constructing a vast conceptual distance between colonial subjects and citizens at home as well as reducing the use of authoritarian tactics in the colonies, all without giving up on what Lugard would later describe as the "use" of "wealth" in the "tropical regions of the earth." Maine's intervention began with a deep, comparative, juridical archaeology in which he argued that the West and the non-West arrived at legal codes in different ways and for different reasons. Second, he argued that Western legal codes inherently produced progress, whereas Eastern ones were designed to preserve custom. Third, he reasoned that Eastern societies would naturally resist Western jurisprudence precisely because of its antagonism to their beloved customs. And finally, he returned to the basic assumption that imposing a liberal legal framework on colonized subjects through force or coercion not only defied and disrupted their local social systems but also vitiated the core principles of liberalism. As he put it,

> When . . . the rules which have to be obeyed once emanate from an authority external to the small natural group and forming no part of it, they wear a character wholly unlike that of a customary rule. They lose the assistance of superstition, probably that of opinion, certainly that of spontaneous impulse. The force at the back of law comes therefore to be a purely coercive force to a degree quite unknown in societies of the more primitive type.[9]

Maine therefore recommended that "traditional," "customary," and "native" society be preserved and codified in Britain's colonies. His recommendations were meant to guide policy in a direction that would strengthen imperial legitimacy while also suggesting a sense of respect—if that is what one could call it—for "societies of the more primitive type." The supposedly benevolent character of that respect also strengthened the moral legitimacy of imperialism back home. Instead of undermining the liberal project in favor of a conservative one, Maine's ideas ended up rearranging the horizons of liberal imperialism. By ruling themselves, not according to liberal institutions—which could not, Maine wrote, be "imported like steam machinery, warranted to stand any climate and benefit every community"[10]—but instead according to customs they already understood and valued, the colonized would enter modernity gradually and judiciously.

By not only allowing for but in fact endorsing social systems that contained laws starkly opposed to classical liberal ideals—such as the caste

system in India—Maine's theorizing nevertheless expanded and reinforced the ideological scope of liberalism as an *ism*. As Mantena writes,
"In its most ambitious articulations, indirect rule as political theory
was institutionally grounded in a policy of decentralization and philosophically justified as a form of cosmopolitan pluralism."[11] This pluralist
sensibility led to the subtle alteration but also reinvigoration of liberal
sensibilities concerning benevolent trusteeship. Protecting and preserv-
ing native society became hallmarks of a new brand of liberalism, one
that could continue promoting a universalist, expansionist agenda while
simultaneously justifying the limits of that agenda. Essentially, liberals
took comfort in the idea that non-Europeans were not being forced to in-
teract with the political economic system otherwise imposed everywhere.
Meanwhile, the ideological standing of concepts such as free trade,
contract law, and individual rights drew strength from their increasing
contrast with the communal rites, patriarchal authority, and the bonds
of consanguinity to which "traditional" societies supposedly clung. Although it would take a few decades and the unfolding of specific events on
the ground, Lugard would transform Maine's ideas into a set of portable
policies that, as Mamdani has long argued, became the authentic form of
colonialism, the quintessential method of managing difference, and the
eventual foundations of postcolonial governance.[12] The fact that indirect
rule was premised on placing subjects outside of liberalism while simultaneously strengthening liberalism forms the basis of what I am referring
to as *periliberalism*.

By the time Lugard put Maine's ideas to work in Nigeria and by the
time World War I had come and gone, British liberals took it for granted
that "societies of the more primitive type" fared better under a form of
rule that respected their "superstition[s]," "opinion[s]," and "spontaneous
impulse[s]." Maine had referred to those as indicators of "the real India,"
and his inheritors in Britain would likewise associate them with "the real
Africa."[13] However, a major technological development in the intervening
years made it possible for real African life, or so many people thought, to
be captured and brought to the United Kingdom.

"THE REAL AFRICAN LIFE"

When the Greville brothers arrived in Nigeria in February 1922, Lagos was
suffering a depression caused, in no small part, by Lugard's (mis)manage-
ment of the colony. Before becoming governor-general of amalgamated
Nigeria in 1914, Lugard had been governor of the Protectorate of Northern

Nigeria, where he famously experimented with indirect rule by employing emirs as administrative proxies. However, proxy rule was poorly suited
to the Southern Protectorate, particularly on the coast, where a classic,
mercantile liberal approach to foreign intervention, practiced among
generally decentralized communities, was well established. In addition to
converting human beings into commodities, mercantilism had fostered
other forms of trade as well as a large class of Western-educated Africans
and plenty of tax collection, resulting in an ample colonial treasury. Regardless, when Lugard's notorious knack for self-promotion earned him
the new governorship, he phased out lucrative forms of mercantilism in
the South and put indirect rule to work everywhere. According to Anthony
Nwabughuogu, "The old methods of assessing colonies — 'administrative
efficiency' and 'economic development' — had been abandoned. New cri-
teria were now established; the degree of strength and stability of 'native
chiefs' and their loyalty to Britain."[14]

Therefore, Britain's sense of what was good for Nigeria went from bad to
worse. The shift had dire economic consequences in the South, leading
to deep social unrest and eventually resulting in major political disasters
like the "Aba Women's War" of 1929.[15] The Greville brothers encountered
a Lagos overflowing with migrants who streamed in from the hinterland
seeking all manner of wage labor. Inflation and unemployment rates
were rising, and the city was transitioning from a thriving trading post to
a mere port, funneling commodities to other markets for exchange.[16] Indirect rule was not so much serving southern Nigerians in their languages
and customs as it was cutting them off from the liberal economy.

As one might expect, these developments received little attention from
the Greville brothers' camera. The few scenes they did shoot of Lagos,
according to Daniel Stephen, gave the impression of "a large African city
easily controlled by Europeans: ordered and prosperous, a place of business where money was being made and where the people were content,
happy, and sharing in the benefits of commerce and 'good government.'"[17]
After filming this version of Lagos, however, the Grevilles moved on to
interior towns, shooting religious and political pageants, the palaces of
kings and emirs, and various extractive industries, including cotton growing and tin mining, both of which relied on forced labor provided by the
heads of various native authorities.[18] At the end of the day the images that
the Greville brothers brought back to London highlighted the very structures of indirect rule without indicating their effects.

Having learned much from the disaster that was their first film, the
Grevilles' Nigeria footage was perfectly suited for the aesthetic horizons

toward which British liberals were increasingly groping. Indeed, metropolitan reactions to the raw footage, which was screened over several nights in 1923, were so positive that space and time were carved out for screenings at the upcoming British Empire Exhibition, which opened in 1924 on 216 acres in the London suburb of Wembley. By that time, empire exhibitions and other kinds of "world's fairs" had become common fixtures of the modern world, but Wembley, argues John MacKenzie, "was the greatest" of them all.[19] Like other exhibitions, Wembley both was motivated by and responded to recent changes in the global balance of trade.

For Britain, the years following World War I were severe for workers, industry, and even capital. Because of an acute domestic recession, coupled with the rise of newly industrialized nations, including the United States and Japan, the passionate free-trade liberalism that had propelled Britain to the apex of the global economy was increasingly muted by currents of nationalist protectionism. The Conservative government that came to power in 1922 sought to close off the import market with a tariff regime, hoping to shore up British industry and then, by turning attention to exports, bolster and expand British finance capital. The enclosure of the domestic market was incomplete, however, for Britain's imperial possessions were conceptualized as commercial halfway houses under the banner of the "commonwealth." Import duties on commonwealth commodities would remain low, placing British colonies, protectorates, and dominions in unique positions within the world economic system. Given their lack of political sovereignty, their constitution as resource hubs, and their subjection to policies that directed most of their trade toward the United Kingdom, the societies of the commonwealth were therefore simultaneously central to and on the margins of global commerce.

Import duties, of course, raised the prices of foreign goods in the United Kingdom, which did not make British consumers particularly cheerful. Thus, to sell this elitist, pro-finance economic agenda to voters, the new government waged a massive public relations campaign.[20] If the nation was going to close itself off from the rest of the liberal world yet continue to develop its industrial and financial capacities, it needed British consumers and merchants to take a substantial interest in the labor, natural resources, consumer markets, and manufactured goods available in various parts of the empire. Wembley served that need in two ways: it provided a physical space within which British consumers and entrepreneurs could learn about and pursue commercial opportunities in various colonial markets, and it aestheticized and made public a new, more modernist, more expansively liberal conception of the empire on which the sun never set. To that end, there was less emphasis on exotic, primitive savagery than in previous empire exhibitions and more emphasis on the impressive customs and industriousness of the people subjected to British rule around the world.[21] The idea was to show that rather than being backwaters in need of technocratic beneficence, British colonies had become potential independent trading partners. Several scholars who have studied the exhibition remark that it therefore peddled an entirely new brand of cultural difference, one marked by spectacles of nobility, heritage, and the myriad honorable—if not quaint—ways of laboring and living within modernity that various colonized people had developed.[22] For Wembley's planners, film was initially considered an experimental and insignificant form of propaganda; however, it emerged from the exhibition more important than ever. As Lee Grieveson, Tom Rice, and Scott Anthony have shown, the 1924 exhibition gave birth to a new screen media form: documentary cinema.[23] Nigeria featured prominently in this process, as not only the subject of the new form but—as we will eventually see—also an important dumping ground for its output.

The Wembley brand of cultural difference was baked right into the design of the exhibition grounds (which, according to some sources, were so neat and so contrived that they left the impression of a vast film studio with numerous sets).[24] The whole empire was on display, but many visitors remarked that the most vividly rendered region was West Africa, housed in a pavilion that was spatially arranged and constructed in a style that was perhaps unintentionally but unmistakably metaphorical of its position in the imperial economy (see figure 1.1). Whereas most of the pavilions consisted of massive white, concrete structures, some with a bit more *oriental* flare than others, the West Africa exhibit was housed within an expansive "Walled City" (as it was frequently billed)—modeled on Zaria—within which the exhibits for Sierra Leone, the Gold Coast, and Nigeria were anatopistically housed. In an architectural review for the *Nation*, Roger Fry panned most of Wembley's ferro-concrete buildings but praised the West Africa pavilion, writing, "Perhaps the nearest approach to any genuine architectural emotion is to be got from the replica of a West African walled town. Here at last are signs of an intelligent sensitiveness to architectural forms. Here the relief of one surface, the recession of another, has intention and a plastic meaning . . . you get a sense of mass, of dignity of scale which marks the triumph of intelligent barbarism over the last work in civilised ineptitude."[25] This infatuation with "intelligent barbarism" over and above "civilised ineptitude" was, of course, characteristic of the new, modernist, liberal expert: an educated professional

FIGURE 1.1. Residents of the "Walled City" at the British Empire Exhibition, 1924–1925. Reprinted courtesy of the Brent Museum and Archives.

who may have been skeptical of ruthless imperialism but who was highly invested in its material benefits and therefore receptive to the sociological redemption of liberalism as a protector of native culture. Just as Picasso drew inspiration from African art, so British liberals drew inspiration from the idea of essential differences between European and African cultures.

Within the walls of the West Africa exhibit, a smaller set of walls enclosed the Nigeria exhibit (again signaling the series of removes from which Nigeria was held in the imperial marketplace). The major scenes on display included a mock village, craft workshops — showcasing leatherwork, metalwork, embroidery, pottery, and carving — and a palm-oil extraction plant, which represented the kind of mechanized apogee to which other forms of indigenous handiwork might aspire. Visitors entered through a series of gates and then followed a path to gawk at natives who were busy working (these "natives" were brought to Wembley to live and work on the exhibition grounds for months at a time). If the point of the exhibition was to establish trade between freely acting British citizens and colonial subjects, the fact that both parties were being corralled into a commonwealth marketplace, and given that imperial subjects had very little sovereign control over their own production or trading vectors, the arrangement was, of course, hardly liberal. One party was the subject of the other party's bemused gaze, not to mention political and economic domination. Moreover, at least one African visitor to Wembley (an anonymous writer, billed as "a well known West African business man; resident in London," probably from the Gold Coast) remarked that the supposedly traditional craftwork and architecture on display were entirely too contrived, that technology and commerce as he knew it in the major trading ports of West Africa had been all but erased from the exhibition.[26] Therefore, Wembley seems to have struggled to resolve liberal interest in native customs and liberal philosophies of straightforward free trade. Was West Africa an established node in the global system of trade, a quaint site of potential investment, or somehow both at the same time?

The accusation of contrivance leveled by the anonymous African businessman subverts an otherwise widespread liberal consensus about Wembley and its ability to represent the empire, a consensus that is particularly evident in comments provided by those who viewed the Greville footage. The reels that Norman and Vincent brought back from Nigeria were edited into several small films, supplied with intertitles, and screened on a regular basis inside a small cinema house built exclusively for the Nigeria exhibit. A senior editor from the trade journal *West Africa* wrote a review of the films in which he remarked, "It is beyond doubt that they will give to 99 people out of every 100 at Wembley who know nothing of West Africa their master impression of the country." With this sentence the writer swiftly and insightfully, if unintentionally, theorizes the conceptual relationship between film and reality, suggesting that what is "real" is a matter of impressions, on which he then expands: "And it was so fatally easy for the film-makers to lay stress on the wrong things, the things which don't matter, but which please the groundlings, the sort of paralyzing 'muck' about plurality of wives and so forth, over which the cheaper sort of London daily 'rags' have been spreading themselves. In each case the performance was a triumph. There is not a wrong or false line or note."[27] This account of the Greville footage demonstrates a surprisingly constitutive theory of film as opposed to a representational one. Some things—such as polygamy—may exist, but they do not matter, he suggests. Therefore, the medium of film is burdened not with representing the world but with making one, and when it does so well, triumphing. His tone also betrays the ascendance of a liberal ideological orientation influenced by indirect rule, in which the highly educated gentleman ought to be praised for being capable of truly understanding colonized people, their relationship to the world, and the ways in which their institutions might be respected and preserved rather than trampled or sensationalized. Mantena calls this "culturalism," which she rightly warns against in contemporary political discourse.[28] One of the things that imperialism does—then and now—is to constitute a spectrum of similarity and difference that determines what qualifies as "culture." Note that the *West Africa* reviewer calls these "master impressions."

Several other reviews of the Greville footage are catalogued in *West Africa*, making it a rich source of material on the interwar liberal ethos. Some of the reviews appear in a regular column titled "A Coaster's London Log," the byline for which always includes the pseudonym 'Spotted' Dog. In one example, bearing the headline "The Real African Life," 'Spotted' Dog further elaborates the relationship between liberal experts and the masses:

> What, I take it, the people of West Africa want to feel is that the public money of their country spent on these films has been spent intelligently and discriminatingly, so as to do the country all the good that is obtainable. They may be given the unhesitating assurance that this is the case. We are shown the real West Africa, in its daily life; with its workers busily turning out their products; its professional men . . . ; its Native Administrations' work at such a delicate testing point as the pension system; and (not least appealing to the British part of the audience) with its overwhelming evidence, none the less telling because not thrust at you by Major Lawrence and his coadjutors, of how immeasurably Africa has benefited by British inventiveness, regularity, and perseverance. The happy result achieved is a series of pictures . . . which Britons and Africans can witness with equal pride and delight.[29]

This analysis drips with the logic of periliberalism. Readers should be delighted, according to 'Spotted' Dog, that public funds have been extracted from West Africans by a government in which they have no representation to create an impression about their lives, which have been placed beyond metropolitan legal and economic norms. Not only is this arrangement productive and modern, but it is also "real." Moreover, because the impression created is uncoupled from the lurid propaganda of T. E. Lawrence ("of Arabia"), it should therefore be particularly satisfying for both "Britons and Africans."[30] After all, cultural differences such as polygamy become "paralyzing" when sensationalized. Much more invigorating, according to 'Spotted' Dog, is an image of cultural difference that is technical yet reverent, even though it supposedly depends on British "perseverance" and the delicate work of "Native Administrations." The effect is to quarantine a zone of culture from direct participation in the world. It is not sovereign—they have no control over their "public money"—but it is theirs. For historians and postcolonial intellectuals, these comments diverge, perhaps rather agreeably, from the more stereotypical colonial language of savagery and darkness. However, 'Spotted' Dog never relinquishes what he refers to as the immeasurable benefits of colonization. The discourse of savagery and darkness wielded by his predecessors may have justified an earlier version of (universalist) liberalism, but 'Spotted' Dog's comments abet the turn to a qualified, variegated, and more insidious brand of that same philosophy.

In another anonymous review of the Greville footage, the writer "perceives" in the "dark of the picture-house" the "familiar profile" of none other than Fredrick Lugard. When the reviewer asked the sixty-five-year-old Lugard for his opinion, he "expressed himself very definitely about the beauty of the pictures and pointed out . . . again and again the significance of certain happenings, the folklore interest of details and the distinctive differences of the many tribes in Nigeria."[31] It is precisely these so-called tribes, we must remember, into which most Africans were forced by indirect rule and to which they had no choice but to turn for legal, political, and economic redress. Lugard's ethnographic assessment is presented as proof of the films' credibility, of their fidelity to the real Africa, and of the right notes that they strike. However, what the films represent—indeed, what they help constitute—is a new version of "Africa" that at this point has become a conceptual category as much as a place, which Lugard helped to invent.

Lugard had much more to say about the Greville films, which he cited as being central to the West Africa pavilion's overall resounding success. In a short essay for *West Africa*, he refers to them as the "most effective agents . . . for familiarizing the British public with the empire." For example, "you can turn from the moving picture showing the weaver, or potter, or smith at work, and see the living Natives plying their industries in a row of native shanties in the courtyard." To highlight the importance of this impression, Lugard then dwells considerably on the difference between the West Africa pavilion and the much smaller East Africa pavilion, housed in a pseudo-military fort. For him, the key distinction (which once again affirms his characteristic knack for self-promotion) is that "the West is essentially an exhibition of the produce, the art and skill in industry . . . of the indigenous African, the East—always excepting Uganda [where Lugard got his first taste of colonial administration but not where he was able to fully implement indirect rule]—is largely devoted to demonstrating what the White man has done in the country and its attractions for further White settlement and industry."[32] What Lugard is praising, in short, is the fact that British rule and its undoubted influence on African industry have been virtually erased from the Walled City. He goes on to argue that although visitors to the West Africa pavilion feel as if they are in direct contact with African people (a sentiment echoed by many visitors),[33] the East Africa pavilion emphasizes the mediating presence of the White man as "settler, planter, and trader."[34] These discrepancies are, of course, the very merits by which indirect rule was defended and how it contributed to the growing ideological capacity of liberalism. It made exploitation invisible. It made the subjection of Africa to the liberal world order seem like an internal African process, not the machinations of White settlers. Lugard concludes his contribution on an aspirational note: "There is a new spirit abroad, and Wembley, by bringing up the British democracy in closer touch with the undeveloped estates and peoples, must be the interpreter of a new and better understanding."[35]

At the heart of the "new spirit" that Lugard championed, which resonates with the general thrust of the exhibition as well as with the Greville films in particular, is the idea that colonies such as Nigeria were increasingly sovereign. That was both true and not true, of course. As political independence drew nearer and the more self-governing that colonies became, the more they were connected to and dependent on the global political and economic order. Meanwhile, colonies were internally stratified, with some regions *enjoying* relatively open access to global trade and some cut off from it, although the latter were essentially sovereign unto themselves. It was the dual sense that colonies were operating according to their own customs while simultaneously plugged into the liberal world order that reinvigorated the project of empire. Visitors were supposed to leave Wembley with renewed enthusiasm for liberal ideals. However, that enthusiasm depended on and reinforced a protectionist, demonstrably unfree economic relationship with Africa as well as the image of African producers as happy, sovereign, and—in their own way—modern. This, once again, is periliberalism. It is, to reiterate, not simply about being peripheral to the liberal world order; it is about being fundamentally and indispensably constitutive of the liberal world order precisely by being held at arm's length from it.

THE CINEMA OF PREFERENCE

When the British Empire Exhibition ended in 1925, a discussion commenced about the fate of the acclaimed Greville films; eventually, a decision was made to reedit and retitle the footage for screening in commercial cinemas, the contract for which was secured by a small firm called British

Instructional Films (BIF). In parallel, the British government created the Empire Marketing Board (EMB) and provided it with a film unit to create new content in the spirit of the Greville films. The mandate was explicitly articulated in pedagogical terms—"to educate our people . . . in an appreciation and knowledge of Dominions and Colonies"—but the plan hinged on the commercial appeal of the footage.[36] Officials hoped the Greville films would continue to elicit the sort of enthusiasm on display at Wembley, even though they knew that nonfiction films had a small popular audience and would therefore be considered with skepticism by the owners of commercial cinema houses. Nevertheless, the BIF employed aggressive marketing tactics on the theory that once the films found their way in front of British spectators, they would prove to be popular. They were wrong. The "Empire Series," as the films were known, performed miserably in the commercial market, and some of them were sent back to the colonies, where, officials further speculated, they might find more-amenable audiences. But documentaries were no more successful in the commercial cinemas of Lagos than they were in London. In both places they had to compete with American feature films, which would prove the bane of British cinema for decades.

I return to documentary film at the end of this chapter, but in the paragraphs that follow I first explore the structures of commercial cinema with which the Empire Series had to compete. Largely a feature of urban life, commercial cinema houses in Nigeria constituted what I am calling a cinema of preference, to which citizens and subjects of the empire had recourse. However, I use the word *preference* somewhat ironically because free participation in commercial cinema was constrained by a number of factors, including censorship, ticket prices, and zoning laws. The cinema of preference was an urban phenomenon, something in which citizens of the empire and people who closely orbited its centers of gravity could choose to participate. Meanwhile, subjects of native authorities, particularly those in the rural hinterlands, could not participate at all. Cinema came to them, and they could choose to attend or not, but an entirely different set of films was made available to them—or, as we will see, was imposed upon them. In line with indirect rule, therefore, two spheres of cinema culture emerged during the interwar period: one constituted within the liberal world order and one without. Both were structurally overdetermined, but if the cinema of preference seemed to have radiated liberal values, that was only because—like liberal values more generally—it acquired the luster of freedom by contrast to the constraints associated with its counterpart, the cinema of imposition, which thrived on the periphery of commercial film exhibition.

If the years following World War I were austere in parts of Europe, they were profligate years for American cinema. In the 1920s, Hollywood ramped up its production not only to serve the growing domestic market but also to exploit otherwise *underserved* markets around the world. The US government became deeply involved in the process, both by helping Hollywood pry open foreign markets and by capitalizing on cinema's glamour to generate interest in American consumer goods, fashion, technology, and political rhetoric. A US State Department employee by the name of William J. Yerby played an important role in bringing Nigeria into that process.

In the early 1920s, Yerby served as the US consul in Dakar, Senegal (then a French colony). He was one of only eleven African Americans in the US Diplomatic and Consular Services at the time, all of whom were appointed to relatively low-profile positions in various Black-majority nations in Africa and the Caribbean. However, he was promoted several times, becoming one of the first three Black Foreign Service officers in US history. He served in West Africa for more than seventeen years before petitioning to be appointed in a more "stimulating climate" in 1924.[37] His name appears throughout the historical record as a major proponent of American commerce in West Africa and, incidentally, as a good friend of W. E. B. Du Bois. Du Bois's correspondence with Yerby and with a common acquaintance of theirs suggests that Yerby had a brusque and discordant personality, but his knowledge of trade along the West African coast was unparalleled. In 1922 he wrote to the secretary for the Southern Provinces in Lagos asking for a list of cinema houses operating in southern Nigeria. His request reveals that the United States' pursuit of hegemony was truly global, long before the cold war. It also places Nigeria in a conspicuous position regarding the emerging relationship among cinema, commerce, and state power.

Yerby's request and the response to it also suggest that the business of cinema was even more entrenched in Nigeria than previously understood. James Burns writes that "by the early 1920s there was at least one permanent cinema in Lagos showing films to 'natives.'"[38] However, the list that the secretary of the Southern Provinces in Nigeria sent in 1922 included six cinemas, five of which were in Lagos.[39] One is simply the name of an individual, B. F. Adesola, and it is unclear what kind of cinema was being operated. However, two others—the Theater Garden and Empire Hall—were major multipurpose performance halls, both of which regularly advertised their film exhibitions in newspapers. In 1921 the Enterprise Cinema Company advertised six nights of film screenings each week at the Empire Hall, which featured, as one ad put it, "Charlie Chaplin, Mary Pickford, 'Fatty,' 'Bunny,' and all the Stars."[40] The remaining two cinemas on the list are the Nigerian Cinema Show Gardens and the Royal Cinema. These two seem to have been the first of Lagos's truly commercial cinema theaters, known as "bioscopes," buildings dedicated solely to the screening of films. Intriguingly, the "Royal Cinema" is a name that persists across accounts of commercial cinema in Lagos up through the 1960s and is commonly associated with a man by the name of S. Khalil of West Africa Pictures Company. A Syrian, Khalil is on record as the owner of various cinemas and the promoter of myriad screenings at locations such as the Empire Hall and Glover Memorial Hall. The Royal Cinema listed in 1922 may or may not be the same one operated by Khalil (since "Royal" was a common name for cinema houses across the world at that time), but if it was, then it was the longest running bioscope in Lagos history.

Despite the fact that Africa's bioscopes were run by entrepreneurs from various nations around the world and operated at the pleasure of European powers, the goal of the US State Department was to make them nodes in an American trade network. This placed them at the center of global commercial competition, as records at the Nigerian National Archives in Ibadan make clear. Among the memos that circulated between various colonial offices during the preparation of Yerby's list is a note to the comptroller of customs acknowledging that "certain British Firms would probably be glad to receive the same information."[41] Here the British can be seen playing catch-up to the American cinema-state complex, which took a very different approach to the confluence of film and state power. As scholars such as John Trumpbour and Ian Jarvie have chronicled, the US State Department had its own liberal empire project in mind.[42] The first director of the Bureau of Foreign and Domestic Commerce, Dr. Julius Klein, testified before a congressional subcommittee that he had once been shipwrecked in Peru and observed that American products were displacing British ones in local markets, in no small part as a result of the influence of Hollywood films.[43] In subsequent years the State Department would work very closely with Hollywood—particularly with the Motion Picture Producers and Distributors of America and its notorious leader, Will H. Hays, to expand Hollywood's global reach. These events ran parallel to British efforts to employ cinema in the name of expanding imperial trade, exemplified by the British Empire Exhibition, although the American approach is distinct in the way that it conceptualized the relationship between nation and audience. Where the British government focused on creating films about the world outside of the United Kingdom in order to nudge British businesses out into it, the US government focused on distributing Hollywood films to the world in order to entice global interests to do business with Americans. Many factors contributed to these approaches, not the least of which were geography and ideology, and I do not mean to suggest that Britain had no commercial film industry or that the British government had no interest in fostering it, but the British were late to the game and essentially had to learn it from their American counterparts.

British officials lamented the expansion of American cinema into British cities, but they absolutely agonized over the expansion of American cinema into the rest of the empire. As Grieveson writes, "The promise of liberal citizenship held out by American films would be, or could be, seductive and disruptive for those varied populations in Britain and its empire who were not citizens but *subjects*. The presumption to liberal democracy so central to the textual economies of American film would be deeply problematic for a colonial power."[44] The depth of the problem that Grieveson notes registered, somewhat revealingly, in the language of race. In conferences and trade publications, countless British officials articulated their fears not so much in terms of the liberalization of the colonial subject but in the corruption of the non-White psyche. After all, the "textual economies" of American cinema to which Grieveson refers emphasized not only the centrality of individual rights but also the profound and potentially disruptive autonomy of characters exercising those rights. As the conservative British government of the time saw it, unfettered pursuit of individual desire resulted in the cinematic depiction of antisocial behavior, including glorified crime, unregulated sex, and institutional corruption. The more the colonial subject was exposed to such images, the more the status of the imperial master was sullied. Hesketh Bell, another former governor of Northern Nigeria, used this provocative phrasing:

> Although we know that a vast deal of harm can be done even to civilized persons by the display of bad pictures, the injury which can be done to primitive people by the exhibition of demoralizing films, representing criminal and immodest actions by white men and women, can hardly be exaggerated. The success of our government of subject races depends almost entirely on the degree of respect which we can inspire. Incalculable is the damage that has already been done to the prestige of Europeans in India and the Far East through the widespread exhibition of ultra-sensational

and disreputable pictures, and it behoves us, therefore, *while there is yet time*, to see that the same harm shall not be repeated in our Tropical African Empire.[45]

These sentiments were echoed repeatedly during the interwar years, as several other scholars have noted. My interest in Bell's argument centers on its periliberal qualities. There is a world of moving images, he suggests, in which trade is free and cannot be controlled, but Africa should be quarantined from it. Moreover, conservatives like Bell were certainly amenable to individual rights, but the extension of those rights seems to have been deeply disquieting for them. Thus, as commercial cinema expanded in Nigerian cities and as colonial censorship regimes rose to mitigate its damage to European "prestige," several theoretical premises of liberal modernity came into question. Should pictures that excite the individual desires of audiences and therefore perform well in an open consumer market trade freely? Or should the state intervene to ensure that the public is exposed to pictures that will support the cohesion and enrichment of the society? Rather than deal with the contradictions head-on, colonial officials moved forward with censorship, raising further questions. Why were the very values that liberal imperialists presumed to impart in Africa withheld from African eyes? Moreover, did illiberal forms of state intervention and censorship undermine liberal governance, or — as otherwise practiced in colonies and postcolonies — did those illiberal moves signal a broader liberal agenda? The separation of the world not only into zones where liberal philosophy could be applied selectively but also into races, with similar restrictions, highlights the racism inherent in liberalism.

Commercial cinema attendance may have been a matter of preference, but it was not an entirely free enterprise. No matter one's race or nationality, a person from any stratum of colonial society could, in theory, *choose* to attend the cinema in a city like Lagos, whether to see or be seen at the pictures. But ticket prices were graded and corresponded with classified seating, creating structural forms of racial segregation. And what was shown was subject to another set of constraints. As we have already seen, the global economy brought more American films to Nigeria than British or Indian ones, but there were further physical constraints as well. The location of a cinema and who could operate it were tightly controlled by the colonial administration. Indeed, multiple applications for cinema permits in Lagos were rejected on the grounds that they would be disruptive to the surrounding communities. Cinemas increased nighttime traffic,

bringing both light and noise to otherwise quiet residential neighbor-
hoods. Additionally, the archive of the commissioner of lands reveals
that by the time World War II broke out, cinema permits were being
denied in the name of public safety. Officials worried that sites lit up at
night would be easy military targets, even though Lagos saw no fighting.
Thus, investors who saw potential in the market for increasing access to
motion pictures were thwarted by a government uneasy about granting
it.[46] Commercial cinema may have been a site of pleasure for imperial citizens during the interwar years, and the consumption of motion pictures
may have been a matter of preference, but commercial cinemas in colonial Nigeria were hardly citadels of liberty.

   The cinema of preference also offered a limited range of content. Its
appeal may have been grounded in what Grieveson calls its "promise of
liberal citizenship," but American liberalism was not necessarily well-
suited to colonial subjectivities. Silent Hollywood cinema often addressed
a spectator-subject for whom traditional values need not compete with
modern, liberal aspirations. Many silent Hollywood films, as Steven J.
Ross argues, featured fantasies of wealth, luxury, and free trade, but they
were tempered by forms of moral resolve associated with the working
class and their supposedly industrious cultural norms. The films arriving
in Lagos from America not only demonstrated the "moral superiority of
the working class while lavishing attention on the glamorous life-styles
of the wealthy," in Ross's words, but also portrayed working people as
"salt-of-the-earth types who taught the wealthy the value of hard work."[47]
These messages may have resonated with American audiences who were
at once dubious about yet covetous of the liberal elite. Meanwhile, most
urban African cinemagoers had been socialized into a system where it
was precisely by rejecting the values of familial communities—especially
indigenous religious values—that one gained access to the benefits of
liberal modernity. As such, the cinema of preference offered what, in retrospect, we might call a keep-it-real fantasy of liberal modernity, which
may have been improbable in the United States but would have been absolutely fantastic in colonial Lagos.

THE CINEMA OF IMPOSITION

Back in London, the Empire Series was exhibited at the Pavilion Cinema
in 1927. 'Spotted' Dog wrote a review in which he states that "so far as
the pictures themselves are concerned," the series was "very interesting
and instructive," but the titles and intertitles supplied "the usual idiotic

note associated with film-making." He had especially harsh words for a film called *Black Cotton*: "I suppose the word black is applied to the African people (whose patience and dignity in the cotton fields of Nigeria, at Zaria ginnery, and round the dye-pits of Kano, might have given a lesson to the film titler), but in the interest of accuracy he ought to be told that there is no such colour as either black or white in the human race. Film educationists cannot educate unless they are educated themselves."[48] Once again, the political correctness of the liberal expert is on ostentatious display—here using a brand of "postracial" rhetoric that may have been progressive for its time but is nevertheless dismissive of the history of race as a means of creating and maintaining inequality and exploitation. Simply put, "black" and "white" were made real by imperialism and because of their association with ongoing economic and political disparities cannot be so easily unmade. Indeed, we might ask what kinds of inequality and exploitation are being simultaneously created and obscured by 'Spotted' Dog's reference to African "patience and dignity."

The story of cotton farming in northern Nigeria is about much more than traditional African handiwork. It is a story about local slave labor, technological transfer, propaganda, government handouts, and tax incentives. Nevertheless, this is the first intertitle of *Black Cotton*: "Cotton produced in the new cotton fields of the Empire is now becoming an appreciable item of the world's cotton supply. The industry in Nigeria, as far as growing is concerned, is a purely native one." Indeed, Kano was, when the footage was recorded, the center of a prosperous textile industry. It drew from local cotton cultivation and manufactured more than two million rolls of cloth per year.[49] The industry was so productive, in fact, that there was little incentive to participate in the imperial export market. However, the United Kingdom—which had its own robust textile manufacturing sector, headquartered in Lancashire, but possessed neither the land nor the proper climate to grow cotton—needed colonial cotton to compensate for global shortages that first appeared after the US Civil War. Eventually, UK textile manufacturers established the British Cotton Growing Association (BCGA), which targeted a number of colonies for production of raw material, including India, Uganda, and Nigeria. In the case of Nigeria the BCGA began by looking to the South, which had decades of experience exporting cotton on a relatively small scale. However, by the turn of the twentieth century, the cocoa and palm-oil trades had become too profitable for southern Nigerian farmers to seriously consider devoting land to cotton cultivation once again. The BCGA therefore turned its attention to northern Nigeria but also encountered several obstacles there. Cotton

was profitable only for those farmers who had access to indentured or
slave labor (as indeed it was in the American South). The colonial government thus chose to look the other way when it encountered local forms
of slave trading, despite official British policy on the matter. In defense of
that position, Lugard wrote the following:

> Such measures may seem to constitute an arbitrary interference with
> natural laws of progress, and even to place the executive in a spirit of
> antagonism towards the full operation of the law. But they are conceived
> in a spirit of equity to the owner, and for the real benefit of the slave. They
> are suited only to a brief period of transition, which can be hastened by
> judicious explanation to master and slave alike. They will not arrest or
> defeat the operation of the law, but only make it more gradual.[50]

This gradualist strategy was in part implemented through the courts of
the native authority, which arbitrated slave-trading disputes. The colonial
government also relied on the headmen of various native authorities to
expand the amount of land on which cotton was grown by getting "every
adult male to put in at least one acre of crop."[51] Tax incentives were then
promised as part of the pitch, as were reduced transportation fees, which
the colonial government promised would derive from the completion of
a rail line between Lagos and Kano. British officials also launched a propaganda campaign claiming that the cotton export trade would be more
profitable than it actually was. And finally, colonial officers gave out free
seeds to interested farmers. When the railroad was completed, however,
it contributed to the collapse of the local transport business and a rise
in unemployment. It brought in yards of cheap cloth from British textile mills, but the quality of imported, manufactured cloth was so poor in
comparison that it only bolstered the preference of Nigerian consumers
for local cloth, which in turn allowed Kano manufacturers to pay relatively high prices for raw cotton in the local market. Nigerian farmers
simply had no incentive to consider large-scale exports. Some historians
have argued that had British buyers offered higher prices for Nigerian
cotton, Nigeria might have become a major cotton exporter.[52] However,
the "purely native" industry celebrated in *Black Cotton* was, in the end, less
a triumph of tradition and more the failure of imperial state protectionism in the face of African free trade (see figures 1.2–1.5).

Regardless, *Black Cotton* depicts a local industry in the process of
transformation under supposedly benign colonial tutelage. As an early
intertitle declares, "During the harvest all the available hands young and

old, are called into full employment," emphasizing the role of the family or village in the enterprise rather than slave labor. Then a long line of laborers is shown carrying bales of cotton on their heads through the cotton fields; later, the line culminates at the foot of a giant pyramid of cotton bales, suggesting at once the grandiosity, indigeneity, and tyranny of the pharaohs. Another intertitle reads, "Great new areas of production await opening up as soon as the Railways now in course of construction are completed." That celebration of technology is then followed by a celebration of the market. One intertitle reads, "The ready market causes the crop to be regarded by natives as a most reliable source of income," while another forecasts, "It is calculated that Nigeria will soon be exporting a million bales of cotton annually." Shots of the cotton being ginned in large metal machines recall the prominence of technology at the British Empire Exhibition and, indeed, a wide range of commercial films of the period. However, before cutting away from the laborers at the gins, a patronizing intertitle declares, "Old methods die hard and some Africans still adhere to a rather laborious manner of ginning." At this point, roughly halfway through the thirteen-minute film, attention shifts to local, artisanal methods of processing cotton, which stand in contrast to the industrial methods favored by the British. Women are shown ginning cotton with sticks and pressing oil from seeds: processes that are described as "tedious" and inefficient. Men are shown gathering massive amounts of cotton into bales and loading them onto train cars. An intertitle reads, "The cotton plant has been in Africa from time immemorial, and a great deal is used by the Africans for local purposes." Women are shown spinning yarn, and men are shown weaving it into cloth on local looms. "They are wonderfully expert in the use of machines of their own construction," effuses another intertitle. The dye pits are shown, surrounded by men dipping cloth in and pulling it out. That work is described with the film's now characteristic rhetoric of tradition: "The secret of these vegetable dyes has been handed down for generations." Finally, the results of the local industry are held up to the camera, as well as reluctantly modeled by several women. As one intertitle recapitulates, "In spite of the great import of cheap European cotton cloth the native weaving industry continues to flourish."

The reality of cotton growing in colonial Nigeria was that the industry might have modernized, and quickly, if its relationship with the global economy had been characterized by actual free trade and equity. However, what the titlers of *Black Cotton* likely understood and what was therefore assiduously avoided in the film is the fact that modern political,

"BLACK COTTON."

Arranged by

BRITISH INSTRUCTIONAL FILMS L^TD

SURBITON, SURREY.

Cotton produced in the new cotton fields of the Empire is now becoming an appreciable item of the world's cotton supply. The industry in Nigeria, as far as growing is concerned, is a purely native one.

The ready market causes the crop to be regarded by natives as a most reliable source of income.

In spite of the great import of cheap European cotton cloth the native weaving industry continues to flourish.

FIGURES 1.2, 1.3, 1.4, AND 1.5. Intertitles from *Black Cotton*, produced for the "Empire Series" by British Instructional Films.

economic, and technological practices had not been adapted to the formidable textile market in northern Nigeria. Instead, the film suggests that local cotton manufacturing, despite being well established in the region, was itself failing to adapt to the modern world. The fact that local people continued to prefer their own methods and products is depicted as quaint and conservative, a formulation that seems to be legible, in hindsight, as a palliative for the wounded ego of British industrial investment interests. Indeed, the title of the film suggests something irredeemably "African," a recalcitrant "Black" version of the supposedly pure White textile industry upon which the modern world was built. Black Nigerian cotton—and by extension a great deal of Nigerian social practice—had chosen, the film insinuates, to remain on the periphery of the liberal world order for its own, undecipherable, customary reasons. Once again, however, the explanation for northern Nigeria's lack of cotton exports follows from the low prices that British firms offered in comparison to those offered by local manufacturers. In the end the image of a recalcitrant society obscures the degree to which the political arm of the British Empire attempted to shape Nigeria into a submissive gear for its economic machine as well as the degree to which that economic machine abhorred truly free trade. In discussing a similar propaganda film, made by the ruling Conservative Party, also intended for British audiences, and also focused on West Africa (in this case, Ghana), Grieveson writes that "images of material connections [between colony and metropole], emphasized through the connective tissues of editing, are central to the visualization of a political economy that positioned empire development and markets as integral to the sustenance of the wealth of the nation."[53] Thus, in the late 1920s, images of noble traditions, coupled with images of modern connections, reinforced the false notion that Africans were free to choose their entrance into, as Grieveson phrases it, "the liberal world system." Instead, being selective about preventing or enabling Africans to enter is what really kept the liberal world system running.

After its failure in commercial cinemas, Black Cotton was retitled and repurposed for another afterlife. Julian Huxley, an evolutionary biologist, was asked to take it with him under the title of Cotton Growing in Nigeria when he traveled to East Africa as an education consultant in 1929. Huxley was given three films by the Empire Marketing Board to screen at government schools, each film more aesthetically complex than the last, in order to assess audience comprehension and appraise "the value of the cinema for educational and propaganda purposes."[54] Cotton Growing in Nigeria was supposedly the simplest of the three films, and it elicited a

number of fascinating responses from students, which they provided in
mandatory essays on the screening events. One Tanzanian student wrote
that "we found that the people of Nigeria are now civilized as I saw women
picking the cotton from the pods and put in the sacks, and how they gin it
by machines called gins."[55] In Uganda, a twenty-year-old medical student
named S. N. Lameka wrote the following:

> The method of growth of cotton in Nigeria in the first stage is almost
> alike of ours in this country, but from harvest to made-up lint or even
> to a garment in the hands of the natives themselves became gradually differ-
> ently when compared with ours. . . . They themselves dress in their own
> European-made looking clothes, manufactured every inch in their
> own land, with their own hands and brain. While the Cotton Industry
> in Uganda is grown by Natives themselves and shipped for foreigners,
> *and that is all.*[56]

Indeed, the cotton export trade was more robust in Uganda than Nigeria
during the interwar years, but this — once again — has less to do with a
failure of "their own hands and brain," as Lameka put it, than with the
exploitative structures of the colonial economy. Large swaths of Ugandan
land were under the control of European cotton plantations, and many of
the gins in Uganda were run by Indian manufacturers.

According to Christopher P. Youé, the strong export market for
peasant-grown cotton in Uganda — very much the opposite of what pre-
vailed in northern Nigeria — was a side effect of competition among British textile manufacturing capital, agricultural capital, and new forms
of Indian manufacturing capital.[57] British textile manufacturers had a
strong lobby in London in the form of the BCGA, and they were therefore
more successful than other European settlers in Uganda at securing political assistance for their sector of the economy. They were also waging
a high-profile fight against increasingly independent Indian entrepreneurs who — as they saw it — put the United Kingdom's reputation at risk.
In the end, however, British manufacturers were unable to convince the
holders of the purse strings in London that British-owned plantations in
Uganda should receive ongoing government assistance. Plantations were
more capital intensive than small farms and were thus more prone to
market volatility than peasant cotton production, which the government
considered to be flexible and resilient. What that really meant was that
British politicians made the following calculation: if British settlers produced cotton with government assistance, then the government would

be compelled to protect prices, but if African smallholders produced cotton, no protection would be needed. In other words, risk was never factored into the formula when it was African peasants doing the farming. Moreover, buying Ugandan cotton out from under Indian manufacturers at prices greater than Indians wanted to pay Africans but far lower than British buyers would have paid to British settlers allowed the government to simultaneously position itself as developmentalist trustee (to Ugandan peasants), self-interested nationalist (to British manufacturers), and superior imperialist (to Indian manufacturers). Essentially, Ugandans did not manufacture textiles from their own cotton because Britain ensured that Ugandan manufacturing failed. What Lameka's comments reveal, in the face of such illiberalism, is just how attractive liberal ideals regarding self-sufficiency could be. The "hands and brain[s]" of Nigerians are celebrated by an African on the other side of the continent because they seem to represent a degree of sovereignty. It is good, his essay suggests, for Nigerians to make their own clothes, "manufactured every inch in their own land," but we must remember that Lameka's realization is made possible by the mediated representation of an embattled industry. Colonial cinema did not simply obscure the reality of colonialism; it contributed to the creation of another reality in which self-sufficiency was celebrated as a core value, not just a way of coping with economic isolation.

In spite of their intentions, colonial film producers could never claim to create the exact subjectivity they attempted to address. Nevertheless, modes of address do tend to inform the conditions in which subject formation takes place. As Jonathan Beller puts it, the very act of looking is a form of labor. He argues for recognition of a "cinematic mode of production," in which spectators are not passive receptacles of ideology but in which—through actively learning the medium and becoming expert on it—they "learn the rules of the dominant social structure."[58] That dominant social structure involved, according to Peter Morton-Williams—an ethnographer commissioned by Britain's Colonial Film Unit to study the reactions that rural Nigerians had to pedagogical films—"a sort of wish-fantasy."[59] In my reading of Morton-Williams's observations, the prospect of remaining within local communities and abiding by established social values while simultaneously accessing the material benefits of liberal modernity was the primary motivation for rural Nigerians to engage with and become expert on the development messages of colonial propaganda films. In other words, whereas indirect rule and colonial cinema were conspiring to offer imperial subjects their own version of modernity, outside of the liberal world order, those subjects expressed interest in gaining direct access to the benefits of liberal modernity, particularly as a means of elevating their status above nearby communities. But local competition for, say, having the biggest maternity hospital in the area only entrenched the ethnic affiliations fostered by indirect rule and also depoliticized technical and social innovation. In fact, gaining access to the material benefits of liberal modernity did not necessarily mean entering the liberal world order at all. Instead, the material desire that Morton-Williams observed, coupled with the modes of address that were consistently employed by colonial cinema, suggests a subject position that might be described according to ongoing preparation for the liberal world order. Colonial films cultivated a desire to reform oneself fundamentally—to get clean, work more efficiently, build the right home, and collaborate with the right institutions—in order to eventually gain access.

Nowhere, perhaps, is this message more clearly articulated—at least in the realm of colonial cinema—than in *Daybreak in Udi* (1949, dir. Terry Bishop), the Crown Film Unit (not Colonial Film Unit) production that won an Oscar in 1950 for Best Documentary. Its primary audience was not in Africa; rather, *Daybreak in Udi* was one of several films produced at the same time as the cinema of imposition but through different bureaucratic structures and with different aesthetic sensibilities. And although colonial films made for African audiences were themselves a mixed bag, comprising different styles championed by different bureaucrats—with men like Huxley and Morton-Williams calling into question the simplistic approach developed by men like William Sellers of the Colonial Film Unit—the social positioning and modes of address associated with both kinds of colonial cinema reinforce the notion of screen media as global, liberal gatekeeper.[60] Indeed, if *Black Cotton* was designed to celebrate self-regulation and entrepreneurship among Africans, *Daybreak in Udi* was designed for self-gratification among the British as well as other members of the liberal world order. As Femi Shaka argues, it differs from films aimed at African audiences by depicting modernization not as a British mandate but instead by representing "Africans as initiators of development projects." And although Shaka praises *Daybreak in Udi* for this step forward, he nevertheless criticizes it for two important steps back. The film tries to "absolve the British colonial authorities of their responsibilities" while constituting "a disingenuous attempt to pass the buck of development to indigenous communities even though they do not control the apparatuses of government and revenue collection."[61] Here then lies an intriguing observation about periliberalism's favored modes of address.

As Shaka notes, a generative way to understand *Daybreak in Udi* lies in free indirect subjectivity, although he does not use those terms. The film's plot depicts the construction of a controversial maternity hospital, which is requested by a small group of Udi residents and then built by their labor with funds solicited from the colonial government. It is also opposed by a local faction of traditionalists who descend on the new hospital during its first night of operation in the form of *egwugwu*: ancestor masquerades. Three women are inside, a pregnant woman and a midwife from Udi, as well as Iruka, a Nigerian nurse from outside the community: she was sent to Udi as a government expert and is part of the colonial bureaucracy, but she is not British. Shaka argues that because the midwife and Iruka are both given several point-of-view shots, spectators are invited into their experiences of the egwugwu siege. He also writes that "even though the midwife enjoys similar narrative authority through spatial articulation in this sequence, Iruka's display of courage and imagination, when it matters, is what is foregrounded in the sequence."[62] However, I would argue that the two work together. What qualifies the point-of-view shots as examples of free indirect subjectivity is precisely the ambiguity associated with their close proximity or the way the narrative voice shifts so freely during the film's climax. The result is a kind of claim in which local capacity building, in the context of colonial self-absolution and disingenuousness — or what Mantena calls "alibis of empire" — engenders both acute fear, as experienced by the midwife, and "courage and imagination," as experienced by Iruka. Running in parallel with the cinema of imposition, therefore, *Daybreak in Udi* — with its primary audiences in Europe and America — illustrates the ways in which the liberal world was invited to understand the developmentalist anxieties of Nigerians yet pass the development buck on to them anyhow. Meanwhile, Nigerians were invited to celebrate receiving the buck.

The scholarly literature on *Daybreak in Udi*, and colonial propaganda cinema more generally, is rich and well established.[63] The recurring argument is that the practice of imposing cinema — in which correspondents loaded projection equipment into vans and drove out into the colonial hinterland, often with native translators in tow, to bring imperial messages to imperial subjects — and the content of the films shown — such as lessons on hygiene, agriculture, and modern living — were scornfully patronizing and blatant about their paternalist modernization agenda. However, the project of modernization often contradicted the project of protecting and promoting traditional institutions, which characterized indirect rule. Brian Larkin has described this dialectic in temporal terms, as a tension between the dual processes of "preservation" and "transformation," but it helps to simultaneously hold on to a spatial metaphor adapted from the "world systems" approach of inside and outside.[64] If liberalism depends on an outside space of preservation while generating an inside space of transformation, then the tension that Larkin observes may, in fact, resolve itself.

What I am calling periliberalism emanates from a process where liberal experts in the metropolitan core develop a preference for cultural artifacts that celebrate the dignity and industriousness of peripheral, imperial subjects, even while those subjects are pushed further and further from the central ideals of liberalism. Meanwhile, peripheral subjects in one location may be invited to look upon their counterparts in other peripheral spaces—whether in different colonies, in the cities, or in communities nearby—with similar reverence for the dignity and industriousness of liberal self-sufficiency. The binary logic of transformation and preservation is thus pegged to the idea that each force's opposite is operating somewhere else, somewhere outside of *here*. This perspective explains how Nigeria can be both a key node in the liberal world order yet marginalized from it. And, of course, valuing industriousness and self-sufficiency is not a foreign or outside introduction to Africa. Nevertheless, as the example of *Black Cotton* suggests, the relative isolation of African industriousness and self-sufficiency from the global system of free trade could be promoted as a colonial value even at a time when the evolving contours of modernity required the globalization of productivity everywhere. Either Africa would enter the global economic system on strictly dictated imperial terms or it would not enter at all. And although that is clearly an illiberal position, both options were somehow supposed to represent rational, dignified, modern choices for Africans.

(IM)PENDING SOVEREIGNTY

By the 1950s, as the imperial project morphed into the commonwealth project and as colonies prepared for political sovereignty, such concepts as dignity, self-sufficiency, and cultural heritage became the cornerstones of many African nationalist discourses. Indeed, the argument that Africans could manage their own economic resources in their own ways would be central to the argument that they could manage their own politics. When independence did arrive, however, the discourse of self-sufficiency folded under itself into what James Ferguson calls the "paradoxes of sovereignty and independence," the idea that self-rule can be twisted into a form of blame directed against African governments for economic underperformance over which, in reality, they have little control. Capitalism's reach is global, and sovereignty from its processes is nearly impossible, even when those processes are indirect. For the most part, it is according to the whims of major corporations and powerful nation-states that small nation-states acquire and build wealth. Yet because they are ostensibly sovereign, in political terms, they bear the blame for their failure to build wealth. Since the waning days of colonialism in Africa, therefore, excessive concern for concepts such as liberation, independence, and sustainability has diverted international political attention away from the lack of economic development, capital investment, and industry—in spite of ongoing resource extraction—that began in the colonial era and persists today. According to the logic of periliberalism, African poverty becomes easily explained as a product of "their own hands and brain" rather than an alibi for the most criminal policies of liberalism. Indeed, periliberalism thrives on what Ferguson refers to as "the depoliticization of poverty."[65]

As I have argued in this chapter, documentary cinema emerged in Nigeria and the United Kingdom simultaneously. In both places, however, documentary films competed with commercial films, primarily British and American ones, for attention. This relatively early cinematic landscape overlapped with the changing political and economic landscape of British liberalism, especially the turn to indirect rule and increased willingness to use protectionist mechanisms to influence market dynamics. In aesthetic terms—as exemplified by films edited from the Greville brothers' footage, as well as *Daybreak in Udi*—the result was a mode of address in which Nigerians, other Africans, and even Euro-American liberals were invited to celebrate imposed isolation from global trade as a triumph of local self-sufficiency. Promoting "real African life" became a smoke screen for removing Africans from the discussion about how they would participate in the exploitative processes of global capitalism.

During formal decolonization in anglophone Africa, the cinema of imposition was transferred to the newly "sovereign" nation-states of the continent. The case of Nigeria is perhaps the most profound, in which the formal and structural features of colonial cinema laid the foundations for the continent's most expansive television network. Obafemi Awolowo, the prominent anticolonial nationalist who served as premier of the Western Region of Nigeria, led his government to create a mobile cinema unit based on the British model. He then prodded his party to pursue mass-media broadcasting, embarking on a project—before colonialism had even ended—that would result in Africa's first television station south of the Sahara.[66] In the next chapter I examine the rise of postcolonial Nigerian state television through the lens of key figures who shaped the medium, as well as one of its most iconic programs, *The Village Headmaster*. The story of that show and its creator, Segun Olusola, reveals how the paradoxes of sovereignty dogged Nigerian screen media well into the postcolonial period.

2 Emergency of the State

TELEVISION, PEDAGOGICAL IMPERATIVES,
AND *THE VILLAGE HEADMASTER*

"Trade still follows the flag." So reads the lead of a newspaper advertisement that G. B. Ollivant, a subsidiary of Unilever, ran in the *Daily Times* of Nigeria on October 1, 1960: the day Nigeria became a sovereign nation-state (see figures 2.1 and 2.2). The ad directly references previous ones taken out by other Unilever subsidiaries, which featured similar copy: "Trade follows the Flag," a common assertion and underlying premise of British liberal imperialism. During the 1924 Empire Exhibition, for example, the Royal Niger Company ran ads picturing its flag flying over a bucolic scene of colonial mercantilism, complete with riverside warehouses and steam from shipping barges floating up through oil palms. In the 1960 Ollivant ad, Nigeria's new flag—green-white-green, rendered in newsprint gray—flies over a modern harbor with skyscrapers and cargo ships. From warehouses and barges to towers and cargo ships—progress indeed! Yet if the older ad explicitly endorses a relationship between imperialist domination and free trade, the Independence Day ad suggests that although sovereignty may reconfigure trade, it does so in more semiotic than structural terms.

Scores of companies took out newspaper advertisements like Ollivant's on Independence Day, each one expressing congratulations to the new nation, claiming that the future was bright and that political change would in no way dampen business prospects. In fact, many ads proudly and unironically proclaimed that the very corporations that had benefited from the colonial dispensation were not only poised to benefit from the new one but also, as an ad for the Kingsway chain of department stores put it, "proud of the past."[1] To propose, however, that the publishers who printed the ads, the entrepreneurs who did business with the publishers, or the consumers who read the newspapers were resigned to the idea that independence was in name only would grossly mischaracterize

Trade
still
follows
the
flag

The flag of independence, now flying proudly
over Nigeria, marks a splendid record of progress.
G.B.O. have traded successfully in Nigeria for
100 years, helping to develop Nigerian businesses
and training large numbers of Nigerian
managers and technicians, thus bringing
benefits to the whole country.
In congratulating Nigeria on her
achievement, G.B.O. look forward to
another 100 years of successful
trading under the new flag.

G·B·O BRANCHES
THROUGHOUT
NIGERIA

G. B. OLLIVANT (NIGERIA) LTD. P.O. BOX 144 LAGOS

FIGURE 2.1. G. B. Ollivant advertisement artwork, appearing in the *Daily Times* of Nigeria on October 1, 1960.

the atmosphere on October 1. Without a doubt, independence was a moment of euphoric optimism for many Nigerians and outside observers. It may be true that sovereignty is full of paradoxes,[2] and it may be true that some of those paradoxes are signaled in the media produced at the time, but those are largely contemporary truths emanating from the history that played out after independence. In 1960 it would have been perfectly acceptable to assume that liberalism had submitted to the symbols of a new power, that trade would now follow the dictates of a novel form of sovereignty, one emerging throughout the global South. Perhaps one way to understand the paradox is through what Lauren Berlant calls "cruel optimism," the idea that what you desire is "actually an obstacle to your flourishing." To extend James Ferguson's argument, the desire for sovereignty—to be left alone and to have the power to choose one's fate—may have denied Nigeria and other nations access to the very liberal order that created them; nevertheless, the optimism of independence also describes, as Berlant writes, "a scene of negotiated sustenance that makes life bearable as it presents itself ambivalently, unevenly, incoherently."[3] Indeed, optimism is a key feature of periliberalism, as the following chapters of

THE FLAG GRANTED IN 1886 TO THE GOVERNMENT OF THE NIGER TERRITORIES

The British colours in the first quarter were in accordance with the charter. In the fourth quarter was the Niger Company's device, triple in form, triple in motto (the words " Ars, Jus, Pax " are on it) and triple in colour (yellow letters on black ground, within a red circle to signify the protection of the British Empire).

" Trade follows the Flag "

The Niger Company are merchants, shipowners, transport agents and mining experts, and advertising agents. They have branches in every place of importance in the country. They act as agents for some of the biggest business houses in Great Britain.

From their Liverpool office The Niger Company arrange export of everything needed for the Nigerian market. From Lagos they carry through the despatching of Nigeria's minerals and products generally. From Burutu they run an up-to-date passenger

and transport service on the Niger and Benue Rivers.

Nigeria is a market of eighteen million consumers. As civilisation advances the natives' horizon broadens ; they have increased purchasing power and with it a desire for increased comfort.

Language is no difficulty. The native who cannot read, quickly recognises trade-marks and learns to associate them with the goods so branded. He is a keen judge of value, ready and anxious to buy British produce, because he knows from experience that it is a sound investment.

For all information about Nigeria—one of to-day's great markets—apply to :

THE NIGER COMPANY LTD.
ROYAL LIVER BUILDING LIVERPOOL

Chief Nigerian Office: THE NIGER COMPANY LTD., LAGOS, NIGERIA, WEST AFRICA
London Office: THE NIGER COMPANY LTD., LEVER HOUSE, LONDON, E.C.4

FIGURE 2.2. Advertisement artwork for the Niger Company, appearing in *West Africa* on June 28, 1924.

this book attempt to clarify. Even if postcolonial Nigerian screen media have, or have had, much in common with colonial media—which is the crux of this chapter—postcolonial Nigerian screen media, from television to video film, have attempted not only to make life bearable but also to make it *meaningful*, or at least give meaning to the process of bearing the ambivalence, unevenness, and incoherence that define modern life everywhere and in particular ways in Nigeria.

Nigeria already had one regional government television network on Independence Day, and another was coming on line as the fireworks exploded overhead. The origins of those two networks, in the now-defunct Western and Eastern regions, are relatively well documented—at least we know a good deal about when, why, and how Nigeria's nationalist politicians channeled public funds into establishing what were some of the first television broadcasting facilities in Africa.[4] Television was conceived as a developmentalist institution, the best way to ensure rapid and extensive education of the new citizenry, although as Liwhu Betiang points out, "From inception in Nigeria, TV has existed for the subversive use of political leadership against the people it pretends to represent."[5] Because Nigerian television was a state-run enterprise, operating within an oil-rich country that has been governed for much of its history by military dictators and, when not, by a structurally corrupt kleptocracy, Betiang's characterization is perhaps unsurprising. Less often discussed in the scholarship on Nigerian television is the *what*. By what means, exactly, did political leaders use television to subvert the nation, if in fact they did so? What kinds of programs were broadcast? What do those programs look like? What do they say? In short, what is or has been on TV in Nigeria? Because of poorly maintained archives and a general reticence on the part of Nigeria's broadcasting bureaucracy to discuss its history, these have been difficult questions to answer. Nevertheless, in this and all the chapters that follow I offer sustained readings of some iconic Nigerian television programs, episodes of which I have been fortunate enough to acquire—haphazardly—over the past several years.

To be clear, the kind of research undertaken by scholars such as Betiang, who has methodically traced the various political processes that gave birth to and shaped Nigerian state television over half a century, is critical for media studies in Nigeria.[6] For example, it is essential to know that Nigeria's first station was founded by the iconic anticolonial nationalist and Progressive Party leader Obafemi Awolowo, who saw television as intrinsically modern, a way of proving to outgoing colonial officials, local constituents, and antagonistic forces in the federal government that his party had mastered liberal democracy and development. I have argued elsewhere that such an orientation positioned elites like Awolowo as gatekeepers between the liberal world order and the Nigerian people who sought to deliver modernity in carefully planned packets.[7] I have also written about some of the content that was broadcast by the Western Nigeria Television network (WNTV) and later by the Nigerian Television Authority (NTA), linking that content to films produced by the British Colonial Film Unit (CFU). My recurring argument has been that Nigerian television inherited its social and political posture from colonial cinema, attempting to instruct the people of Nigeria about their position relative to the liberal world order. Previously, however, I have said little about the possibilities of Nigerian television and the ways in which locally produced content attempted to realize them. Following the lead of historians like Fredrick Cooper, therefore, I seek here to visualize the paths that seemed to be opening up for Nigeria's first television professionals at the time of independence.[8] What did they want from the medium, and what kinds of content did they create to realize their desires? After all, whether or not those desires turned out to have been obstacles to the flourishing of Nigeria, it is important to understand the long-lasting effects they have had on the aesthetic configurations of Nigerian screen media culture.

In the first part of this chapter I take a renewed look at the early history of television production in southwestern Nigeria by considering it through the eyes of two key figures, Adebayo Faleti and Segun Olusola. Both were consummate storytellers. In the days immediately before and after independence, they were employed as screen media technicians and bureaucrats, but their major interests lay in the crafting of narratives and philosophy, attested to by their later careers. Faleti has been less influential in federal government circles than Olusola, but he was already involved with government-sponsored screen media when WNTV was launched. He then worked for many years in subnational state television and eventually played an influential role in the Nollywood video boom. His experiences therefore straddle all the major periods of Nigerian screen media history. Meanwhile, Olusola was directly responsible for many of the paths pursued by Nigerian state television. He was instrumental in the establishment of both regional and federal broadcasting networks. He created one of the most enduring television stories in Nigerian history, *The Village Headmaster*. And he was a celebrated statesman, eventually becoming Nigeria's ambassador to Ethiopia. Along the way, Olusola delivered scores of speeches and published several essays in which he established a relatively coherent body of media theory. After accounting for what I have learned from personal conversations with Faleti before his death in 2017 and from close readings of Olusola's biography, speeches, and essays, this chapter turns to episodes of *The Village Headmaster* in order to understand the way that Nigerian state television seems to have imagined its public.

FALETI AND THE FOUNDATIONS
OF STATE TELEVISION

Adebayo Faleti was thirty years old when independence came to Nigeria, and he already had a great deal of professional experience with screen media, particularly in education, translation, and film exhibition. In 1956 he was hired as a film commentator for Awolowo's Government Free Cinema scheme, a touring exhibition system explicitly modeled on the CFU. Faleti's job was to drive to Yoruba-speaking communities in the Western Region, set up and commence film exhibitions, and then "kill" (as he phrased it) the English-language sound track, allowing him to translate and explain concepts in Yoruba. The content that Faleti translated included educational documentaries from abroad and English-language propaganda produced by the Western Region government, including *Self-Government for Western Nigeria* (1958), a short documentary that is often referred to as a sort of contrived conversation between nationalist elites and their constituents, strategically produced for British eavesdropping.[9] Awolowo refers to that film as one of his great achievements, which made his government the largest film producer in Africa at the time and "having the largest government cinema audience as well."[10]

Awolowo's party, the Action Group, hoped to further expand and harness its vast audience when it established WNTV in Ibadan one year before independence. The official reason for doing so, as many media historians have noted, was to redress the iniquitous control that colonial officials exercised over broadcasting.[11] But radio was the more popular and widely consumed medium of the time, and television broadcasting was extremely expensive. Therefore, what television represented was more than just access; it was a marker of prestige. As various accounts of the era never fail to note, WNTV touted its prestige through the vainglorious motto "First in Africa," to which the motto of the Eastern Nigeria Television Network (ENTV), "Second to None," bombastically responded.

Faleti was invited to apply for a position during the development of WNTV, and he was eventually hired to review and edit films for transmission—many of them, once again, purchased or on loan from abroad. In the beginning the station was a public-private partnership, with expertise, content, and half the initial capital outlay provided by Overseas Rediffusion: a London-based, global commercial radio and television corporation headquartered in repurposed buildings on the site of the 1924 British Empire Exhibition in Wembley. The managing board of the Western Region station was initially composed as a bilateral balancing act, in much the spirit of other decolonization initiatives, with three members from the Western Region Government and three from Overseas Rediffusion.[12] The operational staff was almost entirely Nigerian, although a few advisors were recruited from the United States International Cooperation Administration (ICA), a forerunner of USAID. Faleti was supervised by an ICA agent named Janet Hyde-Clark, who went on to advise other fledgling African television stations on behalf of the US government. Apparently, Hyde-Clark valued Faleti's keen sense of cinematic aesthetics. Faleti told me that his experience with cinema went far beyond his professional duties. During his years as a film commentator, Faleti lived in an apartment in Agege that overlooked the famous Pen Cinema, which later became a church and then a fast-food restaurant.[13] As was often the case in those days, the Pen was an open-air establishment, and each night Faleti was able to watch the latest films from his apartment window. Projectionist by day and spectator by night, Faleti had quickly become one of Nigeria's great experts on the medium of film.

By 1961, the partnership with Overseas Rediffusion dissolved, owing to ideological differences between the Western Region Government's progressive, public-service, educational agenda and the television corporation's commercial imperative, which favored the transmission of well-produced content from the United States and the United Kingdom, content that tended to maximize advertising revenues. As Faleti recounts, on their way out the door his British bosses accused the Nigerian staff of having "trade union tendencies." The company also believed, according to Faleti, that it would take no less than three years for Africans to learn how to run a television station on their own. Certainly, the split with Overseas Rediffusion led to some chaos at WNTV, but several accounts of the station's early years note that Nigerian personnel mastered the equipment and processes within months. During the reorganization Faleti was reassigned to the radio division, which had opened in May 1960, where his skills in English-to-Yoruba translation were in great demand. In the years that followed he finished a degree at the University of Ibadan, prolifically produced content for radio and television, and was eventually promoted to controller of programs. He also continued to write creatively in Yoruba, which he had been doing for years, and went on to become one of the most influential writers in that language.

As a creative artist and film expert trained by the postcolonial bureaucracy, Faleti embodies many of the contradictions that will be central to part 2 of this book. He learned film through Awolowo's government scheme. He learned small-screen aesthetics and video technology through his time in state television broadcasting. But he is also an independent artist, known for several stinging critiques of the colonial project and the postcolonial Nigerian government. However, key to Faleti's conception of his art is a pedagogical imperative. Films should have an "influence on morals, culture, and patriotism," he told his audience at a lecture in 2009.[14] At the event he also lamented the fact that Nigeria had resorted to making films on video, calling instead for a massive infusion of government funds in order to produce viable content for "international film festivals." That argument is not uncommon among Nigerian intellectuals and even some filmmakers, but Faleti is certainly not in the majority within Nollywood. Many of the industry's pioneers have shown very little interest in festivals, choosing instead to make low-budget commercial films for purely and unapologetically pecuniary purposes. Yet Faleti's interest in morality is shared widely within Nollywood. One major purpose of this book is to understand the historical context of Nollywood's ongoing pedagogical imperative. Whether or not a link can be proven between state television and video film, pedagogy was undoubtedly central to the ascent of television broadcasting.

Within two years of independence the prestige associated with television had infected every major governmental jurisdiction in Nigeria. By the end of 1962, Radio Kaduna Television (RKTV) was broadcasting to the Northern Region, and the federal government, based in Lagos, was broadcasting on the Nigerian Television Network (NTV). Stations were also being established in nations such as Sierra Leone, Northern Rhodesia (now Zambia), Tanzania, Kenya, and Côte d'Ivoire. As one of Faleti's American colleagues at WNTV, George Arms—an ICA consultant to the educational division—blithely phrased it,

Academicians need no longer debate whether it is a good idea for Africans to have television, and economists need no longer concern themselves with its invidious effect upon the balance of the economy and the warping of the purchasing power of a new country. Together they should address themselves to the HOW of this medium—how to get it used, once it exists, for soundly educational and informational purposes, for news, for nation building, for language teaching, for the thousand and one tasks that television is ideally suited for in largely nonliterate communities, instead of observing its use only as an expanded distributor of ancient film series featuring a never-never land where cowboys, murderers, cuckold fathers, luxurious sirens and craggy cops extrapolate themselves unmercifully every twenty-six and one-half minutes. But it won't be easy, friends; it won't be easy. I made a speech once a long time ago, in which I said "Americans *want* entertainment by television. Americans *need* education by television." The same goes for Africans, and in spades.[15]

Despite his casual American style, Arms echoes the sentiments of colonial film officials (see chapter 1), who gravely lamented the idea that Africans would consume commercial entertainment programs from the United States when what they really needed was instruction, in just about everything, from mathematics and English to sewing and hygiene. Arms's emphasis on *how* in this early moment presages the subsequent scholarly focus on the politics and developmental impacts of Nigerian television at the expense of attention to *what* aired. Indeed, the developmentalist sentiment on display in Arms's comments went unchallenged pretty much everywhere in the years following independence. It certainly informed the Western Region government's continued investment in television, despite the fact that it steadily lost money. It also informed the expansion of television in Nigeria over the next four decades.

In Arms's formulation both Americans and Africans *need* education by television, but what is unclear is why Americans also get what they *want*: entertainment. Does Arms exhibit a periliberal sensibility, in which Americans enjoy the benefits of liberalism while Nigerians occupy a marginal dispensation with entirely different needs? Do Africans not also deserve entertainment? And is American entertainment television not also a source of morals, culture, and patriotism? If both societies need education, perhaps the difference between what American and Nigerian spectators receive from television depends on the institutional configurations of production. Perhaps states, particularly postcolonial ones, are capable only of broadcasting normative versions of the values cited by Faleti, while commercial industries are capable of being less orthodox and much more adaptable. If so, Americans get entertainment because production is commercial, whereas Nigerians get education because production has mostly been statist. Certainly, there is some truth to that formulation, but as William Mazzarella argues—pointing to the analogous case of Indian television and its transition from state bureaucracy to commercial industry—the scholarly tendency to juxtapose statist and commercial capabilities tends to underwrite the ideological legitimacy of each.[16] It implies that only the state can elevate the society to new heights and only the market can deliver what people really want. More critically, it succumbs to a representational theory of mass media as opposed to a constitutive one. In the representational model, a media text's effectiveness is measured by the degree to which it mirrors its spectators' lives and desires. State media tends to do it poorly because it is focused on cultivating restrained political aspirations. Commercial media does it well supposedly because it will show people anything they are willing to pay to see. Meanwhile, television, video film, and other screen media actually play key roles in *constituting*, not representing, the everyday realities, desires, and aspirations of the spectators they address. They fill the air with words that the culture then uses to speak. Faleti's experience with ICA experts and his subsequent nostalgia for government media suggest that WNTV's early emphasis on instructional programs—championed by outgoing colonialists, local politicians, and expatriate advisers—constituted a sign system and social space within which the screen would long perform the role of teacher. Therefore, one of the things the screen constituted was a particular relation between media and spectator. If Faleti embodies the contradiction between art and state-sponsored media in mid-century Nigeria, perhaps no other person embodies the media-as-teacher ideal more than Olusola, the first director of programs at WNTV, with whom Faleti worked closely.

OLUSOLA AND THE VILLAGE OF STRANGERS

During the late 1950s, while Faleti was driving around the Western Region in a cinema van, Segun Olusola was plying the same roads with a tape recorder. He began working at the Nigerian Broadcasting Service (NBS) in 1955 and was soon assigned to produce a radio documentary about the ways in which educated Nigerians remembered their school headmasters. The NBS was originally an arm of the colonial government but was later reorganized on a public model, much like the BBC. The Nigerian Broadcasting Corporation (NBC), as it was renamed, was the first public colonial radio network in the vast British Empire, and it invested heavily in developing on-the-ground capacity.[17] Rather than rebroadcast BBC or commercial content from Britain, the NBC sought to train a large staff of Nigerian personnel, comprising some 415 individuals, to develop original content.[18] Olusola's documentary, called *My Headmaster*, which aired in 1958, was part of that push. It consisted of interviews with various eminent personalities as they reminisced about the school administrators who had initiated them into the world of Western letters. Of course, headmasters in those days were more than just school administrators; in some small communities they were the primary representatives of government, and, as such, they often performed the functions of mayors or district officers. At the beginning of formal colonialism, most headmasters were expatriates, but by the dawn of independence many were Nigerians, men (and sometimes women) who were positioned as models of, and even gatekeepers to, modern citizenship.

The *My Headmaster* project apparently made a lasting impression on Olusola, who at first privately and later professionally nurtured ambitions to create a new story revolving around the key social role played by a local headmaster in a small roadside village. According to Olusola, the idea for the story struck him in 1964 as he drove from Ibadan to Lagos.[19] Five years prior, he had been lured from the NBC in Lagos to WNTV in Ibadan—roughly two hours north by road—to serve as the first director of programs at Awolowo's new station. But when the federal government caught the TV bug and launched its own station, Olusola was invited back to Lagos to serve as controller. En route to the interview, Olusola recalls that he drove past his hometown, Iperu—a small town established by workers who had built the Lagos-Ibadan expressway at the turn of the century—and as his car whizzed past, the idea struck him to set his story of an iconic village headmaster in just such a place. He intended to pitch the idea at his interview but forgot because of a case of jitters. Nevertheless, he went back home and drafted a script, which he hoped to develop as soon as his duties began. However, the project was delayed another four years for various professional reasons, not to mention the chaos that followed the military coup of 1966. The first episode of *The Village Headmaster* aired in 1968, and in one incarnation or another it remained on the air in Nigeria until 1990, making it one of the most constant and abiding screen media narratives in the history of the nation.[20]

The narrative energy and social significance of *The Village Headmaster*, as developed in Olusola's "master" script and carried through to the first episodes, proceeds outward from the point where its geographical location and main character intersect. Indeed, the title of the program represents a skillfully distilled and sharply focused signifier of that intersection. The "village" that Olusola creates is a rich, suggestive concept with infinite ability to engender politically salient story lines. It is simultaneously small and large, old and new, local and global. It is designed to make the connotations of the village national as well as make the image of the nation village-like. Similarly, Olusola's "headmaster" is a concept full of contradictory political implications. Embodied in his person, profession, and social status are the simultaneously liberating and oppressive forces of Western education and the liberal world order. He is designed to highlight the international postcolonial entanglements of the village-like nation and the paradoxes of modernity, but he is also meant to somehow rise above them all. In the master script, Olusola describes the village of Oja as a "no man's land," a place where "everybody is a stranger."[21] It is only thirty years old, having been established just before World War II and, like Iperu, was originally a labor camp for the men building a highway. It is located in the Southwest, the Yoruba-speaking part of Nigeria, so it has "developed along Yoruba traditional patterns," says the script, but as descendants of labor migrants, Oja's inhabitants are drawn from throughout the nation. So there are men, and this is their land, but the village is a "no man's land" in the sense that the place cannot be claimed as part of anyone's cultural patrimony. The Yoruba institutions that help unite the community are more superficial, modern conveniences than deep social structures. For example, the institution of the *oba* (roughly, "king" in Yoruba), whose title is oloja of Oja, is a "very modern tradition" indeed.[22] Olusola describes him as "very young . . . at 30" and adds that he "seems to have been planted to act this role."[23] As such, the oloja is conceived less as a spiritual and cultural authority figure than as a political figurehead requiring constant reauthorization. As Olusola writes, "All efforts will be made to protect and sustain the Oloja's political leadership following several unsuccessful attempts at local political government."[24] However, by inventing a so-called traditional ruler—in order to approximate political sovereignty—the Oja community has essentially reproduced the colonial system of indirect rule. Yet despite an inclination toward political defensiveness, the master script reveals that Oja is not a particularly important village because "the highway never materialized."[25] The village's native authority system therefore helps it function in a dispensation where the community was created by various legal, political, and economic processes to which it now has little access.

Despite the prominence of Yoruba institutions, the villagers claim different ethnic backgrounds and speak a great deal of English. In this way, *The Village Headmaster* epitomizes the notorious "federal" style of Nigerian state television, in which ethnic surnames, regional styles of dress, and even certain linguistic flourishes function primarily as fungible cultural capital.[26] That style, of course, was also integral to several other intellectual projects in the early years of independence, including the cerebral dramas of Olusola's close friend and collaborator, Wole Soyinka. In his play *The Road*, for example, Soyinka muses on a similar roadside location featuring a similar mix of characters and cultural capital; nevertheless, he grounds his multiethnic nation-statism in a Yoruba mythopoeia that is as deeply cultural as it is inventively idiosyncratic. James Gibbs actually takes issue with Olusola's "bolt from the blue" account of his inspiration for Oja's "no man's land" setting, suggesting that Olusola copied it from Soyinka's radio series *Broke-Time Bar*, a precursor to *The Road* that Olusola helped Soyinka produce in Ibadan. As Gibbs notes, however, *The Village Headmaster* "has always had sufficiently distinctive qualities in its *dramatis personae*, setting, tone and mood to acquit it on the charge of plagiarism."[27] A more generous reading of the relationship between Olusola's television program and Soyinka's plays would, in fact, suggest that both men derived inspiration from their collaboration and, more importantly, from the generative idea of a small roadside community. Likewise, a more stimulating research question would ask why the image of a village, set near a highway, has so much narrative potential. The thesis that drives my reading is that the village allegorizes a community generated by modern forces—here, a promised highway, with all its connotations of industry and mobility—which would not have been possible without the village's inhabitants (after all, they built the highway), yet their community remains external to and unable to fully participate in the modern forces that the highway represents. The roadside village is quite simply a metaphor for periliberalism.

The gatekeeper between village and highway, or nation and modernity, is the headmaster. Olusola imagined the original headmaster, Gabriel Fagade, not only as a teacher but also as a pastor, an organist, and, most important of all, "a genial forty-year-old settler of quarrels."[28] He established the Oja school some twenty years before the events of the first episode, meaning that he arrived just a decade after the formalization of the office of the oloja. However, this relatively minor difference in timing animates one of the major contradictions that the show allegorically explores. The village is new and multiethnic. The political authority that governs it is young and barely legitimate. Nevertheless, villagers have developed a sense of autochthony, projected onto the office of the oloja, to which the headmaster cannot lay claim. He is the bearer of Western letters, music, and religion. He works tirelessly to contain social disruption. He travels often to the nearest metropolis, Ibadan, to take and bring back messages for the federal government. He is essential to the functioning of Oja, especially its modern institutions, but he is reminded again and again that he can never call it home.

The plot of the master script fully develops this dilemma. It revolves around an outbreak of yellow fever, euphemistically referred to as "the stranger," which sets off chauvinist suspicions that nearly drive Fagade from the village. In the end the oloja confirms Fagade's citizenship by offering to bestow upon him a chieftaincy title; meanwhile, in his house, Fagade's "wife," Clara (he is a widower living with a woman he has never formally married), attempts to scandalize his daughter by telling her that despite having what appears to be a Yoruba surname, Fagade hails from a small ethnic group in the East. These intrigues are set against the arrival of a mysterious letter written in French that one of Fagade's employees— the daughter of another recent eastern immigrant—has been busy translating since the opening scene. When it is eventually read aloud to the oloja, the letter reports that Oja is one of six villages to which the "Headquarters of International Human Rights" has been invited by the federal government of Nigeria to see the "harmony that exists among the various tribes."[29] What the master script masterfully establishes, therefore, is the strategic usefulness of both nativism and multicultural liberal nationalism, depending on one's objectives and the resources at hand.

These contradictions, established in Olusola's master script and his original character sketches, remained key to the show's profile throughout its run. Fagade was played by Ted Mukoro from 1968 to 1972, after which Olusola created a new headmaster, Ife Araba, played by Femi Robinson from 1972 to 1984. In the character sketch for Araba—part of a proposal for a renewal of the program, called The New Village Headmaster—Olusola describes the second headmaster much like the first: "His antecedents are not known and are source of materials [sic] for investigation and although he was born and brought up in a Yoruba community, he is a 'stranger' in almost any community." However, Olusola emphasizes that the headmaster's strange quality is a result of his Western education as much as his vague origins. He is described as a "philosopher-teacher-spiritualist" who considers Oja's social organization a "text for his philosophical studies to which he applies a most inquiring mind."[30] The third and final headmaster was Cosmas Aderibigbe Ali, played by Justus Esiri, from 1984 to 1990 (Esiri would go on to star in dozens of Nollywood video films, some of which are discussed in this book). In a 1986 episode, Chief Eleyinmi, the Oloja's second in command—hilariously played by Funsho Adeolu— scolds Aderibigbe with the lines "Whatever you are, whatever book you have read, you are a stranger in Oja. And you will always be a stranger here." In other words, local achievement does not a local citizen make. Quite the contrary. Not only has his (neo)colonial education ensured that Aderibigbe can never become one of the villagers, but modernity has in fact produced a nation and a man who cannot belong to one another. The headmaster's alienation is redoubled in a village where *everyone* is a stranger. Because the show was created by a Western-educated government official working for one of the most prominent developmental state apparatuses in Africa, *The Village Headmaster* has a lot to say about the ways in which elites may have understood and responded to—and perhaps lamented—their positions in postcolonial society. Historians, ethnographers, and literary scholars of Africa have repeatedly commented on the postcolonial elite's alienation from the rest of society, but the stories that men like Olusola tell in scripts and in novels do more than represent that phenomenon; they actively constitute the set of relations within which periliberal subjectivities thrive.

EMERGENCY POWERS

Olusola may have modeled Oja on his hometown of Iperu, but Oja Village—as an allegorical symbol—is invested with far more dynamism than Olusola saw elsewhere in rural Nigeria. In a 1964 speech at King's College, Lagos, he described his own rural upbringing as the antidote to urban life. He equated the geographical space of the village with the past. Tradition and culture, he claimed, are firmly rooted there. He called the village setting "a perfect system born of generations of experience and observation of natural physical causes." Finally, he expressed a desire to keep Nigeria's villages "intact" so that able-bodied men would not be lured away to big cities, resulting in a situation where "old and tired men are left to till the earth and protect the women."[31] Indeed, the intensive urbanization of Nigeria—from which Olusola and the members of his audience at King's College had no doubt benefited and that was expanding exponentially at the time—presented a number of challenges for the country, particularly in food production and housing. However, urbanization also presented opportunities, many of which still have yet to be realized. Had cities not been built according to the dictates of indirect rule, they might have been more capable of handling waves of immigration and productively employing the subsequent agglomeration of labor. Instead, postcolonial migration has tended to reproduce what Ato Quayson refers to as the "spatial nexus of the colonial template" on varying scales.[32] Inadequate housing, zoning, and transportation arteries persist, making urban immigration compoundingly burdensome for citizens and officials alike. In 1964, as he spoke to a room full of elites, Olusola called for "emergency action" to stem the tide.[33]

Because Olusola was a television producer, his proposed emergency action involved the broadcasting of filmed content. In his speech he referred to a study—one he had helped conduct three years prior—of rural Nigerian spectators' reactions to various television programs. As part of the project, researchers posed the following question to a hundred members of an unnamed village fifteen miles from Ibadan: "If you could grant one gift to each Nigerian baby born today, which of the following would you choose: (a) Wisdom, (b) Wealth, or (c) Good Health?" Thirty-five villagers chose wisdom, seventeen chose wealth, and forty-eight chose good health. The respondents were then shown a program called *The Brains Trust*—modeled on a BBC program of the same name—in which a panel of experts discussed the same question. The consensus of the panel, according to Olusola, was that "Good Health was the wisest choice and no panelist thought wealth was worth anything on its own."[34] The next morning, the researchers surveyed the villagers again, and this time an astonishing seventy-six chose good health but not a single person chose wealth. Olusola cites these findings as evidence of the extraordinary power of television to influence village minds and manufacture social cohesion—and perhaps consent—betraying his investment in the modernization ideology that reigned supreme at the time. In this case, however, villagers were essentially instructed by government propaganda to suppress their material aspirations in favor of their bodily well-being, suggesting a biopolitical rather than redistributive imperative.[35] Likewise, the animating assumption of the project, the idea that internal migration and its effect on public health constitute a "state of emergency," seems to be a formulation that Olusola borrowed from the French.

A similar experiment in rural television and national development was conducted in France in 1956, subsidized by UNESCO and unironically titled "State of Emergency." In UNESCO's report on the project, French villagers of the time were described as illiterate, inarticulate, and dirty. Their homes were depicted as old, run-down, and unsanitary. More significantly, the report laments that French villagers produced little more than they consumed—failing to generate surplus value—while being highly resistant to modern farming techniques. In the minds of rural French citizens, it seems, there was no emergency at all. So it might be more accurate to think of the state of emergency envisioned by postwar global elites—in France as in Nigeria—as an emergency of the state (see figure 2.3). At issue was the ability of modern governments to harness both the productivity and attention of the nation without being overly nationalistic (after all, cultural nationalism was regarded by some with deep skepticism in the immediate postwar years). In France, bombed-out cities and industrial zones could not handle waves of migration from the countryside, so the countryside had to be made into a major site of production as well as an attractive place to remain. Thus, for different reasons, France and Nigeria both needed television to create (a fantasy about) the enabling conditions in which village life would seem fulfilling within an economic system otherwise increasingly antithetical to rural life. The material fortunes of villagers were not likely to swell, but staying in good health and good spirits would go a long way to alleviate pressures on urban infrastructure.

The UNESCO report notes that "the chief difficulty in planning the telecasts was to find a subject that would interest both the wine-grower and the farmer, the labourer and the engineer, the village family and city television audiences, for there is only one television network in France."[36] This difficulty has particular relevance for Nigeria, where—despite the initial proliferation of subnational state governments and the television stations they operated—programming was increasingly centralized. By 1976, all Nigerian television stations would be subsumed under one federal network. As centralization increased, therefore, the key lesson that Nigeria seems to have drawn from the French example is the idea that good programming could appeal to urban and rural audiences equally. After many forms and genres were tried in France and opinions were recorded several times, the consensus was that programs should focus on modern farming techniques and machinery, which made rural life seem relevant to urbanites and urban industrial products central to rural living. The periliberal character of the French strategy is striking: with modern technology, villages would enter the modern world, although they would not enter the *urban* world. Indeed, the urban world would benefit from keeping the rural world out. In the end the UNESCO vision would become more applicable to the Nigerian context than Olusola could have possibly imagined in 1964. By the 1980s, one of the NTA's most popular programs, *Cock Crow at Dawn*, was explicitly produced to accompany the "Green Revolution," an early neoliberal project in which modern farming techniques were promoted across the Third World in order to cement postcolonial dependency on First World seed and machinery manufacturers.[37]

If a state of emergency calls for minimizing dissent, Olusola was nevertheless well aware of the dissonance that could, and often did, swirl

'STATE OF EMERGENCY'

TV TEST TUBE
(Cont'd)

UNESCO-Cassirer

AN EASIER LIFE for countrywomen was the subject of one of the "State of Emergency" programmes. Yet a survey among tele-clubs showed that more women than men are opposed to modernization. Left, Roger Louis, tele-club organizer turned producer who arranged the programmes.

THE evening of January 7, 1954, marks an important date for a group of small French villages some 60 miles from Paris. On that evening farmers, rural workers and local officials were crowded together in their town halls and schools to "have a look at the television". They were there for the opening of a new television series called "State of Emergency" which had been prepared for their tele-clubs by the Radiodiffusion-Télévision Française and Unesco. The series was a unique experiment which had as its goal the introduction of mechanization on farms, and modernization of living conditions in villages.

The joint project grew out of a Unesco decision to produce a series of educational programmes aimed at rural populations, to evaluate the results and to publicize them for the benefit of governments, educators and television producers throughout the world who are trying to find the best ways of using television for adult education in rural areas.

Why did Unesco choose a group of French villages for its experiment? Firstly because the conditions there seemed to offer an ideal "testing bench". It is no mere chance that tele-club associations had sprung up mainly in the country where the need for new kinds of entertainment has become more pressing as countryfolk have become more aware of the greater amenities of town life. Secondly because the economic and cultural conditions of the little villages to the east of Paris reflect a way of life that is roughly the same in many other countries.

Isolation, material handicaps and financial and social problems, all too common in Europe and elsewhere, are barriers to a badly needed modernization.

Thus the lessons and conclusions drawn from a pilot project conducted in France through the tele-clubs would, with some adjustments, very probably serve as a guide for the introduction of television into the country areas of many of Unesco's member states, and at the same time would be of help to other countries embarking on similar educational experiments.

The chief difficulty in planning the telecasts was to find a subject that would interest both the wine-grower and the farmer, the labourer and the engineer, the village family and city television audiences, for there is only one television network in France. Finally, it was decided that the series should demonstrate the vital problems confronting French agriculture and the need to introduce modern methods for their solution.

All the problems would be presented in a framework of "true life stories" and in nearly all the programmes their main lines would be explained through the experiences of living people. In many cases farmers came to the studio. Viewers, for example, were introduced to M. Lecomte whose son had joined the army and left him, at an advanced age, to work his farm alone.

A small farmer and an industrialist discussing credit, revealed both sides of the question. Whether the subject was the re-allocation of *(Cont'd on next page)*

9

FIGURE 2.3. First page of the article "State of Emergency," published in the *UNESCO Courier*, May 9, 1956.

around television broadcasting. In a 1978 speech at the NTA Festival of Television Drama, he described a number of ways in which his agenda as a television producer had been resisted over the years. In one case a 1960 production of Soyinka's *My Father's Burden*, a satire of political corruption, was met by "an official attempt to stifle its production" yet aired anyhow. In the following six years, Olusola acerbically observes, political corruption in Nigeria did not wane. In another case a scene of adultery that he staged in a televised play met with public outrage, not only for depicting a fictional immoral act but also for broadcasting images of an actual married woman—the actress—in bed with an actual married man—the actor. Finally, Olusola recounts that in a televised production of J. P. Clark's *Song of a Goat*, the crucial culminating scene in which Zifa, the protagonist—played by Ted Mukoro—slaughters a real goat caused such an uproar that the network did not run a repeat of the production for five years. The effect that audiences can have on a producer therefore prompted Olusola to speculate that "perhaps it is the society that influences television drama and not the other way round." However, rather than celebrate the power of audiences—and, by extension, the emerging Nigerian public—Olusola instead cites these examples in order to double down, more than a decade after his speech at King's College and almost two decades since the experiments in France, on the concept of state emergency powers. As he concludes, "The Executive presidential system, itself an expression of our yearning for some firm political leadership, implies that all the tools necessary to prosecute a developing economy must be made available to the political leadership."[38]

Ultimately, Olusola rejects the two best-known models of public television, the BBC in the United Kingdom and the Public Broadcasting Service (PBS) in the United States, in favor of a more authoritarian, developmentalist version of mass mediation. He also qualifies the value of Euro-American liberal norms such as press freedom, private media ownership, and artistic license. Those norms may serve certain kinds of social systems, he concedes, but Nigeria is distinct. As a "conglomeration of well developed homogenous groups attempting to survive under one modern nation-state," the country must concede emergency powers to its leaders. He continues:

Our emerging nation-state is in a state of war externally against highly developed nation-states of all political isms whose interests are being rapidly eliminated by the prospect of our emergence, and internally against ignorance of a most pernicious species—because we do not recognize our ignorance.

The instruments of war at this moment do not consist of machine guns and tanks, lawyers and diplomats, bankers and money fixers: all, invariably, products of our external aggressors. This is a battle for the minds of the people, a war of ideas and television broadcasting or the control of it is central to the armoury.

Television producers, dramatists, and the ideas managers of Nigerian Television should all be part of this vast arsenal of weaponry—in order to achieve a society that can truly be a modern nation-state.[39]

Instructive in these comments is Olusola's sketch of a world order threatened by and thus hostile to the emergence of sovereign nation-states in Africa. And although his characterization of the Nigerian public—as an ignorant mass against which an all-out propaganda war must be waged—may be hard to endorse, the Euro-American public broadcasting models he rejects were—at the time—similarly "authoritarian, classist, and statist," according to Michael Cramer. However, what really matters about state and public television, in Cramer's estimation, is their "utopian" horizons, the promises they make about the possibilities open to a well-informed, cohesive society, which—even if they have historically been subverted—"we can call on the future to fulfill."[40]

Cramer's account of "utopian television" depends in large part on the idea that artists and intellectuals are invited to participate in and leave their mark on public broadcasting. However, Olusola notes that his declaration of war may rankle artists, who refuse "to be caged—raging to fly free." "They have my best wishes," he deigns dismissively before softening a little and committing to work with artists who understand the nature of the crisis.[41] Of course, Olusola's characterization of the crisis, especially the external threat, is not without merit. It may be unnerving to see a statesman declare war against his fellow citizens, but Olusola is beyond reproach for leveling accusations against the "first" and "second" worlds, both of which were waging massive media campaigns attempting to win hearts and minds across the planet. Moreover, as several political theorists have argued, the state of emergency, or "exception," is actually the "paradigmatic form of government" in modern times.[42] During the cold war, therefore, the state of exception that Olusola claimed would have given lasting power to the gatekeeper state, not only to ensure its sovereignty and remain nonaligned but also to then turn around, imagine, and address a public that needed specialized attention until such time as it could "truly be a modern nation-state."

The notion of a "gatekeeper state," once again, comes from Cooper, who in recent work describes it as a viable form of statecraft only because of the "extreme asymmetry in economic relations between Africa and the industrial countries." Guarding the gate has indeed allowed the relatively young and weak states of Africa to assert Westphalian sovereignty against various kinds of external influence, but Cooper reasserts that it has also allowed the state to wield repressive influence over the lives of its citizens. "Development was too important," he writes, "as a source of manipulable patronage resources and as a symbol of the state's gatekeeper power to be allowed to take a course toward private accumulation or toward letting trade unions, farmers' associations, and other organizations independent of the state take the initiative."[43] As part of the gate, therefore, Olusola's conception of television as a "weapon" places it on a kind of social rampart. Done right, it fends off unwanted outside influence and fosters public confidence. As Cooper points out, however, development turns out to have been as much about tamping down internal initiative and maintaining state control of the gate as it has been about unleashing the potential of the citizenry. The public that Nigeria's foremost architect of state television has imagined, at least according to his many speeches, is evidently periliberal. Its members do not live in a modern nation-state and must therefore wait outside of the liberal world order, with all of its self-righteous political ideals, until their chance to participate or to respond effectively to its processes eventually arrives. In his work as a content creator, however, Olusola did not simply seek to address a periliberal public (although he did so); more importantly, his programming—as I will show in the next section—seems to have been designed to create an opportunity for the public to identify with and therefore concede to—but also prop up—the gatekeeper developmentalist state.

THE VILLAGE HEADMASTER

The central premise of Olusola's most successful and memorable creation is that its modern, educated, authoritative hero is forever embattled. The village headmaster does thankless work on behalf of a mostly ambivalent, sometimes openly hostile community, but his dedication never wavers, and he is always rewarded in the end. In the first iteration of the show, Fagade's qualifications are called into question on several occasions, and multiple characters attempt to get him fired. By the late 1980s, in *The New Village Headmaster*, little had changed. In one episode a local government council tries to get the headmaster and his entire staff sacked because students have scored poorly on a federal exam ("A Path of Honour"). In another, a master seamstress refuses to release Ali's daughter and his niece from their apprenticeship ("Freedom Ceremony"). She accuses Ali of encouraging the girls to usurp her authority as a master craftswoman once they have graduated. The only person who can reason with her is the oloja, who reminds her that he controls the market hierarchy within which she works. The show's drama thus revolves around a critical tension between the developmental state, embodied by the headmaster, and reactionary, local elites who seek to undermine it at every turn. That tension may indeed be one of the most clichéd narrative engines in modern African storytelling, although the poles are also frequently reversed. A small cadre of local elites, who are supposedly dedicated to *real* African values, are just as often pitted against the invasive forces of a reckless Western modernity. As we have seen, colonial cinema productions such as *Black Cotton* (see chapter 1) construct a periliberal resolution to this tension by fashioning a mode of address in which nativist resistance to modernization is neither reactionary nor authentic but represents the crucial concept of sovereignty, therefore absolving Western institutions—both foreign and local—from the mandate and responsibility to intervene in or support the social systems they have isolated. In contrast, *The New Village Headmaster* confronts nativism head-on, although it also fails to challenge periliberalism. As I argue below, the show ridicules vestiges of indirect rule—especially customary courts—not because it prefers to champion global citizens, networked to the liberal world order, but because it wants to prepare citizens for life on the edge of a world order into which they may one day qualify for entry. Moreover, the developmental state institutions that the show celebrates are the gatekeepers that will ultimately determine what the process of qualification entails. Customary courts may seem relevant to people's lives, the show suggests, but they cannot make people modern.

In the seventy-eighth episode of the series, titled "Heroes, Villains, and Others" (1986), the third headmaster, Cosmas Aderibigbe Ali, is accused of illegally raising funds under the guise of a community development project to pursue his own personal ventures. Three men in particular—the chief judge of the local customary court, Chief Eleyinmi; a local government councilor, Bamishe (Dele Ogunmiluyi); and a close relative of the oloja, Dagbolu (Dan Imoudu)—conspire to turn the entire village against Ali. What most worries the three conspirators, who are so pompous and inept that the show invites spectators to laugh at them with derision, is not that the headmaster might bend federal rules or that he might abuse his social position—none of which he does, of course. Rather, they seem to be particularly worried that he actually has the power to mobilize the village and raise the funds necessary to complete a major project. The show's mode of address invites spectators not just to celebrate the headmaster's efforts but to identify with him while simultaneously reviling any effort to impede his progress.

The episode begins with an exemplary convergence of screen media techniques that brings the show's mode of address into focus. An official letter has just been delivered by courier to Ali, who opens it while striding into his parlor (see figure 2.4). As he reads, a single-stroke drumroll, played on a Western-style snare, rattles the sound track. The camera angle is flat, providing a medium shot of Ali, who faces right so that spectators see his profile and the letter equally. Then he turns slightly, almost facing the camera. The drumroll plays once more, stops, and then again, each time longer than the last. Every drumroll is also followed by a short, almost imperceptible double thud, perhaps on the kick drum

FIGURE 2.4. *The New Village Headmaster*. Ali reads a letter from the Schools Management Committee.

of a trap set. Ali looks up, consternation clearly visible on his face. As he broods, there is a knock at the door, and four people enter, members of a fund-raising committee who have come to discuss their plans for a bore-hole in Oja. Ali hands the letter to Mr. Garuba—the senior teacher at his school, endearingly played by Joe Layode—who reads it aloud:

Dear Mr. Ali,

It has come to the notice of the SMC, that you, as headmaster of Oja Community School, are illegally collecting funds from parents in the name of school development. You are well-aware of the Ministry of Education's instructions, to parents and teachers' associations, particularly head-masters, that under no circumstances should levies be collected for any school development. You will please explain in writing within 24 hours why disciplinary action should not be taken against you.

The Schools Management Committee, it seems, is under the impression that Ali's project, which is meant for the entire village, with which his teachers are assisting, and—as spectators later learn—which has been endorsed by an extension officer from the Ministry of Health and Rural Development, Miss Ebibi, is some kind of private infrastructure project for either him or his school. The official prohibition against such a project would have been designed to mitigate corruption or the use of an official office to solicit funds from ordinary people, as well as to ensure that all construction projects tied to federal institutions are carefully vetted. The letter implies that even if the money were used to enhance the school, it would be illegal for not flowing through the proper channels. As the members of the committee reveal, however, rumors are circulating in town that the money will be spent not on the school—sanctioned or not—but on sending Ali's son abroad for medical treatment or perhaps for building a clinic to be run by Ali's wife, Fatima. All this is a total surprise to Ali. Therefore, the letter is a bombshell. The drumrolls that play as he reads it allow spectators into his affective state as it unfolds.

The initial, short bursts of drum rattling seem to signal the agitation that would inevitably accompany the opening of an official letter addressed to its reader. The first one begins before Ali has laid eyes on the text. The next one seems to accompany Ali's reading of the letter's salutation. As he continues to read, the drumrolls are longer and longer. The final one extends beyond the act of reading, as Ali looks up and reflects. Nevertheless, most of the drumrolls align with steps of the decoding routine. The three long rolls synchronize with the three long sentences of the letter. The kick-drum sound at the end of each one imitates punctuation, perhaps a period (or "full stop"). The narrative eye of the program does not show us the letter, nor does its ear provide Ali's inner monologue, as if quoting him while he reads. Instead, the drumrolls provide access to Ali's emotions while the visual signs narrate his act of reading. Therefore, the subjectivity offered is indirect and freely so. It is not an open window into Ali's subjectivity; rather, it is mediated by the distinction between eye and ear. Yet it also provides free access to both subjectivities, as if the narrator were temporarily slipping into and out of Ali's head space.

Ali's reading of the letter also contrasts with other readings. Besides Mr. Garuba, both Miss Ebibi, the rural extension officer, and Oja's other local government councilor, Mr. Balogun—who serves on the borehole committee—are handed the letter as the plot unfolds. Both read in silence, grinning or snickering here and there, signaling their recognition of the letter's absurdity. But their readings are narrated strictly in the third person. No drumrolls or other audiovisual conventions offer spectators access to their subjectivities. The headmaster is the only one given the opportunity to tell his experience of the story along with the narrator's.

The letter, of course, is central to the plot of the episode. Ali will have to prove to the relevant state institutions that he is working in the name of his community, not in his own self-interest, and that the borehole is not intended for the school alone. To the members of his committee, Ali wonders aloud, "How can one help this community without being branded a crook or a fake?" That question is also central to the show's chosen mode of address. By granting spectators access to Ali's emotions at the very moment he reads the letter, *The New Village Headmaster* invites spectators to sympathize with his paradoxical subject position, raising even more questions: Can development proceed from representatives of the state without looking paternalistic? Will people ever trust someone telling them what they need and asking for their money to get it? And if people object to the agendas of bureaucrats, is there a higher authority to which they can appeal? Moreover, in addition to accusations that Ali is misusing the people's resources, he also fears the power of the higher-level bureaucrats under which he labors. Thus, when spectators are allowed to enter, however briefly, into the subject position of the village developmentalist at the very moment when these questions are being raised, they are invited to see two overlapping layers of postcolonial statecraft. There is the enterprise of development, and then there are the politics.

By the end of the episode, Ali has proven to everyone that his motives are pure. His superiors not only endorse the borehole project; they
also attend the fund-raising ceremony. Eleyinmi also reverses course.
He returns to the oloja's palace, hobbled for having danced excessively
at the ceremony, and declares, "That man they call Aderibigbe Ali is
a fantastic man. His types are rare in any community." A major source
of Eleyinmi's newfound reverence for Ali comes from learning that Oja's
borehole will be the first in the region, putting their village far ahead of
others nearby. We can hear echoes of Peter Morton-Williams's research
on colonial cinema's rural audiences, in which interest in infrastructure
projects followed less from what the infrastructure provided than from
the status it conferred and the gaps it closed between citizen and subject.
Eleyinmi is not exactly jockeying for liberal citizenship status, but he is
no die-hard nativist either. As the key figure of comic relief and ridicule,
he is a parodic counterbalance to everything the headmaster represents.
If the headmaster is serious, single-minded, and dedicated, Eleyinmi is
preposterous, inconsistent, and pretentious. Part of identifying with the
headmaster's subjectivity, then, is gaining an affective sympathy for
the sense of exasperation that Eleyinmi frequently elicits. Indeed, Eleyinmi is a character worth considering at some length.

Chief Nicodemus Ologbenla Eleyinmi is a judge on Oja's customary
court. He often describes himself as the "chief justice" of the court, conspicuously borrowing the language of English common law. In fact, one
of Eleyinmi's most memorable characteristics, and the key to much of his
comedy, is his propensity for linguistic aggrandizement and malapropism.
His catchphrase, if it can be called that, is "legal jurisprudence," which
he seems to use in every other sentence. His entire public presentation is
premised on the idea that no matter what he is discussing, he is the one
bringing "legal jurisprudence" to bear on the matter. His voice is high-
pitched and breathy; his speech is halting. He tends to talk at length,
meandering through labyrinths of terminology and regularly painting
himself into a rhetorical corner. He is almost always wrong, but he is successful at convincing others to go along with him or, at least, preventing
them from being able to counter his arguments. He is also visually comic.
The late Funsho Adeolu, who played Eleyinmi from 1972 to 1990, developed the idiosyncrasy of pulling his arms inside his capacious *agbada*
so that his gestures are hidden from view, producing a kind of tent-like
effect that centripetally diminishes his physical presence. At one point
during "Heroes, Villains and Others," Eleyinmi, Bamishe, and Dagbolu
are bent over a table discussing the building plans for a new customary

FIGURE 2.5. *The New Village Headmaster*. Eleyinmi folds his arms inside his agbada.

courthouse. Eleyinmi giddily anticipates the space in which he and his peers will be "soaked in terminological inexactitude of criminal law and jurisprudence." Bamishe then notes that this is the place where "judges will be writing evidences [*sic*]," but he suddenly becomes somber, suggesting that Eleyinmi will have trouble writing anything. Why? Bamishe mischievously pulls his arms inside his own agbada, imitating his friend (see figure 2.5). Without a word, Bamishe's gesture asks the question: how could Eleyinmi ever hold a pen with his arms inside his clothes? Everyone doubles over with laughter.

Customary courts are, of course, a holdover from the colonial era and a foundational component of indirect rule. Originally called "native courts" in Nigeria, these institutions were designed to settle disputes—over land, other kinds of property, and marriage—that arose between native parties or, in some cases, between one native and one nonnative party. On paper, the idea was to provide colonized subjects the opportunity to live according to the norms and axioms derived from their cultural heritage. In reality, however, customary courts created a distinction between African subjects and non-African citizens, defining the limits of liberal jurisprudence and often forcing the creation of hybrid, Frankensteinian legal codes that were neither indigenous nor liberal.[44] Eleyinmi's inventive language signals his incomplete relationship with both the indigenous social system and the liberal world order that impinges on it. He often bills himself as the oloja's second in command, but the oloja—now elderly and accordingly wise—barely tolerates Eleyinmi's spurious behavior. Eleyinmi may preside over the customary laws of Oja but not over all of its customs or many of its laws. Therefore, in one sense Eleyinmi is socially impotent, like El Hadji Abdou Kader Beye in Ousmane Sembene's *Xala* (1975). Although Eleyinmi is not literally impotent the way El Hadji is, both are, in the more important allegorical sense, powerful and esteemed figures whose authority seemingly derives from nowhere, neither from abroad nor from the local community. Eleyinmi is clearly not an agent of the state, like the headmaster. Meanwhile, the oloja props him up, entertains his eccentricities, and tolerates his council but then usually contradicts him. In the final balance sheet, Eleyinmi is an elite with no constituency. And this is the man, we cannot forget, who reminds Ali that "whatever you are, whatever book you have read, you are a stranger in Oja. And you will always be a stranger here." Eleyinmi's comic position in the narrative thus augments the show's mode of address by inviting spectators not only to laugh at him but to do so from the perspective of the headmaster, the representative of the developmental state, which regards Eleyinmi as quaint and absurd—necessary, perhaps, but anomalous all the same.

One final note about the oloja. The producer of *The New Village Headmaster*, Dejumo Lewis, played the *Kabiyesi* (the Yoruba term of address for an oba, used frequently in the show) as a slow-talking, perceptive, and supremely just figurehead. He would go on to play a supremely just oba in the widely renowned video film *Agogo Eewo* (2002), made by the equally renowned director Tunde Kelani. When Eleyinmi and his accomplices suggest that Ali might be using the borehole funds to build a clinic for his wife, Lewis's Kabiyesi wonders why that should matter if, in the end, the money goes to help the community. Indeed, although the oloja of Olusola's master script is conceptualized as an implant, someone who is barely legitimate, Lewis's oloja, some twenty-five years later, has fully established his moral authority. He too is comic. He often undercuts Eleyinmi to hilarious effect. And Lewis adopts his own physical idiosyncrasies for the performance, such as habitually reversing two steps, in order to build momentum, before launching himself forward, especially when ascending to his throne. Thus, if the original oloja embodied the system of indirect rule, the creation of ostensibly indigenous institutions where they were otherwise absent, the oloja of the final incarnation of the program has become a tradition in his own right, handed down over several decades to multiple actors, not to mention loyal viewers. *The New Village Headmaster* may invite its spectators to identify with an embattled developmentalist state, trying in vain to make Nigeria into what Olusola calls a "modern nation-state," but it also cements the effects of indirect rule. The oloja comes across as quaint, but more sympathetically so than Eleyinmi. Noble and sagacious, he is the preserve of knowledge and values — or custom — under which people can safely shelter until the headmaster finally opens the way to the liberal world order.

"THE VIDEO SHOCK"

During the years that Justus Esiri played the village headmaster, the middle to late 1980s, Nigeria suffered a severe economic crisis. During the "oil shocks" of the previous decade, state revenue from crude production had peaked, inflating the country's economic portfolio. The value of the naira soared, and the state made several infrastructural investments, including expanding the NTA (although it squandered and siphoned off plenty of oil money too). Over the course of the next decade, however, oil prices steadily dropped, and revenues dried up, laying Nigeria's weak structural conditions bare.

As the process played out, Olusola observed that the oil boom had "made every other household in the city centres affluent enough to own not only a television set but also a home video player." At the time, most of the content available for viewing on a "home video player," or VCR, was imported (and then illegally dubbed), usually from the United States and Hong Kong. The first local videos produced for mass-market distribution were music videos, featuring the stars of Nigeria's vibrant and globally influential popular music scene. In an essay titled "The Video Shock," Olusola wrote that "for the television broadcaster, the Nigerian home video culture is a nightmare which could have literally deprived him of his job were the job market realistic. As it is, he is kept in business only because television is a public service, state-owned venture."[45]

In hindsight, of course, this was a faulty forecast. What Olusola lamented was that home video almost exclusively provided foreign content. State-owned television provided plenty of foreign content too, but it also produced and aired a great deal of local content. For him, that was the beauty of state media: sovereignty. It staved off the invasive tendencies of the market. What Olusola could not have seen coming was a home video culture that almost exclusively produced local content, which is what began to emerge in the late 1980s. When *Living in Bondage* arrived in 1992, it represented a new kind of sovereignty, one independent from outside forces but not closed off to outside influences. The question that remains, to which part 2 of this book is addressed, is whether or to what degree video film altered the configurations of sovereignty that obtain for a postcolonial nation created by but without direct access to the liberal world order. To put it another way: Does trade still follow the flag? If so, what flag?

Part II

3 "No Romance without Finance"

FEMININE MELODRAMA, SOAP OPERA, AND THE MALE BREADWINNER IDEAL

In April 1991 *Checkmate* debuted on the NTA at 8:00 PM on Thursdays. It quickly became one of the most widely discussed soap operas in Nigerian television history. When it premiered, the Lagos *Guardian* covered a press release distributed by the show's creator, Amaka Igwe (then Isaac-Ene). She declared that her program—despite the fact that it was produced independently, was underwritten by Lever Brothers, and was merely broadcast by the NTA—would continue the developmentalist tradition of the state television network. As Igwe wrote, *Checkmate* was designed to "mirror happenings in our society with the view to providing positive reinforcements of valuable norms: such as good business ethnics [*sic*], fidelity in marriage, good child-rearing techniques, etc."[1] These genuflections to developmentalist rhetoric were likely strategic, given the increasingly tense relationship between independent producers and the NTA at the time.[2] It was simply in Igwe's best interests to present *Checkmate* as a public service, whereas in fact she later fully embraced the Nollywood business model precisely because it allowed her to circumvent the NTA and its paternalist mandate. In the years that followed her move to video film, as Igwe wielded massive influence over the commercial film industry, she regularly and unapologetically reminded her critics and interrogators, as she did for me in 2010, that her primary motivator was straightforward financial gain. She made stories, she said—and very good ones by most measures—because she wanted to make money. Full stop. Indeed, a cursory look at *Checkmate* reveals that if it had anything to say about good business ethics, marital fidelity, or child rearing, it was certainly not by mirroring "positive reinforcements." The show's characters regularly engaged in corporate espionage, cheated on their spouses, and abused or neglected their children. If *Checkmate* was designed to cultivate prosocial norms, then the method it used might be described not as mirroring but as *foiling*, in which norms are advanced by sensuously developing and then summarily castigating examples of their transgression.[3]

Consider *Checkmate*'s depiction of "business ethics." The series revolves around Anne Haatrope (Ego Boyo, née Nnamani), who, along with her two brothers, Benny (Francis Agu) and Richard Jr. (BobManuel Udokwu), control their father's large investment firm. As the first episode commences, Anne and Richard Jr. are returning from the United States, where they have been living for several years while their ailing father received medical treatment. During those years Anne built a successful company of her own, to which she plans to return. However, she and Richard Jr. find that Benny, who has been at the helm of Haatrope Investments in their absence, has run the family company into the ground. The books are a mess, revenues have not been collected, and a major creditor is threatening to call in a loan. There are several scenes in which Benny drinks whiskey and snorts cocaine. He is oblivious to the fact that their Uncle Vite (Olatide Ajayi Jiyeh), Richard Sr.'s brother, is embezzling company funds and trading secrets with a competing firm. Anne must therefore stay in Nigeria to right the ship. As she does so, quite expertly, she discovers that a rival investor, Segun Kadiri (Richard Mofe-Damijo), seeks not only to outbid her on every deal but to destroy Haatrope Investments entirely. Kadiri forces Anne into a shadow business war where several underhanded and even illegal techniques become necessary. She strategizes against Kadiri like a chess grandmaster, which gives the show its title, but she is hardly a paragon of capital investment ethics, whatever those might be.

Likewise, marital fidelity finds few paragons amongst *Checkmate*'s cast of characters. One of Richard Jr.'s old friends, Akpan Edem (Tunde Euba), is a student at the University of Lagos, where his father, Monday (first played by Zulu Adigwe and later by Norbert Young), is a lecherous professor: a stock character in Nigerian popular culture. He is caught several times in compromising situations with students, but for much of the first season, Monday's wife, Eno (played by the show's original producer, Tammy Abassi), is stoic in her loyalty and patience. Similarly, one of Richard Sr.'s old business partners, a developer named Tajudeen Adebowale Fuji (Kunle Bamtefa), is a staunch patriarch and polygamist with three wives—one of whom he marries during the first season—and more than a dozen children. Early in the show's run, he is obliged to take in a child from one of his affairs, a deaf teenage boy, against which his second, and most insubordinate wife, Peace (played by the famous highlife singer, Pauline Njoku), protests vehemently—though in vain. Fuji's senior wife, Moji (Toun Oni), tells Peace that "children is children, whether inside or outside wedlock." Fuji's household is thus chaotic and mutinous, and it constitutes the show's comic relief. His wives and children scheme—often jealously against one another—to extract money from him while he maneuvers to hoard his wealth and chase women. A friend of Fuji's son calls the place "Fuji house of commotion," which would eventually become the title of a situation comedy spin-off, also produced by Igwe, which debuted in 2001. Once again, however, if Checkmate is designed to promote marital fidelity and child rearing, then it does so by (often hilariously) developing their foils.

Despite Anne Haatrope's position at the center of the narrative, the emotional heart of the story is Anne's friend, Ada (Mildred Iweka), whose devoted and earnest husband, Nduka (Bimbo Odulaja, later Manuel), refuses multiple opportunities to cheat on her, even though their loving marriage bears no children for its first few years. It is not uncommon in screen media and other forms of Nigerian popular culture for infertility to pose a greater threat to a marriage than infidelity. Nduka's mother (Obiageli Molobe) thus comes to town one day with a young woman whom she wants Nduka to marry, precisely to produce a grandchild, but Nduka refuses. Ada is subsequently paralyzed with insecurity about her femininity, and she regularly questions Nduka's sincerity, although he proves it again and again, often by cooking meals, something he can do much better than she. Meanwhile, Ada seeks solutions, first in the form of traditionalist medicine and then through a Christian Aladura prophet. Eventually, she does become pregnant, but spectators also learn that Nduka's mother has ulterior motives. Ada is an osu, a member of an untouchable caste in Igbo custom, and even though she comes from a wealthy family and even though Nduka's devotion never waivers, their marriage has caused his mother endless grief back home in the village.[4] She is therefore relentless in her attempts to tear the couple apart. The struggle between Ada's love for dear, unassailable Nduka and her contempt for his meddling family sends her into a spiral of self-pity that shapes one emotional arc of the series. Several visual and audio cues—which I explore later in this chapter—suggest that the indirect subject of Checkmate is Ada's precarious femininity and its correlation with her husband's (in)ability to provide adequate material support. The barometer of "valuable norms," as Igwe puts it, seems to be Ada's incipient nuclear family and whether or not it can withstand a host of external social pressures. Moreover, the modalities by which Ada's struggle is addressed to spectators, as I will argue here, laid the foundations for two strains of melodrama—a feminine mode and a masculine mode—that would become central to the development of Nollywood.

This chapter begins by sketching the cultural stakes of melodrama, drawing from several accounts of the mode's history and social significance. The feminine and masculine melodramatic modes of Nollywood, described in this chapter and the next, operate by constructing forms of gendered suffering and then proposing calculated responses. This chapter also includes a brief sketch of the history of the term *soap opera* and its relationship to the modern processes that have created Nigeria, illustrating the political dimensions of the form. Then, returning to *Checkmate*, I demonstrate that Nigerian state television promoted the feminine melodramatic mode by broadcasting certain kinds of content that indirectly emphasize the correlation between femininity and male breadwinning. That particular indirect subject would remain a key feature of Amaka Igwe's video films and subsequently a large corpus of Nollywood films, especially those made by Emem Isong, one of Nollywood's most prominent producers. In some of Isong's iconic films, the male breadwinner ideal promises to regulate masculinity for the benefit of femininity. However, in addition to being the measure of a man, the breadwinner ideal is the measure of access to a liberal form of life largely unavailable in Nigeria. Thus, as I will explain in chapter 4, soap operas may have brought certain images of feminine power to Nigerian television screens, but they have also incited a fierce rhetorical backlash.

MELODRAMA AND THE RATIONALIZATION OF SUFFERING

The standard denotative gloss of *melodrama*, drama with song (*mélos*), is already at play in the story of Nigerian screen media and free indirect subjectivity that is unfolding in this book, but so too is the standard connotative gloss. The drumrolls that play when Cosmas Aderibigbe Ali reads the letter from the Schools Management Committee in *The New Village Headmaster* (see chapter 2) not only invite spectators into Ali's subjectivity but also offer extra-realist access to his emotions. To call that access "extra-realist" is to acknowledge that human beings are capable of making inferences about other people's emotions only from the things they say or do; we do not hear with other people's ears, see with their eyes, or feel with their feelings. In melodrama, however, it seems as if we do. And even when musical sounds are not a factor—as in the novels that Peter Brooks studies in his widely influential *The Melodramatic Imagination: Balzac, Henry James, Melodrama, and the Mode of Excess*—the text may address its audience by offering access to emotional content that feels contrived, that draws attention to its extra-reality by being bigger, more obvious, more gestural, and more formulaic than most people are accustomed to in everyday life. The reason for doing so, according to Brooks, is to seek moral order in an otherwise murky moral terrain. If realism is motivated by a desire to "possess the world by understanding it," as Christine Gledhill phrases it, melodrama is motivated by a desire to make moral sense of a world that cannot be possessed.[5]

Gledhill's seminal work on screen media modalities, and melodrama in particular, suggests that the mode is essentially epistemological, a way of getting to know a world that often defies our logocentric impulses. Perhaps unintuitively, then, melodrama shares its worldview with postmodern, poststructuralist approaches to signification, although melodrama also takes its stand, Gledhill argues, "in the material world of everyday reality and lived experience." In that way melodrama shifts attention from the limits of language to the social uses of signifying. Words may constantly fail us as we attempt to apprehend reality (therefore providing us with perhaps the only reality we can ever know: a socially constructed one), but the pain and pleasures of real life nevertheless call for an aesthetic rendition that, if not real, feels *true*. Gledhill quips that melodrama "operates on the level not so much of 'Yes, but . . .' than of 'So what!'"[6]

Brooks argues that there is a legible history underwriting the urge to respond to "So what!" He claims that melodrama emerged in the eighteenth century to address specific ruptures of modernity, especially the shift away from "sacred" systems of moral regulation. The culmination of the Enlightenment in the French Revolution, he writes, "marks the final liquidation of the traditional Sacred and its representative institutions (Church and Monarch), the shattering of the myth of Christendom, the dissolution of an organic and hierarchically cohesive society, and the invalidation of the literary forms—tragedy, comedy of manners—that depended on such a society."[7] The epistemological project of melodrama therefore constantly creates instances of moral singularity in what he calls a "post-sacred" era. As influential as Brooks's arguments have been, however, many scholars have worried about their applicability beyond modern Europe.

Certainly, there are obvious pitfalls to consider when applying theoretical approaches generated in the context of European history to non-European forms of cultural production, but the worries expressed by some critics when it comes to melodrama appear to be unnecessary. To see how, let us first note a few examples.

Wimal Dissanayake's edited collection on Asian cinematic melodramas includes several chapters exploring the possibility that twentieth-century Asian films draw upon forms of sensational address that predate the modern era.[8] Dissanayake also suggests that Western liberal ideas about the relationship between individuals and families contrast with Asian traditions of constructing the self within and through the family unit. Nevertheless, the cinematic texts that are studied in his volume do not simply reproduce some kind of traditional aesthetic; instead, they highlight tensions between older forms of address and new ones, as well as competing ideas about individualism and the importance of family. Dissanayake notes that there is no correlate, as far as he knows, for the word *melodrama* in any Asian language. Thus, whether or not melodrama is older than modernity in Asia is difficult to demonstrate, but one thing is clear: melodrama *thrives* in a modern context where values regarding family and social organization are fragmented and fluctuating. That instability ultimately underlines Brooks's historical argument. Even if modernity did not produce melodrama, modernity demands a kind of truth that melodrama seems well positioned to address.

In the case of Africa, scholars such as Moradewun Adejunmobi and Birgit Meyer are less concerned with the independent precolonial emergence of a form equivalent to melodrama (indeed, they are both heavily invested in Brooks's formulation), but they call into question the applicability of his notion of the "post-sacred." As Adejunmobi writes, "We do not, at this time, have a post-sacred era in Africa. On the contrary, the dominant idioms in many African societies today for confronting political and institutional failure draw from the realm of spirituality. Likewise, morality in most Nigerian video films in English is explicitly tied to religion and often to Pentecostal theology."[9] Notice that in Adejunmobi's account, spirituality *confronts* politics and institutions; it does not constitute them. In Brooks's conception of the sacred era, however, religion and the state converge not just often but in general, a premise to which I will return shortly.

Finally, Agustin Zarzosa—in his work on melodrama writ large, but with specific reference to Mexican screen media—laments that Brooks's emphasis on modern Europe and the emergence of a post-sacred order there "universalizes the manifestation of melodrama as a bourgeois mode of experience."[10] For Zarzosa, melodrama is a fundamental mode of human understanding that may become useful during certain historical moments but does not have an easily documented history. His critique is simultaneously cultural, temporal, and material, calling into question the idea that melodrama *emerged* anywhere. However, what concerns me is the role that modernity has played in making melodrama the preferred aesthetic mode of screen media storytelling. As Linda Williams convincingly argues, film studies has long contrasted melodrama with supposedly more "classical" ways of telling stories, but melodrama is actually the "backbone of popular global cinema"; it is "the rule" and not the exception.[11] From that perspective, Brooks's historical approach remains useful. Perhaps it is true that melodrama did not emerge solely from bourgeois Europe, but—whether we are referring to Asia, Africa, Latin America, or anywhere else—modernity seems to have made melodrama more useful than ever.

As I understand Brooks's argument, the post-sacred era in Europe, which followed the French Revolution, did not destroy various pillars of the sacred or even deface them in many people's eyes. Rather, the singular association between religious institutions and juridical institutions, and their combined ability to regulate morality on a very large social scale, became fragmented. No longer were the church and the state coterminous. Today, many people locate primary moral authority in formal religious institutions—that has never gone away, whether in France or Nigeria—however, the existence of a secular state brings at least one other authoritative voice to the discussion of moral subjects. Brooks's conception of the sacred era could describe any theocracy or any society where some kind of sovereign figure claims a divine right to rule, but this is not to say that moral debate would be absent from either configuration; rather, the terms of the debate, according to Brooks, would be regulated under one umbrella of institutionalized power. Meanwhile, in a post-sacred era, even when the state is relatively weak, it still vies with and often supersedes institutionalized spirituality. For example, the Nigerian state may be characterized by what Adejunmobi calls "political and institutional failure," but it retains a great deal of influence over criminal prosecution and still claims a monopoly on violence. Therefore, Nigeria can indeed be described as a post-sacred society not because religion has been diminished or the state is hegemonic but because the two compete. Even when the state loses, it is there, hovering, both materially and conceptually, as a potential source and arbiter of moral discourse. Furthermore, the very establishment of Nigeria as a nation-state assembles under one social system people committed to different religious institutions, which has, in fact, prompted several attempts to re-create a sacred order, such as instituting Sharia law in some northern states. Even in those cases, however, Sharia courts are augmented by customary courts, and there is significant ambiguity about applying the law to non-Muslim residents of the states in question. There has even been some popular debate about whether the legislation authorizing Sharia law, which was passed through the parliamentary system, actually violates Nigeria's constitution: a debate that pits different moral authorities against one another.[12] Therefore, no single framework for moral authority exists in modern Nigeria. This stands in stark contrast to the forms of social organization that operated in the same space before the modern era. Indigenous African religions have always been complex and internally contradictory, like all religions, but in ways similar to Brooks's conception of premodern Europe, many African societies assumed no separation between spiritual discourse and the constitution of social and political power. As Jacob Olupona writes, "For adherents of African traditional religions, such a separation is neither desirable nor possible, because religious beliefs inform every aspect of life."[13] Today, indigenous religious systems still exert varying degrees of pressure on the lives of many Nigerians — as illustrated by Ada's *osu* status in *Checkmate* — but they compete with imported systems. Therefore, it is not the loss of a particular moral voice but the condition of polyvocal morality that calls for a melodramatic intervention. Moreover, this is the condition of modernity everywhere.

A modern world system composed of distinct nation-states, featuring various religious institutions and infused with capital's own discourses about the sociality of accumulation, labor, the body, the natural environment, time, and more, provides many proliferating forms of moral discourse. And whereas some narrative modes not only accept but also embrace the resulting ambiguity, melodrama tends to seek a resolution. As Brooks writes, it becomes "the principal mode for uncovering, demonstrating, and making operative the essential moral universe in a post-sacred era."[14] This universe is what he elsewhere refers to as the "moral occult," a value system not readily apparent at the surface of daily life. And as Meyer observes, occult and surface depend on each other. In many African video films informed by a Pentecostal worldview, she shows, the process of revealing the moral occult depends at least as much on constructing the imagery of the surface as it does on digging below it.[15] For example, family dysfunction needs to be fully and painfully developed before melodrama can unearth the forces that shape it and then draw moral conclusions about them. As such, the moral occult is a realm always under construction, not simply a set of premodern codes to resurrect. In fact, Brooks is steadfast that after modernity the sacred social order will never be reestablished. Therefore, melodrama is not a form of archaeology but a fully modern project of the new, meant to help us cope with the present.

Brooks's historical approach is critiqued by Zarzosa, in part to resolve what he calls "problems of cultural translation."[16] I have been similarly tempted to conceptualize certain aesthetic forms outside of history, as the transcultural effects of encoding human consciousness—what I have elsewhere called "ideological impulses."[17] The idea is that they may cohere in specific moments to specific discourses, which can be traced historically, but they appear to have no documented historical emergence. As Zarzosa puts it, melodrama is neither "a historical nor a universal form: it is simply a dramatic solution to a persistent problem," namely the "unhappy consciousness," a concept that he draws from Hegel. In Zarzosa's rendition, consciousness seeks freedom from the oppression of the social world (what in Hegelian dialectics is often referred to as "servitude") through various dramatic modes. For example, the stoic mode seeks freedom within the self. Meanwhile, the skeptic mode actively negotiates the contested space between a variety of imposed and self-generated features of subjectivity. Finally, the devotional mode, which often manifests in religion, "counters obedience with obedience," substituting a "divinized master for the worldly master." Zarzosa argues that melodrama is different from all of these; it responds to oppression by pitting ideas against one another, by essentializing, amplifying, and dramatizing virtue and evil in order to arrive at a new set of ideas that can ameliorate the suffering caused by social oppression. Melodrama does not reveal a long-lost moral order, according to his approach; it redistributes morality in an attempt to arrive at a formulation that causes less suffering both at the personal and social levels. Zarzosa's argument intersects with Brooks's where the ubiquity of suffering meets the pervasiveness of certain modern institutional formations, such as the nation-state. Melodrama may draw inspiration from individual suffering, but any redistribution it seeks will be routed through the actual institutions capable of paradigmatic change. The modern fragmentation of institutionalized morality thus compounds the problems associated with social oppression, calling the mode into ever greater service. If moving images are the quintessential media of modernity, then it should come as no surprise that melodrama is their quintessential mode. Likewise, there is a deep resonance within cultural studies for Zarzosa's claim that the world of melodrama is "a world in which ideas inflict suffering and, consequently, the epistemological quest is not for an idea that might reveal the essence of things, but for one that might obliterate suffering or, at least, for an idea that might give suffering a rational sense."[18] After all, once the rationality of suffering has been systematically described, it may be systematically undone.

However, undoing suffering is not always the goal of rationalization. Indeed, addressing a normative position from which modernity is continuously suffered and never ameliorated is the organizing principle of periliberalism but not, by the way, for neoliberalism. In neoliberalism—and its attendant popular, visual cultural forms, including self-improvement reality television and superhero films—inadequacy and victimization often create the enabling conditions by which self-interested, arrogant, and even dismissive attitudes to social relations become morally justified. Neoliberal modes of address may acknowledge suffering, but only so that it can be overcome and, perhaps, foisted by a hero onto others: always the "evil" ones, of course.[19] Thus, neoliberalism sometimes looks like an attempt to rationalize suffering—because suffering makes the hero strong—but the ultimate goal of neoliberal narration is to efface that suffering. To truly *rationalize* it, as in periliberal forms of cultural production, is to inhabit it, to narrate suffering so that it becomes a persistent, commonsense feature of experience. But why would anyone watch that? How could it possibly be pleasurable?

The purpose of this chapter is to begin describing the ways in which independently produced Nigerian state television serials and several subsequent Nollywood video films have addressed themselves to a public that, they imagine, can indeed glean pleasure from inhabiting and rationalizing the very personal suffering produced at the interface between public and private life. Melodramatic screen media texts about families and romantic relationships, I argue, posit a set of conditions in which the suffering of women, in particular, could end; nevertheless, they place greater emphasis on the dignity and righteousness of inhabiting that suffering until the right conditions for its amelioration are met. In a modern liberal world order, where knowledge of the means to reduce many kinds of suffering is widely distributed but the conditions to use that knowledge are not equitably shared, virtue and evil must be continually *redistributed*. It becomes virtuous to not only suffer initially but to endure suffering indefinitely. Likewise, evil may be attributed to the perpetual-motion machine of suffering, but it is also redistributed to any mechanism that short-circuits that machine. In exploring this redistributive process I hope to address a perennial problem in Nollywood studies, where we struggle to understand why video films that seem to denigrate female characters can be so popular with female spectators.[20]

My approach involves returning to the aesthetic practices of successful Nigerian soap operas—especially *Checkmate*, which aired in the early 1990s—in order to develop strategies for reading the emergence of Nollywood films that, at first glance, posit femininity as suffering. The paradigmatic Nollywood example I arrive at near the end of this chapter is the influential antiromance *Games Women Play* (2005). As Jonathan Haynes notes, because of the way that early video films were produced, melodrama does not simply index an ideology that is being mass-mediated to Nigerians from abroad; instead, it is bubbling up through informal production.[21] Melodrama has been made into a local form of address, where the word *local*, nevertheless, cannot but imply a relationship to something known as *global*.

"SOAP" AND "OPERA": MEANING AND MEDIUM

Soap opera is often, if erroneously, considered the feminine melodramatic form par excellence, an association with profound ideological implications. Certainly, experts on the subject are less categorical, and soap operas were of course not the first or the most spectacular renditions of melodrama, but in the 1930s and 1940s mass-media critics, particularly in the United States, implied a strong correlation between the melodramatic features of detergent-sponsored radio serials and women spectators, to whom the serials' accompanying advertising was targeted, which cemented the association. Their work thus brought femininity to the center of melodrama and subsequently contributed— perhaps unwittingly, though sometimes apparently not—to the feminization of such concepts as emotion, advice, and morality. In one extreme case the Lazarsfeld Bureau of Applied Social Research employed psychoanalysis to arrive at the conclusion that women related to soap, both as commodity and narrative form, through a kind of "lack."[22] The fact that such a lack was located at the intersection of domesticity, commodification, and nonwage labor constructed women as passive, incomplete participants in the economy, even though the economy fundamentally relied on their active participation. By the 1980s, soap operas would become a major site of feminist, poststructural epistemological revision, which has laid the groundwork for all subsequent serious studies of the form.[23] Today, soap opera is understood as a form that may rely on the vague notion that femininity is marginalized within the political and economic processes of modern society but centers femininity anyhow, suggesting that it is at the core of modern culture.[24] As in periliberalism, therefore, soap operas explore a set of signs that are constitutive of a system that endures only by holding them at arm's length.

There are many ways besides melodrama that screen media can explore and redress the marginalization of femininity, and television soap operas are so plentiful and common around the world that we cannot attribute to them a fixed set of defining characteristics that will apply across all or even most examples. However, the generic designation is itself instructive. Both *soap* and *opera*, separately and together, suggest a narrative structure and means of mediation invested in redistributing the moral capital associated with femininity's place in modern life. If femininity, as a social and ideological construct, can cause suffering, then soap opera can reveal the rational sense of that suffering. Furthermore, there is no a priori reason, as feminist media studies have argued, that such revelations cannot also lead to the amelioration of suffering.

To begin with, the *soap* in *soap opera* obviously signifies the companies and brands that have sponsored countless global examples. In Nigeria the major sponsors of soap operas have been Joy, a PZ Cussons brand, and Lux, a Unilever brand. Unilever is the largest consumer-goods company in the world, reflecting the merger and acquisition of several margarine and soap companies over the course of more than a century. Central to all the major products in its portfolio are plant oils, particularly palm and coconut oil, which come from tropical countries such as Nigeria, and which have greased the gears of the modern global economy since it first sputtered into motion. As Anne McClintock evocatively documents in *Imperial Leather: Race, Gender, and Sexuality in the Colonial Contest*, the companies that first exploited tropical plant oils for modern food and hygiene products were also among the first to translate commodities into brands and brands into advertising, a process that put soap at the very center not only of capitalism's consolidation but also the late nineteenth-century liberal venture to salvage the embattled project of empire. Like the formulation of indirect rule and the formalization of colonial holdings (see chapter 1), soap advertising was propelled by a claim to have conquered the globe—in the past tense—while simultaneously pursuing authorization to conquer the globe in the future. McClintock refers to this contradiction as the "myth of first contact."[25] Soft body soap, a commodity made available to most Victorians only by the violent domination of vast conquered territories, industrial-scale plantations, and the systematic exploitation of slave labor, was depicted in newspaper and magazine advertisements as a civilizing agent arriving on an unexplored

FIGURE 3.1. Artwork for Pears' Soap advertisement, which appeared in the *Graphic* on April 30, 1890.

coast as the vanguard of a clean, modern, whitewashed capitalism at which dirty, half-clothed natives could only wonder with surprise. Which came first, the soap or the empire? By (re)constructing the non-European person, as one famous print ad did, not as the subject of an entrenched if thinly stretched empire—and certainly not as its citizen—but somewhere beyond empire, somewhere outside the liberal world order, in a place to which soap might float from a shipwreck (itself a breakdown of that order), only then could the imperial project continually justify and reauthorize itself (see figure 3.1).

Indeed, whereas Victorian advertising imagined a zone outside of liberalism, inhabited by *dirty Africans*, the companies that later became Unilever were as embedded in that zone as any institution possibly could be. They constituted many of the first waves of European trade with coastal West Africa. They built the colony of Nigeria. They got rich at Independence. They got even richer bringing *Checkmate* to millions of viewers. And their wealth continues to grow, making Unilever Public Limited one of the most powerful firms on Nigeria's stock exchange, not to mention in the world. Lux has sponsored soap operas around the globe and has been endorsed by film and television stars from the United States, Nigeria, Bangladesh, India, the Philippines, and numerous other countries. Beyond femininity, domesticity, commodification, and nonwage labor in Nigeria, soap also signifies the cataclysmic violence of imperialism. Even as the colonial project concluded and its violence was disavowed, soap packaging and advertising repeatedly returned to imagery of tropical exploration and the racialization of bodies, suggesting that clean, bourgeois liberalism is somehow still possible—at least for the White, Euro-American subject. Meanwhile, the same combination of imperial violence and modern cleanliness correlates with a much more dissociative condition in Africa.

In *Lifebuoy Men, Lux Women: Commodification, Consumption, and Cleanliness in Modern Zimbabwe*, Timothy Burke argues that "the costs of the type of hygiene invested in soap have been constituted by its associations with the bodily disciplines of colonialism, of decades of mission teachings and domestic training, but the desirability of soap also comes from the same sources."[26] To this mix could be added the visual investment in hygiene made by various colonial cinema units, which produced scores of films on housekeeping and body washing. It may be a long way from Zimbabwe to Nigeria and from colonial cinema to television soap operas in the 1980s; nevertheless, the relationship between the bars of Lux soap sold in colonial Rhodesia and the ones sold in contemporary Nigeria develops from significant conceptual overlap, not to mention their material connections. If, by 1980, soap and personal hygiene were no longer invested with the disciplinary regimes of colonialism and mission work, soap's desirability was still constituted by reference to the very world order that generated colonialism and missionaries. For example, the soap commercials that ran on Nigerian television in the late 1980s and early 1990s may have trafficked in the predictable values of glamour, wealth, cleanliness, and feminine sexuality, but just as or more importantly, they stressed the value of international social status and travel. In Lux ads, Patti Boulaye could be glimpsed performing to White audiences and mingling at multiracial parties that do not seem to have been held in Nigeria. Meanwhile, Joy soap ads featured the "Joy Girl" song, in which a man's voice twangs to the timbre of country music:

Hey, Joy Girl
No matter where you're going,
Everywhere your fame is growing,
With your beauty, internationally.
It's got that Joy Girl quality.

The emphasis on internationalism exhibited in these ads may follow from the long-standing association between soap and a glamorous life beyond the reach of its consumers; however, where the markers of that world have often been class-based in Euro-American advertising—rich White women selling soap to middle-class women—they gain an extra level of racial and geographical coding in Nigeria. *International* is shorthand for *oyinbo*, meaning not only foreign but also Euro-American, often White, of or pertaining to the liberal world order. The "soap" of Nigerian soap operas is therefore a visa, an all-access pass to a world from which its consumer-spectator has been spatially excluded.

The *opera* in *soap opera* signals melodrama, a comparable way of identifying a story told through song. Of course, that is not the only connotative meaning of *opera*, and singing has rarely been essential to radio or television serials, but the term, as it is used in the modern broadcasting context, stands in for the kind of clichéd, formulaic, extra-realist emotional performance so often associated with melodrama. So why not call them soap melodramas? The story of how *opera* came into the nomenclature for soap-sponsored serials is incomplete, but it is nevertheless useful because it points to the importance of the form's preferred modes of address, over and above its typical content. In 1938 Charles A. Maddry, a minister in the southern United States, referred to daytime radio serials as "soap tragedies" because, he wrote, "it is by the grace of soap I am allowed to shed tears for these characters who suffer so much from life."[27] Maddry notes that some of the programs aired at the time were sponsored by lard, bean, and flour companies, but it makes some sense that, given the historical processes I have just traced, "bean tragedies" did not emerge as the genre's favored designation. A year later, an article in *Newsweek* referred to radio melodramas as "soap operas," continuing Maddry's emphasis on soap companies, as opposed to other advertisers, but shifting from the genre of tragedy to the medium of opera, perhaps drawing on the term *horse opera*, which some in Hollywood labeled westerns. From there the designation seems to have been settled, although the change from genre-specific to medium-specific nomenclature is nonetheless illuminating. What matters in soap opera has less to do with what happens in the story—whether hubris attenuates heroism, for example—than how we are invited to attend to the narrative—for example, with our affective attention concentrated by music or, more often, other nonverbal cues. As Brooks argues, tragedy is a genre relevant only to the sacred period, no longer applicable in the modern world (despite what Raymond Williams might have to say).[28]

Taken together, *soap* and *opera* form a compound signifier of quintessentially modern forces. The nomenclature calls for emotional investment by audiences and critics—based in Nigeria certainly, but elsewhere too—on such a scale that moral redistribution becomes possible, particularly in stories that reference the violent constitution and sequestration of gendered domestic space within the liberal world order. Through public airwaves, commercial interests speak in private places about intimate forms of consumption. Ideas about gender, sex, bodies, families, and the relation of each to the public sphere are pitted against one another in order to ameliorate some suffering, to rationalize other suffering, and, most of all, to sustain attention for the purposes of selling products that prepare one's body and one's home for the modern public sphere. In that way the boundary between public and private is constantly shifting, resulting in the continual redefinition of individual, family, and society. Soap operas and their association with the forces of modernity and colonialism, combined with their redistributive mode of address, thus open up the possibility for significant play with ideological signs. As Amaka Igwe's press release suggests, perhaps unintentionally, Nigerian soap operas may be broadcast by the developmentalist state, but they seek moral order in an immorally modern world.

CHECKMATE AND THE "GOLDEN AGE"
OF NIGERIAN TELEVISION

Although any serialized broadcast narrative about the members of a relatively coherent social network could be described as a soap opera, many
critics of Nigerian television agree that something specific emerged from
the NTA in the middle to late 1980s that specifically invites that designation.
The Village Headmaster, some might say, is a kind of soap opera. The same
could be said of *Cock Crow at Dawn*, the green-revolution agricultural-
development series that aired in the early 1980s. But in 1984 Lola Fani-
Kayode independently produced a serial called *Mirror in the Sun*, for
which the NTA agreed to help her find a sponsor on the condition that
NTA staff coproduced the program. PZ Cussons eventually signed on and
directly paid production costs. Unfortunately, the show fell apart within
a year, a result often attributed to the NTA's disruptive involvement in the
project.[29] Thirty years later, Clarion Chukwurah, one of the stars of *Mirror in the Sun*—who also starred in several celluloid films and eventually
went on to a successful career in Nollywood—told me that her experience on the show directly influenced her public stance against government subsidies for Nigerian film production.[30] Nevertheless, as Barclays
Foubiri Ayakoroma recounts, the impression the show left behind was
indelible. The viewing public seemed to want more content in the same
vein, which, according to Ayakoroma, offered "exhibition of modern
trends in fashion, social life, as well as glamorous ladies and gentlemen,
who became instant role models." This was very different from the village
settings and transparently developmentalist tone of previous NTA hits.
Ayakoroma also provocatively claims that *Mirror in the Sun* was "a true
reflection of the putrid moral life of the society."[31] Of course, the same
could be said about some of the supposedly recalcitrant antiprogressives
in *The Village Headmaster* or *Cock Crow at Dawn*, but soap operas were not
designed to elevate the status of the bureaucratic state by contrast to the
rest of society's "putrid moral life." Instead, by constructing an elaborate
surface culture where dysfunctional, if beautiful, families threatened to
fall apart—week after week, in perpetuity—and then digging below that
surface to grapple with the foundational social problems that made life so
"putrid," Nigeria's soap operas introduced a new kind of developmentalist discourse to state television. Instead of attempting to build a nation
on the image of a strong state, they contemplated—often indirectly—the
features of a strong nation and then wondered whether the state had any
ability to foster them.

Of all the soap operas that characterize the so-called golden age of Nigerian television, *Checkmate* has the most enduring legacy. *Mirror in the Sun*, despite its enormous influence, was a flash in the pan. Fani-Kayode's second serial, *Mind-Bending*, was a four-part miniseries. After that, she had trouble finding sponsors for new programs.[32] *Behind the Clouds* was conceived at the NTA and starred several actors from other NTA programs, such as *Cock Crow at Dawn*, but it was beset by all manner of personnel problems and lasted only two years.[33] *Ripples*, perhaps *Checkmate*'s greatest rival, aired on Friday nights for thirty minutes. It ran for five years (1988–1993), suggesting a significant viewership and consequent support from sponsors. The show's creator, Zeb Ejiro, went on to become one of the biggest moguls in Nollywood and is now commonly known as "the Sheik." However, *Checkmate* occupied the most coveted spot on the NTA's schedule, Thursdays from 8:00 to 9:00 PM. It also attracted the most-sought-after sponsor in the industry, Lever Brothers. And *Checkmate* was the last of these soaps to be developed, so its legendary status could be read as a culmination of everything that came before it. Nevertheless, as a testament to *Checkmate*'s popularity, in 1992 the National Electoral Commission (NEC)—which was in the midst of conducting the country's first parliamentary elections in a decade, the result of yet another military coup—piggybacked on *Checkmate*'s viewership in order to transmit crucial voting information to the nation. Knowing that millions of citizens were directing their attention to TVs, the NEC broke in at 8:00, just as *Checkmate* was about to start, to address the nation. Writing about the incident in the *Guardian*, Sola Osofisan trumpeted, "Fact rode to victory on the back of fiction."[34]

My use of the term *golden age* follows from countless references made in passing by Nigerian friends but also documented on the internet—in chat rooms, blogs, newspaper articles, and YouTube channels.[35] However, the idea that Nigerian television *peaked* in those years indicates a profound irony. The economic crisis of the post–oil-shock decade made it impossible for the NTA to produce a large amount of its own narrative content. In addition to pursuing deals with independent producers, the network made several bulk purchases of Latin American *telenovelas* that had already been dubbed into English. The NTA's shifting acquisition model expanded the aesthetic horizons of Nigerian television and encouraged a small number of talented artists to experiment with televisual aesthetics, but corporate sponsorship and the network's right of refusal also placed clear limits on the risks that independent producers would take. The programs those producers created may not have been primarily motivated by developmentalism, but their content was broadcast only if the state saw developmentalist potential in it. And as noted in the beginning of this chapter, producers sometimes provided the language, perhaps superficial, to describe that potential. However, the evolving developmentalist discourse that independent producers participated in was as much a sign of the times as it was an injection of new blood into the network. Such, once again, are the "paradoxes of sovereignty and independence."[36] Over the course of the 1980s, Nigeria weathered the whims of the global economy poorly, so the state stepped back from television production, creating a vacuum into which new forms of international and local programming poured. And as the developmental state weakened, governmentality gave way to what Gregory Mann calls "nongovernmentality."[37] According to Charmaine Pereira, the military regime of Ibrahim Babangida, which came to power in 1985 and instituted a structural adjustment program (SAP) a year later, oversaw a proliferation of nongovernmental women's organizations with oblique relationships to the state. However, she argues that "in an international context where economic aid and professed sympathy for the rights of women are increasingly linked, the championing of 'women development' should be recognised for the opportunism that it represents."[38] In such an environment, soap operas could be rationalized as developmentalist television if they broadcast images of empowered women and also helped the state alleviate budget shortfalls by triggering certain forms of international aid, as well as allowing it to assert sovereignty by casting the entire enterprise as internally driven. This was neoliberal developmentalism. Regardless of state television's new horizons, however, the primary mode of address remained periliberal, for the disparity between the assumptions that guided the international agenda and the actual lived experiences of spectators was so great. Soap operas could temper liberal fantasies about what Pereira calls "professed sympathy for the rights of women" by allowing spectators to *gawk* at empowered women while simultaneously inviting them to *identify* with steadfast, tolerant, and morally patient women.

Consider the distinction between Anne and Ada in *Checkmate*. Anne is rich, well educated, and fashionable. Most of the powerful men with whom she butts heads at Haatrope Investments treat her dismissively, but she gleefully defies their expectations. Her major rival, Kadiri, slowly becomes her love interest, although her social position and American-style bravado make her status within their budding heteronormative relationship not just more equitable than the norm but perhaps superior to her man's status. Anne therefore epitomizes liberal life in the changing world order. She is an empowered figure, unmoored from social expectations, which both liberates her but also underplays the importance of social and familial networks. Instead of inviting spectators to identify with Anne, therefore, *Checkmate* holds her at a slight distance. The camera work and audio rarely offer an opportunity to inhabit her subjectivity. And her love life, in which smoldering hatred ignites the passions of desire, is too spectacular as well as too formulaic to be entirely sincere. All of this is encapsulated in a shot that concludes the opening credits of each broadcast. Anne stands in a glamorous setting—a well-appointed bar in some episodes, a balcony overlooking the lagoon in others—clad in designer threads. She turns and looks directly into the camera, raising a glass of wine and slightly tipping her head. On the sound track, a soaring march performed by an orchestra elevates the moment.[39] By toasting her spectators—whom she not only acknowledges but also sees as distinct from her—Anne may very well honor them, but she does not identify with them.

Ada Okereke is Anne's oldest and dearest friend. Like Anne, Ada was born into a wealthy family, but instead of pursuing power and prestige, she married a humble schoolteacher and found work in a bank. She and Nduka live in a small apartment where Nduka pampers her, though largely without condescension. In several episodes he enters a scene by emerging from the kitchen wearing a frilly apron and raving about something simmering on the stove. When Ada cooks, however, she always manages to burn something. Therefore, Ada's life is also a kind of fantasy, but it is one with which spectators are pointedly invited to identify. Indeed, far more than any other character in *Checkmate*, Ada and her consciousness frequently take over the subjectivity of the program, several examples of which I will explore in a moment. Also, Ada's marriage may be unconventional, but its eccentricities only highlight the very conventional challenges it faces. At first, she and Nduka struggle to conceive. When that happens, they struggle against extended kin. Unlike Anne, therefore—whose struggle with a hateful business rival, with whom she falls in love, is extraordinary—Ada must withstand some of the most ordinary social pressures facing modern Nigerian women. Her husband's devotion, signaled not only by his cooking but also by his many attempts to shield their marriage from outside influence, suggests that what makes Ada a worthwhile character study, what will sustain interest in and identification with her story, is the question of whether she can form an ideal alliance with Nduka against the cruel world. That turns out to be a monumental challenge.

In the following paragraphs I trace Ada's negotiation of that challenge through four substantial instances of free indirect subjectivity. My method of analysis could be described as indulgent because it invites the reader to devote significant attention to the unfolding of audiovisual elements—as I describe them in text—and perhaps glean some of the pleasure that accompanies serious investment in the formal features of the show. To not only observe Ada's moral conundrum, as illustrated in the opening paragraphs of this book, but also to get a sense of the suffering, the emotional process by which she arrives at the idea that she must leave her devoted husband, the reader must allow free indirect subjectivity an opportunity to demonstrate its potential.

Two key moments of free indirect subjectivity in *Checkmate* involve a black cat. The first time it appears, Nduka's mother has recently told Ada that her family is *osu*. Ada paces around her parlor and then sits, the camera zooming in to a close-up, while the image of her face dissolves to a flashback (much like the scene from *Living in Bondage* described in the opening of this book). In Ada's flashback, Nduka's mother, shown from a third-person point of view, hurls insults: "*Amaosu*, vampire!" These names might have seemed like exaggerated mudslinging when they were spoken, but Ada is slowly realizing their valence. *Amaosu* is the full signifier for her family's proscribed status. When the image dissolves back to Ada in her parlor, she rises and walks to her bedroom. As she enters, hymn-like organ music fades from the sound track, and Ada looks quickly to the left, then to the right, as if she has heard a sound but cannot pinpoint its source. Suddenly, her eyes grow wide and settle on something beyond the frame. A Wurlitzer organ stinger reverberates on the sound track, and the image cuts to a black cat sitting on a windowsill, as if seen through Ada's eyes. The image then returns to Ada as she screams and runs out of the room. In the following shot she closes the door to her bedroom and rubs her eyes as if she is not sure of what she has seen. After holding her hand to her chest for a moment, Ada looks to her left, and the image cuts to her Bible sitting on a shelf, once again seemingly shown from her first-person point of view. She crosses, grabs the Bible, and holds it to her chest while the last drops are wrung from the Wurlitzer and several cymbal crashes shake the sound track. The experience seems to have convinced her to call a friend, who had previously offered to take Ada to an *Aladura* prophet on Bar Beach. Ada not only visits the prophet but also purchases holy water and drinks it in the hopes of conceiving. Therefore, her eventual pregnancy may lift her spirits, but it is also presented through the convention of free indirect subjectivity—from mother-in-law, to black

FIGURE 3.2

FIGURE 3.3

FIGURE 3.4

FIGURE 3.5

FIGURE 3.2, 3.3, 3.4 AND 3.5. *Checkmate*. Shots and countershots. Ada sees a cat on her windowsill (figures 3.2 and 3.3). Ada sees her copy of the Bible (figures 3.4 and 3.5).

cat, to Bible—as fortification against the wicked meddling of extended-family members (see figures 3.2–3.5).

Later, when those family members meddle once again, the freely indirect, subjective vision of the black cat returns. This time, Nduka's mother has brought support. Her husband (played by the veteran actor Sam Loco Efe) begs Ada to "release" his son. Much more than their marriage is at stake, he argues; Nduka's entire family is tainted by Ada, causing them bitter social strife back home. Ada begs her father-in-law to stop, crying "Enough!" as tears come to her eyes. Then she clutches her chest while organ music, once again reminiscent of the Wurlitzer sound so often associated with silent cinema and early soap operas, fills the sound track. Ada's eyes grow wide, and the image, using the same first-person point of view as before, cuts to the black cat sitting on that same windowsill. Briefly, the image returns to Ada before showing another flashback, this time of the Aladura prophet. The conceptual link between Ada's pregnancy and her meddling in-laws is now cemented, raising several questions: Will her child ever have peace with a family like Nduka's? Will Ada ever be a proper mother, and will she ever have a proper nuclear family if she and Nduka cannot prevent this kind of outside influence? When the visions finally end, Ada runs from the parlor to her bedroom, where she climbs a chair, attempting to retrieve her suitcase, but falls onto her belly and writhes in pain. Credits roll.

In the next episode Ada will be lying in a hospital bed, which by this point in the series has become a common image. The same episode that ended with her cliff-hanger injury began with Ada in the hospital for a different reason—she had passed out upon receiving confirmation from her own mother that her family is, indeed, osu. Therefore, Ada seems to be perpetually under bodily threat. However, that first hospital stay also had a positive outcome because it inadvertently produced knowledge of Ada's early-stage pregnancy. Moreover, one of the most important and stylistically complex moments of free indirect subjectivity in the entire show follows closely upon the heels of that revelation.

The scene in question opens with a medium shot of Ada reclining on her hospital bed, perusing a pamphlet on breast-feeding. She is happily coming to terms with the idea that she will be a mother. She then lays the pamphlet down, slowly rises, and walks to a small table, where a vase of flowers sits next to a greeting card. As she takes the card in hand, the image rapidly and uncharacteristically cuts back and forth between a profile shot of Ada standing in the hospital room and shots of Nduka sitting in their apartment. The camera then zooms in on Ada's face as she stands

FIGURE 3.6. *Checkmate*. Ada looks up at her doctor.

holding the card, and her eyes roll back in her head. At that point the transition to a memory seems to be complete. The choppy editing ends, and the screen is fully inhabited by a flashback in which Nduka professes his love for Ada. Then other flashbacks follow. Ada sees herself and her husband having dinner at a fine restaurant, followed by a rare exterior shot of the two of them running on a beach. Each scene is shown from a third-person perspective, but before the scene at the beach ends, the sounds of a door opening and Ada greeting her doctor are superimposed over the flashback. In that brief moment, spectators may be seeing with the narrator's eyes, as it were, but they are allowed to hear with Ada's ears, inviting them to identify with her as she descends from her reverie. Much of the action that follows is presented in the third person, but one curious shot, seemingly from Ada's perspective as she looks up at her doctor, fractures the narrative voice (see figure 3.6). Seeing with Ada's eyes, spectators hear her speak words, the meaning of which she seems to be fully realizing for the first time. "I, Ada Okereke, will someday be called 'Mommy!'" she gushes. Ada then thanks her doctor profusely, who modestly deflects the praise, sending most of it to God—and, in a classic patriarchal move, a little to her husband.

This complex version of free indirect subjectivity accompanies Ada's full realization of her maternal status, but one more important instance accompanies her related realization that femininity relies not on motherhood alone but on the status of one's husband. The scene with which this book opens occurs during Ada's second hospitalization. Nduka comes to visit, and while he is sitting by her side, bent with contrition for his family's actions, Ada strokes his head, and the mode of address begins to inhabit her subjectivity, freely and indirectly. "I've got to leave you," spectators hear her saying as if she is telling secrets inside her own head. She then sees another set of flashbacks featuring Nduka, once again shown in the third person, in which he tells her he loves her, yet she replies, still in her own head, that she must consider her personal welfare as well as that of their baby. As the flashbacks continue to roll by, Ada repeats to herself, "I've got to let you go. I've got to let you go." In this pivotal scene the marriage at the heart of *Checkmate* is called into question by the husband's inability to make life bearable for his wife and child. His devotion and deference are not enough to make him what Carmela Garritano, drawing on the work of Stephanie Newell, refers to as a West African example of the "ideal husband" and "romantic hero."[40] Fertility cannot save the marriage either. Ada's maternal glee has morphed into protectiveness. Of course, several characters advise Ada to stay with her loyal and kindhearted husband, and perhaps some spectators, if not many, will agree. But the issue at the heart of the story, the force underneath the surface of Ada's tumultuous emotional state, involves the instability of Nduka's masculine status.

Nduka thus operates as a foil for the ideal husband, though not in the Manichaean sense sometimes attributed to melodrama. He is not a *bad* husband, but he simply cannot change the conditions that prevent him from being ideal. He is monogamous in the most ideal ways—loving, devoted, and sexually potent—but he cannot make his marriage neolocal, and he is not the household's breadwinner. In the very first episode, when spectators are introduced to Ada and Nduka, the first two conversations they witness concern, on the one hand, Nduka's devotion—he cooks breakfast for Ada before leaving for work—and, on the other hand, the meager wages he earns: Ada refers to him as the only engineer in Nigeria teaching at a secondary school. Nduka is modest; unemployment rates are high, he notes, and building projects are scarce. "But you're the best," Ada tells him, yet Nduka replies, "Thanks for the vote of confidence, wife. It's unfortunate, though, you're not an employer." Here they both express a desire for Nduka to earn better wages, but they are not the ones positioned to make that happen. In another scene, halfway through the first season, Nduka tells Ada that he has just refused help from her father to replace their dilapidated car. He declares, "I want to be a man, in my own rights, not bought and kept by my wife and her family." Nduka's determination here illustrates that extended-family members have many ways to interfere with a marriage. It also illustrates that financial independence is crucial not only for neolocality but also for the sustenance of heteronormative gender relations defined in liberal terms: "a man, in my own rights." As Nduka presents it, therefore, buying a new car for his family is a matter of manhood, and the fact that he cannot do so on his own, at least not yet, runs parallel to the fact that he cannot stop her parents, or his for that matter, from interfering in their marriage. Moreover, the fact that Ada's fate hinges on Nduka's ability to be a man in his own rights, over which he has so little control, means that Ada will have to continue suffering until conditions change. Rather than bring money into their marriage, as Merit will do in *Living in Bondage* (see chapter 4), Ada will choose to deepen her maternal suffering. Unlike her friend Anne, therefore, who seems to control her own destiny, Ada can only tolerate hers. And by inviting spectators into Ada's subject position, through several moments of free indirect subjectivity, while tying her fate to her husband's, *Checkmate* does not simply assert the patriarchal order; it displaces the suffering of femininity onto the category of the (failed) husband. Were he truly independent—not just financially but socially as well—Ada's suffering would end. However, Nduka's inability to win his family's bread is less about his personal aptitude than it is about social and material conditions he cannot control. Moreover, the history of those conditions points to the breadwinner ideal's profound ideological status.

THE CONFOUNDING PERSISTENCE OF THE MALE BREADWINNER FANTASY

The male breadwinner is less an actual person than a social ideal grounded in Victorian conventions of family and economy. It depends on Christian ideas about monogamy, modern ideas about the nuclear family, and industrial capitalist ideas about wage labor. More than simply the idea that men should support their families materially, the breadwinner ideal stresses that one woman must perform enough unpaid domestic labor to free up one man to sell his labor outside the home, both of which are essential if their family is to play its proper role as a consuming unit in the market economy. The male breadwinner ideal was introduced in Nigeria through colonial capitalism and its pretensions to liberalism. That is not to say that gendered hierarchies arrived in Nigeria with colonialism.

Historical and ethnographic research on premodern West African economies has established that although the fruit of men's labor may have been
ideologically overvalued and although men may have asserted patriarchal
authority in their households, precolonial forms of patriarchy are not interchangeable with the modern conception of breadwinning.[41] In what is
today southern Nigeria, the productivity of women may have long been
subordinated to the productivity of men, but women have also enjoyed
many forms of economic autonomy, as laborers in their own substantial
gardens and farms, caretakers of their own livestock, producers of their
own commodities, traders of their own goods, and feeders of their own
children. Today, women all across southern Nigeria participate heavily
in the productive capacity of the economy and contribute substantially
to household wealth. Therefore, in this region the configuration of gendered labor that is usually associated with the breadwinner ideal is more
imagined than real. Yet that was also true in Victorian Britain when breadwinner ideology coalesced, as well as in other places where it has been
promoted.[42] The idea of the male breadwinner signals an evanescent
social fantasy but one that must be seriously considered in relation to
Nollywood because it appears so often on the screen.

Checkmate actually equivocates about the breadwinner ideal, suggesting that a man who could earn enough money to be "a man, in his
own rights"—providing for and protecting his monogamous, neolocal
marriage—may represent the potential end point of feminine suffering,
yet the show simultaneously explores the possibility that feminine suffering continues precisely because the local economy cannot produce such
men. Ada rationalizes her suffering by accepting that she has no power
to change these structural conditions. In several Nollywood video films,
however—which I explore later in this chapter and which bear formative
and aesthetic relationships to Checkmate—women are allowed to enjoy
the benefits of breadwinning men, although the ideal is qualified in other
ways. By different means, then, both media forms promote feminine tol-
erance and patience in the face of an unproductive economy, yet from a
purely developmentalist perspective that message is confounding. Why
not promote feminine entrepreneurship and public service? To be clear,
there are some Old Nollywood films that have done so, and more and
more New Nollywood films also do so, but a major current of the video
film phenomenon suggests that gender relations can be effectively measured by the earning potential of men as well as their commitment to
spend those earnings on one woman and her children. At issue here is
not a reflection of gender norms in southern Nigeria and not necessarily

the aspirations of women either; instead, the breadwinner ideal seems to represent the kind of fantasy that sustains not only economic systems but gender systems as well. Moreover, to understand gender differentiation and its social construction in any particular place and time, as Joan Wallach Scott argues, "We have to ask how, under what conditions, and with what fantasies the identities of men and women—which so many historians take to be self-evident—are articulated and recognized. The categories then will no longer precede the analysis but emerge in the course of it."[43] Over the course of this chapter and the next, therefore, the categories of "feminine" and "masculine" are not simply assumed but emerge from attention to the ways in which fantasies about gender relations have been articulated in Nigerian screen media.

Before returning to screen media, however, I pause here to reflect on the shifting conditions under which gender fantasizing has taken place in Nigeria. Ethnographers and historians who study gender and marriage in the region bring important diachronic sensibilities to the subject, helping us understand not just that gender is socially constructed but also how, over time. For example, the anthropologist Daniel Jordan Smith argues that although contemporary marriages in southern Nigeria differ in many ways from those of past generations, the most important difference has to do with the fact that modern couples see marriage as their own project, based primarily on love, while their parents' generation was more likely to understand marriage as a social project rooted in extended-family structures. This shift is not, of course, simply about time and progress. Following the introduction of wage labor and Christianity, discourses about marriage in southern Nigeria disentangled themselves from concepts associated with kinship networks, they exchanged polygamy for monogamy, and they exaggerated the economic contributions of men, although the concept of fertility has remained extremely important. Smith provides the example of Ifeoma and her husband, Chibueze: "Chibueze worked in a nearby town in a white-collar clerical job in a government office. They had built their own modest house and lived near but independently from extended kin. By all appearances, with four healthy children, her own small business, a house, and a respectable reputation in her community and church, Ifeoma had achieved the ideals of modern Igbo womanhood."[44] Smith's focus on Ifeoma's achievements at the end of this passage is significant. She measures her femininity, he tells us, according to her reputation, her industriousness, her fertility, her independence from kin, and her breadwinning husband, which casts "womanhood" as a multimodal achievement. Factoring a breadwinning husband into the equation is not simply about patriarchy. On the contrary, a "white-collar clerical job in a government office," as Smith phrases it, is not only a modern development in Nigeria; it is in fact rare, a form of employment that has not been easy to land even under the flourishing of state bureaucracies that took place during the first two decades of independence, let alone today, after the hollowing out of the Nigerian state by structural adjustment. Formal-sector employment may have briefly been materially responsible for the construction of a certain kind of Nigerian masculinity, but material conditions have changed. Why then has the ideal not changed as well? Indeed, for men to espouse a breadwinner ideal based on formal-sector employment would jeopardize the ideal. Men are more likely to work in the informal sector, where regular wages are not guaranteed. However, for the social construction of femininity the scarcity of formal employment actually raises the stakes of breadwinning. Ifeoma's sense of feminine success is therefore elevated by the idea of achieving something singular, by associating the "ideals of modern Igbo womanhood" with rising above the local standard. Likewise, it weaves a fantasy around the subject of masculinity. Even when couples like Chibueze and Ifeoma can achieve it, soap operas such as *Checkmate* suggest that the fantasy could unravel at any moment.

Lisa Lindsay's work on the history of the colonial railway in southwestern Nigeria helps explain why the male breadwinner ideal is so robust when its material basis is so delicate. The progression of her argument, which I follow at some length here, illustrates the importance of struggle in the development of ideology. According to her analysis, through their struggles with the colonial state some Nigerian men came to think of themselves as breadwinners. Meanwhile, some women, through their own struggles with the colonial state, as well as their struggles with Nigerian men, came to understand the breadwinner ideal as strategically useful. Thus, even when the struggle ends and in spaces where it has not taken place, it can contribute to the fantasy—not universal, not eternal, but available—to which various constituencies have had persistent recourse in the process of, as Lindsay puts it, "working with gender."

In the Yoruba context that Lindsay studies, men have long been required to amass small fortunes in order to get married, but a successful marriage has also depended, for many generations, on a wife's ability to bring resources into the home, often through market trading.[45] As the colonial project unfolded, however, men migrated to trading posts in search of money for marriage and were incorporated into the modern system of wage labor. At the railway, British officials seized on the idea

that extended kin and wives played key roles in the financial constitution of local marriages and used it to discriminate against their Nigerian
employees. Officials reasoned that local men did not require the kind of
breadwinner wages typically paid to British workers, who had no immediate recourse to extended-family assistance.[46] However, the same officials
eventually realized that their discriminatory pay scale was incommen-
surate with the empire's larger project of "modernization." As Lindsay
writes,

> But by the mid-1940s and beyond, European observers no longer favored
> workers' kin as sources of security that could justify low wages, and in-
> stead began to see the extended family as a drain on employees' resources
> and wives' financial autonomy as problematic for reproducing a working
> class. By the 1950s and into the 1960s, the expansion and stabilization of
> urban labor coincided with the flourishing of modernization ideology.
> The stabilization and modernization ideals held that a committed urban
> wage earner would focus on his nuclear rather than extended family and
> that breadwinner wages would make earning a male activity and repro-
> ducing (in its broadest sense) a female one.[47]

Instead of reflecting family structures, therefore, wage labor could be
used to *create* them. Lindsay also points out that Nigerian laborers were
not simply pawns but were active players in this process.

In the early 1940s World War II caused a spike in inflation, to which
Nigerian railway workers and other civil servants responded by agitating
for higher wages. Meanwhile, the colonial state attempted to manage rising commodity costs through price controls and food distribution, which
negatively affected market traders—most of them women—who became
increasingly vocal in local politics. As southern Nigerian men and women
struggled to wrest concessions from the colonial state, the masculine discourse of higher wages clashed with the feminine discourse of price de-
regulation. Did men deserve better pay in order to win bread for their
families, or did women deserve price protections in order to contribute
more to their households? Eventually, the breadwinner discourse pre-
vailed, resulting in a new gendered conception of labor that, as Lindsay
writes, "define[d] 'worker' as a masculine category."[48]

Meanwhile, the spread of Christianity also afforded men and women
opportunities to appropriate and contest discourses of the nuclear family.
Missionaries promoted monogamy, with special reverence for scriptural
doctrines like Genesis 2:24, which states that "a man shall leave his

father and his mother, and shall cleave unto his wife."[49] The choice to be monogamous and live apart from extended kin, to have neolocal families, thus came to be associated with "enlightenment" and full participation in the modern economy.[50] Meanwhile, Christian doctrines about monogamy were packaged with Pauline notions about gendered hierarchy. As one of Paul's letters to Titus argues, to be a good wife is "to be self-controlled and pure, to be busy at home, to be kind, and to be subject to their husbands, so that no one will malign the word of God."[51] Given the typical division of labor in southern Nigerian marriages, however, being "busy at home" was and is less beneficial than market trading and other forms of nondomestic labor. Therefore, the path pursued by many women has not been doctrinal so much as it has been strategic, yet part of that strategy has often involved willingness to appropriate the breadwinner ideal where necessary. At the nexus of the cash economy, agitation for family wages, and the colonial construction of workers as masculine, some Christian women have asserted their agency by demanding remuneration from men they have married. As Lindsay writes,

> [Men's] financial potency, real or exaggerated, contributed to wage-earners' masculine self-esteem and their sense of importance relative to women. Divorce cases from the 1940s and 1950s show that women became exasperated with husbands who did not meet their material obligations, and lack of sufficient financial maintenance was the most frequent reason women gave for leaving their husbands. In contrast, wage-earners who brought home steady paychecks were often seen as good mates because they could be good providers.[52]

Many women thus used breadwinner discourse to simultaneously access economic security and regulate the behavior of men. The sentiment that modern life consists of finding a man who can afford to keep a woman, and only *one* woman, has become a discourse that many Nigerian women wield skillfully and by which many Nigerian men measure their masculinity. The popular colloquialism "no romance without finance" is still regularly invoked today to describe modern orientations to marriage.[53]

By far the most significant argument that Lindsay makes, however, is not that some women and some men have found the breadwinner ideal useful but that it persists discursively in the face of such a short-lived material career: "The ideal of modernization, and with it, modernizing families—helped to shape gendered aspirations that simply cannot be fulfilled under present political-economic circumstances."[54] Meanwhile, the postcolonial Nigerian government has repeatedly enacted policies that favor nuclear families and male breadwinner households, perhaps hoping to create the circumstances that would fulfill gendered aspirations but in reality often punishing citizens by way of tax and inheritance laws for circumstances beyond their control.[55] Indeed, as the oil boom ended in the 1980s and the Nigerian economy collapsed, and as the government pursued structural adjustment, the economic crisis led to a gender crisis. This was the context from which Nollywood emerged, and as it did, many important films seem to have fantasized about a resolution to the crisis that was embodied in a kind, handsome, devoted husband with a great job who could afford to keep his wife at home. To reiterate, however, this fantasy may have nothing to do with the social aspirations of real women; rather, to fantasize about breadwinner husbands is ultimately to fantasize about a set of social conditions that could ease gendered suffering—at least in certain regards. Nollywood, as I will now show, seems to have sustained this fantasy long past the break with state television.

CHECKMATE'S CHILDREN: VIOLATED AND GAMES WOMEN PLAY

The mode of address on display in *Checkmate* is melodramatic in its insistence on the emotional experiences of its characters, its separation and elevation of quotidian social pressures to the categories of good and evil, and its attempt to redistribute goodness to those men who are capable of building a strong, independent, nuclear family while redistributing evil to the conditions that undermine men's breadwinning capacities. *Checkmate*'s mode of address is also feminine in the sense that it invites spectators—of any gender—to identify with a female character and, more importantly, with a constructed sense of her distinctly feminine experiences within a supposedly ideal heteronormative conjugal relationship. Amaka Igwe would reproduce this feminine melodramatic mode of address in some of her work in Nollywood, most notably *Violated* (1996), which was by far the most successful video film of its time.[56] The modal relationship between *Checkmate* and *Violated* also registers at the level of cast. *Violated* stars Ego Boyo and Richard Mofe-Damijo, the actors who played Anne Haatrope and Segun Kadiri in *Checkmate*. Likewise, Mildred Iweka, Kunle Bamtefa, Toun Oni, and Ruth Osu—who starred in *Checkmate* as Ada, Fuji, Moji, and the maid at Haatrope House, Nana Kofo, respectively—also have major roles in *Violated*. Unlike *Checkmate*, however, Boyo and Mofe-Damijo constitute the emotional heart of *Violated*, and the gendered relationship to wealth is polarized. This point of comparison matters precisely because, as more than a stand-alone text, *Violated* participates in a wider visual culture where the overlap between actors and characters contributes to the ways in which those characters might be understood.

Haynes's description of *Violated* in *Nollywood: The Creation of Nigerian Film Genres* is superb, so I will offer no extended summary here, although some background information and analysis of a few plot points are essential to my argument. More importantly, my objective here is to build on and push Haynes's reading in new directions. For example, Haynes notes that the film was marketed to Lagos elites and enjoyed a public premiere at the MUSON Center, the most prestigious venue in the city. That strategy, he wryly suggests, masked the film's more general appeal to ordinary-market women, who are said to constitute Nollywood's core audience.[57] I would add that Igwe's marketing strategy therefore reproduces a contrast between wealthy and middle-class women that features in the film itself, and was also embodied by Anne and Ada in *Checkmate*. If the film is addressed to ordinary women, then its aspirational sensibility—its depiction of extremely wealthy people living lives that ordinary spectators might not otherwise see and might covet—is amplified by the idea that wealthy people also enjoyed the film, that they would also spend their money to see it—and conspicuously, in public no less. Instead of a caricature of Nigeria's petro-elites, therefore, *Violated* could be imagined as part of elite culture itself, not only lending to the film some invaluable cachet but also contributing to the pleasure of being addressed as an indirect subject. The film might suggest that a lot needs to change in order for Nigerian women to enjoy the good life; nevertheless, it offers them a small piece of the good life to enjoy in the meantime.

Boyo's character in *Violated*, Peggy, is a working girl in love with Mofe-Damijo's Tega, heir to a massive banking fortune. Tega's father has passed away, and his mother (played by veteran stage and screen actor Joke Silva) serves as trustee until Tega can produce his own heir apparent. Mama Tega opposes her son's relationship because Peggy has "no name," no known family history. Tega should return to his ex-wife, Tessy (Funke Adepegba), his mother argues, because Tessy is the daughter of the bank's most important client. He does not obey, so Tega and his mother quarrel for most of the film, and he is cut off from his inheritance. Tega does not mind, however, as he has set out to make his own fortune, launching a company with his friend, Sam (Ahmed Uwhubetine). Therefore, what makes Tega ideal is his devotion not only to Peggy but

also to the breadwinner concepts of neolocality and financial independence, even at the expense of his actual financial status. In the end, however, Tega will prove himself to be the ideal husband by achieving both
without forfeiting his inheritance, not to mention by having a child with
Peggy. Nevertheless, the path to the perfect nuclear family is complicated
by Peggy's sordid past. As the film progresses, spectators learn that she
was orphaned at ten, was taken in by a middle-class couple, and was raped
at fifteen by the husband, Amadi (Bamtefa). Peggy became pregnant and
gave birth to twins, whom she abandoned in a village, where an elderly
woman (Oni) kept one child, a girl, and took the other, a boy, to a nearby
hospital. There, he was sold to a middle-class woman, Sumbo (Iweka),
who had just lost her own son in labor. (Indeed, the film opens with
scenes of Mildred Iweka in a hospital bed that vividly recall her scenes
from *Checkmate*.)

Unlike *Checkmate*, in which the primary character (played by Boyo)
is not the story's emotional center, *Violated* places Boyo's character—a
working woman—at the heart of the story and invites spectators to identify with her. Knowledge of Peggy's secrets is revealed piecemeal through
exquisite storytelling that often relies on images from her dreams, which
means that she is the primary character into whose subjectivity spectators
are given a glimpse. Otherwise, the camerawork and editing are mostly
understated. The arc of Peggy's story involves coming to terms with her
past in order to be fully prepared to marry Tega. Meanwhile, Mama Tega's
arc begins with condescension toward Peggy, turning to outright contempt, before finally settling into acceptance. In the end she is a paragon of grandmotherhood. However, Tega changes very little. From the
start, he is philosophically opposed to marrying for class status, he is
steadfastly devoted to Peggy, and he is willing to risk his entire fortune
for love. His resolute and very liberal morality pulls Peggy through her
struggle to come to terms with her past, as well as his mother's journey
from greedy matriarch to nurturing mother. Tega has every opportunity
to achieve breadwinner status in spectacular fashion, but he chooses the
more difficult path of starting his own business and providing emotional
as well as financial support to a woman with low social status. Peggy may
have been violated, but as Haynes argues, the story is less about her preparation for motherhood than her preparation for marriage.[58] *Violated* is
about getting the perfect man.

Haynes also writes that Nollywood films such as *Violated*, as well as
the television soap operas that preceded them, "make a claim for—to
create and expand—an autonomous space within women, where purposes

are found and decisions are made, a basis from which they come to terms with their patriarchal societies."[59] Therefore, the feminine address of Nollywood melodramas does not condescend to spectators; rather, it invites identification with female characters who, despite hitching their stars to men, make empowered decisions about their own lives in liberal if not quintessentially neoliberal fashion. As I see it, Tega operates in *Violated* less as a guide for masculine behavior than as a nonpareil by which female spectators might measure their own men and their own claims to modern femininity. However, that gender model is almost entirely at odds with lived experience in southern Nigeria, not simply because, in this particular fantasy, Tega is so fabulously rich or because, in reality, the society is more bluntly patriarchal than he appears to be (let us be clear, every society is more bluntly patriarchal than Tega appears to be). And it is not simply because highly educated, romantic, devoted, rich men who can support one woman financially and emotionally, who can withstand the pressures of extended family and the economy, and who also resist the temptation to lavish their money on other women are so rare; rather, it is because the liberal economic and political conditions necessary to produce men like Tega are not widely distributed in Nigeria. Haynes agrees that the film "propagandize[s]" a conjugal family ideal, but he argues that "the film's wild inflation of living standards really just provides a pleasurable décor for a struggle based in essential family relationships, in the standard manner of international cinema and television." Rather than wealth being central to the gender model on display, he claims that the model "has been so widely disseminated in Africa by Christianity and popular culture that it is no longer the exclusive property of a particular class."[60] However, I would argue that the model works as propaganda, that it thrives in popular culture precisely because power, especially class power, remains a key component of the model, not to mention the configurations of popular culture. I understand the gender model on display as a form of privilege, in which Tega is not simply a good man but one whose capacity for goodness is substantially underwritten by his social and financial status.

To reiterate, the concept of a male breadwinner is obviously not radical or utopian, yet it can be realized only in a context of regular living wages, which is presumable in some places where the ideal has thrived but is not presumable in much of contemporary Nigeria. In that sense, Tega represents not just the ideological position of the bourgeoisie but also the transformative potential of the well-paid working man. As Peggy becomes pregnant and after she has the baby, several scenes in *Violated* are constructed around Tega returning from work to greet Peggy, who has been at home all day. She cooks for him and otherwise manages their domestic lives, relying on his income to do so. At the beginning of part II of the film, Peggy urges him to reconcile with his mother because she is "tired of counting kobos" while his business venture gets off the ground. In a short scene in their bedroom she makes it clear that she did not marry him for his family's money, yet their conversation suggests that Tega must be strategic about how he will, as he puts it, "sustain this family." Peggy does not tell him what to do, nor does she find a way to generate income herself. Instead, after eliciting anger from Tega about his ability to win bread, she silently embraces him. In subsequent scenes, when she does leave the house during the day, it is to begin the search for her children and put her moral house in order. That, the film implies, is the primary labor she must perform to keep the household going.

Meanwhile, Tega's behavior may be extraordinarily benevolent, but he is insistent that his vision of work, class, and marriage is not "socialist." His business partner, Sam, reminds him that even though Tega opposes marriage for the purposes of class status maintenance, the freedom he advocates depends entirely on his class status. "Until you stop wearing your fancy suits," Sam scolds, "and very expensive designer clothing, stop driving your flashy cars, using your mobile phone, your fat expense accounts, and you ride the bus like everyone else to get to where they're going, then I'll understand you actually know what you're talking about." In other words, Tega may not be interested in class, but he is not abolishing it either; instead, he misrecognizes values that derive from his class status as some kind of personal morality. Wealth does more, it seems, than simply decorate the fantasy in *Violated*. In fact, the film suggests that if more men had access to wealth, there would be more good marriages. Therefore, a very key difference between *Checkmate* and *Violated* is the fact that whereas *Checkmate* invites spectators to suffer along with Ada as her husband fails to win material and emotional bread, *Violated* invites spectators to identify with Peggy as she sorts through her own moral issues in preparation to enjoy Tega's bread. Thus, where state television suggests that the ideal subject position is one of waiting, patiently and tolerantly, Nollywood begins to suggest that it is possible to create the moral conditions for material achievement.

Violated illustrates one of the key ideological innovations of Nollywood. If NTA productions such as *The Village Headmaster* invited spectators to identify with the developmentalist state and to sympathize with all the pressures it faced in securing liberal life for its citizens, and if

independent productions such as *Checkmate* invited spectators to identify with citizens who know and have seen liberal life but are waiting for
their version of it, Nollywood often invites spectators to do more than
sympathize or wait. *Violated* specifically invites spectators to identify
with a woman who, in order to enjoy the kind of liberal life embodied
by a breadwinning man, must get her own moral house in order. Peggy
must directly confront the immoral things done to her by powerful men
as well as the immoral choices those actions have caused her to make. In
the end she finds her son living with Sumbo and agrees to let him stay so
that he can grow up with the only family he has ever known. Peggy has
also retrieved her daughter, who, along with the child she conceived with
Tega, becomes part of their emerging, idealized nuclear family. Peggy's
story is therefore about a life within reach but one that can be seized only
when she has become an expert of herself. This is a neoliberal version
of periliberalism, a seeping of newer values into the general condition
of being held at arm's length from liberalism. The story still emphasizes
the value of living conditions that are unavailable to the vast majority of
Nigerians, but instead of trying to understand how government wants
to create those conditions or waiting to see if government can succeed,
Violated suggests that if individuals want to enjoy liberal life, they should
get busy creating the conditions to do so.

   As several scholars have noted, Nollywood's vision of personal morality may be generally rooted in a pervasive Pentecostal ethos, but *Violated*
deals with morality in pointedly secular terms. Of course, the explosion of
Pentecostalism in the post-structural adjustment era speaks to the mutually reinforcing messages of self-regulation inherent to both discourses.
Nevertheless, *Violated* demonstrates that some early Nollywood films deal
with moral themes outside of religion. That squares with arguments made
by anthropologists such as Ferguson and Smith, who have convincingly
argued that in much of African sociality, issues related to governance
and economics have long been discussed in moral or "social relational"
terms.[61] Contrary to Enlightenment discourse about the science and rationality of creating wealth or wielding power, many Africans—according
to the ethnographic literature—have conceptualized social relations in
ways that, using more contemporary terms, might be described as forms
of "social justice." Ferguson invokes Comaroff and Comaroff, who claim
that "producing people, relations, and things" in Africa is the "work" one
does in "producing oneself."[62] Likewise, Karin Barber has observed the
same dynamic at work in the Yoruba traveling theater, where honest, incre-
mental work is depicted as the foundation of a good social disposition

as well as moral wealth, whereas quick money constitutes the path to immorality. As Barber argues, however, Yoruba theater artists in the 1980s struggled to create convincing visions of good wealth precisely because there was no apparent model for it in the actual society.[63] In terms of the theoretical and methodological orientation of African cultural studies, therefore, the use of moral discourse in *Violated* does not simply reflect the cultural discourses available to its spectators; it also participates in constituting those discourses. But it does more than that. It participates in constituting a subject position that bridges the impasse between fantasy and reality. If conditions of liberal life are desired yet there is no model for a woman who can go out into the world and create those conditions, then it becomes a moral and therefore prosocial choice to work on oneself, to prepare one's subjectivity for another social force— here embodied by the ideal man—who may come along at any moment and make liberal life possible. So Nollywood's neoliberal innovations may create space within the fantasy of gender for more individual agency, yet they do not change the fundamentally periliberal orientation of the local address.

In the final pages of this section I turn to one of the most famous Nollywood feminine melodrama films ever produced, *Games Women Play* (2005). It received several nominations for the first set of African Movie Academy Awards. It has also made at least one visible top twenty list of the "Best Nollywood Movies of All Time."[64] Several critics cite *Games Women Play* as a paradigmatic vehicle for patriarchal values.[65] However, more than an indictment of feminine behavior, as the film's title suggests, *Games Women Play* is concerned with defining the ideal breadwinning man and the rules by which women must play to get and keep one. In terms of wealth and (sexual) devotion, the film has as much to say about men's games as it does about women's.

Games Women Play was written and produced by Emem Isong, a graduate of the University of Calabar whose highly successful love stories have made her a major player in Nollywood. By 2005, she was regularly working with Remmy Jes Productions, the dynamic marketing unit run by Rob Emeka Eze, who, along with the virtuoso director Lancelot Oduwa Imasuen, had cornered the market on relatively high-budget romances starring the most-well-known actors in the industry. *Games Women Play* spawned a series of pseudo-sequels, including *Games Men Play* (2006) and *Reloaded* (2009). Then, after a string of successful films with Remmy Jes, Isong established her own production company, Royal Arts Academy, which became one of the most prolific and high-profile institutions in

Nollywood. Isong's films regularly featured the industry's biggest celebrities at the time, including Genevieve Nnaji, Omotola Jalade Ekehinde, Desmond Elliot, and Stella Damasus (all of whom star in *Games Women Play*), as well as Monalisa Chinda, Uche Jombo, Majid Michel, Nse Ikpe Etim, Jim Iyke, Van Vicker, Ramsey Nouah, and Rita Dominic. Those celebrities, Isong admitted, do not work for small fees, implying that her production company has significant resources to wield. And not only do her films seem to sell well on the streets; they also seem to have influenced other filmmakers. She pioneered a style that has essentially become the Nollywood norm.[66] *Games Women Play* therefore represents one of the most lucrative and influential branches of early Nollywood. Portrayals of the occult, precolonial villages, or crime—the subjects of the next three chapters of this book—may have attracted substantial outside attention to Nollywood, but the celebrity romance may be the genre that propped up the industry during its most crucial and formative years.[67]

Isong's approach to filmmaking adds a layer of complexity to the mirror thesis proposed by Amaka Igwe, whose legacy Isong—consciously or not—has inherited. In her office in Lagos, sitting behind a large desk, Isong told me that "I write what I see. I mirror society. Some of these things are happening, and there is no need of us trying to live in self-denial, saying it's not happening. It's there."[68] She thus vehemently distances herself from the developmentalist tradition of state television. Her role as filmmaker, she suggests, is not to show people what they should be or what they should avoid, but instead to show them what they are. In a context where developmentalist state media long dominated screen culture, therefore, that straightforwardness is, in a sense, revolutionary. And indeed, Isong's sentiment is part of what makes Nollywood distinct from most of the African screen media that preceded it. However, there remains a very deep morality in Isong's vision that aligns with the content shown on state television, especially examples like *Checkmate*. Society may be full of immorality, but Isong does not simply mirror it. In fact, her films suggest that what may be "happening" in society is that certain forms of liberal life—complete with autonomous subjectivity for women and men, companionate marriage, and enough wealth to make breadwinning a choice, not to mention fancy suits, flashy cars, boutique restaurants, and even well-equipped gyms (things that Haynes refers to as being "too 'oyinbo'—foreign, White")—can be and often are achieved by immoral means.[69] Her films thus imagine spectators who are indirectly subject to liberalism, who are invited to take pleasure in various depictions of liberal life, but who can also take (greater?) pleasure in the idea that having limited access to liberal benefits is part of a morally superior path through life.

The most immoral and memorable game in *Games Women Play* is initiated by Candace Bassey (Genevieve Nnaji), a famous film actor who makes a bet that her fiancé, Temi (Desmond Elliot), will never cheat on her. She asks her unmarried friend, Yvonne (Omotola Jalade Ekehinde), whom Temi does not know, to attempt to "seduce" him in order to prove his loyalty. At first, Temi is incorruptible, but with Candace's incessant prodding, Yvonne becomes an increasingly capable flirt and eventually wins Temi's affections. When Candace realizes that the game has gone too far, however, it is too late. Temi rejects Candace and in the final scenes of the film embarks on a new relationship with Yvonne.

Candace's profession is meta-cinematic: she is essentially a version of Nnaji, the actor who plays her, whereas Temi is a defense attorney and Yvonne is a stockbroker. Like *Checkmate*, therefore, the film's titular subject arises from a spectacular, elite romance. There may be more than one game in the film, as the title suggests, but Candace's game is by far the most extravagant and the most game-like—with rules, an end point, a sense of fun, and opposing sides. Her opponents include Yvonne and their friend Emma (Stella Damasus), who is shocked at first but then bets against Temi and seems to relish the chaos that Candace—the stereotypically narcissistic actor—has brought upon herself. As the game plays out, however, Yvonne's acquiescence and Temi's eventual infidelity are, like the romance between Anne Haatrope and Segun Kadiri in *Checkmate*, too spectacular to be convincingly realistic or relatable. Much more convincing is the secondary "game" in which Emma is embroiled. Her story is also spectacular, but it includes more relatable elements that are focused on a domestic setting while several moments of free indirect subjectivity invite spectators to identify with her. Like Ada in *Checkmate*, Emma is the one character in the film who is part of a companionate marriage and a nuclear family when the story begins. Her journey and the invitation for spectators to participate in it point to the indirect subject of *Games Women Play*.

The film opens with Emma picking up her twin children from school. She drives a Mercedes-Benz, and they return to a magnificent house. Emma's husband, Damian (Zack Orji), runs some kind of data analytics firm that apparently nets him millions of naira in income, although very little about his work is explicitly depicted. The lack of specificity about Damian's work, like Yvonne's generic yuppie profession, recalls Barber's insights, noted earlier, about the silences of Yoruba traveling theater. Such wealth simply cannot be made to seem real. By all accounts, however, Emma has achieved a normative ideal version of femininity. Her only work is in the home—indeed, she laments the amount of work required of Candace and Yvonne—while her husband brings home plenty of bread. Damian is also charming, supportive, and devoted. One of his employees, Ada (Ini Ikpe), attempts several sexual encounters with him, but he never relents. "I am married, and I intend to remain so," Damian tells her. However, all of this conjugal bliss is jeopardized by the fact that, like Peggy, Emma's moral house is out of order.

Damian announces one day that his old friend, Bill (BobManuel Udokwu), has just returned from the United States, where he was wrongly imprisoned for seven years, and will be staying with them until he can land a job. Bill has picked up an American accent, recalling Udokwu's character in *Checkmate* (indeed, Udokwu's industry nickname is "Mr. Hollywood"). When Bill enters the house and he and Emma lay eyes on each other, the sound track is suddenly filled with the synthesized sound of an electric guitar, wailing with pinch harmonics (a relatively common but unmistakable sound, typical of heavy-metal music, sometimes referred to as "squealies"). The effect is quintessentially melodramatic. Emma shouts "Jesus!" Then a close-up displays Bill's hand as he drops his luggage. Both characters stare at the other, wide-eyed.

Over the next several scenes, spectators learn that Bill and Emma were previously married and that they formerly went by the names William and Emerald. They met in Ireland and then moved to the United States together, where, in an attempt to gain a green card, Bill lived with and pretended to be married to an Italian American woman. Invoking Nigerian spectators' familiarity with Hollywood, the story proceeds with the allegation that Bill's sham wife "got mixed up with the wrong mob," members of which detonated a bomb at her house. Bill was not there at the time and was subsequently convicted of her murder until, after seven years in jail, the mob's boss was arrested and exonerated Bill. However, Emma knew none of this at the time. She believed that Bill had been killed in the blast, and just a few weeks afterward she met Damian, who was vacationing in New York. They quickly fell in love and got married.

It takes a bit of convoluted discussion, but Emma eventually establishes that she could never have known what happened to William, making her moral conundrum convincing. Who is her real husband? Is it the successful breadwinner with whom she has built an ideal marriage or the man she met and married first, a man who had to leave their home and live with another woman precisely because he could not win bread? Now, that man is back, still without breadwinning potential but with a legal claim to Emma. These questions are further complicated by the fact that Emma never told Damian about William, which means that any resolution will depend on Emma's ability to admit her mistake, divulge her secrets, and achieve moral clarity. Unfortunately, Emma fails to do so, eventually going so far as to sleep with her first husband, Bill, under the very roof that Damian's bread has built.

The depths of Emma's moral predicament begin to register the first day that she and Bill find themselves alone in the house. Emma is busy polishing her furniture when Bill approaches. As Emma turns toward the next piece of furniture, she notices Bill standing there, and the image cuts to a shot from Emma's perspective, tilting upward from Bill's feet to his torso. The frame then returns to a shot of Emma as her head completes the upward movement associated with the previous shot (see figures 3.7–3.12).

During that brief moment in which the camera inhabits Emma's subjectivity, the synthesized sounds of pinch harmonics play once more. At this point, pinch harmonics have become one of the most frequent and meaningful sonic motifs in the film. Each time they play, they are associated with either a literal threat to Emma's perfect nuclear family or a threat to the ideological image of companionship that she has constructed for herself. They play, for example, when Candace proposes the game with Temi and Yvonne, shocking Emma's sense of romantic fidelity. Indeed, the pinch harmonics seem to register an emotional reaction to various events in the story that might be described as exclusive to Emma, as if she were co-narrating the film. They even play when Emma is not present, as when Damian rebuffs Ada. The first time it happens, Damian leaves the room, and Ada watches with a look that suggests she will try to seduce him again. The camera focuses on her face, and those piercing pinch harmonics wail, as if Emma's subjectivity, in addition to the camera, were observing Ada. To be clear, there are other moments in the film when the synthesized sound of a guitar accompanies conjugal tension, but the pinch harmonics are reserved for those moments that bear directly on Emma's situation. The result is a sense that along with the third-person narrator, Emma's subjectivity is freely and indirectly seizing various opportunities to tell the story. Like a Nabokov novel, it is as if Emma is begging spectators to judge her with mercy—though judge her they will.

In an awkwardly contrived twist, spectators learn that Emma gave birth to her twins not long after her marriage to Damian, meaning that the children could be Bill's. The last thirty minutes of the film therefore consist of a courtroom drama in which the children's paternity and Emma's

FIGURE 3.7

FIGURE 3.8

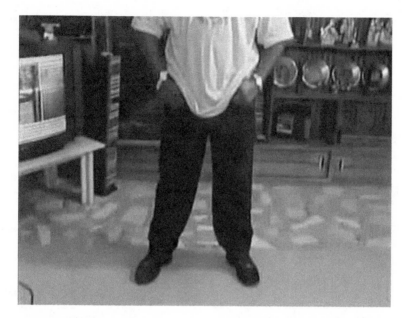

FIGURE 3.9

FIGURE 3.10

FIGURE 3.11

FIGURE 3.12

FIGURES 3.7, 3.8, 3.9, 3.10, 3.11, AND 3.12. *Games Women Play*. Emma regards Bill. The image moves from third-person perspective (figures 3.7 and 3.8) to point-of-view (figures 3.9 and 3.10) and back to third-person perspective (figures 3.11 and 3.12).

moral character are put on trial. Having found Emma and Bill together, Damian is furious, demanding custody of the twins and calling Emma "Jezebel." However, that particular biblical gloss of femininity is hardly unique in the story. When Ada proposes to become Damian's next wife, he tells her: "I have heard about scheming women, but, my God, you certainly take the cake. They say God created women and since then he has not rested, and it is true. How can he rest with shameless serpents like you prowling the face of the Earth? Thank God I've been delivered from the clutches of all you daughters of Jezebel." By the time Damian utters these words, Candace and Temi have also split. Temi shows interest in Yvonne, but at the very moment he learns about the game, he refers to her as a "sneaky, slimy snake." Thus, when Emma's trial finally commences, the major signs of femininity on display have all invoked the biblical Fall.

When it comes to "negative" significations of femininity like these, Jane Bryce has produced one of the most convincing arguments in Nollywood studies to date. Rather than indications of gendered sentiment in the society at large, she argues, Nollywood's femininity is "an ambivalent sign for an era of transition, signifying both social depravity and the desire for social transformation through radical change."[70] Nollywood thus both participates in and signifies what she calls a "crisis of patriarchy." The courtroom drama at the end of Games Women Play might be read as an attempt to resolve that crisis, therefore reinforcing patriarchy, but it does so in a way that also regulates masculine behavior. Damian and Temi are ideal because they would never countenance infidelity. Moreover, Nigeria's crisis of patriarchy is not in and of itself the major social problem addressed through signs of femininity. Indeed, the crisis of patriarchy derives, as Bryce suggests, from an overarching crisis concerning the society's inequitable position within the world economy.

The final sequence in Games Woman Play constructs a remarkable version of the moral occult in a post-sacred context. Temi is Damian's attorney, which brings the two major games in the film together. Candace and Yvonne are present to support Emma. Everyone's fate therefore seems to depend on Emma's in some way. First, Temi cross-examines her, questioning the fact that she slept with Damian as soon as she met him, only weeks after her husband had died, or so she thought. The gallery reacts disapprovingly, but Emma insists that she slept with Damian only after he proposed marriage. Then Damian is cross-examined by Emma's attorney (Samantha Ovuehor), who brings Christianity into the courtroom by way of emphasizing the modernity of the postcolonial justice system. "Thank god for Christianity, Mr. Damian," she says. "Because under the African

religion the offense you have just committed would have earned you instant death, by hanging. Did you know that?" Her question suggests that
"under the African religion," spirituality and state justice were concomi-
tant. Damian answers in the negative, so she explains, "You took another
man's wife away for eight years." Of course, Damian insists he never knew
that Emma had been previously married. Moreover, he ups the ante on
the purported modernity of Nigeria's justice system. When Emma's attorney refers to a proverb, which says that "only a child can say who its
father is," Damian insists that there is one more source that can speak:
DNA. Then, just before the judge (Oduma Francis Mike) orders everyone
to submit to DNA testing, eight-year-old John (Valiance Mowete) asks
to address the court, which the judge allows. John says, "Our parents
taught us not to lie, that lying is for the devil, but one of them is lying
right here in this court. I don't know who." The judge then promises John
that the state will not give him the wrong "daddy." All the arguments of
the trial therefore pit the moral discourses of state authority, precolonial
religion, and Christianity against one another, juxtaposing each of them
with the cold rationality of science. Morality here is indeed fractured, but
as the trial wraps up, the film digs even deeper.

During closing arguments, Emma's attorney claims that Bill and
Emma have been reunited by God and that Damian is not the father
of the children because he "is only a custodian that God used" to bring
Bill and Emma back together. Meanwhile, in Temi's final repudiation of
Emma, he summarizes her actions: "A man comes into her house. In less
than two months, she is caught, pants down, with him in her matrimonial
home. Women have never ceased to amaze me." Neither party is censured
by the judge. Both religious fatalism and condescending misogyny pass
without comment. And then, when the judge hands down his sentence,
claiming to apply the law and science to the case, he too seeks a new moral
order:

> [Emma] is a woman of no morals, a disgrace to womanhood, who has suc-
> ceeded in putting her children in a great psychological trauma that will
> be very, very difficult to erase. Such attitude or behavior from a woman
> should not be tolerated in a civilized society like ours. The twins, John and
> Jill, have a right to private and family life, as enshrined in Chapter 4, Sec-
> tion 35, of the 1999 constitution of Federal Republic of Nigeria and should
> not be tossed around like a coin. From the DNA test carried out, the result
> shows conclusively, and without any shadow of doubt, that the father of
> the twins is none other than the defendant, Mr. Damian Okafor.

The judge then awards custody to Damian and visitation rights to Emma. The courtroom begins to empty, and the children run to Damian, who embraces them. Temi stands at his side. The homosocial tableau of the two men and the children constitutes the final image of the film, but just before the credits roll, the screen is inscribed with the customary Nollywood invocation: "To God Be the Glory."

Isong maintains that she does not reproduce the final invocation lightly. She is entirely forthcoming about her Pentecostal faith and the fact that in her writing, "most issues are resolved through Christ." Furthermore, she claims that this is in consonance with the society at large, though not without the slightest tinge of cynicism. As she puts it, "Nigerians, we're quite religious, in quotes, so you can't divorce some of our stories from religion." The "in quotes" here suggests a self-awareness about the post-sacred nature of her complex society. Yes, many Nigerians tend to be exuberantly religious, but there are lots of ways to be religious, not to mention several other moral orders to consider. The final judgment against Emma suggests that a new morality resides somewhere between avoiding psychological trauma, creating a civilized society, and glorifying god.

Emma's fate may seem severe, but melodrama often relies on such extremes, calling spectators to look deeper than the surface, in which Emma could not have known about Bill's survival. Below that surface it is clear that Emma gained access to an almost perfect version of modern femininity and risked it all by keeping secrets from her ideal man. Damian does not demand subservience from Emma so much as he demands moral clarity, which Emma can achieve only on her own. But what if she had told Damian about her previous marriage when they met? Would he have loved her as much? Would he have ever married her? In *Violated*, Peggy discloses her secrets to Tega before anything terrible happens, so he stands by her. Emma's failure, on the other hand, seems to result from entering marriage without moral clarity, suggesting a total lack of faith from the very beginning in the norms of the breadwinner ideal.

CELEBRITY'S NIGHT OUT

Not only does *Games Women Play* explore the moral occult but it also posits the interface between surface and occult in the medium of the television screen. Early in the film, before she commences with her game, Candace is interviewed for a fictive television program called *Celebrity's Night Out*. Spectators are invited to watch Candace preparing for the interview and

witness her behaving like a spoiled child. A makeup artist spills foundation on her blouse, and she explodes with rage. She then appears on the
show—cinematically twice removed—*acting* gracious and poised. The interviewer invokes Candace's mega-celebrity status, calling her the "golden
girl of the Nollywood home video" and acknowledging the "press men,
photographers, [and] people running here and there wanting to catch a
glimpse of you." He then refers to a film in which, according to some fictional fans, Candace was not acting but "playing herself, true to type" as the
"bitchy daughter of the vice president." At that moment, Candace looks
into the camera and asks her public, "Do I look like a bitch?"

Who knows what the fictional television audience thinks? However,
real spectators have just seen her off camera, and they know better. So
does Yvonne, who is watching *Celebrity's Night Out* at home on her television. The film cuts from Candace's interview to a shot of Yvonne, sitting
on her couch and remarking to herself, "Candace Bassi, she can never
change." A large projection-screen television fills the far wall of Yvonne's
parlor, from which the program radiates. Those who follow Nollywood
closely would be unlikely to miss a number of jokes embedded in this exchange. The actor who plays Yvonne, Omotola Ekehinde, has starred in
several films with Nnaji, suggesting that she knows her quite well. During
the early 2000s she was also Nnaji's rival for the position of Nollywood's
biggest diva. Indeed, Ekehinde is the one with a reputation for being difficult on set.[71] Yet another joke will be apparent only to the well-informed
Nollywood spectator who recognizes that Candace's interviewer is none
other than Imasuen, the director of the film. In that role he is tasked with
managing Candace's character, but as interviewer he is unable to render
her the same way spectators know her. Imasuen is thus, literally, an interviewer, providing a connection between his view of Candace and the
public's view of Nnaji. This inter-viewing makes the medium of the video
film and its relationship to television hyper-apparent. Uncannily, this becomes true on an even deeper level for the critic or industry insider who
knows Isong's crew, or the spectator who takes the time to methodically
decode the film's credits. The men who play the makeup artist (Temisan
Etsede) and production manager (Emeka Duru) on *Celebrity's Night Out*
are the very men who perform those roles for Isong's production company. (I did not recognize them on first viewing but did so, with a feeling
of revelation, after having spent a week on the set of another Isong production in 2010.)

As Birgit Meyer points out, "hyper-apparent" media do not necessarily confound the ideological content of a message. Meyer suggests a

reinterpretation of Marshall McLuhan, arguing that certain mediations in Africa reveal a "complete consonance between [the] medium and what it conveys."[72] For born-again Christians, in particular, who seek immediacy with the Holy Spirit, television can enable a supplicant to be touched by god, as when one lays one's hands on a television set while an on-screen pastor prays. This kind of linkage between media technology and spiritual immediacy may also carry over from spiritual discourse to discourses of the family. Isong claims to be mirroring society, but her viewers often claim that what appears in video films can actually *constitute* social relations. As Carmen McCain notes, many viewers and critics expect Nollywood to construct and positively reinforce national culture by producing celebrities who are role models for citizens. In some cases, viewers argue that if they know stars behave immorally off screen, they will not watch their films.[73] Therefore, it would be overstating the case to claim that Nollywood *produces* indirect subjects of the liberal world order who must resort to the concept of morality in order to temper their desires for liberal life. Nollywood does not have that kind of power. However, it does seem to imagine such spectators and address itself to them. McCain's observations suggest that along the way, Nollywood can accomplish more than exploring the moral occult. It can also accomplish more than pitting ideas against one another in the search for a new distribution of morality. *Games Women Play* addresses a public clearly understood as local and invites it into the fictional field of the film, much as Bollywood melodramas do, according to Ravi Vasudevan.[74] It then allows that public to identify with the subject position of precarious femininity, thus inhabiting the razor's edge of periliberalism. The spectator is invited to enjoy an experiential possibility where liberal life is at hand but constantly exceeds one's grasp. The best defense, it seems, is to retreat into one's moral fortresses until conditions change.

4 Breadlosers

MASCULINE MELODRAMA, MONEY MAGIC, AND THE MORAL OCCULT ECONOMY

Establishing shot: a massive, modernist mansion—painted beige and brown with Spanish accents—looms over a gravel driveway bordered by a lush, tidy lawn. Dissolve to an interior shot: a tall man in a fine tunic and matching trousers parts a red curtain and walks toward the camera. Cut to a long shot of a large, well-furnished parlor. Two women and several children are spread across a succession of elaborate, neobaroque sofas and chairs. The tall man enters the left side of the frame and orders one of the children to make room for him on one of the sofas. Close-ups then establish that one of the women is middle-aged and the other much older. This is the household of Chris Amadi (Charles Okafor) in the spectacular Pentecostal horror film *End of the Wicked* (1999, dir. Teco Benson). The younger woman is Chris's wife, Stella (Hilda Dokubo); the older one is his mother (Patience Oseni). The tableau of people scattered across Chris's furniture suggests that an imbalance of gendered authority threatens the orderly outward appearance of his home.

Chris speaks: "I have gathered all of you here to know exactly what is going on in this house." Stella and the children have been tormented by vivid, bloodcurdling nightmares, but Stella is skeptical of Chris's resolve. She accuses him of doing too little to address a problem that, as she frames it, puts the lives of her children and herself at risk. The dialogue devolves into a bombastic verbal scrimmage, which communicates—if not much actual information—the unyielding tension that permeates their home. Chris's mother simply looks on until he finally appeals to her: "What have I said to warrant this kind of rubbish, this kind of outburst from Stella?" "It's enough, my son," she pleads, although Chris remains indignant. He shouts, "It is not enough!" and stands, wagging his finger. "I am the man of this house," he insists, "I provide everything that is needed in this house . . . but when it comes to taking action in this house, Stella will not allow me to take authority."

Spectators already know that Chris's anger is entirely misplaced. The film's opening sequence establishes that Chris's mother is the one causing the nightmares. She is a witch known as "Lady Destroyer" in a cult that worships Beelzebub (played by Alex Usifo Obiagbo, with titanium-white face paint and a bright-red, blood-soaked chin). Their coven meets in a forest that appears to be located in some kind of parallel dimension. Lady Destroyer flies there at night in a corrupted physical form, as if rotted and disfigured from years of evil servitude. There, she and the other witches receive instructions from Beelzebub and seek his assistance with their various malevolent schemes.

End of the Wicked has become something of a global phenomenon for two parallel reasons. One of the most spectacular plotlines involves child witches, core members of Beelzebub's cult, who wreak havoc in their parents' homes. The film was produced by the media arm of a Pentecostal church in Calabar, Liberty Foundation Gospel Ministries, which is run by Helen Ukpabio, a preacher known for her controversial prophecies about child witches. Along with her films, Ukpabio's sermons and books have contributed to the persecution and abandonment of hundreds of actual children in southeastern Nigeria over the last two decades. Several humanitarian organizations have stepped in to care for the children, one of which was featured in an award-winning BBC documentary, *Saving Africa's Witch Children* (2008, dir. Mags Gavin and Joost van der Valk), which—despite drawing valuable attention to the plight of the children—exoticizes Nigeria, Pentecostalism, and Nollywood in ways that are as unsurprising as they are unanalytical. Meanwhile, in a similarly sensational and paternalist if less condemnatory vein, *End of the Wicked* is often celebrated by connoisseurs of global B-grade horror.[1] The innovative use of makeup and special effects, along with a willingness to unflinchingly depict animal sacrifices and sexual imagery, makes it feel as if the film is designed solely to shock and titillate. Certainly, *End of the Wicked* provides many salacious, hair-raising thrills, but it is addressed to its spectators as a form of revelation. "This film is coming to you by the special grace of God," reads an opening title screen. "There have been several near successful attempts by the powers of darkness to stop it, because of its great expositions."[2] More than excite spectators, therefore, *End of the Wicked* offers its audience a window into the occult forces that supposedly impinge on families like Chris Amadi's.

The great irony of Chris's claim to household authority, which is based on his supposed generosity, is that he addresses it to his mother. Lady Destroyer, it turns out, is the agent of a system specifically designed to destabilize the fantasy of a modern nuclear family and the breadwinner ideal that sustains it. At some of the coven's meetings, for example, the gathering functions as a spiritual court of family law, with Beelzebub as magistrate. In one scene Lady Destroyer steps forward to plead her case against Chris and his status as head of their household. Her accusation is worded so straightforwardly it is confounding: "He gives me everything that I need. He feeds me, shelters me, and clothes me." She then produces material evidence of Chris's ability to provide, on which Beelzebub rules in the language of liberal jurisprudence.

> I have found the accused guilty of all the charges leveled against him. The evidence before me proves beyond any reasonable doubt that the accused, Chris Amadi, is truly the son of Lady Destroyer. The food, clothes, and some other things shown to this great spiritual court prove that our Lady Destroyer is being taken care of by Chris. I now find him guilty of all the charges, according to spiritual laws, and consequently sentence him to life imprisonment with hard labor.

The life of bondage imposed on Chris thus seems to be the penalty for providing "everything that is needed" in his house, which of course raises several questions. Is Beelzebub, and "spiritual law" more generally, offended because Chris provides for *more* than his nuclear family (taking care of his mother too) or because he is a successful provider in general? And why is providing such a heinous crime? The film does not make it clear. Nevertheless, Chris is relentlessly tortured and eventually killed during a cult ritual. Near the end, Chris's sister comes to visit, bringing her fiancé, Emeka (played by a young Ramsey Nouah, who would later become one of Nollywood's leading heartthrobs and eventually an influential director), to meet the family. Lady Destroyer again requests help from Beelzebub to undermine the couple's relationship, suggesting that the main offense against Satan is their modern companionate marriage. Likewise, the subplot about child witches bears on the central theme of breadwinning and nuclear family structures. After all, witchcraft has long been associated with surplus feminine social power in societies across the globe, suggesting that the depiction of child witches in *End of the Wicked* evokes the possibility of surplus *immature* power. Modernity amplifies that surplus, creating conditions in which the supply of "bread" fails to meet extant demands. All of this calls the nuclear family and the breadwinner ideal into question. What are its possibilities, and what are its limits?

The language of Pentecostal discourse in southern Nigeria is dominated by the concept of "winning," where life is a war between forces of light and darkness, where even the simplest achievements must be attributed to God's ability to defeat Satan.[3] Individuals, small groups, and colossal gatherings of people regularly and publicly pray for God's help in conquering the forces that would otherwise prevent them from passing exams, traveling safely, finding spouses, attracting customers, receiving official documents, and more. In many Nollywood movies inflected by that worldview, however, modern men cannot win. In their pursuit of breadwinner status, they may tragically fall into money-magic cults (as in *Living in Bondage* [1992], discussed in the introduction to this book and later in this chapter). And if they somehow avoid that pitfall and do become successful breadwinners, they may be destroyed by satanic powers operating within the home. In fact, the very act of breadwinning, according to *End of the Wicked*, invites Satan's judgment. In this imagined landscape it would be much safer, it seems, to give up on the ideal altogether.

Films like *End of the Wicked* and *Living in Bondage* are not always billed as stories about family life. Jonathan Haynes, for example, discusses them separately from a genre he specifically calls "family films," under which he includes titles like Amaka Igwe's *Violated* (discussed in chapter 3). Yet he also acknowledges the porous construction of genre boundaries in Nollywood, noting that families are the central preoccupation of most video films and that occult and other supernatural themes cut across the industry's various categories.[4] Haynes's assessment of the overlap is infallible; nevertheless, occult sequences tend to be so spectacular that they can distract from some of the other thematic preoccupations of certain films. If an occult sequence features children or money, for example, then the film in question may be treated as a film about child witches or money magic—in or outside Nigeria. *End of the Wicked* is studied mostly for its use of horror conventions and its role in the child witch phenomenon.[5] (Likewise, in informal discussions several Nigerians have told me they remember the film precisely for its horror and especially for the insidious way that its child witches use sweet treats to seduce new initiates. The singsong chant, "Puff-puff, puff-puff," one friend told me, still rings in his ears.) When scholars focus on the social dimensions of the occult sequences in African video films, they often invoke the vast body of scholarship on "occult economies," in which the prevalence of stories in African newspapers and popular culture about occult practices corresponds with tumultuous economic shifts taking place under neoliberal capitalism.[6] For example, Lindsey Green-Simms describes *Living in Bondage* as "a Mephistophelian tale about the illegitimate accumulation of wealth in the postcolony."[7] As *End of the Wicked* points out, however, that association is not always direct. In an altogether different reading of *Living in Bondage*, Paul Ugor writes that "although Andy comes across as 'greedy,' his real ambition, especially within the context of an African mega polis like Lagos, is to make decent money that will enable him to lead a good life, and as he himself explains, to have his wife driven in a good car while she goes grocery shopping." Ugor emphasizes the lack of employment opportunities available to Andy and young men like him all across Lagos. However, notice that Andy is motivated primarily by a desire to provide for his wife, Merit. Elsewhere, Ugor notes that Merit is the one bringing money into their home, which ultimately leads him to conclude that Andy is suffering from the infantilization of having women and parents support him financially (Andy thus serves as an index, in Ugor's account, of youth unemployment).[8] I find Ugor's reading extremely insightful and methodologically generative, yet Andy's suffering may have less to do with infantilization than with a particular kind of emasculation, especially in regard to his status in his marriage. Therefore, the indirect subject of both *End of the Wicked* and *Living in Bondage* would be masculinity, which though undeniably related to questions of economy, operates at a slight remove. In these stories greed may be a secondary impulse originating from or at least intersecting with the primary impulse to be a *real man*.

This chapter further explores masculinist modalities in some of Nollywood's most iconic occult video films, including *Living in Bondage*, *Ashes to Ashes* (2001, dir. Andy Amenechi), and *Billionaires Club* (2003, dir. Afam Okereke). Those modalities, as I have demonstrated in the introduction, often become particularly legible in moments of free indirect subjectivity. Furthermore, as a seminal Nollywood narrative, *Living in Bondage* has been so influential that its core plot—in which a man pursues wealth in order to provide for and elevate himself in relation to his wife, to the point that he destroys his wife and therefore the very reason for pursuing wealth in the first place—has become a significant Nollywood motif.[9] The masculine mode of melodramatic address, which characterizes *Living in Bondage* and is carried through to several later video films, dialogically interacts with the feminine mode, particularly in the case of television soap operas such as *Checkmate* but also subsequent Nollywood films such as *Violated* and *Games Women Play* (see chapter 3). For more than a decade, at least, a highly visible group of Nollywood films seems to have countered the feminine melodramatic mode and the demands that the feminine mode places on masculinity by questioning the very morality of modern family life. Therefore, both the feminine and the masculine modes are melodramatic in the sense that they seek the moral occult in a dispensation otherwise characterized by contradictory and inconclusive moral discourses on the subjects of gender and power. The masculine melodramatic mode, I will illustrate, is less about being a man than it is about languishing under the rhetorical formulation that *real men win bread*.

LIVING IN BONDAGE: BACK TO THAT STACK

The opening scene of *Living in Bondage*, which tends to attract a great deal of scholarly attention, establishes the value system within which many of the film's characters operate. Andy Okeke sits in his parlor and delivers a lengthy soliloquy lamenting his "miserable existence." He has worked for four companies and a bank, but he has resigned from each job because none could pay him what he feels he deserves. He then took up independent trading, without success, while all his business partners went on to buy Mercedes-Benzes and rise to important social positions. Andy therefore wonders whether his suffering is preordained or if he is bewitched. His devoted wife, Merit (Nnenna Nwabueze), enters the room and, before feeding him his dinner, assures Andy that he is not bewitched—but he cannot be consoled. He will later explain that his obsession with money is about being able to provide his wife with luxury goods, even though they live an otherwise comfortable life. At the beginning of the story, therefore, Andy emphasizes that his natural right to win bread for Merit is being impinged upon by forces he cannot yet name.

On the street, Andy runs into an old friend, Paul (Okey Ogunjiofor), and they have lunch together, at which Andy further elaborates his value system. He narrates his life story by first noting that he does not own a single car and that his house is not "fine." He also concludes that his wife is the only thing he can boast with. In that order, then—car, house, wife—Andy organizes his orientation to the world. Paul is not married, yet he has plenty to boast with, including the right kind of car and the right kind of house. So as different as their lives have turned out, they subscribe to similar values. Paul therefore promises to help Andy.

Back at home, more opportunity lands in Andy's lap. Another old friend stops by with an investment proposition, but Merit is immediately skeptical, which she expresses when a woman they call "Aunty" (Chizoba Bosah) stops by to visit. In her role as mediator between Merit's skepticism and Andy's insatiable greed, Aunty instructs Andy to "settle down and live a good life." But his rebuttal is illuminating. Andy acknowledges that Merit is the perfect wife, but his problem is that *acknowledging* her is not enough:

he wants to *reward* her by purchasing a car, he wants to take her to the
market and buy her whatever she desires, and he wants to "repay her for
all the good things she's done." Therefore, threaded through Andy's value
system is a transactional impulse for which Merit then provides further
context. She says that if she wanted a car, she would have bought one herself, instead of giving money to Andy over the years. Andy then changes
the subject, discussing in portentous terms the way other men have made
money through Satanism, which he claims he could never do. The scene
ends without a resolution to the fact that Andy is not simply "green-eyed,"
as he puts it, but he seeks money to pay back and perhaps cancel out the
financial investments his wife has made in their marriage. If Andy is a
sympathetic character at all, therefore, it is because his greed is prosocial:
he wants to be a good man (by a specific set of metrics); he wants to be
restored to breadwinner status.

   Andy does therefore invest in the scheme against which Merit has
taken a stand, and he does lose all the money. Meanwhile, Merit is harassed at work by her boss, Ichie Million (Francis Agu), who tries un-
successfully to seduce her with cash and jewelry. Quite separately and
without remark, Andy attends Ichie's birthday party with Paul and falls
further into the orbit of rich and unscrupulous people. That night, back at
Paul's house, Andy pledges that he will do absolutely anything for money
and then stays over, having a sexual encounter with a woman named Ego
(Ngozi Nwosu). The contrast between Merit and Andy is now crystal clear.
Merit is precisely what her allegorical name implies: worthy of the most
sincere, loyal, and responsible life partner. Andy is not the man for the job.

   When Andy finally follows Paul to the source of his wealth, it turns out
to be a satanic cult—as many spectators, of course, already know, whether
clued in by foreshadowing, by the film's packaging, or having heard about
it by word of mouth. The cult leader informs Andy that he must sacrifice
his wife to join them and become prosperous. Andy is initially horrified,
but he eventually accepts their terms. As I describe in the introduction
to this book, Andy slowly summons the *courage*—cowardly as it is—to
participate in his wife's murder, and after doing so he immediately begins
to live a lavish lifestyle. He marries Ego (incidentally, the Igbo word for
"money"), but Merit's ghost haunts him, causing Andy to faint at the end
of the film. The enigmatic cliffhanger culmination of *Living in Bondage*,
much like Ada fainting at the end of an episode of *Checkmate*, seems to
have augmented the film's popularity. Kenneth Nnebue, the film's producer, followed it with *Living in Bondage 2*, a year later, although he was
unable to convince all of the cast and crew to return to the project.[10]

Therefore, Ego is written out of the story, and Andy marries a third wife, Chi, to whom Merit's ghost also appears. Slowly, Andy is driven further and further into madness by the apparitions, which simultaneously represent spiritual retribution and his nagging conscience. Near the end of the sequel he is living under a bridge and eating trash, but salvation is ultimately supplied by evangelists who scoop him up, take him to their church, and pray him into a confession. The story ends with Andy and his saviors singing an Igbo hymn, "*Onye Nworum Yaa*" ("He has done it for me").

The emphasis that critics tend to place on the money-magic theme in *Living in Bondage* follows from the spectacular nature of the money rituals. As Haynes writes, *Living in Bondage* "established the first great Nollywood thematic complex—'get rich quick'—and its signature genre, the money ritual film."[11] Such films are often said to have visualized a modern, urban oral tradition that otherwise only ever circulated in rumors. In point of fact, however, money ritual stories and horror aesthetics were already being visualized on state television—most notably in a serial drama called *Hot Cash* (ca. 1984–1988), which depicted the ghost of a young orphan boy known as Willie-Willie (Innocent Ohiri), who was sacrificed in a money ritual and then returned to seek revenge on his killers. The use of jump cuts to depict Willie-Willie's materialization, as well as the iconic white gown he wears, was part of a visual culture system already giving shape to popular imaginaries of occult power when *Living in Bondage* was released. Indeed, Merit's white gown suggests that *Living in Bondage* reproduced as well as improvised on a prevailing visual culture of the occult. Similarly, the red and black decor that marks the ritual space in *Living in Bondage* was already part of the visual culture system of Yoruba traveling theater, as well as the stock imagery of state television productions such as *Tales by Moonlight* (1984–present), both of which regularly used red and black cloth or paint to mark occult ritual spaces. Nevertheless, the depiction of an actual satanic ritual, with church-like features—including chanting, prayers, and priests—as well as a sound track reverberating with otherworldly nondiegetic effects, does seem to have arrived on most southern Nigerian television screens with *Living in Bondage*. Subsequently, those aesthetic features became commonplace in Nollywood depictions of the occult. They also became emblematic of the industry, particularly to outside observers for whom the idea of satanic cults was exotic, reminiscent of a beloved kitsch version of horror, or both.[12] So the moments in the film that have attracted the most attention are, unavoidably, the cult meetings, three of which appear in

Living in Bondage 1, whereas one indoor ritual, one outdoor ritual, and one meeting in the ritual space appear in the sequel.

However, the cult scenes tend to function in the narrative as emphasis rather than major plot developments. The first cult scene follows a more consequential sequence, in which Merit tells Andy that she will travel home to solicit money from her family and then runs into Chief Omego (Kanayo O. Kanayo), a wealthy member of their community, at a high-end shopping plaza. When Merit leaves home, Andy is visibly irritated that his wife is planning to ask her parents to salvage their financial prospects. On the way, Omego offers Merit a different path to financial stability by proposing to set her up with a fashion boutique in exchange for sex. Not only does Merit deny him but she loudly and publicly embarrasses him, accusing Omego of sacrificing his mother to a money-magic cult. Indeed, this is not the first time that Merit has invoked the existence of such cults. Aunty, also at the store, comes to Merit's aid, and together they denounce Omego's "blood money." The film then cuts from the image of Omego, cowed by the encounter, to the cult leader, arms spread in a commanding pose of power. Omego is in the room. Andy's entrance, tragic as it may be, is actually more predictable and pathetic than it is astonishing or harrowing. The priest then explains to Andy that he will need to sacrifice his wife, after which various members of the cult testify to the sacrifices they have made and the ensuing wealth they have enjoyed. Therefore, the setup is solid. Andy will do anything Paul tells him to do. Merit has emasculated him by seeking money in her village. And sacrificing a woman is how most rich men have accumulated their wealth. The cult scene, in the end, is almost purely spectacle.

At the end of the meeting the priest offers a benediction, and then the image cuts to a close-up of Andy sitting in his parlor. This is the first of two homologous scenes, the second of which I described in the introduction to this book. In this first one, classical European art music dances on the sound track—Bach's *gavotte en rondeau* from the Partita No. 3 for violin, a nimble melody that leaps, shuffles its feet, and leaps again before tumbling down a steep hill. The camera slowly zooms to an extreme close-up on Andy's forehead, and then the image dissolves, effectively saying, "Andy was thinking about. . . ." He recalls his courtship with Merit in two scenes filmed at a verdant park. The camera captures Andy and Merit at a respectful neutral angle, though actively zooming in and out, and therefore suggesting a highly interested, third-party gaze. This is not Andy's subjectivity. When the image dissolves back to Andy's forehead, however, we hear his voice while his face remains inert. Rather than watching a monologue, as in the opening scene of the film, and rather than being shown his memories as if quoting them, we are hearing Andy's thoughts, meaning that the subjectivity offered is free and indirect. "I should have listened to my wife's advice," Andy tells himself. This initial invitation into his subjectivity therefore emphasizes the fact that Andy is subordinated to his wife, not necessarily in a negative way, at least not at this point in the film, but he is increasingly coming across as a weak person who is unsure about what path to pursue, whom to listen to, what to stand for. He loves Merit dearly, so he resolves to borrow one of Paul's cars and solicit a prostitute to pass off as Merit for the ritual. After he does so, and after the prostitute, Tina (Rita Nzelu), torpedoes the ritual by invoking the name of Jesus—during the second cult scene in the film—Andy's ruse is discovered, and he is issued the aforementioned ultimatum: he will bring his wife to the next meeting, or he will die. There is a brief scene in which Tina returns to her apartment and tells her roommate that she is leaving the sex trade, that she will henceforth worship "the name of Jesus," which has just proven its immense power to her. And then, once again, Andy is in his parlor deep in thought when classical music plays once more and the image dissolves to a flashback. As described in the introduction, Andy recalls the priest's interdiction, but his reverie is broken by the sound of Merit knocking at their door. She has come with ₦50,000, provided by her family, which represents a potentially game-changing injection of funds into their foundering marriage. However, the money clarifies Andy's thinking. He could run away with Merit, always wondering when the cult would find him, or he could accept the cult's terms and move on to the next stage of his life. A resolution seems to be found in that stack of cash. He looks at it, the camera zooms in on it, he hears the words of the priest, and he makes his decision (see figures 4.1 and 4.2). Of course, having a partner who is capable of generating such a game-changing subvention is a blessing, or so many spectators are likely to think, but Andy has been presented throughout the film as greedy and insecure, regularly wearing a hangdog, pleading look on his face. For a man who wants to make more money than his wife, to buy her a car and take her shopping, the money Merit lays on their table is, therefore, tainted by emasculation, which steels his resolve. And so he follows through with his premeditated lie. The next scene, the third and final scene of occultism in the first film, provides the image of Merit's begowned body lying on the cult's altar. Andy is now an accomplice to murder.

The spectacular occult scenes of Living in Bondage invite so much attention that they seem to suggest Satanism has transformed Andy from

FIGURES 4.1 AND 4.2. *Living in Bondage*. The stack of cash (bread) that Merit brings home (wins).

a devoted husband to a killer. Moreover, the fact that the ritual's purpose is to generate wealth, which it does effectively, therefore suggests that wealth itself—its foundations, mechanisms, and temptations—change Andy from a good person to a bad one. But more than ninety minutes of narrative, in which Andy is carefully constructed as a supremely unsympathetic character, a weak and sniveling man, proceed before the first cult scene. The various opportunities the film provides to understand Andy's value system—his opening monologue, his lunch with Paul, his conversation with Aunty and Merit—all make it difficult to construe him as ever having been really *good*. Of course, Andy does not want to kill Merit; he genuinely loves her, but he is also primarily motivated by the impulse to gratify his material desires—"My body needs more money than the peanuts they were paying me"—and obtain greater social status. So does the cult turn him bad? When the supposedly pivotal scene finally arrives, Andy hardly even features in it: his only role is to carry two bowls of Merit's blood to the chief priest. At that point, Andy has been absorbed and effaced. He is one of them. But his weak and insecure demeanor has not significantly changed.

If the cult is not the *source* of evil in Andy's life, if Andy is already a flawed character with avaricious predilections and little courage, then the cult may be understood as deepening or amplifying Andy's choices. In that sense it is truly occult, a sign system that digs below the surface of social edifice to uncover its underlying logic. It is for this reason that we must reconsider the importance of that large stack of cash that Merit brings into their home. Rather than scenes of magic, the image of Merit's money—and the moment of free indirect subjectivity that accompanies it—encapsulates something definitive in Nigerian visual culture history. *Living in Bondage* may have offered sensational and indelible images of money magic, but the film's narrative is driven by the logic of that stack. As we will see, the injection of similar funds from the wife or her family into the companionate marriage at the heart of a story drives the violent logics of several other occult films. However, two contextual issues are worth considering before turning to them.

"HAVE YOU FORGOTTEN THAT I AM HEAD OF THIS HOUSE, THAT I MARRIED YOU WITH MY MONEY?"

There is a well-developed ethnographic lexicon for understanding the relationship among money, extended family, and the constitution of a marriage. Some of the most widely used terms are *bride-price* and *dowry*. Let us be clear, there is no obvious reason why Nollywood would invoke these terms, especially in the same way that ethnographers do, but the underlying practices associated with these terms are sometimes important factors in Nollywood scripts. Take, for example, the film that cemented Emem Isong (the writer and producer discussed in chapter 3) as a major Nollywood screenwriter, *Emotional Crack* (2003, dir. Lancelot Imasuen). The plot of that film revolves around an incipient companionate marriage between Chudi (Ramsey Nouah) and Crystal (Stephanie Linus, née Okereke), which is strained by Chudi's physically and emotionally abusive behavior.[13] The abuse eventually drives Crystal into the arms of a woman, Chudi's mistress, a fact that has attracted the attention of many scholars, thus contributing to the film's canonical status.[14] When Crystal's mother (Patience Ozokwor, often referred to as "Mama G," a character she played in Gabriel Moses's 2002 film *Old School*) attempts to extricate the bruised and battered Crystal from the marriage, Chudi protests, "You have no right, whatsoever, to come into my house and kidnap my wife. I am legally married to her and I paid her dowry!" Crystal's mother promises that the elders will return Chudi's money, although she begins with what is really the right question: "What dowry?" Indeed, how could a husband pay his wife's dowry? Strictly speaking, a dowry is a payment or gift given to a woman by her parents or other members of her natal family that she takes with her when she moves into her husband's home. Dowry systems are generally practiced in societies where women's labor is not nearly as lucrative as men's, such as large-scale agrarian societies, in which a woman's departure from her natal home will not severely impact its productivity. Instead, under such systems, property-owning families extend and diffuse their accumulative power through dowries by *purchasing* the best possible husband for their daughter and ensuring the transfer of wealth to their grandchildren. In Africa, by contrast, women's labor has generally been vital to household productivity; therefore, the customary transfer of wealth at marriage has been in the form not of a dowry but of a *bride-price*. In a bride-price system a man and his family provide a payment or gift to the wife's family in order to compensate them for lost productivity as well as enable the wife's brothers to marry wives of their own. Therefore, what Chudi means to say is that he paid Crystal's *bride-price*, though his use of the word *dowry* is less about misconstruing ethnographic terminology than it is a matter of popular, colloquial speech. *Dowry* is often used in contemporary Nigeria, perhaps because it sounds more polite than "bride-price." After all, many of the payments made at the beginning of contemporary Nigerian marriages, particularly among the middle class, which is depicted in films such as *Emotional Crack*, are symbolic more than compensatory: a nod to the idea of tradition but not an actual economic necessity.

The issue of bride-price plays a small but important role in *Living in Bondage*. Chief Omego is a rich man and a polygamist, who essentially uses his wealth to *buy* wives. Haynes notes that the discord between Omego's first and second wives over the fact that he has taken a younger third wife recalls the discord in Chief Fuji's house in *Checkmate* (see chapter 3).[15] Indeed, the resemblance is critical to the film's address. And it is so strong that it cannot be completely coincidental. Omego's first and second wives are, in terms of physical appearance and conduct, uncannily similar to Fuji's wives, Moji and Peace. In the first episode of *Checkmate*, Fuji reminds Peace that he paid "heavy dowry" when he married her. Likewise, the reason for including the scene of Omego's home in *Living in Bondage* is essentially the same as the reason for including Fuji's home in the plot of *Checkmate*. It highlights the supposed order and emotional bonding possible in companionate marriages by contrast to the supposed disorder and jealousy that stereotypically characterize polygamous homes. As Chief Omego argues with his wives, he asks them, "Have you forgotten that I am Head of this house, that I married you with my money?" Like Fuji, he is referring, of course, to the bride-price paid for each of them, but the way he does so suggests that he translates custom into the idiom of breadwinning. Of course, being the head of a polygamous household and being a breadwinner are not the same thing, nor is paying a bride-price the same as winning bread, but in the context of southern Nigerian popular culture, the intersection and overlapping of these terms are instructive. A character like Chudi in *Emotional Crack* can plausibly make the claim to have paid for his wife because having the means to do so is easily equated with being what might be called good "marriage material."[16] In *Living in Bondage*, when Merit's family provides her with the ₦50,000 that she presents to Andy, it therefore functions essentially as a dowry, which undermines Andy's status in customary terms while simultaneously undermining his quest to become a breadwinner in modern terms.

THE *CHECKMATE* CONNECTION

The actor who plays Chief Omego in *Living in Bondage*, Kanayo O. Kanayo, has a small role in *Checkmate* as Okosun, the banker who handles the Haatropes' line of credit. He also features prominently in other films considered in this book—including another film discussed in this chapter, *Billionaires*

Club—and he is generally considered one of Nollywood's biggest stars. But Kanayo is not the only actor from *Checkmate* to appear in *Living in Bondage*. At least three others play significant roles in both productions. Francis Agu, who plays Ichie Million in *Living in Bondage*, Merit's boss and the feted millionaire to whom Paul introduces Andy, also plays Benibo, the eldest Haatrope sibling, in *Checkmate*. In the opening credits of *Living in Bondage*—which aesthetically imitate the opening of a television program—Agu is pictured behind a large desk, looking every bit the unscrupulous executive he plays in *Checkmate*. Agu also features prominently in the next masculine melodrama in this chapter, *Ashes to Ashes*. Meanwhile, the actor who plays Benibo's younger brother, Richard Jr.—BobManuel Udokwu—plays a member of the cult in *Living in Bondage*. Like Agu, Udokwu also has a major role in *Ashes to Ashes*. Then there is Ruth Osu, who plays the devoted maid at Haatrope House in *Checkmate* and one of the Okeke's neighbors in *Living in Bondage*. In both cases she is a counselor and moral standard. And finally, the woman who plays Nduka's mother in *Checkmate*, Obiageli Molobe, plays the "cult mother" in *Living in Bondage*. Like Ruth Osu, there is a kind of consistency to her character across both texts. She represents *bad* religious traditions—indigenous Igbo classism in *Checkmate* and Satanism in *Living in Bondage*—but more than that, she represents the power animating a key threat to masculinity. In *Checkmate* she drives a wedge between Ada and Nduka. In *Living in Bondage* she demands Merit's murder.

The point here is not simply that *Checkmate* launched many Nollywood careers—which it did—nor simply that Nollywood shares a large pool of talent and signifiers with state television—which is both true and a major thread of this book—but, more importantly, that *Living in Bondage* can be seen as dialogically related to *Checkmate*. The Omego-Fuji connection suggests that *Living in Bondage* draws from a television strategy of family comparison in order to focus attention on the virtues and potential problems of modern companionate marriages. Meanwhile, the Agu and Udokwu connections are even more suggestive. *Checkmate* was still running strong, churning out new episodes each week, when *Living in Bondage* was released, late in 1992. Both of the wealthy Haatrope brothers, one a philandering drug addict with a churlish wife and the other a fun-loving, earnest, but womanizing bachelor, appear on videotape as members of a satanic cult. And while it is not the same actor, the Omego character who so resembles Fuji is not only a prominent member of the same cult but is widely known and impugned for his pecuniary and sexual avarice. And in both texts an overbearing woman constitutes the major threat to a man's realization of breadwinner status. At the levels of themes, visual tropes, and popular culture personalities, therefore, *Living in Bondage* appears to pull back the curtain and look behind the personas of television's leading men. Whatever *Checkmate* had to say about the connection between marriage and business ethics, *Living in Bondage* unfolds and rereads. Where do the rich, handsome men who flash across the tube every Thursday night during prime time get their money? From Satan? And who is Satan's agent? One's mother-in-law? What does all of this say about the status of modern masculinity?

ASHES TO ASHES: PURIFYING MASCULINITY IN THE FIRE OF SOCIAL JUSTICE

If Francis Agu plays a kind of meta-character, an executive in *Checkmate* who, when *Living in Bondage* went looking behind the curtain, turned out to be the sort of man who might very well sacrifice a loved one for wealth, then *Ashes to Ashes* speculates about the unfolding of that process. Agu's character, Osita, dearly loves his humble and devoted wife, Abigail (Chiega Alisigwe), but he is not a breadwinner, and he desperately wants to be one. In his pursuit of money, however, he is lured into money magic and ends up destroying Abigail. As Haynes has noted, their story is "quite precisely and completely the story of *Living in Bondage*, dropped into" the vigilante genre.[17]

The term *vigilante genre* describes a set of Nollywood films produced in the late 1990s and early 2000s and inspired by headlines about one particularly prominent vigilante gang, the Bakassi Boys, which operated in southeastern Nigeria. As several scholars have noted, the gang occupied an ambivalent space in popular consciousness.[18] It responded to a number of pressing criminal threats facing ordinary people, which the ineffectual Nigerian police and other government agencies were entirely unable to address. The gang was therefore endorsed by several local politicians, and its members were often treated like heroes. Of course, the Bakassi Boys killed people rather than turning them over to the police, and sometimes their victims were later found to be innocent. In order to collect information, they also tortured people from all walks of life. And they often engaged in political violence on behalf of their patrons. Therefore, films such as *Issakaba 1, 2, 3,* and *4* (2000, dir. Lancelot Oduwa Imasuen) suggest more than a little ambivalence about vigilantism, although they mostly lionize the phenomenon, constituting a vision that, as John McCall notes, may be "romanticized and fanciful" but "no more so" than bureaucratic visions of returning to an effective formal justice system.[19] *Ashes to Ashes* is a multipart film, consisting of three, five, or six installments, depending how you count (one installment may span two VCD disks, but in some cases each disk begins with a title screen). One of the genre's characteristics, then, is its proliferative capacity to encompass a vast range of subplots and therefore social concerns. The "story of *Living in Bondage*," as Haynes describes it, occupies only the first third of *Ashes to Ashes*, disks one and two, but it sets in motion, humanizes, and invites personal identification with the apocalyptic spiritual battle to which the later parts of the film are devoted. If the fate of the world depends on the good power of vigilantes overcoming the evil power behind corrupt religious and political leaders, the companionate marriage, modeled on *Living in Bondage*, grounds those abstract powers and gives them immediate social significance.

Ashes to Ashes does not begin with its Andy-like character, Osita, soliloquizing about his financial and social status, but almost. The film opens with a spectacular action sequence in which a group of armed robbers besieges a small community. Halfway through the robbery, vigilantes, here called the "Mbassi Boys," descend on the robbers and send them scattering. However, the vigilantes will not reappear for another twenty minutes, when they infiltrate the robbers' hideout; in the meantime, their presence lurks in the background of the other stories in the film. Immediately following the opening spectacle, the image cuts to a framed portrait of Osita and Abigail hung on the wall and overlooking the proceedings of their home. As the camera slowly zooms out from the photograph, Abigail enters the frame looking worried. The image cuts to a close-up of a plate of food, barely touched, before returning to Abigail. "Sweetheart, what is it?" she asks. The image then cuts to a medium shot from behind Abigail—as if it were the portrait looking out onto their home—showing Osita sitting on a sofa beyond her, in the background. Like Andy, he stares into the distance. At first he will not talk to Abigail, but when he finally does, he snarls about their living conditions. Like Merit, Abigail is patient and reassuring. She tells Osita that they are doing fine, especially with the income she brings in from her work, but like Andy, Osita is unmoved. He says he promised her more, and his inability to bring in greater income means that he has broken his promise. So Osita and Abigail are much like Andy and Merit, although Abigail does not feed Osita in this scene—instead, he will not eat—and Osita is less pathetic than Andy, exhibiting a kind of righteous indignation about his lot in life.

Also like Andy, Osita has learned of an investment opportunity for which he does not have enough capital. He acknowledges Abigail's "understanding" and "support," but he tells her that "the best money can buy is what I wish for you and my family." Abigail assures him that everything will turn out fine, and then the film cuts to a radically different scene. A preacher has been brought to a small village compound to root out some kind of evil that is plaguing the inhabitants. In the dark of night he prays "in Jesus's mighty name," sprinkling holy water on the ground, which helps him locate several auspicious places where he then commands his assistants to dig. As the villagers look on, the diggers uncover ritual objects, raising shouts of incredulity and "amens" from those gathered. Finally, the objects are burned as the preacher continues chanting spells in order to break the bond between them and the family in the compound. The narration then returns to Osita and Abigail's living room. Abigail enters with the very money that Osita needs for his investment scheme. She has embezzled it, she reports, from her workplace, noting that it will not be missed until the end of the month. If Osita's scheme pays off, no one will be the wiser. Once again, therefore, a wife is shown handing a massive stack of cash to her husband. However, the scene of the preacher, spliced between the exposition of the husband's insolvency and the wife's infusion of cash, raises the melodramatic stakes of the story. The preacher literally digs below the surface to uncover the occult power that interferes with domestic life. And like the opening sequence that features the Mbassi Boys, the scene of the preacher now inhabits the moral landscape of the film, suggesting multiple clashes of evil and benevolent power. What kind of forces, this editing asks its spectators to consider, seethe just below the surface of Osita and Abigail's marriage, as well as the money she brings into it?

The next scene begins to scratch that surface. Justus Esiri, the actor who played the third headmaster of Oja Village in *The New Village Headmaster*, plays the role of a diabolical sorcerer who impersonates a Christian prophet. According to Haynes, Esiri's character is modeled on the real-life figure Eddy Okeke, a con man and false prophet who not only made headlines for his antics but also was hunted down and decapitated by the Bakassi Boys in 2000. Several stories that circulate online claim that the final showdown between Okeke and the gang was a metaphysical cataclysm, which the vigilantes won only because their spiritual leader was more powerful than Okeke.[20] In *Ashes to Ashes*, editing introduces this kind of indomitable malevolent power in between the image of Abigail handing Osita a large stack of cash and the image of Osita arriving at a warehouse to assess the return on his investment. Not only has the money disappeared, like Andy's in *Living in Bondage*, but Osita turns out to have been suckered by a 419 scam, the kind of advanced-fee fraud that has become a staple narrative device not only in Nigerian popular culture but also in the global pop culture conception of Nigeria—think email fraud (I have more to say about 419 in chapter 6). Osita stands in the driveway of the warehouse, arguing with its guards, claiming to have met people there just a few days before to confirm the pending arrival of a shipping container. The guards, of course, have never heard about a shipment and insist that the warehouse has been derelict for years. As the severity of the situation dawns on Osita, he collapses at the base of a tree, and then Abigail's words ring in his head: "You can use it and clear the goods, but I must get it at the end of the month." In this moment of free indirect subjectivity, where the dissociation of image and sound creates a sense of ambiguity about who is narrating the story, Osita occupies the subject position of not just the dupe but also of the pathetic, failed husband.

Osita may have started out indignant about the opportunities available to men like him, but the 419 scam quickly reduces him to a state even more pitiful than Andy's. In one beautifully choreographed scene, he is shown buying a bag of *garri* (fermented cassava powder), poor man's food, at the market. As he collects his change, he temporarily and unknowingly sets the bag down on a sharp spike so that as he walks home, grains of *garri* pour from the resulting hole and paint a meandering white line along the road behind him (see figure 4.3). The action is filmed from a solemn low angle. Osita is too distraught to notice, but when he enters his parlor, Abigail glances from him, to the bag, to the floor, with a profound look of pity on her face. Osita, realizing what he has done, drops the bag, falls into a chair, and breaks down crying. It may not have been bread, precisely, but Osita did not bring home the staple food, and he certainly did not win. In the meantime other men have been visiting the "Prophet" and, in order to get rich, have been instructed to bring the heads of loved ones, while the Mbassi Boys continue to track down and ruthlessly execute criminals.

Osita visits a friend, Marvin (Kunle Coker), to ask for money, but Marvin cannot help. Instead, he directs Osita to their old pal Amechi, played by none other than BobManuel Udokwu. As in *Living in Bondage*, Udokwu's character is involved with money magic. Osita asks him, "How do you people make this kind of money? I seem to be the only one struggling so hard yet making nothing." Amechi and Marvin double over with laughter, after which Amechi replies, "It could be you are struggling too

FIGURE 4.3. *Ashes to Ashes*. Osita spills (loses) garri (bread) on the road as he walks home.

hard, in the wrong direction." Then the film cuts to a scene of Osita and Abigail at home, where Osita brandishes his own large stack of cash. Projecting himself into the breadwinner ideal, he tells Abigail, "Soon I'll be able to buy you all those wonderful things I've always wanted to buy for you." Apparently, Amechi has promised to introduce Osita to his pastor, who performs miracles, but Abigail, like Merit, is suspicious. Presciently, she knows it is all too good to be true. And when Amechi finally takes Osita to meet the Prophet, Osita says, "My wife has been very patient with me, but I'm afraid that if I don't provide for her the way I should, I might lose her." And at the end of the meeting he reaffirms that "I'll do anything, as long as it puts food on my table." However, when he finally learns what he must do, some weeks later, Osita is as tormented as Andy. He asks the Prophet directly, "What then is the use of the wealth, if she must die for me to be rich?" — a question that, once again, signals the idea that greed can sometimes be prosocial. He does not simply want to win; he wants to win bread for his family.

Osita, like Andy, is also given an ultimatum: he must bring his wife or die. As Osita subsequently struggles with his conscience, the film seems unable to help itself from flirting with free indirect subjectivity. Osita lies awake at night, and the screen offers a black-and-white third-person flashback of his meeting with the Prophet. But when the image returns to his bed, with Abigail lying nearby, the words of the Prophet continue to ring in Osita's head. Suddenly, he is indignant once again, no longer the miserable sod, and when Abigail asks what is wrong, he barks at her to leave him alone. Like Andy, therefore, his fortitude—condemnable as it is—coalesces in this moment of free indirect subjectivity. Osita then has a dream in which the Prophet antagonizes him, claiming to be everywhere. And just before Abigail wakes him, Osita sees himself from the Prophet's perspective, zapping his own body with electric current as if he identifies somehow with the malevolent power that is preying upon him. Later that morning the Prophet again appears to Osita, in his waking state, reinforcing the ultimatum. Abigail rushes into the room, but only Osita and viewers can see the other man standing there. *Ashes to Ashes* therefore addresses its spectator much like *Living in Bondage* does, though with an even greater sense of scale. It asks viewers to ambiguously inhabit the subject position of the man at the center of the story, sympathizing with his die-hard ambition to become a breadwinner—"If I don't provide for her the way I should, I might lose her"—yet it also suggests that the spectator will be able to understand how such ambition so easily leads to evil.

When it comes time to perform the ritual, there is no cult or deadly weapons. Instead, the Prophet asks Osita to blow powder at his reflection in a mirror. It is his own self, the scene suggests, upon whom he is working. However, Abigail's image eventually appears in the mirror, begging Osita not to follow through. Of course, he does. At her funeral, Abigail's family accuses Osita of murder, once again signaling that money magic is apparent, if not perfectly visible, to all. Then the final element of the motif is introduced. Although Abigail died in a wax print dress, her ghost appears to Osita in a white hooded gown. Indeed, there are three scenes that feature Abigail's ghost. In the final one, Osita asks her to appear more often and stay for longer periods of time. He attempts to embrace her, but she disappears. Thus, the social configuration that Osita has been pursuing the whole time—a textbook companionate marriage in which he could "provide for her" and "put food on [the] table," in his own words—turns out to be an apparition. He can have the marriage, or he can have money, but not both. Osita finds a gun and heads to the church to kill the Prophet, but it turns out that the Prophet can magically evade bullets. Then the Mbassi Boys enter, and the leader, Gagwo (Segun Arinze), accuses Osita of "dining with the devil with a short spoon." Osita is taken away, and the *Living in Bondage* motif is complete.

The next two parts of the film dramatize the increasingly spectacular, magical war between the vigilantes and the Prophet. The Prophet is in fact eventually beheaded, but the source of his power remains a threat. There is a bad *igwe* (Igbo king—see chapter 5) in the land, who, with the help of a sorcerer, has tapped into the same malevolent forces. As in popular stories about the Bakassi Boys, the Mbassi Boys therefore bring in their own spiritual leader, Ubaka, to finish the battle (and the gang is referred to as the "Baka Boys" in the second and third parts of the film). Ubaka is played as stoic and erudite by Sam Dede, who also plays the vigilante leader in the *Issakaba* series, very much cementing his persona in the genre. In *Ashes to Ashes*, however, Dede also plays the role of Ejima, the bad igwe's general, putting on a thick Igbo accent and speaking mostly in Pidgin. On his way to the bad igwe's sorcerer, therefore, Ubaka must confront Ejima. Masterfully edited, the scene of Dede's good character facing down his bad character culminates with the bad one's beheading. From there, Ubaka, Dede's good character, goes to challenge the bad igwe's sorcerer, Okute (Chika Anyanwu), and after vanquishing him Ubaka destroys his evil shrine. These sequences feature very few women, none of whom play major roles in the story. Instead, *Ashes to Ashes* becomes a story of pure, distilled masculinity, a contest to identify the best, most powerful man among a host of possibilities. Moreover, the fact that Dede plays two pivotal, opposing roles suggests that the battle over masculinity is, ultimately, a battle with the self, a battle to manifest the best version of one's masculine potential. Ubaka may destroy all the symbols of evil at the end of the film, but the semiotics of masculinity remain clearly tied to abstract, spiritual power.

The questions that a film like *Ashes to Ashes* raises are related to the relationship between the *Living in Bondage* motif and the horizons of occult power. Real men (like Ubaka) control the occult; they are not subject to it. Moreover, such real men do not seem to be burdened by wives or children. Nevertheless, the social context into which these films are released and to which they are addressed is one where masculinity is essentially inconceivable without wives and children. What makes Osita pathetic and thus legitimizes his capture by the vigilantes—somewhat like the events that necessitate Andy's salvation—is the pursuit of a form of masculinity in which a husband is defined by his ability to bring the greatest portion of money into his home. That such a pursuit leads to one's demise, where gendered collaboration and pooling incomes would work better, might suggest that occult films promote an ideology of gendered equity, that those men who recklessly pursue gendered financial hierarchy must be stopped. However, where Andy is eventually saved by the church, Osita is imprisoned (and maybe even extrajudicially executed—the film does not say). So if the vigilante genre explores fantasies of social power in which justice is an achievement greater than the state can realize but is ultimately grounded in spirituality and resolutely prosocial—and if *Ashes to Ashes* focuses primarily on the masculine contours of social justice, featuring men who fight it out on increasingly cosmological planes—then Osita and his breadwinner ambitions seem to be included, and arrested, in order to uncouple masculinity from breadwinning. The film imagines and addresses a local public in which marriage and masculinity are closely aligned, but it explicitly develops a narrative in which the man who pursues money to provide for his wife is less of a man than the one who pursues his status relative to other men. If the feminine melodramatic mode discussed in chapter 3 promotes the breadwinner ideal as the economic benchmark of an effective society, the masculine melodramatic mode on display in films such as *Living in Bondage* and *Ashes to Ashes* suggests that the breadwinner ideal limits a man's ability to contribute effectively to society. Breadwinning may elevate a man above a woman, but it also ties a man's status to a woman and to prevailing economic conditions. Of course, the construct of masculinity can only be relational, it has meaning only in relation to the construct of femininity and within a social context, but these films seem to fantasize about the possibility that it perhaps might not be. Maybe being a man means tapping into forms of power larger than the familial or socioeconomic. Maybe a *pure* form of masculinity can be found in the pursuit of a pure form of social justice. The masculine melodramatic mode seems to redistribute good and evil in such a way that the social pressure exerted by the breadwinning ideal is evil, whereas finding power outside of the family and social pressure makes a man good. Masculinity is thus made to endure in spite of conditions that might undermine it. The final film that I consider in this chapter suggests that for a man to truly contribute to social justice, to truly be *good*, he must not only abandon the breadwinner ideal; he must also be released from all material concerns.

BILLIONAIRES CLUB: TO GOD BE THE GLORY

Like *Ashes to Ashes*, *Billionaires Club* (sometimes *Billionaire's Club*) recycles the *Living in Bondage* motif and embeds it in a new kind of discourse. It also introduces several innovations that both amplify and call attention to different features of the male breadwinner ideal. Likewise, *Billionaires Club* serves as an especially fine example of Nollywood's iconic serializing style, particularly as it congealed during the early 2000s, leading up to the industry's famous crisis of overproduction and underdistribution.[21] The film's plot is long and intricate, leaving no stone unturned. Indeed, like many writers of the period, the screenwriter of *Billionaires Club*, Constance Daniels, seized the opportunity offered by Nollywood's turn from VHS to VCD, and the need to distinguish one's work in an oversaturated market, to invest in expansive and prolific storytelling. The story is attributed to the film's producer, Sunny Collins, but the end product, built on Daniels's script, essentially consists of three feature-length films that tell one, unified, unbroken story, 317 minutes long. Although the pacing drags in places and there are several twists and turns, little is superfluous. Every subplot counts, although I will not explore them all here.

The intricate plot of the film centers on Zed (Tony Umeh), who is lured into a money-magic cult, the titular "Billionaires Club," although the story actually begins with Victoria (Chidi Ihezie), the woman he will eventually marry and in whose ritual murder he will begrudgingly yet placidly participate. In fact, Zed is not introduced until ten minutes into the film and does not become a major character until nearly the thirty-minute mark. Instead, the setup is all about Victoria and her overbearing mother, Njideka (Patience Ozokwor, who plays more or less the same character she plays in *Emotional Crack*). Victoria is unmarried and lives in Lagos, while Njideka, back home in the East, frets constantly about Victoria's advancing age and inability to land a husband. They seek a resolution in their faith, which appears to be ecumenical. Together and separately, they repeatedly pray for god's help, but in one scene they pray in their parlor, which features a reproduction of da Vinci's *The Last Supper* and a poster from a Pentecostal church headquartered in Oregon. In another scene, Victoria prays in church before a crucifix and a statue of the Virgin Mary. Given the film's primarily Igbo cast and crew, as well as the theme song's liberal use of the Igbo language, the ecumenical form of Christianity on display might be read as pan-Igbo, given that Catholicism is more prevalent in the East than elsewhere in Nigeria. Regardless, Victoria's faith is a prime mover in this story, bringing the kind of Christian salvation on display in *Living in Bondage* back to the center of the money-magic plot. Instead of the husband's salvation in church, however, the resolution in *Billionaires Club* comes from Victoria's ability to not only personally forgive Zed but also procure god's forgiveness as well. In part II, Zed suffers a long and repulsive illness, caused by his relationship with satanic forces, while Victoria stands in a computer-generated landscape of blue and white light, holding her infant child in her hands and pleading with

"Innocence" to release her husband. Zed then also becomes a spirit and returns to the Billionaires Club in order to destroy its members once and for all. In each film featured in this chapter, therefore, occult power requires an equally powerful spiritual response, although it can take the form of Pentecostalism, vigilante magic, or a more nebulous form of Christian gnosis.

What definitely does not change from film to film is the reason the protagonist seeks wealth and joins the money-magic cult. Zed, like all the others, is desperate to be the breadwinner in his house. However, the focus on Victoria early in the film amplifies Zed's predicament. She is under great pressure to marry not only from her mother but also from her friends and even the employees of the styling salon she owns. Luckily, her prayers come to fruition, and she meets two suitors in back-to-back scenes. One is Zed, a kindhearted but struggling chemist (pharmacist) who runs a small kiosk near Victoria's house in Lagos. The other, Charles (Ifeanyi Udokwu), is a well-dressed managing director of a bank. When Victoria discusses these options with her friend, Evelyn (Princess Egu), she receives the following advice: "You must use this opportunity to make yourself comfortable for a lifetime." When Victoria replies that despite the fact that Zed can barely stock his humble pharmacy, she prefers him to Charles the "M.D.," Evelyn is livid. "What!?" she cries out. "Victoria, are you out of your mind? For God's sake, this guy is below your standard. Can't you see? Victoria, open your eyes." Evelyn then storms out, begging to be counted out of any wedding involving Zed. Njideka is also initially hesitant to allow her daughter to marry a man of so few means, although she eventually relents. Victoria's great mistake, the plot suggests, is that she marries for love rather than for a potential breadwinner. Charles the "M.D." makes real money in a legitimate sector of the economy. Had Victoria gone with him, perhaps none of the subsequent events would have come to pass.

Zed is indeed kind and devoted, just like Andy and Osita. But also like them, Zed's kindness turns to malice when his wife subverts his breadwinner aspirations. Victoria's salon is more prosperous than Zed's pharmacy, and she agrees to lend him money to expand his business—far more than he imagines she could spare. After a two-year time jump, spectators are shown Zed's new shop as well as the couple's new home. Victoria is expecting a baby, and they seem utterly contented. But one key indicator of (upward) mobility—as in so many forms of popular and even literary culture, their car—remains a problem for Zed.[22] He still drives his Peugeot 504—an iconic vehicle in postcolonial Africa—which teeters on the verge of death. The centrality of the car to Zed's sense of social status, what Lindsey Green-Simms refers to as "postcolonial automobility," is carefully established in several pivotal scenes.[23]

Immediately following the birth of their child—which is indicated by a scene of Victoria in the hospital cooing over her newborn—the image cuts to a shot of a tire vulcanizer's roadside operation and then slowly zooms out to reveal Victoria, sitting in the passenger seat of Zed's jalopy and holding the baby, with the door open, as they wait for service. The next cut is to the inside of a luxury SUV, driven by a finely dressed man (Kanayo O. Kanayo) who passes by the scene of Zed and Victoria and suddenly stops. He approaches them and asks Zed if he attended the University of Lagos. It turns out, of course, that they are old friends, just like Andy and Paul, meeting on the road where everything about the difference between their class statuses can be condensed into the cars they drive. Kanayo's character, Don, is a slightly updated version of his character from *Living in Bondage*, Chief Omego. He tells Zed that his cosmopolitan appearance has nothing to do with international experience: "You don't need to get out of this country to transform yourself; it's just within you." From here the motif's standard set of events plays out. Don invites Zed to a party where he will see how the rich live. Victoria—whose name Don mysteriously seems to know before they are properly introduced—is, however, immediately suspicious. Ominous music plays as Don drives away and Zed shows Victoria his invitation to the "Billionaires Club." In the following scene, as Zed prepares to leave for the party, Victoria dresses their baby. The imagery suggests that domestic peace is threatened by masculine avarice.

One of the film's key innovations is its addition of a child to the companionate marriage at the center of the *Living in Bondage* motif. Whereas the other films in this chapter exclusively explore the relationship between a potential male breadwinner and a financially secure wife, *Billionaires Club* raises the stakes of winning bread. As discussed in chapter 3, wage labor and Christianity may have introduced new ideologies of marriage and gender in southern Nigeria, but what has not changed, it seems, is the significance of fertility. Why, then, has the money-magic-companionate-marriage motif often ignored this feature of the social and intimate landscape? As I have constructed it, the primary narrative engine in these films runs on a modern form of masculinity that combusts when it encounters feminine financial independence. However, feminine financial independence, as we have established, has deep roots in most southern Nigerian cultural formations. Therefore, what impinges on it is not patriarchy per se but the specifically Victorian patriarchal ideals that color contemporary visions of the good life in many forms of southern Nigerian expressive culture. Children may constitute an important part of the mixture, but they are not strictly necessary for the kind of combustion that takes place in the machinery of modern masculinity. Nevertheless, Nollywood's masculine melodramas also run on the constantly revolving question of whether an aspiring breadwinner would eliminate those for whom he would win bread in order to win bread. If one's bread is not simply for one's wife, but for one's child, then more than just gendered, hierarchical status matters: so too does a man's virility. By juxtaposing scenes of Victoria and the baby with scenes of Zed's jalopy, *Billionaires Club* seems to ask whether it is a car—a key sign of financial solvency and therefore status—or a family that makes a man seem more virile. The way the film then meticulously answers that question makes *Billionaires Club* especially noteworthy.

When Zed arrives at the sprawling hotel complex where the billionaires' party is taking place, he is stopped by several gatemen, some dressed in military fatigues, which is not uncommon in Nigeria but which also, of course, recalls the ongoing association between financial and (para)military power that has defined so much of Nigeria's postcolonial history. The gatemen cannot believe that the man driving this dilapidated car could have been invited to the occasion inside. An SUV then pulls up behind Zed's car, prompting the head gateman to instruct, "Park this scrap [or is it "this crap"?] over there," until Zed's invitation can be verified. The SUV zooms past haughtily. This is followed by a succession of well-edited close-up shots, which reveal that Zed uses a screwdriver, kept on his dashboard, to open the Peugeot's door, which is but a steel skeleton that was relieved of its bulky vinyl casing long ago. Zed stands and verifies his identity, but the gateman still insists that Zed park his car outside the compound. "As you can see," he says, "there are a class of cars here. We don't have any space for yours, sir." Zed protests furiously until Don, who has just arrived, comes to his rescue. The gatemen are instructed to move Zed's car for him, while Don walks Zed to the entrance of the main building. On the way, Zed remarks, "Man, these cars are wonderful!"

Inside, a slowly gyrating mass of overly dressed, corpulent men shower US dollars on several young and scantily clad women. Zed tells Don that he feels uncomfortable, so they walk back to the car park. Don then puts it as simply as he can: "You must be a man, Zed. Opportunities do not perch; they come once in a lifetime." Zed replies that he will do whatever it takes to eliminate the kind of embarrassment he felt at the gate.

Therefore, by equating his sense of masculinity with being able to park his car among those of other men, Zed seals his fate. He *will* come to Don's office in the morning to begin his journey into the Billionaires Club, and in so doing he *will* stake his claim to masculinity on the idea that bread itself matters more than for whom it is won. Back home, Victoria distrusts the recent turn of events. And the following day, when Zed meets Don, he finds that the leader of the Billionaires Club is there: "Billion," he calls himself, played by one of Nollywood's most recurrent icons of patriarchal masculinity, Pete Edochie (see chapter 5). Billion demands Zed's baby, and the now predictable sequence of events follows, including key moments of free indirect subjectivity.

As with *Living in Bondage* and *Ashes to Ashes*, the film asks spectators to identify with the protagonist as he considers his choices. Can Zed really sacrifice his child to become rich? For what purpose, then, is the money? He and Victoria live comfortably. Why then must he have one of those magnificent cars that other men drive? Is it for his own pride or in order to prove to his wife, to whom he owes his modest financial success, that he can be a man in his "own rights, not bought and kept by my wife" (as Nduka tells Ada in *Checkmate* when they discuss a similar predicament of money and automobility)? Is Zed's masculinity measured in comparison to other men? Or is it important that Zed bring more resources to the marriage than Victoria does? If so, winning bread may be less about providing for family than it is about attaining status: not just social status but once again *gendered* status both within and without the home. In order to explore similar questions the other films discussed in this chapter use free indirect subjectivity to flesh out the ramifications of an ultimatum: kill or be killed. However, *Billionaires Club* dispenses with the ultimatum and focuses on the potential productivity of human tragedy or the harnessing of fate. Billion predicts that Zed's baby is terminally ill, and when Zed returns home, the baby is indeed very sick. (Did Billion cause the malady? We do not know.) Therefore, what Zed is forced to consider is whether his child's death should be in vain or should lead to his own success. That is when the now-conventional moment of free indirect subjectivity unfolds, although it does so in ways subtly different from others examined in this chapter.

Zed affectionately cradles the child in his arms while the camera takes a leisurely twenty-five seconds to zoom in on his face, inviting the spectator to devote at least some attention to the musical score, which features a slow, sad organ adagio rolling along in a minor key. The image then dissolves to a flashback on Billion's prognosis for the baby, in which Edochie's voice is augmented by ominous reverb. When the flashback ends, Zed is shown crying, though mournfully rather than desperately. The camera then zooms back out, once again very slowly, and the rolling organ music bounces into an allegro tempo. Zed's tears seem to transform into tears of subtle joy. The music therefore either reflects or, indeed, constructs his buoyant state of mind, as if his subjectivity—already focalized once by the echo of Edochie's voice—is again available for indirect access. Meanwhile, the camera allows spectators to assess Zed's face from a third-person perspective. He has made up his mind, and he seems to be at ease about what awaits him.

Zed tries to convince Victoria to stay back while he takes their baby to "the hospital," but she insists on accompanying him. She is therefore furious when they arrive at Billion's mansion instead, and her anger spirals into desperate torment as Zed hands their sick child to members of the Billionaires Club. Meanwhile, Zed continues to wear a look of serenity on his face. Victoria is left alone while the men convene upstairs and the gruesome sacrifice plays out. When they return without her baby, Victoria rages, and a pair of security guards remove her from the scene. They take her to a room where one of the guards sees a sacrificial blade, picks it up, and kills her. Meanwhile, Zed cheerfully embraces and shakes hands with several members of the club, his membership dues now paid in full.

The club then fakes a car accident, which serves as cover for the fates of Victoria and the baby. Zed hands his and Victoria's businesses over to his employees. They suspect that Zed has become a ritualist, calling the accusation "unanimous," although that does not stop them from accepting his gifts. Once again, it seems, the occult does not so much introduce evil into the social landscape as it accentuates the avarice already lurking below the surface of the social. Zed then makes plans to marry a new woman, but his parents protest vehemently, declaring that it is too soon. And when his fiancé, Oby (Oge Okoye), explains her relationship with Zed to her own parents, she emphasizes the fact that Zed is generous, providing her with everything she wants. It therefore seems that Zed has finally achieved what he has so desired: a neolocal marriage in which he has obtained breadwinner status. However, back home in the village, Victoria's mother, Njideka, begins to see visions of Victoria. Her ghost, it seems, cannot rest.

So ends the first part of the three-part *Billionaires Club*. To avoid belaboring the process of analysis, the remainder of my discussion of the film focuses on the role that free indirect subjectivity plays in the depiction of Zed's demise and subsequent salvation. In part II Zed is married to

Oby, they live in a sprawling mansion, and as Victoria's mother describes it when she wails—addressing no one in particular, the camera closely orbiting her tear-soaked face—Zed drives "a fleet of the finest cars in the whole wide world." Indeed, Zed no longer needs to feel embarrassed in any parking lot anywhere. He has achieved a particular ideal of manhood. As usual, however, his new life quickly becomes a torturous one.

Victoria's ghost, drenched in blood and holding her baby, appears to several characters, including Billion and then Oby's sister, Ebere (Constance Daniels, also the film's screenwriter). Victoria's presence is clearly menacing in both cases. With Zed, however, it is slightly different. She sits outside his window at night holding the baby, who cries incessantly. Otherworldly sound effects roil the sound track. But Zed is the only one who can hear the crying. He tries to drown it out with music but to no avail: the crying seeps into his ears, ears that spectators are also invited to use. These moments of ambiguity, in which the narrative unfolds through both first- and third-person accounts, complement the earlier moment of free indirect subjectivity, the one that accompanies Zed's initial contemplation of the occult. It is important, *Billionaires Club* and other films suggest, to indirectly inhabit a man's subjectivity both when he considers killing his partner in order to become a breadwinner and while he suffers for being a breadwinner without having a real family to enjoy his bread.

When Zed complains to the billionaire brotherhood about his haunting, they laugh and reveal that they too suffer, in different ways, from their association with Satan. It is simply the price that one pays. In fact, so normalized is their perspective that the film implies Zed should simply accept and find ways to cope with Victoria's haunting. Billion admits that there may be methods of minimizing occult repercussions, but they come with their own costs. Zed ignores the costs and decides to sacrifice his left arm in order to expunge Victoria's ghost; however, when his arm begins to disintegrate, he tries to have it treated medically. Then, in a rueful conversation, Billion and Don note that scientific meddling in an occult process only makes the occult stronger. The disintegration thus spreads until Zed's entire body is covered in gruesome sores, and he lies in his parents' compound, dying an agonizing death. This is when Victoria's ghost appeals to "Innocence" to forgive Zed, and he subsequently transitions to the spirit world. Just before he dies, however, as Victoria looms over Zed, spectators see her through his eyes: another key moment of free indirect subjectivity (see figures 4.4 and 4.5).

His parents, sitting nearby, cannot see what he sees and therefore can only glean the extent of Zed's mistakes from the way he speaks to the apparition. As part II concludes, an intertitle, attributed to the producer, Sunny Collins, fills the screen: "Brethren, be contented the way of the Lord has made you. For the Lord God can never make mistake. The gift of Devil can only destroy you but the gift of god is full of joy. Accept Jesus Christ today." Several Nollywood producers, including Kenneth Nnebue, are known to have become preachers. Several others, like Helen Ukpabio, are known primarily as preachers. However, Collins represents something even more ubiquitous (indeed, to the point of being banal): the filmmaker with a Pentecostal sensibility who attempts to instruct his audience, reminding them that all of the magic, all of the evil, all of the hedonism and gore that may appear in a Nollywood film have pedagogical purposes. Yet the invitation to "be contented the way of the Lord has made you" is an invitation to endure the conditions in which not only material accumulation but also breadwinning remains out of the average person's reach. Spectators are invited to see with Zed's eyes as this sentiment is suggested and just before it is explicitly enunciated. "To God," the customary Nollywood inscription begins—which here follows Collins's advice—"be the Glory."

As I have noted elsewhere, another one of the great innovations of *Billionaires Club* is the film's explicit articulation of the money-magic cult with a globalized economic system and, in particular, a system rooted as much in the global South as in the North.[24] Although Zed ascends to his status as spiritual warrior in part III of the film, the brotherhood is suffering inexplicable deterioration. Billion is forced to call in the cult's "superintendent," who arrives in a private jet. He is played by Avinaash Bhavnaani, a Nigeria-based car salesman of Indian descent who has appeared in several video films (including *The Master* [2004, dir. Andy Amenechi], discussed in chapter 6). Bhavnaani speaks Hindi in several scenes in *Billionaires Club*, suggesting that the cult's provenance has at least something to do with India. However, his power is not enough to save the brotherhood. Zed's ghost, wielding a whip, sows havoc among the brotherhood, causing several members to run away, go mad, or die. To defeat Billion, however, Zed enlists the help of the police. But in the final moments of the film, when the police commissioner confronts Billion, he cannot prevail without Zed's assistance. Billion, master of the occult, disappears and reappears at will, evading the commissioner's bullets. But when Zed's ghost steps into the commissioner's body, he is able to detect and mortally wound Billion. Therefore, the climax of the story stitches the power of Christian redemption and resurrection together with the power of the state in order to overthrow the powers of Satan

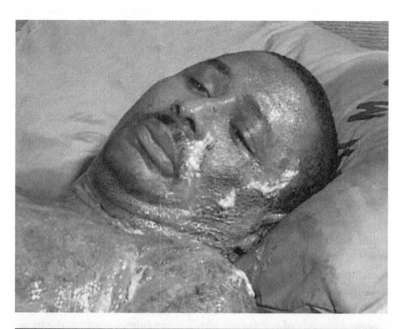

FIGURES 4.4 AND 4.5. *Billionaires Club*. Shot, countershot. Zed sees Victoria's ghost.

and international finance. The disarticulation of finance capital from the global North and the glorification of Christianity—which is here embodied by Zed (not Victoria), who fills the screen, wearing a fine western suit and a derby, brandishing a whip, just before the credits roll—tempers any critique that the film might be making about money and modernity (see figure 4.6). Rather than directly indicting the Euro-American–dominated liberal world order for the limited number of choices available to modern Nigerian men, *Billionaires Club* assumes an indirect perspective. Formerly colonized subjects, from Nigeria to India, seem to generate their own methods—informal, underground—to create and circulate wealth outside of the liberal world order. These developments call for a rereading of Don's comments when he first enters the story: "You don't need to get out of this country to transform yourself; it's just within you." Although Don implies that Zed must find his inner devil, the culmination of the film implies that the modern Nigerian man's best recourse, in a dispensation uncoupled from the world economy, is to find his inner Jesus. And given Sunny Collins's textual preaching, that is clearly a message of complacency, not one of revolution. Part III also culminates with the usual inscription: "To God Be the Glory."

FIGURE 4.6. *Billionaires Club*. Zed's spirit surveys the world.

THE CONTRADICTIONS OF MODERNITY

It should come as no surprise that commercial filmmaking in Nigeria tends toward gender normativity. But in the final assessment of films like *Billionaires Club*, we need a more nuanced approach than discourses of normativity and revolution can capture. The feminine melodramatic mode, as I argued in chapter 3, tends to celebrate the potentiality of a male breadwinner ideal not because women want to submit to men's productivity but because if the ideal were achievable, then Nigeria would actually be part of the liberal world order. Meanwhile, if the masculine melodramatic mode functions as a backlash, it is less about lashing out at women than at the breadwinner ideal itself. Stories of men who turn to the occult in order to become breadwinners and subsequently destroy those for whom they would win bread equate breadwinning with Satanism. And given the conspicuously modern, liberal character of the breadwinner ideal, Nollywood's masculine melodramatic mode therefore implies that there is something satanic about modern gender norms. However, the crux of the matter is in the disjuncture between modern ideology and lived experience in Nigeria. If the local economy cannot support actual breadwinners and the men and women who make families together must therefore pool their resources, then the breadwinner fantasy is actually antisocial. It has the potential to neutralize the very real, very important economic contributions that women make to families and to society more generally, not to mention the contributions they make to the subjectivities of men. Therefore, normativity could be turned into a form of resistance. If men cannot achieve breadwinner status, as alluring as it seems, then they must collaborate with women. Together, men and women can fight for a mutually beneficial economy, not simply for access to the exclusionary and unjust structures of the liberal world order. At the end of the day, gender may be a retrogressive construct, but taken together, Nollywood's feminine and masculine melodramatic modes of address suggest that the power of gender can transcend family and even nation to *engender* power of a much greater sort. It could help eclipse liberalism.

Regardless of the hopefulness that could be read into these films, however, we must consider the fact that given the very real allure of the liberal world order, these films accrue pessimistic meaning as part of Nollywood's local address. From 1992, when *Living in Bondage* was released, to 2003, when *Billionaires Club* came out, as the deprivations of structural adjustment became normalized and as a system of government by military dictatorship transitioned to a system where former military dictators are democratically elected president, these films seem to have taken an increasingly grim view of the status of men in a supposedly liberalizing society. Where Andy finds salvation—although he has still lost his wife and fortune—Osita finds persecution, and Zed—despite his ascendant spiritual power—finds a slow and painful death. Indeed, for Zed, full realization of his potency and virility seems to come only with full removal from the world. But is removal productive? Is it enough, we must ask, for any group of men and women anywhere in the world to fight for their own just economic system within their own nations, or "native authorities," as it were? Is it enough to escape the material conditions of this unjust world? Or rather, for Nollywood's imagined public, should the fight not be, at least in part, for full membership in a world that could not exist without them?

5 Specters of Sovereignty

EPIC, GOTHIC, AND THE RUINS OF
A PAST THAT NEVER WAS

A young Pete Edochie emerges from an earthen structure with a thatched roof, faces the camera, and strikes a bold pose, eyes angled to the sky. "Let them shoot what they will," he announces. "They will never get me." Unlike his character in *Billionaires Club* (discussed in chapter 4), this Edochie character intends to evade bullets not by recourse to occult magic but rather by taking his own life before "they" arrive. He is alone in his family compound, speaking to himself, but also to spectators, of course. In fact, the spectator-subject imagined here has long known what will happen but has never known precisely what this particular character is thinking, certainly not at this critical juncture. Regardless, the narrative does not offer its spectators access to the character's subject position; instead, the character speaks in the form of a soliloquy so that a third-person narrative perspective can relay his stated motivations. According to a purely audiovisual analysis, therefore, the subjectivity offered is unambiguously conventional and stable. However, the soliloquy also assumes its spectators' heavy investment in and knowledge of the context. *You may already know what is about to happen*, it suggests, *but not until now did you know why.* The scene's mode of address is therefore subtly destabilized. Spectators know the character so well that his short declaration of intent may offer a flash of insight into his narration of himself, a possible though more complicated instance of free indirect subjectivity.

Edochie's soliloquy is one of the most radical interventions made by the NTA in its 1986 adaptation of Chinua Achebe's 1958 novel *Things Fall Apart*. Edochie plays Okonkwo, the part-tragic, part-epic hero at the heart of the narrative who has just killed a messenger of the colonial government and who will, before he can be tracked down and arrested, hang himself. Achebe's novel provides very little insight into Okonkwo's dreadful decision. What readers do know is that he is foremost among a group of men in Umuofia who advocate war against invading colonists. After Okonkwo kills the messenger, however, none of the others take up arms—instead, they break into "tumult." The novel tells its readers that Okonkwo suddenly realizes that "Umuofia would not go to war," so he "wiped his machete on the sand and went away."[1] On the next page, his close friend, Obierika, finds Okonkwo's body hanging from a tree. The temporal jump suggests but does not provide a direct connection between the villagers' hesitation and Okonkwo's suicide. However, the gap between the two is profoundly generative, allowing readers an opportunity to participate in and perhaps identify with several different possible trajectories toward Okonkwo's fateful choice. Resignation, spiritual liberation, self-sacrifice—these and many other terms might describe Okonkwo's motives. In the NTA adaptation, however, the gap between Okonkwo's two actions is filled and its trajectory is tightly constricted. His subject position is named and justified. His narrative arc is given a distinct political valence. All of this may have a galvanizing effect, at least for some spectators, but it also isolates Okonkwo from the possibility of robust forms of subject identification.

As the adaptation proceeds, Edochie's Okonkwo returns to his house, retrieves some palm wine, and approaches his family shrine. There he pours libations while pleading with his gods to "let my cause remain alive." In the novel, one possible explanation for Okonkwo's suicide is the realization that his cause is, in fact, dead. By pleading to let it live, the NTA's Okonkwo claims the status of a martyr, one whose cause might live long beyond himself. He then goes on to define the scope of his martyrdom in terms of political sovereignty: "We simply ask to be left to live our lives our own way." By providing indirect access to Okonkwo's subjectivity this way—allowing him to voice what is otherwise an unspoken thought process—the NTA betrays a transparently postcolonial political imperative.[2] Indeed, the reason to identify with a figure like Okonkwo, the television adaptation suggests, is that although he exhibits several flaws, including violent antisocial hypermasculinism, he has never wavered in his commitment to fighting colonial invaders and, by extension, to supporting anticolonial nationalism. Of course, even if more Nigerian men had been as committed as Okonkwo during the colonial period, it does not necessarily follow that the arc of imperial history would have bent much differently. The massive imbalance in raw, mortal power between imperial Britain and villages such as Umuofia is indisputable. Moreover, the adaptation suggests that the fight for political sovereignty also entails a fight for the right to embrace Okonkwo's flaws or, at the very least, to be free from outside judgment while dealing with them internally. That too squares with nationalist politics in the postcolonial period, in which several African governments and leading intellectuals, including in Nigeria, have attempted to discredit global liberal discourses regarding issues such as women's rights, children's rights, LGBTQ+ rights, and disability rights by casting them as breaches of national sovereignty or as Western impositions. Therefore, what the state television network seems to have focused on in its adaptation of *Things Fall Apart* is the difference between a present moment — defined by contradictory global relations as well as political connections — and a past that could have been isolated from them.

One of the most iconic genres in Nollywood, often called the "epic," perpetually restages this contrast between a sovereign past and an implicitly interconnected but dominated present in ways that evoke the NTA's adaptation of *Things Fall Apart*, especially the enduring image of Edochie as a precolonial figure of authority. I have made a version of this argument elsewhere, although in previous writing I focused on the intersection of politics and the supernatural or the ways in which images of magic figure into Nollywood's epics and occult films as indices of the social forces impinging on a hero at the threshold of a new political order.[3] Indeed, many Nollywood films set in the kind of precolonial past depicted in *Things Fall Apart* tend to imagine heroes battling malevolent spirits and vengeful gods, or vanquishing human enemies with the help of supernatural aids in order to (re)establish a functioning system of social rights and obligations within a relatively self-contained political community. I have also argued that films like *Billionaires Club* could be described as epics because the primary problem facing a hero like Zed—which he ultimately overcomes—is the dislocation of moral authority and political legitimacy in a modern, urban, or national community (see chapter 4). Indeed, the kind of money-magic cult to which Zed sacrifices Victoria is often interpreted as a cipher for the moral bankruptcy of "millennial capitalism," against which the Nigerian state is helpless and over which Pentecostal millenarianism might prevail.[4] Recall the moment in *Billionaires Club* when Zed—who has died and been reborn as a spiritual warrior—literally inhabits the body of the police commander in order to execute Billion and thus reestablish the moral authority of the state over a nefarious global economic cabal. Zed also relies on the supernatural to cross the threshold of a new political order. Therefore, it would seem as if the Nollywood epic has at least two variants: one set in a version of the precolonial past, which is already widely referred to as "epic," and one set in contemporary times, which may be referred to on the street as "occult," "juju," or "money magic" but is not necessarily understood to be a genre in and of itself. Elsewhere, I have been tempted to call it the "contemporary epic."

Beyond the comparisons I have made in previous work, I could add several other linkages between contemporary occult films such as *Billionaires Club* and precolonial epics. For example, the music that plays in director Andy Amenechi's occult vigilante film *Ashes to Ashes* (see chapter 4) during the scenes in which the false prophet visits his evil sacred grove also features in two of Amenechi's epics—one, the early and influential *Igodo*, made two years before *Ashes to Ashes*, and two, *Egg of Life*, made two years after *Ashes to Ashes*. In both of Amenechi's precolonial epics, that eerie, unsettling music, reverberating with the sound of distant horns and pierced by prickly electronic effects that bring to mind a vision of insects crawling, plays during scenes in which heroes navigate evil forests. All three films are produced by OJ Productions, which seems to have kept the track on file and repeatedly activated it to create a certain mood, which, moreover, bridges the world of contemporary occult powers and the ancient forces of evil that lurk in the deep, dark bush.

Despite modal connections like these, however, there are many significant modal *differences* between occult video films set in contemporary times and epics set in the precolonial past. At the level of character development, for instance, several epics spend much less time on the interior states or affective relationships between major characters, opting instead for more-archetypal strategies of characterization. Also, the role that occult power plays in epics is less, well, occult. There are still hidden forces at work, some of which can be ascertained only through specialized knowledge, such as divination, but many of the supernatural forces that feature in Nollywood epics are perfectly capable of making themselves known to anybody at any time. So "occult" rituals, including divination, may be common in precolonial epics, but gods and spirits also freely and visibly traverse the landscape of the genre, openly intervening in people's everyday lives. Instead of offering spectators a glimpse behind the curtain, as it were, or digging below the surface of reality, many epics tend to depict a world manifestly subject to and primarily shaped by supernatural power. That power may serve the same purposes for the heroes of both occult films and epics, but in a number of films it is addressed to its audience through different modalities, which may attract different kinds of attention.

In this chapter I argue that a useful way to explain the modal difference between the occult films I explored in the previous chapter and the selected epic films I turn to here is—somewhat paradoxically—through the language of what literary critics have named the *gothic*. That claim is paradoxical in the sense that films such as *Living in Bondage, Ashes to Ashes*, and *Billionaires Club* exhibit distinctly gothic characteristics, especially the hero/villain at the center of the story (Andy, Osita, Zed) and the ghost (Merit, Abigail, Victoria) who haunts him. Nevertheless, Nollywood epics are more tantalizingly described as gothic in terms of the way they treat individual subjectivity, family structures, and spatiotemporality. I should note here that in the case of spatiotemporality I am not just thinking about the genre's typical setting: a village in the forest exhibiting few, if any, signs of contact with the outside world. Nollywood epics offer their spectators an entirely unique approach to the concept of time. As several critics have noted, it is an ambivalent approach, neither completely celebratory nor dismissive of the past.[5] In fact, the past in the Nollywood epic is a *space* unmoored from the dictates of chronological history; it is a construct, precolonial only in the sense that it shows no material signs of the modern economy from which colonialism derived and upon which it was sustained. Otherwise, it is a space where English is used copiously and modern forms of social tension are navigated. Moreover, the Nollywood epic seems to construct a past less for the purposes of inhabiting it than to explore ideas about the present. And in that sense the past haunts the present in ways that lend themselves to recognizably gothic conventions. So as Nollywood epics wander through the landscape of their constructed temporality, they seem to discover the ruins of a previously unknown society, one full of princes, palaces, and palanquins. Those features, so rare in southern Nigeria's recorded history but so common in Nollywood, suggest that global conventions of the gothic may be doing practical social work in contemporary Nigerian popular culture. They also suggest, as I demonstrate in this chapter, that Nollywood has assembled an idiosyncratic vocabulary with which to address its imagined spectator-subjects in terms of their relationship to the persistent question of political sovereignty.

THE GOTHIC MODE OF ADDRESS

As a European literary-critical term, "gothic" signifies in ways similar to melodrama. Critics tend to locate the rise of a gothic mode in the aftermath of the French Revolution.[6] However, where melodrama is said to stage the redistribution of morality in a post-sacred era (see chapter 3), gothic stages the return of a much older sacred order. Named for the ethnic Germanic Goths who participated in the collapse of the Roman

Empire, what critics often describe as gothic literature emerged centuries later, during the Enlightenment, to address fears of a new anticivilizational invasion often figured less in terms of a marauding horde than in terms of an internal awakening, the rise of latent pagan power haunting the ruins of classical and medieval architecture. So whereas modern European readers turned to melodrama in search of new moral horizons, they turned to the gothic in search of a shared past, one that predated Christianity but one that also explained from within why centuries of Christian theocracy had given way to something new in the modern period. In the gothic novel, Enlightenment readers could be simultaneously delighted and horrified by the idea that Christendom was but an interruption of a longer, more vicious continuum of history. The heroes of gothic literature, who explored crumbling castles and vine-covered cathedrals searching for magical potions and holy relics, who found within old buildings elaborate traps, hidden labyrinths, vengeful ghosts, and unspeakable family secrets, and who made Faustian bargains with the devil in order to wield terrifying tyrannical power, struggled with a version of modernity that seemed to be but part of one long, protracted history of savagery. Gothic stories gave the furiously changing and deeply unsettling social climate of early capitalism a context, an anchor, and a sense of temporal scale.

Given gothic's scalar tendencies, narratives composed in its mode tend to seek morality *not* by digging below the surface of individual lives but by allegorizing massive social and institutional forces. Unlike its cousin melodrama, therefore, the gothic mode assigns degrees of goodness and evil to *systems* such as social class—especially, during its emergence, to the rise of the merchant bourgeoisie and the decline of the aristocracy. In England, for example, seventeenth-century gothic literature was famously preoccupied with mysteries of primogeniture, which played out over the generations, resulting in noble lines that had become shadows of their former glory. Nineteenth-century gothic literature would attract new readerships by staging the fall of the empire rather than the aristocracy. Now sometimes referred to as examples of the *imperial gothic*, novels such as H. Rider Haggard's *She* (1886) explore a realm of pagan power that ran parallel to European paganism but was hidden in the darkest heart of Africa, where it was not merely an alien force but one that had been incorporated into the very constitution of the empire. Rotting from within, it was only a matter of time before the imperial project, like the Christendom before it, faded back into a longer narrative of vicious, savage history.

Nollywood epics tend to inhabit similarly scalar temporal settings, often invoking gothic conventions to link the contemporary moment

with a distant past that is itself haunted by an even more distant and indeterminate past. In this chapter I demonstrate that gothic temporalities
can be used to address subjects of national history, often according to the
nation's most mythical foundations, in which Nollywood is no less interested than is state television. However, what might be a fairly straightforward interpretation is complicated by the fact that Nollywood epics
are often invested in certain gothic conventions that, at first glance, do
not seem to apply to Nigerian history, particularly those conventions associated with thrones and royal bloodlines. In fact, one of the most per-
plexing issues in the study of Nigerian video film epics is the predictable
prominence of an *igwe*, or king, in the social landscape of the precolonial
Igbo village.

"*Igwe*" is an honorific term of address in the Igbo language, used to hail
a paramount leader to whom people might otherwise refer as "*eze*" or
"*obi*." In the part of Nigeria where those terms originate, however, such
paramount village leaders, especially kingly ones, have rarely been recorded. Yet the igwe character is a predictably central feature of most
Nollywood epics. Indeed, the word *igwe* has taken on the characteristics
of a title precisely because it has been uttered by so many on-screen characters in so many films as they have bowed before so many enthroned
village potentates. Jonathan Haynes notes that *igwe* has even become an
ironic, comic form of address, used all across Africa, to indicate anyone
who appears to be or dresses like a Nigerian: "This is all Nollywood's
doing. It has created probably the most widespread image of traditional
African kingship for the whole continent."[7] Therefore, one of the key
questions here is why Nollywood's interest in the deep temporal foundations of the nation includes a form of "traditional African kingship" that
only cropped up here and there, not in the form and not nearly as often
as the films suggest, particularly in the locations where the films are set.[8]

Nollywood's invention of fantasy monarchies is all the more intriguing
because such institutions contradict a nationalist narrative about history
that prizes indigenous African forms of representative democracy, social
mobility, and economic equality. That nationalist narrative is corrobo-
rated by many examples from the historical archive, but it also tends to
cite Achebe's novels, which — despite their status as fiction — are of course
carefully researched and, more importantly, so compellingly written that
they have become widely cited standards. As Daniel M. Mengara writes,
"Achebe uses creative license to manufacture a fictional universe in which
Igbo responses to colonial intrusion are depicted with such a high degree
of poignancy that his narrative manages to lend itself a remarkable degree
of epistemological plausibility."[9] In a famous scene in *Things Fall Apart*,

for example, British missionaries ask for the king of the village and are told there is none: "We have men of high title and the chief priests and the elders." This passage suggests two things: one, that the concept of a village king is a colonial invention or imposition (read: indirect rule) and, two, that the citizens of Umuofia know more about democracy than their supposedly liberal invaders. The latter is buttressed by a well-known saying, "*Igbo enwe eze*" (The Igbo have no kings).[10] Therefore, Achebe's novels never mention a person or an office called "igwe." Instead, they elaborately depict patriarchal councils that meet to debate village politics. They offer many scenes in which elders take important decisions to the entire citizenry, in some cases numbered in the thousands, for a vote. Furthermore, admission into the council of elders is not based on heredity. As Achebe describes it, any man could achieve a title by, essentially, purchasing it through the honorable distribution of his wealth.[11] If a man accumulated a certain amount of resources through his own hard work and good fortune, he was not only able but also expected—and therefore enculturated to want—to inject those resources back into the community by throwing an elaborate ceremony and feast, at which he took his new title. With each cycle of accumulation came a newer, more elevated title, the acquisition of which gave a man greater political authority but also minimized the degree to which he could ever accumulate economic power. In Nollywood epics, however, the almighty igwe wields enormous economic power in addition to his fantastic political authority.

Of course, the fantastic power of the Nollywood igwe aligns with the fantastic nature of the epic genre. From the handful of scholars who have critically engaged Nollywood epics, one common theme has emerged: the genre's sense of history should not be taken literally.[12] Certainly, there are epic films that fictionalize historical events, including *The Battle of Musanga* (1996, dir. Bolaji Dawodu) and *King Jaja of Opobo* (1999, dir. Harry Agina). Haynes and Barclays Ayakoroma both refer to them as historical epics.[13] But Haynes also proposes another subgenre, legendary epics, to which he assigns the vast majority of Nollywood films set in precolonial villages. Ayakoroma uses a similar schema, although he further subdivides the latter. Some legendary epics refer to well-known narratives from the oral tradition, such as *Sango* (1997, dir. Obafemi Lasode), which depicts the Yoruba myth of a king's ascension to the status of thunder god (kings are much more common in Yoruba history than Igbo history), whereas others invent completely new narratives, which Ayakoroma calls "fantasy" epics.[14] Their plots may draw upon well-known motifs, but fantasy epics tell new stories in new ways, often in order to maximize the amount of supernatural spectacle that can appear on screen. Nomusa Makhubu describes this phenomenon as the result of processes of "theatricalizing" and "spectacularizing" the village, a practice in which many postcolonial artists and cultural elites have long engaged for the purposes of reclaiming a form of African subjectivity, parodying colonial fascination with African social forms and fashioning an alternative rationality for modern African subjects.[15] Therefore, the igwe may simply be a symbol on par with many other symbols derived from the ideological construction of the African village as a site of alternative modernity.

Besides igwes, however, another significant distinction between Achebe's epic novels and the typical Nollywood epic is that whereas Achebe ultimately brought the villages of his "fictional universe" into contact with societies far beyond their borders, Nollywood's epic villages are generally insular. Aside from some of the "historical epics," which depict well-known internecine wars or colonial encounters, epics mostly focus on social problems internal to a single community or two closely related communities. Haynes writes that "it is extraordinary the extent to which the horizon of these films is conceived of as nothing more or less than the village, imagined as a bounded entity riven by internal conflicts and/or tension with an outside force."[16] The overarchingly claustrophobic mise-en-scène of the genre therefore seems designed to suggest that the community is utterly—and ahistorically—isolated from Europe, the Middle East, and the many trade routes that connected the precolonial African continent. However, this distinction between history and story both feeds upon and reinforces the genre's investment in igwes. In short, the Nollywood epic's gothic mode of address hinges on the visualization of a sovereign who rules a sovereign society.

Although Achebe's Things Fall Apart is also very much interested in the possibilities and limits of political sovereignty, it is averse to the image of a sovereign Igbo ruler. However, given the institutional framework from which the NTA's adaptation of Achebe's text emerged, the television version places unsurprising emphasis on and reifies images of political sovereignty. And although the adaptation includes no sovereign rulers as such—no kings—it seems to have set in motion a cinematic process by which indications of sovereign rule would accrue to proud, emphatic, eloquent men—often played by Pete Edochie. As with the igwe in Ashes to Ashes, however, not all of Nollywood's sovereigns are good. In fact, even Edochie plays igwes who utterly fail the communities they rule. Therefore, the past in Nollywood does not function as a foil for the present, not some idyllic space to which modernity may be contrasted, or an age of darkness from which the nation emerged. Instead, the past truly haunts the present, clawing its way into another dimension because it still has some kind of unfinished business.

THINGS FALL APART: GRIEVING SOVEREIGNTY LOST

Things Fall Apart, the novel, was published on the cuff of independence in Nigeria and takes a look at the past in order to say something to local readers and to a global anglophone audience about the possibilities and pitfalls of political sovereignty and the rise of the nation-state in Africa. The novel depicts an Igbo village, Umuofia, before, during, and after the arrival of British missionaries and colonial authorities. Its narrative voice is omniscient, an authority on village institutions and the ways in which they shape people's perspectives, as well as on the inner lives of various characters, especially Okonkwo, the hubristic middle-aged man at the center of the plot. Okonkwo is driven by ambition, especially by his desperate need to eclipse the status of his languid and sentimental father, Unoka. In fact, Okonkwo is so obsessed with his social status and its reflection on his fragile sense of masculinity that he alienates more self-assured men and often dismisses their advice, at times with tragic consequences. Early in the novel, a boy, Ikemefuna—who has been taken from a nearby village as compensation for the inadvertent death of an Umuofian woman—is placed in the care of Okonkwo's prosperous household. But when the high priest of the most influential oracle in the village orders Ikemefuna's sacrifice, Okonkwo ignores the pleas of elders who warn him not to participate. He joins the expedition that is tasked with escorting Ikemefuna deep into the forest, and when the planned execution falters, he finishes the job himself. The sun then begins to set on Okonkwo's prosperity. Several misfortunes befall him, and when the British arrive, he has little authority left to influence Umuofia's response. His fragile sense of masculinity compels him to aggression as other men resist what they seem to consider an unwinnable war. Ultimately, Okonkwo assassinates a representative of the colonial government, and when no one joins his uprising, he hangs himself. The novel concludes with the thoughts of the British district commissioner, who supposes that Okonkwo's story might make for an amusing anecdote in a contemptuous treatise he is composing about the imperial subjugation of West Africa.

A key feature of Achebe's style in *Things Fall Apart* revolves around the insights that he provides into the minds of characters like Okonkwo, the district commissioner, and various other villagers, both individually and collectively. The narrative voice does not remain consistently and objectively omniscient; it indulges from time to time in free indirect discourse or what I have been referring to as "free indirect subjectivity." It is not simply that the narrator of *Things Fall Apart* knows what characters are thinking; instead, in a few select places the narrative voice takes up the subject position of certain characters as if, during key moments, those characters must be given an opportunity to tell part of the story. For example, when Ikemefuna is walking with the men of Umuofia through the forest (unaware that he is about to be killed), the narrative voice moves from reporting Ikemefuna's thoughts about his mother and sister to directly inhabiting his subjectivity. There is a suggestive ellipsis, and then the text reads, "of course, she [his sister] would not be three now, but six. Would he recognize her now? She must have grown quite big. How his mother would weep for joy, and thank Okonkwo for having looked after him so well and for bringing him back."[17] Quotation marks are not used here. The narrative voice has been given over, at least partially, to Ikemefuna, as though he has been handed a microphone. Elsewhere in the novel the narrative voice inhabits Okonkwo's subjectivity— for example, when he wonders why mosquitoes always go for one's ears. He remembers a story that his mother told him about mosquitoes, and his voice takes over the narration, declaring all women's stories silly. In other places the narrator refers to the missionaries' Christianity as a "lunatic religion." Does that phrase come from the subject position of the narrator or from the villagers? It is not clear. And of course, at the end the district commissioner reports that Okonkwo's suicide would make "interesting reading" but doubts how much space he should devote to it. "There was so much else to include," the text reads, "and one must be firm in cutting out details."[18] These particular moments of free indirect discourse turn an otherwise detached, floating narrative voice into a composite of many voices in the story, effectively inviting readers to draw connections among them.

The connectivity of subject positions rendered by free indirect discourse in Achebe's *Things Fall Apart* is reflected at the levels of structure and theme. For example, in the chapter following Ikemefuna's sacrifice, the narrative moves swiftly and effortlessly from a glimpse of Okonkwo's posttraumatic depressive state to a discussion between Okonkwo and his thoughtful friend Obierika about the role that each villager plays in

the community's spiritual life, and finally to a report about the deaths of
Ndulue and Ozoemena, a couple who, according to Obierika, "had one
mind. . . . [Ndulue] could not do anything without telling her." Therefore, built into the structure of the chapter are links between the trauma
that Okonkwo experiences as a result of defying the elders' advice and
the discussion of an interdependent heterosexual couple. Okonkwo is in-
credulous. Of Ndulue he remarks, "I thought he was a strong man in his
youth." "He was indeed," offers their friend, Ofoedu, to which Okonkwo
shakes his head "doubtfully." Then Obierika recalls that Ndulue "led
Umuofia to war in those days."[19] Thus, whereas Okonkwo is skeptical that
a man so dependent on his wife could be a *real* man, all of his friends
see Ndulue as resolutely masculine—after all, he led Umuofia to war, according to Obierika—and implicitly endorse the interdependency of men
and women in their community. Combined with the use of free indirect
discourse, moments like this suggest that Okonkwo's insistence on his
own independent identity, forged in opposition to his father's legacy—
an irony, of course, because Okonkwo's identity is therefore chained to
his father's—is idiosyncratic and counter-normative. Everyone else acknowledges and even celebrates the web of subjective positions that bind
their society, especially men and women. In the end, therefore, Okonkwo
fails to lead his community to war against colonization precisely because
he has alienated himself from his community and has denied that even
those Umuofians who have joined the church—including his own son—
remain deeply connected to him. A war against colonization, some of his
friends seem to have intuited, would—in a very significant sense—be a
war against themselves.

We might accuse Okonkwo's neighbors of apathy or cowardice, but
given the tentative title of the district commissioner's book, *The Pacifi-
cation of the Primitive Tribes of the Lower Niger*, readers are also invited to
consider the possibility that Umuofia has indeed been pacified. Moreover, that possibility is presented so callously in the final lines of the
novel that it clearly invites the reader to condemnation, even fury. Ultimately, the novel does not claim that Okonkwo's resistance should be
dismissed—far from it—but it does acknowledge the difficulty of maintaining a starkly resistant subjectivity in the face of so much material
and discursive power. In such cases human beings more often rearrange
themselves to create affirmative ways of working within prevailing power
relations. In a book on the Nigerian musician and political activist Fela
Anikulapo-Kuti, Tejumola Olaniyan refers to the collision of these subject positions as "enchanting modernity . . . an aporetic situation in which

modernity is simultaneously railed at as an alien, oppressive, and bewitching illusion (a *dis*-enchantment) and as a catalyst for further striving (a *re*-enchantment)."[20] Through free indirect discourse—with emphasis on its *free*-dom, its ability to gambol between character perspectives as well as between individuals and collectives—Achebe's *Things Fall Apart* renders the full, aporetic scope of enchanting modernity.

The NTA miniseries adaptation of *Things Fall Apart*, however, disenchants modernity, making substantial use of free indirect subjectivity, but instead of performing the full range of subject positions in Umuofia, it focuses narrowly on Okonkwo's resistance. First aired in 1986, produced by the NTA's Peter Igho, directed by David Orere, filmed by Yusuf Mohammed, sponsored by United Bank for Africa, and adapted for the screen by Adiela Onyedibia and Emme Eleanya, *Things Fall Apart* was widely appreciated across Nigeria.[21] It also seems to have played a part in establishing Nigeria's "golden era" of television. Justus Esiri played the part of Obierika and immediately went on to star in *The New Village Headmaster* (see chapter 2). Esiri's costar, Funsho Adeolu—who played Chief Eleyinmi in *The New Village Headmaster*—played the important Umuofian elder, Ezeugo, in *Things Fall Apart*. Other notable figures from the miniseries include Sam Loco, who would later play Nduka's father in *Checkmate* and eventually move on to several Nollywood roles, and Nkem Owoh, who would become a writer for the enormously popular NTA situation comedy *Basi and Company*, and then become one of Nollywood's most successful comic actors (see chapter 6). As noted in chapter 3, the years following the miniseries were some of the most productive in NTA history and some of the most warmly remembered. Obari Gomba writes that he and his friends and family "bonded" with television because of the adaptation. He also notes that because of the NTA's broadcasts, "There are lots of Nigerians who have not read their country's greatest novel, but they can tell you the main thrust of the story of Okonkwo."[22] And, indeed, Edochie's commanding presence on screen in the major role is certainly memorable, although some of his gravitas also derives from the fact that whereas the subject position offered by the camera and the sound track throughout most of the miniseries is distant, it has a tendency to inhabit the subjectivity of Edochie's Okonkwo indirectly. Moreover, it rarely inhabits anyone else's. It follows, then, that a hagiographic image of Edochie's Okonkwo is one of the series' most enduring legacies.

Two scenes of free indirect subjectivity in the NTA's *Things Fall Apart* are of critical significance here, and they are closely connected. The first occurs at the decisive moment when Okonkwo kills Ikemefuna. The second follows hot on its heels. The first sequence begins with a low-angle shot of the sky and trees, which tilts and pans to an over-the-shoulder shot of the members of the expedition, who are tasked with Ikemefuna's sacrifice, as they walk down a forest path. Then another low-angle shot, still behind the expedition, establishes that Ikemefuna, carrying a pot of palm wine on his head, walks just behind the leader. The image then cuts to an even lower-angle shot, this time in front of the expedition, as its members walk toward the camera. Only their legs and waists, wrapped in cloth, appear on screen. These ant's-eye views of the procession are then contrasted with two high-angle shots, which give a sense of the expedition's small- ness in comparison to the large and enveloping forest. Finally, another shot in front of the men as they walk toward the camera shows their faces for the first time, although it is a medium-wide shot, and little detail is visible. Spectators are invited to see the procession from several angles but not invited to see its members as individuals. It seems to be a system, a kind of machine plowing through the tropical vegetation.

The machine then shifts gears. The leader of the procession slows and unsheathes his machete. Okonkwo can be seen in the background turn- ing away and modulating his gait. The expedition walks off screen, to the right, while Okonkwo, holding no weapon, slowly fills the right half of the frame. The image then cuts to a high-angle shot of the pot on Ikeme- funa's head. The man behind Ikemefuna swings his machete, missing the boy's head and knocking him and the pot to the ground. "Father, they have killed me," Ikemefuna shouts. There is a brief shot of one of the men looking down, presumably at Ikemefuna, before the image cuts to a me- dium shot, quickly zooming to a close-up, as one man turns around, ma- chete raised, and Okonkwo, just beyond him, swings his machete swiftly toward the ground. The song on the sound track, a minor-key hybrid of Igbo folk-style flute and funk-rock bass, which has escorted the expedi- tion all the way through the forest, suddenly freezes; then two bass pulses ring out, one for each swing of the machete. Okonkwo raises his blade chest-high and stares at it, eyes bulging (see figure 5.1). The camera slowly zooms back as the words of Ezeudu, the elder who advised Okonkwo not to join the expedition, echo across the sound track: "That boy calls you father. Do not bear a hand in his death." Of course, Ezeudu's voice is au- dible only to Okonkwo and spectators. In the novel the narrator explains that Okonkwo drew his machete and cut Ikemefuna down because "he was afraid of being thought weak."[23] However, Edochie's Okonkwo is part of a machine and simply acts, after which—in a moment of free indirect subjectivity, not present in the novel—he is given the opportunity to

FIGURE 5.1. *Things Fall Apart* (NTA miniseries). Okonkwo looks upon his machete while hearing Ezeudu's voice in his head.

reflect. In fact, where the novel simply jumps to Okonkwo's arrival back at his homestead, the television version expands considerably on Okonkwo's unfolding subjective experience of guilt.

The NTA adaptation of *Things Fall Apart* has received very little scholarly attention, a symptom presumably of its limited availability, at least until recently. Four articles examining the adaptation were published between 2010 and 2015, two of which mention—and do little more than that—the next key scene of free indirect subjectivity, a spectacular sequence that follows the image of Okonkwo's bulging eyes fixed on his bloodied machete.[24]

The screen fades to black, and then a diagonal wipe reveals that night has fallen on the forest. The expedition of Umuofian men proceeds past a group of curious figures, dressed all in white, without acknowledging their presence. As Okonkwo wearily plods into the center of the frame, his shadow falls across them. Suddenly, a shriek rings out, and a bright light shines on Okonkwo, against which he defensively raises his hands. The image then cuts to a blinding lens flare, seemingly shot from Okonkwo's point of view, after which he is once again shown, in third person, recoiling from its assault. The shrouded figures begin to dance, and the image cuts to a medium shot as they move into formation.

FIGURE 5.2. *Things Fall Apart* (NTA miniseries). Spirits of the wild appear to Okonkwo.

They all seem to be girls, adorned in expressionist costumes implying they are spirits.[25] On their heads are white lace hoods, and over their bodies are white lace robes, material flowing from their necks to their wrists and down to the ground so that as they move their arms, the effect suggests wings, like moths in the moonlight (see figure 5.2). Howls and shrieks continue ringing out, and the spirits form a circle around Okonkwo, who brandishes his machete. Then a muddled chant rises from the chorus of girls:

> Okonkwo, who spilled the blood of he that called him father, shall we show him mercy?
> Okonkwo, the gods trusted you, honored you.
> Now blood, death, doom. Blood for blood, death for death, doom for doom.

The spirits repeat their chant in different iterations, with increasing amounts of reverb distorting the sound track. Several shots reveal that they not only surround Okonkwo but are scattered throughout the forest. The other Umuofian men are nowhere to be seen. In close-up, Okonkwo is shown cowering from the admonitions of the spirits. And when their chant finally ends, they flap away into the darkness, allowing Okonkwo to stand and recompose himself. As he does, the image blurs and sharpens as if reflecting his own confused sight and then cuts to Ikemefuna's natal compound, where news of his death has already spread. Several women are crying, and a crowd gathers. Ikemefuna's mother, played by Nelly Uchendu—a renowned Igbo highlife and gospel singer—performs a dirge, in which the other women participate. Françoise Ugochukwu describes it as a "Gregorian responsory" that provides greater access to the physical spaces and affective inner lives of women than does Achebe's source text.[26] The dirge concludes the seventh episode of the series, and the eighth begins where chapter 8 of the novel begins, with Okonkwo, lying in his *obi*, drunk and depressed.

The spectacle of the spirits resolutely defies Achebe's commitment to a modernist version of realism. Achebe's slightly untrustworthy narrator regularly mentions the supernatural beliefs of various characters but does so dispassionately, often questioning their validity while simultaneously explaining their social significance. Perhaps the spirits in the television adaptation represent Okonkwo's conscience, much like the white-robed ghosts of Merit, Abigail, and Victoria, who represent the consciences of Andy, Osita, and Zed. But the NTA's spirits also sit in divine judgment over Okonkwo, promising blood for blood, which suggests they are fully supernatural. At no other point in the series are such forces depicted, and Achebe certainly never includes them in his novels. The girls are therefore spectacularly unique, the only spirits made manifest in the entire narrative. Of course, Achebe's novel begins with a reference to one spirit, with which the founder of Umuofia wrestled, giving that particular class of supernatural figures—spirits of the wild—mythical connotations. The fact that on television, similarly mythical figures, also appearing in the forest, haunt Okonkwo in the immediate aftermath of Ikemefuna's sacrifice may suggest that his act rocks the very foundations of the society. Likewise, the fact that spirits of the wild appear exclusively to Okonkwo confirms his status as a kind of epic hero; they also confirm the primordial sources of power that both authorize success and foment failure in the world of the story. But if the NTA version is ultimately concerned with anticolonial nationalism and if Okonkwo fails to rally others to that cause, then the spirits suggest that Umuofia's gods—whose vindictive plans they pronounce: "blood for blood"—are either responsible for the advent of colonialism or allow Okonkwo's revolution to fail. Perhaps this is why he kills himself: not to become a martyr, precisely, but to appease angry gods and save his society. In 1958, when Achebe's novel was published—two years before Nigerian independence—the future of anticolonial nationalism was not entirely clear. However, there was plenty to be wary about in the transition from colony to sovereign nation-state. By 1985, when the NTA adaptation aired, the struggle against imperialism and the discovery of oil had produced a powerful, overdeveloped state that although it had not been able to raise the living conditions of most of its people, still represented—or wanted to continue representing—the glimmer of true national sovereignty. And if Okonkwo is the epic hero of the story, if he is the embodiment of the political community, then he is, if nothing else, the sovereign, the one in whom mythic potentiality is invested for good or for ill.

The two moments of free indirect subjectivity cited here—one, Ezeudu's words ringing in Okonkwo's ears, and two, Okonkwo's apprehension of the spirits of the wild (achieved through several point-of-view shots)— both of which follow Ikemefuna's death, invite spectators to identify with Okonkwo's subject position in one of his most critical hours. By the time the colonial messenger is dead, as Okonkwo kneels in his compound, praying to his family gods, his subjectivity has become a major site of spectators' experience of the story. Of course, Okonkwo is clearly the center of Achebe's novel as well, but in the print version his experience is almost always mediated by the narrator, sympathetic though that narrator may be to Okonkwo's compensatory, over-masculinized psychology. Indeed, in the novel the torment that Okonkwo feels after killing Ikemefuna is reported, not felt. In the television adaptation, therefore, Okonkwo's persecution and the intersubjective spectatorial experience attached to it make his story hyperbolically social. Every spectator is given access to and thus the network's imagined public is invited to identify with not only the guilt that follows Ikemefuna's killing but also the bereavement associated with slowly losing sovereign authority. The "blood, death, [and] doom" that Ikemefuna's killing invites, according to the spirits of the wild, which then inflect Okonkwo's plea for sovereignty near the end, suggest that although Okonkwo must be sacrificed to appease the gods who "trusted" him, his death will nevertheless ensure that his cause does "remain alive." The result is a kind of severance; Okonkwo the complex, flawed character is disentangled from Okonkwo the shining symbol, which defies Achebe's project but reinforces the state's.

Although most of the television content that aired in the years following the NTA's *Things Fall Apart* was set not in the precolonial past but in the contemporary present, and although the first video films to appear in the early nineties were equally contemporaneous (a fact often attributed to the difficulty of depicting the materiality of an era different from the one in which filming took place), the distant past would return to small screens and become a frequent Nollywood setting beginning in the late 1990s. And as Nollywood explored the precolonial spatiotemporal terrain, it seems to have drawn inspiration from both the imagery and the mode of address that characterize the NTA's adaptation of *Things Fall Apart*.

IGODO: NECROPOLITICS IN THE LAND OF THE LIVING DEAD

Among the many ways to understand the project of Achebe's *Things Fall Apart*, particularly at its moment of original publication, is as an invitation to revisit the advent of colonialism during the advent of nationhood, to reconsider the factors that prevented successful resistance to colonization at a time when the emerging nation-state was turning its attention to impending questions of neocolonization. Achebe's book seems to say that if hypermasculine strongmen failed the first time around — as sympathetic as their eviscerating encounter with outsiders may have made them — perhaps they should be considered with continuing skepticism going forward. Given the masculinist tilt of nationalist discourse, changing gender structures prompted by wage labor and Christianity (see chapter 3), and the nascent barracks culture that, in hindsight, we know to have characterized early postcolonial politics in Nigeria, Achebe's warning — not unlike the unwitting prognostications in his 1966 novel, *A Man of the People* — is remarkably prescient.[27] The very simple point of his first novel, although it is masterfully executed, is to revisit the past in order to think through the problems of the present. The 1986 television adaptation did not tamper with that general project, but it did change the nature of the warning. Rather than an advisory against hypermasculinity, the NTA's version — produced, essentially, by the propaganda arm of the military government — revisits and revives Okonkwo's cause in order to continue his aggressive fight. As far as the national television bureaucracy seems to have been concerned, therefore, citizens of a country that faced increasing pressure and derision from abroad — either through the early structural adjustment programs of the 1980s or the human rights admonitions directed at several of their rulers — should continue to stand tall and demand to be "left to live our lives our own way."

If, however, the television adaptation was bound to Achebe's source text even as it constructed a neoteric form of traditional sovereign authority,

Nollywood has rarely faced such constraints. Edochie's Okonkwo can only imply the concept of sovereignty with his words and deeds; his prostration before the gods suggests a kind of divine right never literally claimed. He is therefore not really a chief or a king. When Nollywood began making films set in the precolonial past, however, two major changes had taken place in the years following Achebe's publication of *Things Fall Apart*, which made chiefs and kings more likely character types. For one, the rapid ascent of the video film industry in the late 1990s afforded many of its central figures a great deal of cultural confidence, and as they pursued new kinds of projects, they were emboldened to push formal and modal boundaries. Thus, when Don Pedro Obaseki set out to write his first precolonial epic — which would become *Igodo: Land of the Living Dead* (1999) — he could confidently select from a range of cultural, narrative, and filmic resources, creating characters drawn from wellsprings as varied as modern Yoruba cultural production — including novels such as those by D. O. Fagunwa and films such as those by Hubert Ogunde — as well as Edo and Igbo oral traditions, not to mention the prevailing small-screen visual repertoire generated by the NTA's *Things Fall Apart*.[28] This kind of fearless bricolage allowed video filmmakers to craft not only novel character types but even novel social institutions. Secondly, as Axel Harneit-Sievers argues, the social institution of "traditional ruler," particularly in the Igbo case, had steadily grown in size, prominence, and esteem since the 1970s because of government decree and adjudication.[29] Indeed, a long process of inventing the concept of Igbo kingship quite simply flourished in the oil-boom years. Thus, where the NTA's *Things Fall Apart* was constrained by Achebe's vision of political power, which was itself constrained by a sense of fidelity to certain aspects of history, as well as the context of its publication — which took place long before the explosion of Igbo chieftaincy offices — Nollywood was free to explore changing and imaginative ideas about indigenous social authority.[30]

   Igodo is an important film not only because it is essentially the seminal Nollywood fantasy epic but also because it does more than invent a set of characters and institutions; it offers a kind of reflection on (not of) the process of nativizing postcolonial political authority. It opens with an image of lightning striking from a blue sky. A priest of Amadioha, the Igbo thunder god, stands on a hill, dressed in animal skins, looking down upon a small village. The camera looks over his shoulder, zooming in to take a closer look at the community, which is really just a small clearing in the savannah with a few round, thatched buildings and several inhabitants. After a series of establishing shots in the village, the image cuts to a close-up of a woman in labor. She screams so loud that, cutting back to the priest, he can hear her from his hill. He then descends to the village (lightning still striking all around), locates the newborn, and carries him away. The villagers automatically celebrate, suggesting that the priest's spiritual authority is at once also political, that he has an absolute right to take a newborn child. Later, spectators learn that the child has been named Iheukwumere and that he is considered a gift from the gods, "destined to become igwe of the land." Therefore, the film sets out to fix the anachronistic concept of the igwe and attach to it a discourse of divine right. *Igodo* was preceded by a handful of historical epics, including *The Battle of Musanga* and *King Jaja of Opobo*, but *Igodo*—a much more inventive film, inspired by legends—was a smash hit, effectively launching the "cultural epic" genre, which has thrived in several different forms ever since.[31] However, the central problematic of *Igodo* is not simply the establishment of a divine right to rule but the challenges faced by the throne, which can have ramifications reverberating down through the generations.

In the world of the film, knowledge of Iheukwumere's divine right comes from none other than Pete Edochie, who plays a precolonial *dibia* (diviner). However, he is not simply a character in the film but also one of its two embedded narrators—the other being Igodo, the eponymous hero of the story who recounts the events in which Edochie's character is featured. Indeed, the film is constructed on a complex temporal scale stretching across approximately one hundred years. The elderly Igodo, living in contemporary Nigeria, is summoned to the court of the local igwe in order to shed light on a spate of mysterious deaths that have befallen children in the community. Igodo has an edifying epic story to tell of a similar set of calamities that struck the same community fifty years before and the quest that he and six other men completed to resolve it. In those days, he recounts, the prominent men of the village also gathered at the igwe's palace to seek a solution. And it is there, a flashback establishes, that the town's most revered dibia, Edochie's character, tells the story of Iheukwumere, whose life and death another fifty years in the past has determined the tragic fate of their village, Umuoka.

As Edochie's character explains, Iheukwumere was born and lived in a community far away, "across the mountains of Arochukwu" (ostensibly, the village shown in the film's opening sequence). He came from a poor family, and his divine claim to the throne therefore rankled some of the village elders, who attempted to kill him. As Edochie's dibia narrates the story, Iheukwumere escapes from those bloodthirsty elders and is found in the forest by a hunter from Umuoka who raises him to be a great hunter himself, and thus a very wealthy man by the standards of the day. In Umuoka, therefore, Iheukwumere once again finds himself on track to become igwe, which once again offends local elites. Seven men conspire to frame him for stealing "the igwe's staff of office," a crime punishable by death. Iheukwumere is subsequently convicted and executed in an unmistakably messianic passion play, inviting the wrath of his father—Amadioha, the thunder god—who condemns the people of Umuoka to lose their own children in an unending cycle of inexplicable fatalities. However, the dibia played by Edochie is quite powerful, and he divines a solution to the community's problem. They must retrieve Amadioha's blade, which is kept in a distant shrine, and use it to cut down the large old tree that has grown on Iheukwumere's grave, near the igwe's courtyard. Seven men are chosen to atone for the original crime committed by seven men. Among them is Igodo, known for his flute music, who is played by Norbert Young (the second actor to play Professor Eno in *Checkmate*, discussed in chapter 3). Also chosen is Egbunna, a hunter, played by Sam Dede, hero of the vigilante genre (discussed in chapter 4). The bulk of the story consists of their quest, which proceeds through a number of evil forests in which the men face an array of obstacles that claim various members of their party. Some of the obstacles they encounter include "children of the night" (who recall the spirits of the wild from the NTA's *Things Fall Apart*) and "Ijima," the "twins of death," a sculpture erected in the middle of the forest through which each man must pass. The sculpture used in the film is, in fact, one of several modernist works of Yoruba religious art constructed by Susanne Wenger inside the sacred grove of Osun, near Osogbo.[32] Using Wenger's work in this way, the film further surveys a fantasy terrain, taking well-known symbols of indigenous religion created by a European convert and fashioning them into the ruins of an ancient social system. When the blade's location is finally reached, only three of the men remain: Igodo, Egbunna, and Agu (Charles Okafor). The priest of the shrine demands one of their lives in sacrifice to Amadioha, and after a short debate, Egbunna is chosen. On the way back Agu is destroyed by an evil spirit, meaning that Igodo is the only survivor. He presents the blade to the igwe, and the story of Umuoka's suffering ends—as a tribute, they change the name of the town to Umu-Igodo. And as the long flashback concludes, the elderly Igodo—who has become a hermit—suggests that the recent string of deaths derives from a new offense against Amadioha. Thus, it is not precisely the sins of the past that haunt the present; rather, it is only through knowledge of the past that the sins of the present can be apprehended. Like *Things Fall Apart*, the film conceptualizes history less as a source of contemporary problems than as a storehouse of knowledge from which solutions to contemporary problems might be retrieved.

That storehouse, however, is crammed with myths. Rather than retrieve knowledge of Igbo republicanism, *Igodo* elaborately establishes the contrived idea that if a true ruler, one chosen by the gods, is cheated of the throne, the result will be enduring political instability. The seat of power therefore becomes a noble, unquestioned, axiomatic feature of the social landscape. It is not the office that is rotten but the one who occupies it. Likewise, Egbunna's heroic, epic self-sacrifice—as several critics are wont to mention—seems to serve as a parable for postcolonial leadership. His devotion to the quest, the aid he offers to other men, and his reluctance to seek personal glory are read as standards by which contemporary politicians ought to measure themselves. Indeed, most published analyses of the film focus on the idea that *Igodo* levels a critique at the Nigerian political class's renowned veniality. As Ayakoroma writes,

> The predominant theme in *Igodo* is sacrificial leadership, as reflected in the character of Egbuna (Sam Dede). It is common knowledge that Nigeria has been in search of selfless leadership since independence. . . . Egbuna is portrayed as an unwilling leader, who is virtually forced to assume a leadership position. In other words, he is not overambitious by nature and does not take delight in perpetuating himself in office. Once he accepts the mantle of leadership, he goes all out to ensure the fulfillment of his responsibility as an ideal leader. When the time comes for one of the three survivors to pay the supreme price, through personal sacrifice, Egbuna gladly offers to do that to show that leadership is all about service and sacrifice.[33]

Egbunna may assume leadership of the expedition, but he holds little political power in the world of *Igodo*. The group of men he commands is assembled by and completes their expedition on behalf of those with *real* political authority: the igwe, the dibia, and other titled men. Therefore, Egbunna's sacrifice is undertaken in service to the igwe's project, which— it is critical to note—is not concerned with restoring Iheukwumere's bloodline or any other more rightful heir to the throne. In fact, not once in the film is the reorganization of power discussed. Not once is a sitting igwe threatened. When the quest is successfully completed by Igodo, the knife of Amadioha does no more than register and symbolically atone for past crimes. As Igodo holds it aloft, the image cuts to his aged self, the initial narrator, who sits in the palace of the contemporary igwe. "Determine the crime and find the culprit," he tells the igwe's court, "or the sins of the past shall revisit this tribe." Igodo's words suggest that the new spate of deaths is linked to Amadioha and Iheukwumere, that the divine authors of power have once again been offended by human actions and have once again resorted to taking the lives of children. The film ends with the promise of a sequel that was never made, so if the filmmakers had a clear sense of the new crime, we will never know. But the insinuation that Amadioha and his son still exercise power over local politics is the specter that truly haunts the film. More importantly, the offense against them was not committed by the igwe but by other men with lesser social power. The king abides.

The concept of selfless leadership is a nagging problem in many discussions of Nigerian politics. Perhaps the most famous articulation of that sentiment—which in my experience is otherwise widely repeated in local bars, churches, and university lecture halls—comes from the opening line of Achebe's 1983 political and moral treatise *The Trouble with Nigeria*. Indeed, "The trouble with Nigeria is simply and squarely a failure of leadership."[34] Achebe's claim is made against the notion that Nigeria might be composed of ungovernable factions or citizens, which is the general colonialist sentiment often promoted by Euro-American observers. However, what Achebe's claim fails to consider at length is the structural composition of the state, the national economy, and the relation of both to the global economic order. The trouble with Nigeria, we might retort, is that it faces so many troubles, perhaps the most important of which is a political system that has been unable to reorganize itself from its origins as a colonial-extraction enterprise.[35] Many Nigerian leaders may indeed showcase the most obscene forms of greed and corruption, but they also have every structural incentive to do so. Which matters more, we might ask, the configuration of rewards and penalties, the sources of state revenue and methods of its distribution, the system of justice that reacts when public money fails to flow into the proper channels, or the personalities of those who manage the channels? *Igodo* offers a response far more complex than analyses such as Ayakoroma's—which, to reiterate, is typical. As key moments of free indirect subjectivity indicate, to which I will turn momentarily, the indirect subject of the film is what Achille Mbembe calls "necropolitics," the power over conditions of life and death, which is wielded by all sovereign states but in particularly significant ways in postcolonies such as Nigeria.

Power over life and death is such a critical component of sovereignty that it is both unremarkable and extraordinary. Likewise, the depiction of igwes in *Igodo* and other epic video films tends to be so mundane and normative, and so clearly associated with divine power, that it suggests political power derives from forces preceding the constitution of the community, not from the community itself. However, the Nollywood response to such undemocratic power is characterized by neither acceptance nor resistance. The igwe of *Igodo* is, in fact, a very marginal character. In the face of a massive calamity, the community turns its attention to powerful men who epitomize the local division of labor: hunter, farmer, artist, and so forth. Their goal is not to change the configurations of political power, not to question the legitimacy of the authority that puts their lives at risk, but to find a mechanism that will allow the community to cope, to endure, to retain its most basic set of rights—including the right to live—without challenging a system that does not and will not change. Remember, the full title of the film is *Igodo: The Land of the Living Dead*. As Mbembe writes, "To exercise sovereignty is to exercise control over mortality and to define life as the deployment and manifestation of power."[36] In *Igodo* Amadioha represents this power, and the igwe is merely his custodian. And nowhere, perhaps, is Amadioha's power over life and death more spectacularly performed than in an early scene where Egbunna, who will eventually allow himself to die so that the rest of the community may live, decides to join the expedition.

The idea that Egbunna has no political ambition, promoted by several critics, derives from the fact that in the beginning Egbunna is reluctant to join the expedition. However, that reluctance is selfish. When emissaries from the royal court tell Egbunna that the gods and the igwe have demanded his participation in the expedition, he responds, "The gods? The igwe? Where were those cronies and crooks in the council of the igwe when they took my father's land . . . and gave it to Nwoke! Where were they?" There is no further elaboration of this land dispute, but key here is Egbunna's lack of interest in the plight that his neighbors face. He does not consider the igwe's power legitimate, so he wonders why he should contribute to the igwe's authority, even when the lives of his neighbors' children are at stake. It is only when his own son dies that Egbunna reluctantly joins the expedition. The scene is pivotal.

As Egbunna begins to send the igwe's emissaries away, one of his children comes running with terrible news about Dume, Egbunna's eldest son. Egbunna grabs his gun and takes off, while his wife, Mgbeke (played by Rita Edochie, sister-in-law to Pete Edochie), comes out of the house wailing and collapses in the dirt. When Egbunna returns, holding Dume's lifeless body in his arms, several of the villagers who have gathered around Mgbeke report that while he was gone, she has been "seeing things." She points to the sky. And then an over-the-shoulder shot establishes that what she sees is the image of a white ram in the clouds (see figure 5.3). The image cuts to a medium, high-angle shot of the gathered crowd, establishing the spatial context and the arrangement of bodies in the scene, before returning to Mgbeke. At that point the narration is handed over to the on-screen subjects. A close-up of Mgbeke's face, immediately followed by another shot of the sky—with the spotless white ram now clearer than before—makes it plain that spectators are being invited to see with her eyes.

The image then cuts to a close-up of Egbunna's face, which is also immediately followed by a shot of the sky; however, no white ram appears in what is clearly supposed to be his field of vision (see figure 5.4). Egbunna's sight may be offered up for subject identification, but the distinction between what he sees and what his wife sees serves to build the case that Egbunna is blind to the workings of power. According to Isidore Diala, a white ram is the avatar of Amadioha in Igbo cosmology, and Amadioha is also commonly associated with the sun, meaning that what Mgbeke can see in the sky is the very power that opens the film, the same power that offers Iheukwumere to the people, the same power that has been defied

FIGURE 5.3. *Igodo*. Mgbeke sees the white ram in the sun.

by political corruption and therefore demands compensation.[37] Egbunna may not be able to see it, but he knows what Mgbeke's vision means. He turns and surveys the crowd, muttering to himself, "The white ram. The white ram." And then the shot-counter-shot sequences play out several more times: in one case a computer-generated lens flare sweeps across the frame as Egbunna looks skyward, suggesting that although he looks intently upon the sun, he cannot see the god. (It also recalls the lens flare that Edochie's Okonkwo sees when the spirits of the wild hail him.) Egbunna falls to his knees and cries out, "Amadioha!" Seeing, apparently, is not necessary for believing.

These instances of free indirect subjectivity attend the fulcrum of Egbunna's political subjection, the space between his initial denunciation of the igwe's divine right and his eventual acceptance of that right. It is not that the igwe kills Dume—therefore making Egbunna relent—but that Dume's death legitimates the igwe's commandment, and Egbunna must comply. Ayakoroma and others read the ram as a symbol of Egbunna's fate, his eventual self-sacrifice—rams are favored sacrificial offerings—but that strikes me as a strained reading, an attempt to link an interpretation of Egbunna as the story's hero with what is otherwise a clearly significant but also ambiguous and potentially confusing scene that is clouded by special effects.[38] Diala's insights about Igbo cosmological symbolism provide an Ockham's razor with which to cut through the

FIGURE 5.4. *Igodo*. Egbunna sees no white ram in the sun.

confusion. However, the fact that Egbunna cannot see the ram remains completely unexplained in either the extant scholarship or the ethnographic archive. Perhaps his wife is more attuned to such things. Or perhaps the standard reading of the film provides unintended insights.

Egbunna's heroism is a compromise, an example of what might just be the best that the society can hope for under far less than ideal circumstances. To begin with, his initial unwillingness to join the quest comes not from humility but from political resentment. He simply does not recognize a web of connections involving himself, his community, and political power, or at least the current bearers of that power. He is not interested in atoning for the community's past sins. He joins the expedition simply to redress his own son's death. As such, his assessment of power emphasizes the categories of individual and interpersonal relations rather than structural conditions. The fact that the film's use of free indirect subjectivity invites spectators to identify with him may explain why he is so easily elevated to the status of hero. And as the expedition commences, he certainly does assume a seemingly heroic leadership role. After all, he is a hunter, not only strong but also familiar with the forest and the occult energy that obtains therein. More than anyone else, he is confident in that terrain. Yet his sights never rise above the level of the individual and the interpersonal. One of Egbunna's most sagacious lines is a call for unity in which he invokes the proverbial broom, an object made of many thin and easily broken fronds that, when tied together, become nearly indestructible. However, brooms are not interwoven and interconnected objects; they are assemblages of individual, constituent parts gathered together by one force, one band of leather or cloth, but not otherwise linked. Egbunna believes himself to be the strongest of those constituents. Like a military commander, therefore, he pushes the group relentlessly forward. He rescues his men from danger. And in the end, his messianic self-sacrifice—the second such moment in the film—reads as the culmination of his domineering courage. Indeed, there is a presumptuous hubris in the idea that he makes the *best* possible offering to Amadioha. "I am the leader. I am leading here!" he yells at Igodo when the auspicious moment arrives. Like Achebe's assessment of "the trouble with Nigeria," therefore, *Igodo* is a film that fantasizes about a leader in the image of the late General Murtala Muhammed, the military head of state who lasted one short but somehow fondly remembered year in office before he was assassinated during an attempted coup in 1976. Achebe refers to Muhammed as "ruthless" but also "no-nonsense," traits he comes just short of praising, while nevertheless describing Muhammed's

uncanny ability to discipline the country's infamously "unruly" character as "miraculous." The impulse to not only identify with but also lionize
Egbunna therefore comes across as sympathy for the kind of hard-nosed,
top-down, no-nonsense leadership that Nigeria's military government
repeatedly claimed but rarely succeeded in actually providing to its citizens. *Igodo* was released near the very end of military rule in Nigeria, and
Egbunna's disappearance into the cave of Amadioha recalls Muhammed's
disappearance from (public) life—and entry into legend—in the back of
a black Mercedes-Benz.[39] So why can Egbunna not see the ram?

Egbunna cannot see the ram because he cannot see power for what it
really is. Yes, he does *believe*, but he does not *know*. The film may be a com-
mercially successful, hair-raising action adventure that celebrates masculine self-confidence, but its indirect subjects are political legitimacy and
individual subjectivity. What haunts the contemporary world, the world
of the aged Igodo—which frames the story of Egbunna and his quest on
behalf of the igwe of Umuoka—is a contradiction between structural and
individual power. Amadioha and his aggrieved son, Iheukwumere, have
a hold on Umu-Igodo and will not let go. Mgbeke—Egbunna's wife, who
can see the ram—knows the truth. And we cannot forget that spectators
are offered a chance to identify with her too. The scene of the white ram,
in which the subjectivity of the film narration freely jumps from narrator
to Mgbeke to Egbunna over and over again, thus provides the aperture
though which the film's themes pass. At stake is a conception of the political sphere in which various associations between stratospheric power
and personal agency can be apprehended. Or as Siân Silyn Roberts, writing about differences between the British and American gothic traditions
of the eighteenth and nineteenth centuries, claims, "Nothing less than
the definition of the individual and its claims to moral authority are at
stake."[40]

For Roberts, the gothic is a mode concerned with the extraction of a
modern, autonomous subject from the dark labyrinths of tradition. She
argues that the past haunts the early British gothic novel because the project of extracting individuality from feudalism is incomplete. In antebel-
lum American gothic novels, however, political subjectivity is unfinished
in a different way. It is under construction—on a new lot (which has been
violently *cleared*), as it were—and the nature of the links between individuals or the degree to which they form a political community, if at all, must
be painstakingly thought through. In Nigeria, at the end of the twentieth
century, a similar process of constructing political subjectivities is also at
work, but the question is less about crafting a political community than it

is about (re)claiming space for the constitution of a modern subject. The scene with the ram in *Igodo* establishes that although some people think they have the individual characteristics necessary for leading the community to full sovereignty, others know that sovereignty is a relation, one between in here and out there, between emergent and enduring forms of power, between life and death.

Mbembe's discussion of necropolitics cites Georges Bataille to make the argument that a sovereign, a king, is one to whom the normal limits represented by death do not apply: the sovereign is the one who can violate taboos. In *Igodo* the igwes sit on the sidelines, sending others to their deaths in the name of the community. From a necropolitical perspective, therefore, Egbunna cannot represent sovereignty because he does not defy death. Indeed, for Mbembe the power to defy death takes one of its most spectacular forms through the institutions of colonialism, in which a select few Europeans claimed the right to kill and not be killed, to wage war and expect no retaliation, no recognition of their inhumanity. Indeed, the colonizer, having destroyed people's lives, expected to be greeted with awe and appreciation for supposedly bringing greater humanity to the world. The postcolony inherited the colonial disposition, but Mbembe notes that those necropolitics have now given way to a new form, beginning in the late twentieth century, in which militias, dissidents, and terrorists claim power over death in life. Indeed, theirs is the power to make death apparent where others have already established it, where it is already a fact: in the land of the living dead. Ultimately, the space for agency in this necropolitical landscape comes in the form of control over one's own death. Summarizing Martin Heidegger, Mbembe writes that "one is free to live one's own life only because one is free to die one's own death."[41] At the end of the day, therefore, necropolitics is a normative description of modernity. What makes the histories of slavery, colonialism, and postcolonial terrorism into states of exception, as it were, is the fact that the relational nature of sovereignty—one's right to live one's path to death—is so overdetermined, so dominated by both internal dynamics and external relations.[42] Although Mgbeke may be able to glimpse these relations, Egbunna cannot.

To return to Olaniyan's discussion of Fela, modernity can only be a "catalyst for further striving," particularly in a place like Nigeria, if it can provide the foundations for subject formation that he describes as "authentic." Here, authenticity does not necessarily mean unreconstructedly *indigenous*: it is not some kind of reductive nativism or categorical opposition to the foreign, although it does invoke a kind of autonomy that has been lost through the modern, capitalist processes of slavery, colonialization, and cultural imperialism. Of course, all subjects lack certain forms of autonomy, but in the African case, subjection appears to be doubled, to include not just the *normal* forces of subjection but also a "'forced necessity' . . . to capitulate, appropriate, or borrow."[43] Therefore, "authentic subjectivity" names a kind of politics in which the individual is constituted in relation to structures of power but those structures are not themselves "dominated" and subordinated to other forms of power.

What qualifies as gothic in the modalities on display in the NTA's adaptation of *Things Fall Apart* and the Nollywood video film *Igodo: The Land of the Living Dead* is therefore a sense of authentic subjectivity, a sovereign space beyond the history of colonialism, in which enabling subject positions might be constituted. In *Things Fall Apart*, of course, the colonial project arrests that process, but where Achebe's novel advocates moving forward, claiming new forms of sovereignty, the state television version advocates for the reclamation of sovereignty lost. *Igodo* seems to be invested in both projects. As such, it reveals the antinomies inherent to the very concept of sovereignty. For although sovereignty implies autonomy, it cannot exist, like subjectivity, without its outside, without its recognition by other sovereign entities. Nor can it exist without the kind of death that makes life possible. In *Igodo* all of these tensions condense in the figure of the igwe, the sovereign who makes the community sovereign, yet his position depends on Amadioha, on a power beyond himself that controls life and death. Perhaps Amadioha is the necropolitical sovereign, turning the igwe into a mostly silent, unnecessary figurehead. Therefore, using the igwe character to reclaim some kind of pure sovereignty cannot be achieved in the end. The strongest, most ruthless men in the society may do their best to cope, but the god of a distant shrine maintains dominance. And it is this fundamental problematic, this fact of African modernity—the need for a sense of sovereignty that is definitionally impossible—which remains unfinished, which haunts Nollywood's gothic mode. It is the ruins of what never existed through which the mode's heroes trek.

THE BLOODY MACHETE

In *Igodo* the two igwes—one in the film's past and one in its present—are underdeveloped characters. We know that they cannot come from Iheukwumere's bloodline, but then again it is not clear that bloodline really even matters. As is the case with Igbo social titles, perhaps the two have been elevated to the throne simply by acquiring wealth and establishing strong social networks. In other Nollywood epics, however, the office of igwe is clearly hereditary. As a form of conclusion and a relational way to fully understand *Igodo*, I now turn to two epics that are more or less constructed on the *Igodo* model of sovereign fantasy, although they feature gothic obsessions with the subject of primogeniture. The first, *Egg of Life* (2003, dir. Andy Amenechi), was produced by OJ Productions, the same company that made *Igodo*, and its modal innovations essentially derive from replacing the members of the original expedition with female characters. The second, *Red Machet* (2000, dir. Zeb Ejiro), depicts family intrigue in a context where the igwe's bloodline is nearly sacrosanct, as well as the assertion of sovereignty that arises when two neighboring communities clash. As I consider these two films, I also want to hold on to the idea that *Things Fall Apart* exercises a form of influence over Nollywood epics that may run even deeper than the NTA's adaptation.

In *Egg of Life*, Pete Edochie plays the igwe, to whom spectators are introduced on the day of his first son's birth. Edochie intones, "My son, you will remain the blessed of the gods. You shall lack nothing. You will rule over your people. You will succeed me on the throne. The wishes of the people you rule over shall always remain your command. And may the gods make your reign fruitful." Unfortunately, the prince, Ikemefuna, is an *ogbanje*, a spirit trapped in cycles of death and rebirth. Others like him who dwell in the afterlife beckon Ikemefuna to join them. They are costumed just like the "children of the night" from *Igodo*, who are themselves reminiscent of the spirits of the wild from *Things Fall Apart*. They exert strong control over his fate, and the only solution is for seven maidens to retrieve something called the "egg of life" from the "land of the living dead." The expedition proceeds much like the one in *Igodo*, with only two survivors left after the egg has been secured. They refer to the egg as their "destiny," suggesting that their heroism is sublimated to the fate of the prince. That prince, once again, is Ikemefuna, ogbanje, son of Pete Edochie's character, who is the sovereign of the village. The task that the girls must complete, indeed the reason they find themselves trekking along a forest path, is therefore the resurrection of Ikemefuna.

In a fine and productive reading of Achebe's *Things Fall Apart*, Neil Ten Kortenaar writes that Ikemefuna "resembles nothing so much as an *ogbanje*, one of the spirit children whose home is in another world to which, however much they are loved in this world, they inevitably return." Recall that the first chapter of Achebe's novel ends by foreshadowing Ikemefuna's death, as if it is the heart of the story. Recall also that Okonkwo is

the one who kills Ikemefuna. And recall that Pete Edochie plays the role
of Okonkwo in the NTA's version of *Things Fall Apart*. Finally, recall
that Okonkwo cuts down the court messenger with that same machete
that killed Ikemefuna, wipes blood on the sand, and walks to his own
death. Kortenaar argues that *Things Fall Apart* is essentially the story of
filicide; Okonkwo kills his (adopted) son, but he also kills his own childhood, just as Achebe kills the childhood from which he had to escape—a
childhood enthralled to Western letters—in order to become Africa's
most celebrated novelist. For Kortenaar, filicide signals Achebe's commitment to constructing an enabling postcolonial subjectivity, but we
might also note that it constitutes a decisive split with, even a requiem
for, what Olaniyan calls "authentic subjectivity." As Kortenaar phrases it,
Achebe, like other modern Nigerians, "has had to learn that the world
with himself at the centre has not always been what it is now and that
it has been gravely wounded. The child who knows himself to be at the
centre of the world may actually be closer to the precolonial experience,
when Umuofia was at the centre of its own world, than the old man who
feels the world has become radically decentred."[44] Therefore, the urge to
(re)claim authentic subjectivity may be the urge to atone for, or perhaps
even prevent, Okonkwo's machete from descending twice on Ikemefuna's
head and destroying childhood. There may be a shadow of that urge driving the men of *Igodo* into the forest to recover Amadioha's magical blade.
Perhaps there is a shadow of that urge driving seven maidens into the
forest to bring Ikemefuna back.

Expeditions through forest paths are common storytelling devices,
not only in Nollywood epics but in epic stories throughout the world.
They are amenable to readings that find their inspiration, among other
places, in the work of Joseph Campbell.[45] However, in *Red Machet*, which I
would like to link to *Things Fall Apart*, the epic quest is only a small part of
the story, which is otherwise primarily concerned not only with primogeniture but also with opposing sovereignties. Akunna (Zac Orji), first son of a
recently deceased igwe (Moses Osuji), must kill a lion in the forest, using
the town's legendary red machete, in order to ascend to the throne. When
he successfully commits the sacred act, his blade glows a brilliant crim-
son. But Akunna's younger half-brother, Okoro (Prince James Uche), conspires against Akunna and eventually frames him for the death of a nearby
village's princess. The igwe of the second village, Okeke (Alex Usifo), takes
Akunna into custody and arranges his execution. On a second important
trek into the forest, Okeke's men take Akunna to the spot where, according to the court messenger, named Ogele (Sam Onwuka), "He who lives by

the sword dies by the sword." In other words, they must trek deep into the forest to execute him. However, Ogele the accuser is one of the conspirators who have framed Akunna, an injustice demanding reparations. So when the appointed executioner approaches Akunna, machete in hand, the screen cuts to a first-person shot from the executioner's point of view. The camera moves toward Akunna, who cries out, "I am innocent!" And then the image cuts to a close-up of Akunna's neck as the machete descends, but as soon as it touches his skin, it stops, and a clap of thunder rings out. Ogele falls to the ground clutching his neck, where a huge laceration has suddenly appeared. In the end all is sorted out, and the brothers are reconciled. Free indirect subjectivity is used only sparingly, but to powerful effect. Spectators are given this brief chance to identify with the executioner, the machete wielder, precisely at the moment that the gods intervene to prevent the killing of an innocent man. Indeed, the execution is deflected by the gods onto the man who truly deserves it. What haunts *Red Machet*, much like the knife of Amadioha that haunts *Igodo*, is the potentiality of the blade, the killing machine that authorizes power. But here the gods have perfected the killing machine. Rather than a symbol of capricious power, the machete has been fashioned into a sign of justice. But what happens when we link the executioner's machete from *Red Machet* to all the others? What happens syntagmatically when we link each of these stories through paradigmatic substitutions of the bloody, red machete?

Perhaps no other story in the history of modern Nigeria illustrates the concept of "hauntology" better than *Things Fall Apart*. Coined by Jacques Derrida, *hauntology* plays with the idea that being, that the here and now, is folded onto its past and its future—in French pronunciation, of course, *hauntology* is a near-homophone of *ontology*.[46] According to Derrida, to understand what we are or that we exist is to understand that we exist out of time, out of place. Modernity is haunted, he suggests, by futures that have never come to pass, by prognostications from our past that will never materialize. Likewise, in 1958, when Achebe published *Things Fall Apart*, he sought to reflect upon the future by telling the story of an invented past. He created an isolated village on the cusp of redefining patriarchal power and then subjected it to a modern reality about which it suspiciously had no prior knowledge. In 1986 the postcolonial Nigerian government retold Achebe's story but subjected its hero, Edochie's Okonkwo, to forms of supernatural power in which he had never shown any interest before. The NTA made Okonkwo into a divinely ordained if interrupted sovereign, creating the possibility for a new conception of a past that never was. That past would become an enduring site of Nollywood storytelling, a place to sort through the paradoxes of sovereignty that have long characterized Nigeria's modern present. The future of Nigeria, Nollywood seems to suggest—over and over again, with each new epic film, or at least each new machete—lies in a past that never was. But what if Okonkwo had been able to finish his epic journey? What if he had gone to Mbanta, his motherland, and learned something important about the pitfalls of patriarchy? And what if he had returned to Umuofia a changed man? If *Things Fall Apart* suggests that colonialism interfered with the social and political development not only of Okonkwo but also of southern Nigeria, each of the stories with a paradigmatic relationship to Achebe's novel might be characterized as an attempt to return to and change the arc of that story. The bloody machete, the one that came down on Ikemefuna's head, that came down on the neck of Umuofia's court messenger, may be the same one that lies in the hills of Amadioha, the one that can save the village of Igodo, that can be retrieved to resurrect *Egg of Life*'s Ikemefuna, that constitutes sovereign power in *Red Machet*, and that can never be used corruptly. Put together, these stories suggest that the bloody machete is somehow central to Nigerian ontology and hauntology, that to *be* in modern Nigeria is to be haunted by Okonkwo's bloody machete.

This, of course, obscures the reality that to *be* in modern Nigeria *also* means to be haunted by what Achebe dubs the "iron horse," the bicycle that the first missionary rode into Abame, Umuofia's neighboring village. It is the machinery of modernity that brought so much misery to West Africa. However, the fact that there are no iron horses—no signs of modernity—in *Igodo*, *Egg of Life*, or *Red Machet* suggests that Nollywood is less interested in critiquing the machinery of modernity than Achebe was. Colonialism and its iron horses may be hauntological facts of modern Africa, but Nollywood's local address focuses attention on red, bloody machetes instead. That is, Nollywood seems to be much less concerned with the machinations of capitalism and colonialism or the sins of modernity than it is with the sins of various Okonkwos. This is not to say that video films blame Nigerians for the nation's failures—although something of Achebe's formulation in *The Trouble with Nigeria* certainly endures—but Nollywood, like state television, addresses its public where it is. It may be the case that colonialism came from and produced a world where some people—White, Western, liberal—seem to enjoy a form of authentic subjectivity. And that form of subjectivity may be constructed on the rubble left behind by a war on African subjectivity; it may be cobbled together from material and human resources stolen from places such as

Nigeria. And Nollywood's gothic mode of address may implicitly concede those points, but it does so by inventing and exploring an alternative past, one strewn with the ruins of an authentic subjectivity. By inviting their imagined audience into that landscape, to explore it with a sense of both dread and astonishment, Nollywood's gothic epics beckon subjects away from the gates of the liberal world order, acknowledging their indirect subjectivity but perhaps also trying to transcend it.

6 "What's Wrong with 419?"

COMEDY, CORRUPTION, AND CONSPIRATORIAL MIRRORS

When Amaka Igwe launched *Checkmate* in 1991, she claimed that her show would "mirror happenings in our society." Almost twenty years later, Emem Isong, the writer and producer of *Games Women Play*, told me, as we sat in her office: "I mirror society" (on both moments, see chapter 3). Likewise, in an article that is not about any particular Nollywood film, genre, or mode but rather about the industry's cumulative representational power, Chukwuma Okoye argues that Nollywood constitutes a form of "looking at ourselves in our mirror."[1] I could go on and on. Nollywood people—both inside the industry and around it—regularly suggest that video films reflect something about their spectators back to them.

But screen media are not mirrors. When spectators view screen media narratives, they do not perceive themselves—just something perhaps *similar* to themselves. Even the actor who watches their own film does not look upon themselves in the moment of looking, as one ostensibly does in a mirror. Instead, the screen is a repository for images of conceptual others, objects upon whom the spectator-subject looks long after the fact. Regardless of these "facts," however, several film theorists have suggested that screen media may indeed function *like* mirrors. As the spectator-subject regards the screen, the screen also founds the spectator *as a subject* (metaphorically, one might imagine light reflected from a cinema screen onto the face of the viewing subject, making that face visible and therefore constituting it).[2] The French film theorist Christian Metz offers perhaps the most famous line of inquiry in this regard, arguing that the cinema constitutes a kind of incomplete mirror, one that, as he phrases it, "returns us everything but ourselves."[3]

The foundations of Metz's filmic mirror metaphor lie in Jacques Lacan's work on the "mirror stage."[4] In a theory developed primarily by the observation of infants, Lacan argues that subjectivity is anchored in a misunderstanding of one's ability to regard oneself. A very small child looking in a mirror may see itself as it moves, may realize it controls part of itself, such as an arm or a leg, but makes the mistake of overgeneralizing that observation, thinking it has control over itself as a totality. Likewise, the gaze offered by a great deal of screen media allows the spectator to see only fragments of a world, yet because the spectator identifies with the camera that moves freely through that world, the spectator feels as though they have mastery over the totality of it. Particularly in the case of the standard, omniscient, third-person perspective, screen media—when they want to—allow spectators to go anywhere and see anything. Meanwhile, free indirect subjectivity, from the Lacanian perspective, breaks the mirror of screen media because it creates ambiguity about the subject position of the spectator and whether they have control over the world depicted. Nevertheless, it is the possibility of assuming subjective power in relation to the image—like the mirror that similarly deceives us into thinking we have subjective control over ourselves—that calls for an analogy between screen and mirror. Laura Mulvey has given this hypothesis particularly useful critical substance by explaining that screens tend to invite a masculine gaze, producing a subject position for all spectators, regardless of gender, inscribed within and reproductive of a patriarchal social order.[5] For example, it is by assuming the gaze of the camera, which tends to focus on fragments of female anatomy (rarely the whole) and to assign meaning to those fragments, that subjects of patriarchy are continually (re)founded. Therefore, the cinema *is* like a mirror in the sense that it shows us who we are *in an ideological sense*. But of course we are never just one thing.

In several radical film theories, screen media are often described according to the work they do as part of a technological, social, institutional, and ideological *apparatus*.[6] I have certainly been arguing as much in this book. Nollywood, it seems, functions as part of the total audiovisual and social apparatus of what I have been calling *periliberalism*. However, theorists inspired by Lacan are quick to note that screen media do not automatically and directly produce predictable subjects. The cinema is not, at all times and places, some kind of absolute ideology machine. Nevertheless, even when the subject position that is founded in relationship to screen media is critical or oppositional, it cannot be described as purely resistant. After all, no act of looking at what is presented is an act of total defiance. Indeed, looking is a form of acquiescence to the projection of an image. More importantly, however, there are always many different, often overlapping and competing forms of subjectification bearing upon the look. For example, capitalist subjectification may, from time to time, derive value from promoting certain anti-patriarchal consumer behaviors, inviting a multitude of interlaced subject positions. Therefore, the look may resist *and* reproduce hierarchies at the same time. Even more fundamentally for film theorists inspired by Lacan, subjectification can never be entirely determinate because no position, and thus no method of positioning, is ever final: the meaning of any sign is constantly sliding beneath itself, constantly groping for a signified, never settled. Joan Copjec thus argues the counterintuitive point that if the cinema functions like a mirror, it does so by concealing information. To understand Copjec's argument, we must reconsider how *real* mirrors work.

In the process of gazing upon a reflective surface, the adult spectator will perceive a subject (itself) who is brimming with desires. The reason the subject can detect those desires is that the subject is familiar with itself and moreover knows the powerful force of its desires. Meanwhile, the subject also knows that, given social constraints, many of its desires must be and indeed are concealed from outside observers. Therefore, what we all see when we look at a mirror is a surface beneath which we know, from personal experience, are many hidden meanings. Copjec's argument is that if the screen is like a mirror, then it is not because of what it projects back at us or what it makes us think we can see but because of what it *hides* from us. Perhaps we could say that screens are mirrors to the extent that mirrors are screens.

Subjects founded in relationship to screen media therefore understand, if implicitly, that the cinema, the television, or the liquid crystal display panel lacks a certain amount of representational power: it lacks the ability to show us who we really are. And because subjects understand that the very thing that cannot be represented is somehow defined by desire, they are likewise filled with desire to know what lies beyond the surface of the screen. As Copjec concludes, "The desire that [self-perception] precipitates *transfixes* the subject, albeit in a conflictual place, so that all the subject's visions and revisions, all its fantasies, merely circumnavigate the absence that anchors the subject and impedes its progress. It is this desire that must be reconstructed if the subject is to be changed."[7] To reiterate, Copjec's description of filmic subjectivity foregrounds the idea that screen media cannot fully represent *anything*; furthermore, her description asserts that such a paucity of representational power "anchors the subject," around which fantasies circumnavigate. In the end, screen media may have the capacity to reveal our desires to us and therefore in a very important sense show us who we are, but they do so *not* by direct representation, total mastery, or *reflection*. Rather, screen media offer us the opportunity to gain indirect and peripheral access to the desires from which we are constituted.

In terms of the picture that I have so far been composing over the course of this book about the ways that Nigerian screen media texts address themselves to Nigerian audiences, the convention of free indirect subjectivity might well be considered an effect of or response to the kind of circumnavigating subject position described by Copjec. There seems to be an underlying desire—in Nigeria, as elsewhere—to apprehend the world from different perspectives, for which Nollywood is groping or to which it offers its spectators various openings. Thus, in a very foundational sense Nollywood *is* a mirror of reality, but only to the degree that it is a screen that, having foreclosed on the possibility of fully representing aspects of society or offering total mastery, invites spectators to circumnavigate and glance upon a core set of desires from several angles. Here, the temptation is perhaps just too much to be able to resist invoking Achebe's widely cited description of the relationship between subject and masquerade ("The world is like a Mask dancing. If you want to see it well you do not stand in one place."); however, what I am concerned with here is not how the world can be known but how the world reveals the fullness of its unknowability and, more importantly, its unattainability.[8] According to Copjec's use of the mirror analogy, we might argue that Nollywood is aligned with a set of liberal subject positions—in which, for example, nuclear families with proud breadwinners, arising from sovereign national histories, enjoy the benefits of modernity—but what appears on screen can both offer and withhold visions of that kind of liberalism, as I have been at pains to explain. My ongoing argument is that given the centrality of certain liberal discourses to Nollywood's major modes of address and given that the desires subtending those discourses cannot be fully represented and, more than that, cannot be *fulfilled* until conditions change for many of Nollywood's spectators, video films invite the disavowal and repression of liberal desire, at least for the remainder of what seems like an ongoing interregnum.[9]

There is, however, a tradition of mirroring in Nigerian screen media that complicates the preceding formulation. In this final chapter of the book I turn to comic modes of address, which are featured in a significant number of Nollywood video films as well as several state television programs. In each of the examples I consider, literal mirrors make major appearances in the mise-en-scène, providing very different versions of free indirect subjectivity from those that I have otherwise been describing. In one of Nigeria's most successful television situation comedies, *Basi and Company*, which aired from 1986 to 1990, one particular mirror is frequently and conspicuously used to both signal the concept of vanity and provide analytical depth to the social context within which that vanity operates. Like a secondary narrative perspective—not that of the camera or of any particular character—the mirror in *Basi and Company* quite prosaically shows a different side of the story. It functions like an indirect subjectivity that circumnavigates and provides additional perspectives on the kinds of social processes that have characterized Nigeria's transition from petrostate to debtor nation. Ultimately, however, the circumnavigational mode of address in *Basi and Company* aligns with the formal modalities of state developmentalism precisely because it makes light of and therefore minimizes the possibility of directly apprehending the structural conditions that restrict so many choices in Nigeria. The show's satirical tone is legendary, and it spares no one—including corrupt state bureaucrats—but in the final analysis, *Basi and Company*'s multiperspectival mode of comic address suggests an unsustainable moral equivalence between the corruption of the wealthy, who bend rules to get richer, and the corruption of the poor, who bend rules to eat.

In Nollywood, video films that primarily employ comic modes of address, including critically acclaimed and popular titles such as *Osuofia in London* (2003, dir. Kingsley Ogoro) and *The Master* (2004, dir. Andy Amenechi)—both of which star Nkem Owoh, who was the production manager of, a writer for, and occasional actor in *Basi and Company*—also make remarkable use of mirrors. In both video films, mirrors offer similar circumnavigational access to social norms and problems, but they do so without necessarily offering many perspectives. Instead, the quintessential mirror that appears in Nollywood comedies seems to represent a conspiratorial secondary narrator, an indirect subjectivity that complements and amplifies the satirical and ridiculing voice of the primary narrative perspective. In the case of *Osuofia in London* the two can even merge, offering a singularly scathing reflection on postcolonial subjectivity. Meanwhile, in *The Master* the mirror seems to fracture. An ordinary-looking glass that appears in one early scene, where two brothers engage in an intimate discussion about the corruption to which otherwise honest people must regularly resort, is doubled in the film's climax by representations of video and television technology, a process that I describe in detail near the end of this chapter. Both forms of reflection—the literal mirror and the mirror-like use of visual recording technology—are linked by serving the same critical functions in each scene. Together, they dilate the

aperture of the satire; indeed, rather than focusing on individual behavior, the film's jokes ridicule corruption on a global scale. Thus, where the
circumnavigational mode of address in *Basi and Company* is equivocating,
it becomes expansively populist by the time it makes an appearance in *The
Master*. Both instances seem to address subjects on the periphery of
the liberal world order, but where state television invites its subjects to
tame their expectations, to remain skeptical of their own desires, Nollywood turns the tables: it accuses the liberal world order of greedily preying upon and actively denying modernity to people who not only desire it
but without whom modernity would never have been possible in the first
place. Indeed, comedy may be the most critical of all the modes discussed
in this book.

MADAM'S *PSYCHÉ*: THE EQUIVOCATING MIRROR
IN *BASI AND COMPANY*

Basi and Company was created by Ken Saro-Wiwa, the novelist and environmental activist whose 1995 execution by Sani Abacha's military dictatorship shocked the world. However, it was not only through his activism
and death that Saro-Wiwa called attention to the moral failures of the
Nigerian state. When he fled Biafra at the outbreak of civil war in 1967, he
became a leading voice for national unification and the plight of Nigeria's
ethnic minorities: two closely connected issues. Indeed, the small community of Ogoni speakers from which he hailed in the Niger Delta (what
Rob Nixon calls a "micro-minority") — which tends to have been obscured
in the political and cultural shadows cast by Nigeria's "big three" ethnic
groups (Hausa, Igbo, and Yoruba) — has regularly turned to the national
state for protection and redress.[10] Thus, where Nigerian writers from the
big three have been more ambiguous in their esteem for the postcolonial
state — as concept or fact, aspiration or apparition — Saro-Wiwa repeatedly endorsed strong state power as a bulwark against both internal and
external threats. He also contributed directly to the project of the nation-
state by working as a federal government functionary from time to time
and by publishing novels critical of the secessionist movement. In perhaps the most prominent example of the latter, Saro-Wiwa composed
his widely praised antiwar novel, *Sozaboy*, in a language he referred to as
"rotten English": a version of Nigerian Pidgin. That choice linked a discourse about the inevitability, or at least strategic utility — particularly
for a micro-minority — of English becoming Nigeria's national language, with a critique of the degradation of that language and therefore

the degradation of the national project aligned with it. Regardless, the fact that Saro-Wiwa expressed a preference for strong state power in no way mitigated his antipathy for the havoc the state allowed multinational petroleum corporations to wreak in his hometown. A truly strong state would have offered more protection to his people and to the nation at large. Saro-Wiwa therefore brought an inescapably multidimensional view of many state projects—including Western-style education, the English language, and military power—to his work.

Saro-Wiwa first developed the character of Basi—an indigent, unemployed, but literate and loquacious single man living in Lagos—for a play titled *The Transistor Radio* (which he mounted at the University of Ibadan in 1965, while he was still an undergraduate). He later adapted the stage version for radio and then for television, and finally novelized the content of several television episodes. In Saro-Wiwa's source text, Basi is clearly a trickster figure in a specifically modern sense.[11] He survives in Lagos, where everything is expensive but there are no jobs, by constantly scheming and conning, by using his intelligence and his command of English to extract all sorts of value from the people he encounters daily. Indeed, the Lagos that Saro-Wiwa depicts in the play is hyperbolically corrupt but then only barely so. It is a place that punishes hard work while rewarding wordplay and witticisms. Basi tells his young roommate, Alali, that he once landed a good job in Lagos and was immediately sacked. "What for?" Alali asks. "For getting the job," Basi replies.[12] That absurdity has led Basi to the realization that Lagos's elite "make millions each year by doing absolutely nothing." Therefore, he decides to flout normative ideas about the relationship between work and wealth. His strategy, which is also his motto and has been emblazoned on the T-shirt he regularly wears, is "To be a millionaire, think like a millionaire."

Saro-Wiwa's original stage play pits Basi against a pair of fraudsters whose connivance nearly exceeds his own, suggesting that Basi is less the creator of his own circumstances than an agent who can only attempt to cope with the ones in which he has found himself. Moreover, all the major characters in the play make recourse to the looming threat of, but also well-known corruptibility associated with various government institutions, implying that fraud is more than a way people make do in Lagos; rather, it is the national condition, maintained by state ambivalence and ineptitude. Occupying a central place, literally, in this landscape of fraud and corruption is Basi's landlady, Madam, who in the play speaks Pidgin and is nearly duped herself. If the building that Basi inhabits at No. 7 Adetola Street is the hub of the play's activity—with the primary sets consisting of Basi's apartment and a next-door bar run by a man named Dandy—Madam's apartment hovers directly overhead, linking the two together and providing the pivot around which much of the action turns. She is drinking beer when she knocks on Basi's door, demanding the month's rent. And it is her empty bottle, which she leaves behind, that pulls Basi into a scam concocted by Dandy and his loyal friend, Josco. When Saro-Wiwa adapted the material from his play for television, however, Madam morphed from a beer-drinking bully to a fashionable trend-setter who speaks impeccable English. Saro-Wiwa also invented a civic organization for the show, to which Madam belongs, the American Dollar Club, whose members spend lavishly on social gatherings and invest in various opportunities around town. They praise themselves with the title "Proud Amerdolians," expressing no sense of shame for perpetuating an extroverted sensibility about wealth and economic mobility in Nigeria. In the television show, therefore, Madam's apartment, which still looms over Basi's room and Dandy's bar, is the one place on Adetola Street where everyone comes looking for a "piece of the action," as Dandy likes to say. In fact, Madam's apartment is the only place that the entire cast is likely to gather, even though Dandy's cantina, "The People's Bar," is a more obvious location. To be clear, each major character does indeed make an appearance in Dandy's bar, but they rarely do so at the same time. Moreover, the bar is an unseemly place, a masculine space associated with coping rather than aspiration. Meanwhile, next door, in their humble first-floor room, Basi and Alali do their scheming. But of these three sets, if there is a party to be thrown or a meeting to be held, Madam's parlor—one of many rooms in her spacious top-floor residence—is the place where Basi and company all congregate.

The layout of Madam's apartment and the placement of objects within it are key to understanding the way her mirror operates in the series. The principal axis upon which the layout is constructed extends between her freestanding, full-length mirror (sometimes referred to as a *psyché* or a *cheval glass*) on the left side of the set and, directly opposite it, on the far right side, a large television.[13] In between, two ample armchairs in the foreground face each other, separated by a narrow, rectangular coffee table. On the far side of the coffee table, opposite the camera, is a sofa, behind which—in the deep background of the set—is a dining area with table, chairs, and bookshelf. I should note that each of the three sets used in *Basi and Company* is a classic three-wall set built in a production studio, with the camera usually positioned in the fourth wall, able to move from left to right in addition to panning, tilting, and zooming.

The mirror-television axis central to Madam's apartment thus forms the immediate horizontal plane of the set, with each screen (if that is what we are calling the mirror) marking the boundaries of the action, although of course each screen is also capable of projecting images back into the set (see figures 6.1 and 6.2). Rarely, but in seemingly significant moments, the camera is moved to a location within the set, often positioned at either end of the primary axis and therefore providing an opportunity to see what is reflected in Madam's mirror, as if from the point of view of the television, or conversely to see the television, as if from the point of view of the mirror. It is this oscillation of images and action along one primary axis, extending between two *screens*, that makes Madam's parlor an especially productive site of free indirect subjectivity.

One episode from late in the show's run, which includes several scenes set in Madam's apartment, is titled "Lenders and Borrowers." It begins with Basi (Zulu Adigwe) serenading Madam in her dining area. (Adigwe was the second actor to play Basi, and he is also an accomplished

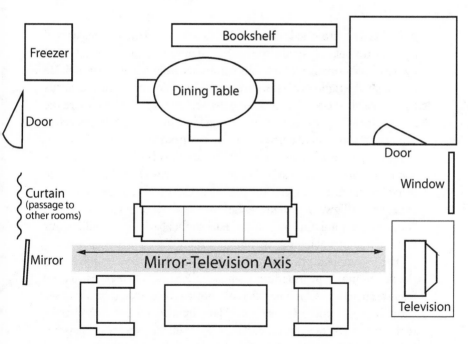

FIGURE 6.1. The layout of Madam's parlor from *Basi and Company*. Image created by the author.

FIGURE 6.2. *Basi and Company.* Screen in screen. Madam's television sits opposite her mirror, in which it is visible.

musician who wrote and recorded the show's second theme song as well as his own album of popular music.[14]) Madam (Aso Douglas) is unmoved by Basi's performance, which falls within his usual modus operandi. He has come, she rightly guesses, to request a loan. Basi nevertheless pleads that he needs the money to "keep quiet" creditors—of whom there are several, including Madam—who are unwilling to "reschedule" his debts. "You mean you want to borrow some money from me," she interjects, "to pay some part of what you owe me?" "That's the idea, Madam!" Basi responds convivially. The canned laughter that Saro-Wiwa employs in the program, in order to suggest the presence of a studio audience, chuckles along with Adigwe as he delivers his lines. Madam then probes further: "But you are a millionaire." "Well," Basi shoots back, "even billionaires have cash-flow problems sometimes."

The series includes many moments like this. At its most foundational, the uncommonly postmodern premise of *Basi and Company* is that its trickster hero *is* a millionaire, that his motto is true, even if he has never actually seen a million naira (or dollars, by which the show's characters often measure value). Therefore, Basi relentlessly seeks loans not because he is poor, although he is that; rather, he has mastered the logic of (neo)liberal finance capital. He may be overleveraged everywhere—indeed, to the tune of about two million naira, he tells Madam—but, depending on how he cooks his books, that means he is actually *worth* as much. After all, who would continue to issue him lines of credit if his *brand* were not so highly valued? Basi goes on to explain that he has "a big deal coming on, a multimillion-dollar deal." Madam then leads him to the sitting area positioned between her mirror and television, where she sits him down and launches into a lecture on solvency and savings (see figures 6.3 and 6.4). As she preaches—evangelizing a version of meritocratic economic thrift, which she and her fellow Amerdolians have completely forsaken— the image first cuts to a close-up and then a medium shot of Madam, each from a perspective just to one side of the television set at the other end of the room. This means that behind Madam—who is sitting in an armchair, leaning toward Basi, who sits on the far-left edge of the sofa, leaning toward her—spectators can see her mirror (her psyché?). In it, Basi's profile is reflected. During the close-up, spectators can see only the version of Basi in the mirror. When the image cuts to the medium shot, however, spectators see both Basis. As Madam and Basi lean toward each other in the foreground, the mirror behind them shows the side of Basi that is otherwise unavailable to the camera. It may be Madam's psyché in the frame, but what it provides is another narrative perspective on Basi.

If the camera eye constitutes the primary narrative perspective in most screen media, a mirror like the one in Madam's apartment allows a fragment of the image to provide another narrative perspective. Traditionally, a narrator is vaguely human, a kind of person, perhaps disembodied, who tells a story in some version of human language. In screen media, however, if the camera is often a narrator and if the camera is essentially a light-manipulation device, then a mirror seems an equally plausible vector for narrative insight. Thus, although written literature may from time to time allow one of the characters within a story to become a narrator, cinema can allow a piece of the image to just as easily take part in the telling of a story. Of course, there is nothing novel about placing mirrors in motion pictures or in any kind of visual art, for that matter. Jonathan Miller, in the catalog that accompanied an exhibition of European paintings that feature mirrors and opened at the British National Art Gallery in 1998, notes that "it is hardly surprising that artists, who deal in representational ambiguities, should have been attracted to the motif of the mirror, and exploited it in many different ways."[15] In *Basi and Company*, the exploitation is clearly deliberate: if the camera had been positioned in just the wrong place, it would have been visible in the mirror. So these shots are not accidental. However, the question is less

FIGURES 6.3 AND 6.4. *Basi and Company*. Basi sits in Madam's parlor, his face visible in her mirror.

about *why* than *to what effect*. In terms of free indirect subjectivity, one effect is that the secondary narrative perspective provided by the mirror *doubles* down on the idea that there is more to what Madam and Basi are discussing than meets the eye. It produces what Achille Mbembe, in his analysis of political cartoons, refers to as a hallucinatory effect. There is "the thing," otherwise described as "reality," and there is its "double," its ever-multiplying, excessive re-presentation. African urban popular culture produces many doubles because it has become, Mbembe argues, a kind of chronotope in which "everything has gone underground. Everything has its reverse side."[16] There is an official version of social organization, and there is a black-market version, a counterfeit that is actually more real because it is the one to which real people have real access in real life. In Madam's apartment—which is a set constructed in the Anambra State Broadcasting Studios in Enugu—television producers have created content to be aired on the state network that provides a realist version of home economics. "He who goes aborrowing goes asorrowing," Madam tells Basi. Simultaneously, however, there is a laugh track (whose perspective does that provide?), and there is a secondary narrative vision, provided by the mirror, of Basi, who seems to understand Madam's lecture less as an admonishment than as a form of commiseration. She begins to say that "borrowing is easier than," but Basi cuts her off. "Oh, Madam, you are so very understanding!" he interrupts, both in jest and earnestness. Borrowing *is* easier (than what?). Adigwe chortles his way through the line, but his character really does believe that borrowing is the answer to his woes. The laugh track seems to agree as it chortles along with him.

If the mirror provides access not to the thing but to our understanding of the desires from which the thing is constructed, then the mirror in Madam's apartment invites spectators to consider Basi's desires, to think about the ways—as Copjec instructs—*his* might resemble *theirs*. Why can't an ordinary man just borrow his way out of scarcity? The rich do it all the time. Governments too. Indeed, this topic would have been transparently relevant at the time the episode aired, just as Ibrahim Babangida's military government stepped back from a disastrous, self-imposed structural adjustment program (SAP). When Babangida came to power in 1985, by palace coup—just before *Basi and Company* hit the airwaves—the Nigerian government was in the midst of negotiating a massive International Monetary Fund (IMF) loan. Babangida canceled it, citing widespread public opposition, but nevertheless implemented many of the IMF's conditions. However, two years of austerity, as it often does, crippled the nation's economy, changing living conditions almost overnight.

Ordinary people were forced to sit up straight and take notice, meaning that any discussion of belt-tightening and borrowing, especially any such discussion broadcast on state television, would have been understood as unmistakably pedagogical and likely condescending.

"Lenders and Borrowers" includes several governmental *lessons* on the fraught topic of economic management. Like Basi, Dandy (Lasa Amorro) also needs a loan. It seems that he has a habit of consuming his stock while he works, with the result that he becomes overly generous, pouring most of his drinks on credit. However, Dandy's open-fisted business model has not attracted more customers. And calling in his patrons' debts does not seem to be a solution, for there is simply no money circulating at this stratum of the society. In the bar, as Dandy looks over his books, Segi (Timi Zuofa)—a young single woman who is friends with all of the men on the first floor and with Madam on the second—admonishes Dandy's profligacy but advises him to seek assistance from Madam.[17] Meanwhile, Josco—Dandy's friend and loyal patron, who is akin to what in Lagos are referred to as "area boys," local street punks—laments that the flow of alcohol should ever cease. Josco is fond of using Dandy's most pretentious professional title, "Leader and Keeper of the People's Bar," and indeed there is a profound significance in this formulation, especially by comparison to Madam and her membership in the American Dollar Club. The People's Bar operates as a kind of mixed economy, one that professes to have "the people's" interests at heart; nevertheless, it must function within a wider commercial system. By extending credit within the bar and drinking his own merchandise, Dandy resembles the Nigerian petro-state of the 1970s and early 1980s, even coming to the realization that he cannot continue to soak his patrons in liquid gold without tending to his own position within the wider economy. When Dandy seeks a loan from Madam, however, he is met with plenty of finger wagging and stern talk about budgeting. The satisfaction of "the people" will have to be suborned to—and thus depend on—Dandy's obligations to Madam and the American Dollar Club, to which he already owes rent and to which his debt payments would be issued. The suggestive possibilities here can be further extended. Consider that in basic macroeconomic terms, the value of the US dollar is inversely related to the price per barrel of crude oil on the world market, meaning that Madam's wealth is measured against, and increases relative to, falling revenue and economic activity in Nigeria.[18] To complete the allegory, then, Dandy goes "aborrowing" because the local economy has frozen up while the very source he turns to for assistance is benefiting from that freeze and therefore has no incentive to help. Instead,

Dandy must learn to cope with the freeze, or so he is told, while the party that assumes responsibility for teaching him is the very one profiting— without performing any other kind of labor or service—from the conditions that he and his customers suffer. This is, once again, the stock and trade of periliberalism.

When Dandy appears at Madam's door, hat in hand, she lectures him the same way she lectured Basi. This time, however, Madam stands in front of her mirror, looming over Dandy, who sits. She instructs him to repeat after her: "Shoddy economic management reflects in our private life. Bad budgeting leads to debt." Dandy, who probably has at most a primary education, is unable to accurately repeat her arcane phrasing, so she throws him out. As Dandy walks through the door, Madam stands with her hands on her hips and a scowl on her face. Behind her, the mirror offers a glimpse of her reverse side: the knots in her *gele* (head wrap), the line of her straight, imperious neck and back. Spectators are not offered a second perspective on Madam's face, another opportunity to identify with her hidden desires, but they are given the opportunity to think twice about her posture, the relative position she assumes, and the authority she claims at No. 7 Adetola Street. The invitation here is to reconsider Madam's positioning as teacher. Spectators know that she too sometimes runs a deficit and even turns to nefarious means to make it up (which I will cover later), so spectators cannot take her pedagogy at *face value*, as it were. In fact, in the second half of the episode, when everyone else has learned that Madam is being stingy and, worse yet, "mean, arrogant, and pompous"—as both Basi and Dandy phrase it—they devise a plan to knock her down to size. Josco (Emmanuel Okutuate), known to pick pockets, is recruited to steal money from Madam's apartment. Meanwhile, Basi assures everyone that he plans to return it to her intact just to remind her that "she is not as bright as she thinks."

When Josco arrives at Madam's apartment, she and Segi are sitting in her parlor discussing Madam's standing in the social order. As Segi phrases it, "It's dangerous to be rich, live among debtors, and refuse to lend money." Fascinating here is the fact that Segi places emphasis not on being rich or the pervasiveness of debt as such but on the refusal to open up lines of credit to the poor, which is the real source of danger for the rich. Indeed, when any capitalist economy freezes up for whatever reason, the rich tend to hoard their capital, deepening the freeze, instead of injecting capital back into the economy. The reason, of course, is that capital wants to accumulate. Rather than letting it slosh over the sides of their buckets, elites tend to use state and international policies to build bigger buckets. Madam simply replies with "I know," after which there is a knock at the door. Like all the characters in *Basi and Company*, Madam has a few catchphrases, and she responds to the knock with one of them: "Come in if you're handsome and rich." Josco enters and greets her with the beginning of another one of the show's formulaic set pieces— "Madam the Madam"—to which she replies, as she always does, "It's a matter of cash." These set pieces are, of course, standard sitcom fare, but they also contribute to the caricature of Madam as someone candidly and unapologetically obsessed with money. After they have been repeated in dozens of episodes, spectators come to realize that Madam can be conned out of her precious cash only when she is *green-eyed* with the possibility of making fast money herself. No such deal is on the table here, so Madam is in relative control.

When Josco walks through the door, the image cuts to a medium shot of Madam sitting in her favorite chair, just in front of her mirror, which offers spectators a reflected view of Josco. Segi leaves, and Josco begins maneuvering. He asks for a drink, for Dandy's bar is dry, and offers to run errands for Madam in return. Madam retreats upstage and pours one drink, then another, during which time Josco searches around for her stash of cash. Finally, Madam tells Josco to wait while she retrieves something from another room, and while she is gone, Josco finds two bags of money under her chair and stuffs them into his shirt. A long shot of the passage that leads from Madam's parlor to the rest of her apartment, next to which her mirror sits, allows spectators to watch for Madam's return while also watching Josco from two angles as he struggles with the large bags of money. Some spectators may desire what he has obtained. Some may also desire to see Josco finish hiding the money before Madam returns. Some may desire to see him get caught. When she finally comes through the passage, she remarks that Josco must be prescient, for how else could he know that she has decided to lend Basi and Dandy the money they have requested? Josco freezes, a look of panic on his face. Madam then continues: "The bags you have with you contain the money." Caught red-handed, Josco replies with his own catchphrase—"Dirty dozen!"— signaling his appreciation for Madam's guile. As he leaves, Madam tells him that she sees like a state: "I am watching you—other people too. So don't try any tricks!"[19]

Back in Dandy's bar, Josco is celebrated as a conquering hero. Meanwhile, Segi returns to Madam's apartment, where she finds Madam preening in front of her mirror. As Madam turns and tells Segi that there will soon be a spectacle to observe at Dandy's bar, the mirror once again offers a view of Madam's straight, imperious back. The image then cuts back to Dandy's bar, where Basi and Alali are holding Josco hostage and threatening him. It seems the bags were filled with ordinary paper, and now Basi and Alali (Tekena Harry MacDonald) think that Josco has kept the real money for himself. Just then, Madam and Segi burst in. Basi feigns allegiance, reporting that Josco has stolen her precious money, at which point Madam delivers the final lines of the episode: "I gave them to him, and I stuffed them with paper. Basi, you have to work hard to get rich!"

What to make of this meritocratic homily? Given the show's affinity for trickster themes, it hardly seems genuine. Then again, Saro-Wiwa is on record extolling the pedagogical value of Basi and Company, which is, in fact, something he also attributes to the trickster genre.[20] He writes that he was inspired to adapt his original stage play for television after seeing video footage of another adaptation by J. P. Clark's PEC Repertory Theater Company. In that version a scene in which Basi and Alali dream about wealth is remediated as a cutaway, where Basi appears driving a car and living in a modern bungalow. Saro-Wiwa reports that "it made an immediate impact in me. This dream of riches by a poor, unemployed man in a basically poor country was valid in 1965 when I had written the play. In the intervening period of twenty years, oil money had introduced terrible habits of fraud, squandermania and foolishness into the country."[21]

So perhaps it is these "terrible habits" that Saro-Wiwa sought to address with Basi and Company. Indeed, in the same self-published promotional bulletin where these words are printed, titled Everything about "Basi and Company": The Most Hilarious Comedy on TV, Saro-Wiwa also printed an article by Karen King-Aribisala, the noted Guyanan-Nigerian novelist and short-story writer, titled "Basi &Co and WAI." King-Aribisala's article aligns Saro-Wiwa's show with the infamous, broad-ranging, state-sponsored social-reeducation program known as the War against Indiscipline (WAI). This program was instituted by the military regime immediately preceding Babangida's, but Babangida chose to continue it, though with fewer federal allocations, for he was simultaneously pursuing structural adjustment. According to the political scientists Adigun Agbaje and Jinmi Adisa, Babangida was less interested in using his military power, as the preceding Buhari regime had done, to enforce practices such as "queuing culture" and "environmental sanitation"; instead, Babangida declared that "the war would be fought 'in the minds and conducts of Nigerians and not by mere symbolism or money spending campaigns.'" In this regard, purchasing episodes of Basi and Company from Saro-Wiwa was more effective, as Segun Olusuola also put it six

years prior, at waging a "war of ideas" (see chapter 2). Both regimes—
Babangida's and Buhari's—nevertheless conceptualized the goals of WAI
similarly. According to Agbaje and Adisa, they were "to guarantee and
strengthen national unity; to instill cultural discipline by discouraging
indolence, disrespect and corrupt and criminal practices and to engineer
consumer attitudes in support of a more self-reliant economy and away
from smuggling, hoarding and foreign currency trafficking."[22]

Agbaje and Adisa note that by advocating for patience in everyday life
experiences, a renewed work ethic, selfless service to the nation, avoiding fraudulent business activities, and the virtues of environmental sanitation, the architects of WAI confused the symptoms of poor economic
management with their causes. Meanwhile, the article by King-Aribisala,
which Saro-Wiwa chose to publish, declares in terms once again similar
to Olusuola's that *Basi and Company* served the state's campaign:

> [The show was] fighting a battle to nurture the mental discipline of a so-
> ciety gone awry. The arena is Nigerian society. The weapon is satire. The
> laurels of victory of that war is a Nigeria in which money is not God, where
> our citizens can utilize their talents not to trick but to assist each other in
> the meaningful task of nation building. . . . Basi represents that element
> of survival and optimism which assisted the Black diaspora in its strug-
> gle against alien lands, peoples, cultures, as far as the Americas. . . . Let
> us be true to our ancestors and give new meaning to the likes of Eshu.[23]

King-Aribisala's conflation of Basi and "Eshu," in relationship to the
struggle of the "Black diaspora," is evocative of the ways in which
trickster narratives have been deployed by Africans as forms of resistance against oppression in the Americas. The genealogy that Henry
Louis Gates Jr. traces between *Esu* and the counter-hegemonic African
American discursive practice of "signifyin" is a particularly strong case in
point.[24] But there is an aporia here.

Can Basi be both resistant and serve as an agent of WAI? Esu, as Gates
makes clear, stands apart from social discourse and interprets it. He is
the deity of the crossroads, the divine trickster figure in Yoruba cosmology, the messenger—depicted on divining boards—between human discourse and that of the gods. However, in Saro-Wiwa's conception, as well
as King-Aribisala's, Basi functions less as an interpreter of social mores
than a discursive reinforcement of them. In that sense, Basi is much more
like the Yoruba tortoise trickster of folk tales, *Ijapa*, than he is like Esu.
Ijapa is classically amoral, flouting norms precisely because he has no

interest in them but nevertheless leaving behind a kind of "moral residue," a set of lessons to be gleaned from his social infractions.[25] Yet inasmuch as the contradiction here is aporetic, Esu is the figure most capable of transcending it. His role, after all, is to open up holes in the fabric of social discourse through which new possibilities might be glimpsed, and in this case he may have actually been doing his job. Expressing sentiments similar to King-Aribisala's, a 1987 New York Times article about Basi and Company featured the title "30 Million Nigerians Are Laughing at Themselves." Saro-Wiwa is quoted as saying that "many rich Nigerians, especially of the political class, have the 'Basi' complex—they are hustling con men."[26] Here, then, is a hole in social discourse. Did the thirty million Nigerians who tuned into Basi and Company every week laugh at themselves or at the political class? It could be that what looks to the New York Times like people laughing at their own society is, from a more contextualized perspective, people laughing at their leaders. Note, however, that Saro-Wiwa describes an elite suffering from the "'Basi' complex," not a social base suffering from the "rich Nigerian" or "Madam" complex. Therefore, the kind of corruption that the show prioritizes seems to start at the bottom, with the Basis, not at the top.

However, it would be disingenuous to claim that Basi and Company fails to skewer rich Nigerians with its satire. Certainly, "Lenders and Borrowers" takes an ambivalent approach to the idea that people like Madam have any right to lecture ordinary, struggling people about profligacy and austerity. Moreover, in other episodes Madam and her greed are clearly the direct subjects of the show's mockery. For example, "Dead Men Don't Bite" and "The Patient" both criticize the elite tendency to spend lavishly on those who may not need it, such as the recently deceased or recently recovered—all for the sake of one's status—rather than distribute wealth to those whose lives would clearly benefit from a cash transfusion. In other episodes, like "Exam Fever" (in which Madam pays Alali to cheat on an exam for her), "The Commissioner" (in which Madam cozies up to Basi because she thinks he has been appointed commissioner), or "The Contract" (in which Madam enlists everyone on Adetola Street to help her forge documents in order to win a government contract), Madam is the key character who is guilty of "indolence, disrespect and corrupt and criminal practices." As advanced by episodes such as "The Proposal" (in which Madam and Basi nearly become lovers), both the rich and the poor in Nigeria, both Amerdolians and common people who live hand to mouth, exhibit what Saro-Wiwa calls "terrible habits of fraud, squandermania and foolishness." Unfortunately, Saro-Wiwa's show, like the

Saro-Wiwa quoted in the *New York Times*, seems to have little more to say than that.

But in a social system built according to the colonial-extraction mandate, run according to an alliance between cynical elites and multinational petroleum corporations, and held in place by the threat of military force, there can be no moral equivalence between the fraud perpetrated by elites, who seek to grow their fortunes, and the fraud pursued by ordinary people, who have no recourse to regular wage labor but who still must feed their children and put roofs over their heads. The television version of *Basi and Company* has attracted only scant scholarly attention, although some critics have either considered it a minor distraction within Saro-Wiwa's oeuvre or, as James Hodapp has recently argued, a "serious" example of Saro-Wiwa's biting social commentary. Hodapp nevertheless concedes that Saro-Wiwa had little wiggle room when it came to working with the federal government: "Basi's large-scale criticisms are couched as criticisms of Nigerian society, rather than of the government, but it takes little digging to expose that the coded Nigerian society includes the Nigerian regime."[27] Indeed, what Hodapp excavates is one of the show's indirect subjects, its willingness to critique not only the regime but also the larger economic system to which that regime is beholden. I have shown here that in addition to digging, one might position oneself to catch the shards of light bouncing off the show's many screens and, by doing so, come to similar conclusions. Regardless, a critique of society that merely *includes* the regime fails to account for the imbalance of power between those with access to the global economy and those without, which is ultimately what made *Basi and Company* amenable to state television broadcasting.

Along the lines of the critique of WAI leveled by Agbaje and Adisa, we might characterize *Basi and Company* as confusing symptoms with causes. Ultimately, the show may have invited spectators to take a second look at society, but for the short-term sake of that society, it also invited spectators to reform themselves, to become experts of themselves in order to someday gain access to the liberal world order. Spectators were not invited to identify with Basi but simply to consider his desires. And because he never fulfills those desires and never improves his station, those desires become emblematic of unrealistic fantasizing. Basi might believe that he can become a millionaire simply by thinking like one, but Madam, who professes hard work and careful economic management, is the real millionaire in the show. Anyone can have the Basi complex, and anyone can be positioned as morally upright for resisting it, but only those who speak like Madam, dress like Madam, and carefully strategize like Madam actually have the millions. After all, according to the show's creator and the WAI agenda it served, it is the "'Basi' complex" from which the society suffers and therefore that it needs to overcome. Nowhere does *Basi and Company* call for an evaluation of the Madam complex; nowhere does it call upon the gatekeepers to open or rebuild the gate.

If *Basi and Company* draws a lamentable moral equivalence between political corruption and personal corruption—in a society, moreover, that is characterized by gargantuan inequality—it nevertheless does something very significant in the history of Nigerian screen media. The trope of the mirror, the fragment of the image that provides a secondary narrative perspective on the primary action of the story, seems to have become part of the DNA of the comic mode of address. Indeed, the image of the mirrored reflection, the addition of a reverse side to the telling of the story, is something well suited to comedy's proclivity for satire and social critique. When put to use in Nollywood comedies, the mirror therefore seems to have been unable to show the reverse side without also undermining the front, the surface, the facade not only of the Nigerian state but also of the global economy, indeed the overarching sociality of modernity, with which the state and its citizens both must reckon. It is to Nollywood's mirrors that we now turn.

THE CONSPIRATORIAL MIRROR IN *OSUOFIA IN LONDON*

Aside from *Living in Bondage, Osuofia in London* may be Nollywood's most canonical film to date. It has been cited as one of the industry's best-selling releases, and many critics seem to find it narratively and aesthetically compelling, not only writing about it in academic books and journals but regularly slotting it into film festival programs and showing it to students. *Mea culpa*, although I am not alone. One of the most prolific and influential critics of African cinema, Kenneth W. Harrow, devotes most of a chapter to *Osuofia in London* in his book *Trash: African Cinema from Below*. Jonathan Haynes discusses it in at least two chapters of *Nollywood: The Creation of Nigerian Film Genres*. And Onookome Okome, another pioneering Nollywood critic, devotes an entire chapter to it in his edited volume *Global Nollywood: The Transnational Dimensions of an African Video Film Industry*. Meanwhile, the film plays a major role in dozens of other articles and book chapters. The reason for its critical attraction perhaps has to do with the complexity of its approach to the concept of subjectivity. The plot is constructed around a classic country-bumpkin-in-the-city motif, but the film also plays with the usual tropes in surprising ways, acknowledging every stereotype about the supposed backwardness of Africa, particularly in comparison to gleaming London, and then asserting that no African need be limited by such stereotypes. One could describe it as a full-throated dismissal of "double-consciousness."[28] As Harrow writes, "Osuofia remains the object of knowing laughter instead of becoming an oppressed victim of racial or modernist prejudice."[29]

In addition to the film's narrative and thematic complexity, its success is no doubt attributable to Nkem Owoh's mesmerizing and side-splitting performance of the so-called *bushman* character. Indeed, Owoh is a very versatile actor. As Haynes notes, he was "part of Nollywood from the beginning."[30] He was also part of state television throughout the so-called golden age. He played a role in *Things Fall Apart*. He was a network "stringer," writing for hit shows like *New Masquerade* (1983–ca. 2001). And he wrote, produced, and acted in *Basi and Company*. Owoh makes a particularly memorable appearance in the final scene of an episode of *Basi and Company* titled "The Patient." The premise is that elites like Madam, the Amerdolians, have a habit of inflating their social status by making large, conspicuous donations at events called "convalescence parties" (at which people recovering from illness raise funds for their medical bills). However, this kind of self-inflation can have wider inflationary repercussions because elites may spend far more than necessary in their bid to outdo one another performatively. Basi thus decides to feign his own illness and recovery so that he too can benefit from Amerdolian largesse, and he recruits a mechanic's apprentice to play the part of his doctor. Everything goes smoothly until the party, when one of the dancing Amerdolians, played by Owoh, recognizes the apprentice and unwittingly foils Basi's scheme. In the early years of Nollywood, Owoh would make a name for himself by writing scripts and subtitles for Igbo-language films, working with such producers as Kenneth Nnebue and Amaka Igwe. In his early on-screen appearances in *Basi and Company*, however, Owoh speaks perfect English, and his comic genius is clearly on display. His dancing is uproarious, and his lines are rib-cracking. He puts on a fine urban accent, and when he speaks, everything else in the room seems to fade into the background. He is also impressively dynamic. One minute his face is deadpan, emotionally illegible; the next, it explodes with a laugh so forceful that it folds his body in two. Owoh would go on to invent the character of Osuofia for an Igbo-language film called *Ikuku* (1995, dir. Nkem Owoh and Zeb Ejiro), but he would reprise it several times—mostly in English and Pidgin—over the next decade. As Haynes notes, one of Osuofia's key characteristics, already evident in Owoh's performance in *Basi and Company*, is garrulousness.[31] He talks and talks and talks. In fact, he never seems to stop talking. Osuofia gets himself into and out of trouble not so much by wit—although he displays plenty of it—but rather by verbal inundation.

There is one major mirror scene in *Osuofia in London*—a classic—and it begins with verbal inundation. I should note that because the film is so widely discussed, I will dispense with a lengthy exploration of its plot and its many significant themes, although a few details are needed for context. Indeed, the scene in question is thoroughly visited by Harrow, complete with screen captures, in his book *Trash*.[32] Regardless, there are ways of thinking about the film and its place in the history of Nollywood's local address that remain to be unpacked. The mirror scene, as is common with scenes of its kind, has the ability to hide as much, or more, than it reveals.

Osuofia is a poor hunter (meaning he is both bad at his chosen occupation and, as a result, impecunious) who lives in Neke Ama Nasa, a remote village somewhere in eastern Nigeria. His brother, Donatus, long ago immigrated to the United Kingdom, where, unbeknownst to his family, he amassed a small fortune. Osuofia learns about Donatus's money at the same time he learns that Donatus has died and left it all to Osuofia—who must travel to London to claim it. When Osuofia reaches London, however, Donatus's fiancée, Samantha (Mara Derwent), and his solicitor, Ben Okafor (Charles Angiama), are scheming to defraud him. As all of this becomes apparent, Osuofia overperforms his distance from modernity—his being out of place in both geographical and ideologically temporal terms—to belly-busting effect.[33] The logic of laughing at such a performance is meant to be parodic, which is signaled by the film's opening sequence, a clear nod to *The Gods Must Be Crazy* (1980, dir. Jamie Uys).[34] However, Osuofia's unmodern behavior protects him, making it more difficult for Samantha and Ben to steal his money. At the end of part I, Samantha resigns herself to marrying Osuofia and traveling back to Nigeria with him in order to embark on a new scheme. Her attempts to both assume the status of Ousofia's wife and simultaneously scheme to steal his inheritance play out in part II. Nevertheless, she cannot penetrate his palaverous and abstruse defenses. Meanwhile, Osuofia grows tired of Samantha as well, so he ends up writing her a check and packing her off to London.

The scene of note begins when Osuofia enters Okafor's office in London for the first time in order to claim his inheritance. Immediately preceding Osuofia's entrance, the film provides a low-angle establishing shot of the Houses of Parliament, suggesting that Ben works for a major firm in the heart of the city. The image then cuts to a medium shot of Ben's desk. Osuofia enters from the right, and Ben rises to greet him. (A boom mic temporarily descends from the top of the frame.) Osuofia is dressed as a village man of title—which, of course, he is not—complete with an *nza* (ox-tail whisk), with which he pats Ben's hand rather than shaking it. They sit, and the image begins to vacillate between close-ups and medium shots of each man as Ben apologizes for not meeting sooner. His British accent is perfectly patrician, which is key to the entire scene. Osuofia is, in fact, confused. The image cuts back to the original, medium shot of Ben's desk, showing Ben leaning toward Osuofia but Osuofia looking around bewildered. He glances behind himself, as if Ben might be addressing another person, and then turns to Ben as the image cuts to a close-up on Osuofia's face: "Are you talking to me? You are talking like Queen Eliza. Look at you. My friend, come down home and talk to me. Look at the fellow Black man like me, my brother. I know you are trying to pretend. Speak a language that I will understand. Open your mouth when you want to talk to me. I am your brother."

Osuofia's accent here, as it has been throughout the film, is a stock device: it is the accent of a semi-educated man from the Igbo hinterland, which is often associated in Nigerian popular culture with Onitsha or Alaba Market traders. The effect of this extended sequence, as Osuofia's backward glance suggests, is that the two men, using two different English accents, speak past each other. Okafor addresses Osuofia in a way that— following Tejumola Olaniyan's use of the word *accent* as both "a distinctive manner of expression" and "emphasis"—could be referred to, continuing Olaniyan's formulation, as "interstitial." It is clearly a British accent, but it has been claimed by a Black man of Nigerian descent and addressed to another Black, Nigerian man, as if it belonged to both of them. Olaniyan writes that the interstitial accent of African cultural studies—which, to be clear, is an intellectual, philosophical accent, not simply a descriptor for variations of spoken language—relativizes and deconstructs rather than affirming or defending "given differences such as 'continent,' 'race,' 'class,' 'nation,' and 'foreign-indigenous.'"[35] In contrast, Osuofia speaks in an accent that aligns with what Olaniyan calls the "affirmative"; it assumes not only a particular correspondence between Blackness and a manner of expression but also a particular affiliation between Osuofia and Ben that furthermore derives from their apparent racial similarity. Indeed, Osuofia accuses Ben of pretending, of speaking in a manner that is not really his. But that is just the setup.

Osuofia—who is obviously illiterate—refuses to sign any papers. As spectators later learn, those papers are actually fraudulent, drawn up in order to dupe Osuofia out of his inheritance. So Osuofia is right not to sign them, although he is not aware of it at the time. Meanwhile, he goes on and on about the currency in which the money is calculated and the method he will use to transport it home. All of this verbal inundation makes Ben boil, so he asks to be excused for a moment and walks off screen, left. The image then cuts to a gleaming public restroom in lavender and white. The camera is pointed at a row of sinks, screen left, above which stretches a long mirror that shows the doors to several stalls opposite the sinks. Spectators first see Ben enter the frame from the left, reflected in the mirror, and then, a second later, from the right. Here, the double precedes the thing. The two Bens continue to walk toward each other but stop just before they converge, put their hands on the countertop, and bow their heads toward one of the sinks. The image then dissolves to a medium, over-the-shoulder shot of Ben, which slowly zooms to a close-up on his face, reflected in the mirror. Ben's reflection looks directly into the camera and speaks in an entirely different accent: a Nigerian accent, urban, inflected with Pidgin. "What kind of stubborn goat is this? Why is he being so difficult? I hate these semi-illiterate foreign clients. They get me so annoyed and give me problems and *wahala!*"[36] The image cuts back to the angle that opened the sequence, once again showing the two Bens looking at each other. "When I get annoyed," he continues in his (dubiously acted version of a) Nigerian accent, "I start to lose my British accent. Mmm. Ehn?" Then, slipping back into the British accent, while the image cuts once again to a close-up of his reflection, Ben continues: "My cultivated, English, natural accent." Back to the two Bens: "And I start to speak like my father." He then assumes the Nigerian accent one more time, exclaiming "And I don't like it! Oh!" Finally, in a sequence that cuts back and forth between an extreme close-up of Ben's reflection and the medium shot of the two Bens standing at the sink, he directly addresses the audience, speculating, "You're laughing at me? You think I have a problem. You think I have a coconut problem" (see figures 6.5 and 6.6). Ben then breaks his engagement with the spectator-subject, begins to splash water on his face, and speaks to himself: "OK, calm down, calm down. OK. OK. Deep breath. Stiff upper lip. God save the Queen." He then reintroduces himself: "Ben Okafor, solicitor." After a quick "Excellent," he engages spectators one last time. In an extreme close-up, he asks, with a lopsided grin on his face, "How can I help you?" Ben then turns toward the camera and walks off to the right of the frame, while his reflection, a

FIGURES 6.5 AND 6.6. *Osuofia in London*. Ben Okafor talks to himself in the mirror.

second behind him, walks off to the left. Just as his reflection was the first to enter the scene, it is the last to leave.

For Harrow, the mirror in this scene functions as a technology of subjectivity. Following Judith Butler, he describes its capabilities in both semiotic (Lacanian) and institutional (Foucauldian) terms, writing that "the mirror provides direct visual images of Ben's role-playing, his rehearsal for the performance, his split verbal and visual self, his subject position that both recuperates and resists the power that chastises and punishes, but that also empowers him."[37] Strictly speaking, however, it is the camera that provides *direct* images of Ben's role playing. The primary narrative perspective allows spectators to see that Ben is standing in front of a mirror, using it to watch his own rehearsal. When the image cuts to a close-up, however, the mirror provides an *indirect* perspective on Ben's performance. It *mediates* between Ben and the camera. The question, perhaps, is whether the (twice) mediated image is actually the more *authentic* one. After all, if subjectivity is always mediated, whether by signs or institutions, then drawing attention to the mechanics of mediation may be more honest than ignoring or attempting to surpass them. However, the mirror also *disappears* in the close-ups. Ben could be gazing directly into the camera as far as spectators know. The close-ups recall the effect that Foucault analyzes in his description of the Diego Velázquez painting *Las Meninas*, which opens Foucault's reflections on epistemology in *The Order of Things*.[38] *Las Meninas* includes a mirror that seems to show two subjects of a painting, which is itself in the process of being created within the world of the painting. It is as if the subjects of the metapainting, which is otherwise invisible in the actual painting, are shown in the mirror and therefore transposable with the spectator who stands opposite the mirror—while the actual spectator-subject, the viewer of the painting, does not, of course, appear in the mirror in the painting. The light-manipulating materiality suggested by the mirror, combined with the complicated formulae of sight lines in the painting, thus makes *Las Meninas* an early—it was painted in 1656—version of cinema's point-of-view shot. It also therefore calls attention to the inverted processes by which subjects are formed and come to know the world. As Foucault puts it, "The profound invisibility of what one sees is inseparable from the invisibility of the person seeing."[39] In *Osuofia in London* it is only because of the establishing shots of the restroom and because of the first zoom from over the shoulder to close-up that spectators are led to believe that all of the subsequent close-ups are produced using a mirror and not, as is perfectly possible, using a camera positioned somewhere opposite the stalls.

To reconfigure Harrow's terms, the *camera* "provides direct visual images of Ben's role playing" while the mirror *hides* "the power that chastises and punishes, but that also empowers him." In fact, the mirror does two things. It gives the brief impression that Ben is the story's narrator, that we are seeing with his eyes while he talks to his own reflection. But it also gives the impression that Ben is talking *to* spectators, looking directly into the camera and addressing the viewing subject. The reflected close-ups of Ben thus constitute incisive moments of free indirect subjectivity, in which it is ambiguous whether it is Ben, in the first or second person, or in a different third-person narrative perspective, who is telling the story. And more than invite subject identification, Ben's direct address to spectators also holds them at a distance, marks them as distinct from him (in much the way Anne's direct address does in the opening credits of *Checkmate*). In fact, when he asks, point blank, whether spectators think he has a "coconut problem" (being dark on the outside, white inside), the distance between image and spectator crystallizes. Meanwhile, the medium shots, in which two Bens are visible, are more conventional.

In the shots that show Ben's profile and back side, standing at the sink, while simultaneously capturing his front, via the mirror, spectators have access to almost 270 degrees of Ben: everything but the right side of his body. In a literal sense, therefore, the mirror does provide more information about him. However, that information is split in two. In the medium shots, the mirror invites spectators to skip back and forth, assessing Ben from different points of view. Following Copjec, the salience of surface calls attention to the fact that something lurks beneath or behind it. Some set of desires must animate Ben's sense of self. He must want something: money, surely, but perhaps something more, something immaterial. In the scene at his desk, Ben appears to suggest that there is no such thing as a Black accent, a Black manner of expression, or automatic affiliation between two Black bodies. In front of the mirror, however, Ben acknowledges that his British accent is a studied affect, a sign of his subjection, and unnatural. He *affirms* that among others of *his kind*—Black, Nigerian, Igbo—there is a prevailing manner of expression, one he can barely suppress. Therefore, what appears to be the power to choose an accent is really a forced choice. It is primarily a case of "power that chastises and punishes," in Harrow's words, rather than power that *empowers*. In the end, therefore, Osuofia is right. Ben is "trying to pretend," and he should "speak a language that [Osuofia] will understand." The mirror proves his point. Combined with the close-ups, the mirror becomes a fragment of the image that confirms what some of the characters are saying and doing.

In that sense it does more than circumnavigate Ben, inviting spectators to consider his desires; instead, it conspires with the primary narrative perspective to deliver the film's full meaning, or at least 270 degrees out of 360.

The mirror in *Osuofia in London*, however, cannot do it all. It invites spectators to circumnavigate and assess a subject from several perspectives, but it never provides a full 360 degrees, and it even holds spectators at bay. Indeed, to understand the figure of the fraudster, the subject who has access to several accents and who uses them to choose between subject positions — thereby reaffirming the situatedness of subjectivity — we must navigate to another point of view, another rehearsal in front of another Nollywood mirror.

"IS THAT NOT 419?": *THE MASTER IN THE MIRROR*

In one of the most robust and productive readings of Nollywood to date, Brian Larkin describes an "aesthetics of outrage" that seems to characterize the greater share of video films, at least for the formative first two decades of the Nigerian industry's history. As he puts it, Nollywood stories tend to be structured according to "continual shocks that transgress religious and social norms and are designed to provoke and affront the audience."[40] Certainly, that description would apply to many of the films featured in this book, from *Games Women Play* and *Living in Bondage* to *Igodo* and *Osuofia in London*. However, Larkin further argues that a similar aesthetic would have been out of place on state television, given that developmentalist discourse aims to uplift and inspire rather than shock and affront. Yet we have seen that outrageous characters, from Chief Eleyinmi (*The New Village Headmaster*—see chapter 2) and Nduka's mother (*Checkmate*—see chapter 3) to Basi and Josco, can be part of the inspirational formula. Even in colonial cinema, as in *Black Cotton* (see chapter 1), inspiration functions by contrast to astonishment, where the wonders of modernity are meant to eclipse the staggering toll exacted on human bodies by long-standing modes of local production. Nevertheless, we have also seen that some African spectators, in places such as Tanzania and Uganda, seem to have found the early twentieth-century Hausa cotton industry, by way of an example, inspiring despite the gargantuan and at times exhausting human effort involved.[41] Likewise, Larkin describes a similar push and pull: "Outrage works through a mechanism of distancing: characters are involved in actions so horrible that one cannot identify with them. But at the same time, it depends on similarity: characters come to their actions by choices made to alleviate real hardship."[42] Here, Larkin is specifically referring to the 2005 video film *The Master*, which stars Nkem Owoh as a poor-trader-turned-419-fraudster.[43] The stock character of the 419 con man is ripe for such treatment because it is an ambivalent sign in Nigerian popular culture. To be clear, the image of the (sometimes email) scammer is reviled by many Nigerians the same way it is reviled (and ridiculed) globally; nevertheless, scammer figures can also be revered. To wit, several popular songs equate scamming with the kind of gangster culture celebrated in some strands of American hip-hop.[44] Thus, whenever *The Master* appears in the scholarly literature, it usually functions as an example of the status of 419 fraud in Nigerian popular imaginations.[45] In fact, a song and music video that Nkem Owoh recorded to accompany the film *I Go Chop Your Dollar* has even been cited in mainstream American news media as proof that Nigerians are willing to entertain the idea that fraud, particularly when it is directed at Euro-Americans, may be considered retributive and therefore legitimate.[46] The question that concerns the final section of this chapter is whether the outrageous antics of characters such as Basi, Osuofia, and Dennis (Owoh's character in *The Master*) invite subject identification or address Nigerian spectators in some other way.

The international interest in a video film such as *The Master* suggests that its address is not simply local, yet it also focuses attention on the fact that Nollywood's local address may be very different from its global address, meaning that distinguishing between the two is all the more appropriate. Mainstream American journalists may express their own form of outrage at Nigerian 419—at least the instances of 419 directed at Americans, which form just a fraction of the overall phenomenon, much of which takes place entirely within Nigeria—but there is a significant conversation taking place in Nigerian popular culture about the idea that whereas local fraud (of the kind committed by Basi and Madam, for example) should be condemned, some degree of sympathy can be maintained for the retributive possibilities of international 419. Indeed, the kind of advanced-fee fraud that Dennis perpetrates in *The Master* does seem to constitute a choice "made to alleviate real hardship," as Larkin puts it, which may have significant local appeal.

When the film opens, Dennis is struggling financially. He lives in the house of his junior brother, Benji (Charles Inojie), who has a salaried job. Dennis, meanwhile, sells *okrika* (secondhand clothing) in the market. Benji comes home one day to find that Dennis has never left the house and, in an act of defiant social inversion, accuses his senior brother of laziness. However, Dennis refutes Benji's accusations on several counts. Long ago, he says, he dropped out of school and worked to pay Benji's school fees, thereby providing the education that led to his brother's formal employment. More recently, Dennis borrowed a considerable sum to go abroad but was deported back to Lagos and rendered *koboless*. And in an even more immediate sense, Dennis argues that the okrika business's profit margins are simply too small to justify long hours spent in the market, not to mention the backbreaking labor of transporting the goods. Therefore, Dennis essentially rationalizes laziness, which comes across—certainly to Benji and probably to many spectators—as outrageous. Simultaneously, however, Dennis's rationalization is detailed and specific enough to invite a sense of what Larkin refers to as "similarity." Dennis runs the numbers and reveals that a whole day's work in the okrika market would net him little more than two dollars per day, which is, in fact, the average income of 92 percent of the Nigerian population.[47] Moreover, the enterprise that earns him this "chicken change," as he puts it, consists of selling the castoffs of the global economy. Is it really noble, his logic seems to ask, to scratch out a living selling foreigners' old clothes, day in and day out? Dennis tells Benji that unless he can get access to more capital to invest in his business, work is a waste of time. In the span of a few minutes, therefore, Dennis paints his plight—and that of most Nigerians—as globally inflected, a symptom of the country's peripheral position within the world economy. Then, in quintessentially periliberal fashion, Benji attempts to temper Dennis's indignation: "You can't change all that by staying at home," he declares. The next day, however, Benji produces the capital that Dennis requires—₦70,000 he has borrowed from the junior staff cooperative at work. That would have come to roughly $550 at the time, hardly "capital" by global or even local standards, but Dennis thanks his brother profusely and sets off the next day to "spend it wisely," as Benji instructs. Unfortunately, Dennis immediately falls prey to an elaborate scam, spending the entire ₦70,000 on kilos of sawdust dressed up to look like bargain-priced okrika. Soon after, he runs into the scammer, Ifeanyi, and tries to have him arrested while inundating him with the kind of silly verbal barrage usually associated with Owoh's Osuofia character. (When Ifeanyi refers to Dennis as a "nincompoop," for example, Dennis repeatedly calls him a "picanoo.") Dennis fails to get justice, but the scammer invites Dennis to his house, a palatial mansion surrounded by gleaming luxury cars and guarded by two beefy young men in tight-fitting shirts. Ifeanyi is played—true to type—by Kanayo O. Kanayo, the tall, suave, eloquent (often dubiously wealthy) gentleman of *Checkmate, Living in Bondage*, and *Billionaires Club* fame. He seems to appreciate Dennis's gift of gab, which is a fraudster's—indeed any trickster's—most valuable asset. So he offers Dennis a chance to prove himself in a complicated scam, which Dennis—who is desperate to pay his brother back and prove himself capable of financial solvency—immediately accepts.

Dennis's first scam is far too elaborate—and ingenious—to recount here, but key to its success is the notion that Nigerian middlemen and aspiring business tycoons are as concerned with their appearance as they are with making money. The dupe—or *mugu* in the local 419 lexicon, as made popular by Owoh's hit song—fails to see through the scam because he is positioned within it as the only shrewd visionary in his sector of the economy. Larkin has elsewhere drawn attention to this aspect of the film, the way it emphasizes the power that social facades exercise in the Nigerian political economy or the fact that sartorial choices and self-presentation may be more important than capital and skill.[48] Needless to say, Dennis performs his role with aplomb and begins to climb the ladder of Ifeanyi's 419 network.

The first key mirror scene of *The Master* occurs when Dennis rehearses for a subsequent role. Like a reverse of the mirror scene from *Osuofia in London*, this one begins with a close-up of Dennis's reflection as he practices his lines. The camera then pulls back to reveal the context. Dennis is pacing around his room in Benji's house, but he has traded his faded okrika for a finely tailored sharp white tunic and trousers. The mirror in which he watches himself is half-length, perched on top of a stereo that sits cheek by jowl with a small television. As with Madam's mirror, therefore, this one shares its visual field with a television screen (precisely the kind of screen from which video film narratives radiate). Equating the two screens in this way might add fuel to the argument that video films are mirrors, but because the mirror is so closely associated in this instance with fraud and impersonation—as, indeed, it is in *Osuofia in London* and *Basi and Company*—it emphasizes the perfidy of reflections and the shell game of the image. Dennis's reflection resembles Madam's and Ben's in another way too: it speaks impeccable English. Dennis renders his line— "No, Mr. Robinson. What you and your people want me to do is completely against bank policy"—in a clear, elite accent. This contrasts with Dennis's usual urban, Pidgin-inflected register. Also like Madam, though less like Ben, Dennis knows how to modulate his demeanor. The first time spectators hear his line, Dennis is delivering it with a hint of pugnacity, but he corrects himself, noting that his words should come across as "cool." At that point, Benji walks in on the rehearsal.

Dennis explains to Benji that he is practicing for "a big business," at which point Benji—much like Merit and Aunty in *Living in Bondage*, who immediately leap to the correct conclusion about Chief Omego's fortune and the pitfalls that await Andy—wastes no time reprimanding Dennis: "I hope you are not planning to go and join these 419 people." Rather than refute his brother, Dennis poses (as he stands in front of the mirror) a much larger question (see figure 6.7). "What's wrong with 419?" he asks. "Is it not people who do 419?" He further explains that 419 is simply "business," that it is not "devils" who do the work but "human beings." This exchange is filmed in close and medium shots, but after Dennis begins to make his case, the image suddenly cuts to a relatively long shot of the room. Benji stands on the left side of the frame, Dennis on the right, with the mirror/stereo/television tableau between them, in the background. In *Basi and Company*, the mirror-television axis forms the extreme boundaries of and structures the primary space of action in Madam's apartment. Here, that axis has been compressed into a single point and pushed deep into the visual field, thus accentuating the agency of the "human beings," as Dennis puts it, in the foreground. It provides a few fleeting glimpses of Dennis's back as he turns away from the mirror and practices his lines, but—aside from the opening shot—it never offers extended alternative perspectives of the characters on screen. Instead, this mirror mostly shows an empty corner of the room. And because that corner lies beyond the camera's frame of reference, the mirror provides greater context for the action within the frame. Indeed, if a mirror placed in the frame of screen media functions as a fragment of the image that provides more information about the narrative, this one emphasizes the fact that although Dennis's rehearsal may be a bone of contention between him and his brother, it is set within a more expansive context than their opposing viewpoints. These two men may make their own story but not necessarily under conditions they have chosen.[49]

As Dennis continues to recite his lines, Benji fulminates about the perils of 419. The two men therefore speak past each other. Benji then crosses the frame and collapses onto Dennis's bed. However, his move does not disrupt Dennis's rehearsal; in fact, Dennis turns and addresses his lines directly to Benji. Meanwhile, the mirror continues to show glimpses of Dennis's back and the far corner of the room. "Now, Mr. Robinson," Dennis continues, "what you and your people want me to do is against the banking policy." The image then cuts to an over-the-shoulder shot as Dennis advances on Benji, who, lying prone on the bed, seems to become the "Mr. Robinson" of Dennis's charade. The younger brother protests:

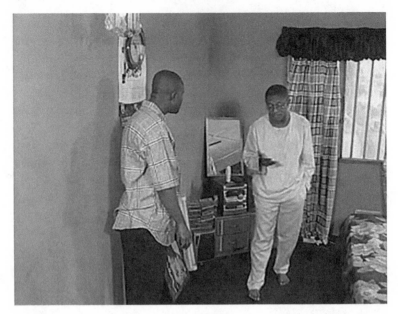

FIGURE 6.7. *The Master.* Dennis and Benji discuss 419 in Dennis's bedroom.

"I am not Robinson, brother. What is it now?" However, Benji's exasperation only fuels Dennis's rehearsal. The more he protests, the more Dennis
can practice maintaining his "cool" demeanor. "Try to understand my own
point of view, Mr. Robinson," Dennis improvises. "It is completely against
the law." The line, its deliverer, its addressee, and their context thus seem
to be more than rehearsal. The way that Dennis and the camera advance
on and corner his brother suggests that Dennis really does want Benji
to understand his "point of view." However, the camera does not enter
Dennis's point of view; it remains beside him, showing his hand as he addresses Benji. Spectators are therefore not invited to identify with Dennis, although they are invited to take his vituperations seriously. What
does Benji (and his "people") want Dennis to do? Honest work? That, Dennis asserts, breaks the "law" of "banking policy" or, to put it another way,
defies the logic of international finance capital. However, Dennis wants
to pursue that logic. After all, he has already argued that predatory speculation is just the work of human beings, not devils. Indeed, according to
Dennis, fraud simply follows the impulses of human nature, so "What's
wrong with 419?"

The placement of Dennis's rehearsal mirror in the corner of his room
and the few shots of characters reflected in it simultaneously emphasize

the agency of those characters and provide expanded information about the structural conditions within which they operate. Rather than providing spectators with another way to see Dennis or Benji, the mirror in *The Master* seems to invite spectators into an enlarged conception of space. In it, characters do the best they can within the circumstances they have inherited. Once again, therefore, the mirror is a technology of subjectivity, but instead of emphasizing the forces that impinge on subjects, it explores the limits of the structures that surround them. This version of subjectivity is less interested in the signs and institutions that produce or mediate the subject than in the development of subjectivity within an arena that has been shaped and circumscribed by signs and institutions. The difference is very subtle, of course, but nevertheless significant. Do signs force themselves on subjects, or do they form barriers out of which subjects cannot break? The magnitude of this distinction is more fully realized in the final scene of the film, to which I will turn shortly.

In the meantime, Dennis realizes just how unique his skill set seems to be. He eventually rises so high in Ifeanyi's network that he branches off into his own deals. Before he does so, however, he plays the major role in a scheme with international proportions and global implications. It begins as he arrives at Murtala Mohammed International Airport in Lagos, accompanied by a large motorcade, to welcome an American investor named Mr. Evans (Sunny Harp). Dennis claims to be the eponymous Murtala Mohammed (who was actually the Nigerian head of state from 1975 to 1976 and whose assassination elevated him to the status of martyr—see chapter 5). He then refers to the federal government airport as his own "private" terminal, which he lets the people use. Once again, this scam is built on the foundational idea that when it comes to doing business in Nigeria, gleaming surfaces make the best veils. Mr. Evans is completely taken in by Dennis's hilariously over-the-top performance of the corrupt *big man*, bloated by oil wealth, who claims to have given the nation its infrastructure as a gift. The scam also hinges on the idea that American oil executives are likely to be ignorant of Nigerian history (should they not know Murtala Mohammed's name?) even when they want to do business there yet will be very aware of Nigeria's infamous corruption and be entirely willing to participate in it. The arrangement that Dennis proposes to Mr. Evans is as follows: the federal government has drawn up a $600 million contract to repair its oil infrastructure. The job can be done— with many corners cut, surely—for $200 million. Mr. Evans will get the contract as long as "Murtala Mohammed," who advises the president, agrees to award it to him. Mohammed's (Dennis's) consent rests on two conditions: Evans must remit $200 million to him and the president, and Evans must spend $30 million of his own money to set up an indigenous shell company to accept the award, which is important because it would give the deal a nationalist aura. Mr. Evans is thus led to believe that if it all works out, he will net $170 million in personal profit. Dennis and his associates further perform their sleight of hand by staging a robbery, in which Evans's briefcase is stolen. Dennis offers to repay everything that Evans has lost, even producing the cash to do so—which further adorns his wealthy facade—but Evans declines. As Dennis returns the money to his own briefcase, he pretends to praise Evans, in Igbo, for his magnanimity. Of course, Dennis is, in fact, declaring his intentions to steal and enjoy Evans's wealth. In the end, Evans loses the contents of his briefcase—$90,000—as well as the $30 million he provides for the shell corporation. The scam nets Dennis more than $9 million, establishing him as a major player in Ifeanyi's 419 network.

From the beginning of the film, Dennis has exhibited an independent streak, never conceding to any set of rules or institutional norms, which makes him a convincing liar but also has other consequences. When he finally goes solo as a 419er, he invites the ire of several "godfathers," who demand a percentage of every deal in order to hold security services and other officials in check. Dennis's refusal to play along thus dooms him. During the second part of the film he enters into what will be his final deal, which involves another fake oil contract, this time with a Mr. Littlewood, played by Avinaash Bhavnaani (the actor who plays the superintendent of a global occult cabal in *Billionaires Club*). The role that Dennis plays in this scam is that of the paramount ruler from a community in the Niger Delta, where oil reserves have recently been discovered. He is willing to help Littlewood get a "prospecting" contract in return for kickbacks as long as Littlewood promises to protect the community from environmental harm. Here, the scam marshals two salient critical discourses that have been central to this study. One is the role played by "native authorities," the paramount rulers whose power was invented or inflated by the colonial system of indirect rule (see chapter 1). The second concerns the fate of people who live on top of the fuel that powers the engines of the global liberal order, which is willing to flout its own liberal norms to pull that fuel out from under their feet. Dennis's lack of interest in institutional norms therefore aligns him with periliberalism but also calls attention to its hypocrisy.

The last thirty minutes of *The Master* bring several of these critical threads together in a spectacular way. Dennis's performance of the "high chief" indexes the argument that indirect rule originally functioned and continues to do so as a form of primitive accumulation, in which zones of the global economy are marked off from the liberal order and are subject to any number of experimental legal regimes. Who needs international law when you have the blessing of the chief? However, when the godfathers, who are furious with Dennis's roguery, allow a normal criminal investigation to proceed against him, they are not exactly condoning the reintegration of such zones into the world's regulatory system. Their ruthlessness further extends periliberalism, the selective gatekeeping that positions most of the people in a country like Nigeria outside of the world order and, all the while, makes that order more functional. What the godfathers assert is their individual power, not the rule of law. Indeed, when the police descend on Dennis, he is at the gate of the international terminal of the airport, and they safely keep him from getting through. He is then delivered to a courthouse to enter his plea, where a number of media outlets are already waiting to catch a glimpse of the famous 419 kingpin.

The final scene of *The Master* opens with a crowd of reporters rushing to see the police paddy wagon as it enters the courthouse compound. Owoh's hit theme song plays on the sound track:

Oyinbo [foreign, usually non-Black] man, I go chop your dollar.
I go make your money disappear.
419 is just a game.
You be the loser.
I be the winner.

Three of the journalists hold video cameras and, as they follow the motion of the truck, turn toward the camera that is telling the story, the primary narrative perspective—which, going forward, I will refer to as the *nondiegetic camera*. For a brief moment, therefore, the reporters' cameras and the nondiegetic camera point at one another, as if reflecting one another or looking in a mirror (see figure 6.8).

Then, as the paddy wagon parks and Dennis is brought out in shackles, the reporters and their cameramen, as well as the nondiegetic camera, gather around it. The score changes to an anxious drone of drums and synthesizer chords as the nondiegetic camera joins the huddle, panning left and right, observing its fellow cameras. Suddenly, any distinction between the nondiegetic and diegetic perspectives collapses. Spectators are shown glimpses of Dennis and the journalists, some of whom hold tape recorders, as well as several bystanders. The mode of address here invites

FIGURE 6.8. *The Master.* The nondiegetic camera observes diegetic cameras.

subject identification with the media and the public. Spectators are no longer watching social issues and positions play out; they are invited to participate in the constitution of culture, the fashioning of Dennis and the 419 phenomenon that he represents.

One reporter asks, "Is it true that you defrauded an American to the sum of $10 million?" to which Dennis's attorney, standing by his side, responds, "My client is innocent until proven otherwise." Dennis then launches his own ill-advised defense: "I am not a fraudster. I'm a straight businessman, and I do business." Another reporter asks, "As a business- man, sir, what do you do?" Dennis replies, "I do business. I deal on deals. If you have a good deal, you get it to me; if I like it, I buy your deal. If you have money to buy my own, I give you my deal, you pay, and that's busi- ness." The reporter follows up: "What sort of deals? Give us an example." "Look," Dennis digresses evasively, "there are people who work for their money, and there are others who make their money work for them. I be- long to the class that make my money work for me. So, if you want to know 'what deals,' you ask my money." Dennis's articulation of capital and class, in which he controls money but money can only speak for itself, illustrates the pivotal Marxist argument that what makes capital conceptually distinct from money or other forms of value is its subjectivity, its idiosyncratic logic, its uncanny ability to intervene in discourse and decide what makes a deal a deal. A third reporter then brushes Dennis's convoluted logic aside and gets to the point: "But then chief, it is widely known that you are an international 419." Dennis's attorney steps in: "My client takes exception to such malicious prejudice," but Dennis cuts her off. "No, don't worry," he soothingly enjoins. "I will answer it. I wish I were a 419. I would have put one or two things right." He then commences with the film's transparently and unapologetically climactic speech, a populist jeremiad about the history of modernity. As he speaks, the score shifts to a tranquil piano arpeggio accompanied by spellbinding chimes. The non-diegetic camera provides glimpses of the people gathered, some of whom turn to one another, miming their positive reactions to Dennis's words:

> What do you call 419, you journalists? They came here, the White man came here, long, long time ago, our great grandfathers, they parceled them, they put them into a chamber, they sent them across as slaves, they sent them to go there and do menial labor. What do you call that? Is that not 419 on the superlative order? And you don't write about it. And you don't ask questions about it. There are banks they call "security bank." Somebody calls government functionaries, soldiers, whatever, that are ruling the country, and they pack it, our own money, that belongs to you and I, they send it over there, they give them cover. What do you call that? Is that not 419? There are people, even now as I'm talking to you, there are people who import goods. If they import goods, they open their goods, you will see rubbish there. Open the container you will not see any good there. All you see is bad. They bring sawdust and nonsense, whatever. What do you call that? Is that not 419? I want you people to think, journalists, think!

Slavery, finance, and periliberalism—Dennis has named them all, though in evasively populist terms. His freewheeling syntax may elicit nods of agreement from many of the bystanders, but the journalists are unmoved. One asks, "Sir, please, I would like to know for how long have you been in this business," to which Dennis replies, "What business are you talking about?" "419 business, of course, sir," the journalist responds. "Did I tell you I'm in 419 business?" Dennis asks. "It's obvious, sir," the journalist shoots back. However, Dennis poses another question, "What is obvious?," and then supplies his own response: "'Four' is not my language; it's not yours. 'One' is not my language; it's not yours. 'Nine' is not my language; it's not yours. They're all foreign. I want you people to open your head and think!"

Dennis then changes the subject, asking the journalist if he is trained, and the fervor of the moment passes. The score returns to the synthesizer drone, and Dennis approaches the steps of the courthouse, pausing just long enough to flash a politician's smile and thumbs-up to some of the bystanders. The reporters follow, begging for more comments; instead, when Dennis reaches the top of the steps, he turns and finishes his lecture: "In any case, it is the greedy people. It is the greedy ones that fall victim of 419. If you're not greedy and do not have intention of defrauding anybody on this nation, they will not fall victim of 419. In any case, I am clean. I am clean!"

Dennis turns and enters the courthouse, followed by several journalists. Some remain outside, including one camera operator and one reporter who have set up to record their final report. Meanwhile, the nondiegetic camera records the entire scene. The reporter mentions that Dennis has hired a well-known "radical" lawyer, which among other things should make the case "interesting." Fade to black. "To God be the glory."

PERILIBERALISM AND CORRUPTION

Dennis's final speech in *The Master* is far more political than most Nollywood films tend to be, yet it is not really all that remarkable. The sentiment that 419 fraudsters intervene in the iniquitous dynamics of the modern world system is somewhat widely shared, not only in Nigeria or Africa but across the global South. And in terms of critical discourse, it echoes the analysis provided by several scholars, including ethnographers of globalization such as Jean Comaroff and Charles Piot.[50] Moreover, like Dennis, the historian Stephen Ellis explicitly links contemporary Nigerian fraud, of the kind that "deliberately target[s] foreigners," to indirect rule. As he puts it, "The actual experience of Indirect Rule in Southern Nigeria especially involved such a high degree of deceit and manipulation as to amount to a training in subterfuge for anyone who had close experience of it."[51] As Ellis frames it, the indirect rule system in the South, like Lugard's experiments in the North (see chapter 1), functioned by hypocritically proscribing any kind of trade in human beings while inwardly tolerating many forms of local slaving. (To be clear, "slaving" means something different from the transatlantic slave trade and, moreover, constitutes a way that many premodern societies across the globe dealt with war captives and other people unmoored from certain community institutions.) As Ellis describes it, all across southern Nigeria during the colonial era,

Nigerians were forced to hide certain cultural practices from British authorities who espoused liberal legal sensibilities; meanwhile, those same
authorities documented many forms of Nigerian indentured servitude,
which clearly violated liberal political principles, but chose to look the
other way in order to continue collecting taxes, running their bureaucracy, and extracting resources for the benefit of a global economy that
may have been created by slavery but had recently outlawed it in order to
move on to new stages of accumulation. In other words, the kind of fraud
on display in *The Master* is born directly from periliberalism. Moreover,
Dennis's speech not only makes that plainly obvious but also suggests that
ongoing fraud is a calculated response.

   If the message of *The Master* is not particularly exceptional, its method
of delivering that message is quite extraordinary. The mirror and television set featured in the scene that takes place in Dennis's bedroom, as
well as the gaggle of cameras featured in the final scene, call attention
to the fact that when the very nature and morality of corruption are at
stake, there is always another perspective to consider, always more of
the context to see, more space within which the accused agents operate.
It is not entirely clear whether the spectator is invited into that context
and therefore allowed to consider their own agency or the spectator is
held at arm's length, given an opportunity to visualize the full context
and observe the way that other agents operate within it. This ambiguity
produces a revelatory kind of free indirect subjectivity. Whereas conventional forms of free indirect subjectivity—such as point-of-view shots
and auditory memories on the sound track—invite spectator-subjects to
identify with specific characters, the mirrored form of indirect subjectivity that I have discussed in this chapter seems to invite spectator-subjects
to identify *as* a camera. However, they are not necessarily invited to identify *with* the camera telling the story. It is as if spectators are allowed to
capture and edit their own sequences, as it were, by toggling back and
forth between the primary narrative perspective (nondiegetic camera)
and secondary narrative perspective (mirror, screen, or another camera). The resulting narrative might be called *conspiratorial* in the sense
that the second perspective conspires with the first to deceive spectators, although I would not consider such deception in entirely negative
terms. The primary narrative perspective of most cinema is itself highly
deceptive—such is the nature of the medium. It frames ideas for spectators at the same time that it presents itself as objective. Meanwhile, mirrored indirect subjectivity pretends to show spectators more information
than one camera can show and therefore pretends to be more objective,

but two or more two-dimensional images do not a third dimension make. So whereas *Basi and Company* purportedly exposes the complicity of all social strata in the corruption endemic to Nigeria but actually provides just two snapshots, one of the rich and one of the poor, seemingly drawing a line between the two, Nollywood plays more formally with the discrepancy between surface and meaning, between facade and desire. State television calls for a subject position that disavows corruption of every type, but Nollywood is not so sure. Corrupt individuals like Ben and Dennis may not be winners in the end, and spectators may not be invited to identify with them, but the use of mirrors and mirror-like technologies invites spectators to *reflect* on the conditions in which corruption flourishes and by which it makes a certain amount of sense.

Nollywood's comic mode of address may not invite spectator-subjects to identify with characters who are positioned on the margins of the liberal world order—as the melodramatic and gothic modes often do—but it does address spectators as indirect subjects of the liberal world order. By asking spectators to identify with several third-person narrative perspectives, the comedies discussed in this chapter invite spectators to attend critically to issues of corruption, fraud, race, and colonialism, as well as objectively consider their own desires. Some Nigerians may desire access to and the benefits of a world system built on the backs of their ancestors and maintained by holding them at arm's length from its benefits, yet comedies also draw attention to the hypocrisy, the corruption, and the profound inequality endemic to liberal modernity. Being placed on the margins of the world system enables Nigerians to reassess that system, or so comedies suggest. And although *Basi and Company* calls for subjects to temper their desires, to avoid participating in the corrupt world system, for the sake of the nation, *Osuofia in London* and *The Master* invite subjects to consider how they might appropriate and apply the terms of the system for their own benefit. As Copjec argues, "The suspicion of dissimulation offers the subject a kind of reprieve from the dictates of law, the social superego. These dictates are perceived as hypotheses that must be tested rather than imperatives that must be automatically and unconditionally obeyed."[52] Therefore, the comic mode may be no more radical than any other, yet at least it shows that periliberal subjectivity, like all subjectivities, is not simply domination but an invitation to agency. Agency is always circumscribed, and periliberal agency is no less so—perhaps more so—but if the entire modern world is a 419 scam and if the pedagogues of the world are scamming on the superlative order, then what, indeed, is wrong with a little 419 of your own?

Conclusion

FANTASIES OF INTEGRATION OR
FANTASIES OF SOVEREIGNTY?

Nollywood is a relatively young film industry that is changing at break-neck speed. There is a Yoruba proverb that says, "If the snail moves, the shell will follow it" (*Bi igbin ba fa, ikaraun yoo tele e*), which I think aptly describes something about Nollywood, though not its pace. Instead, the metaphor of the snail and its shell describes the relationship between Nollywood and state television, the thing from which Nollywood emerged and from which it cannot be disassociated. Nollywood may be moving in many new directions, but the history of state screen media continues to be an important part of the industry's identity. The articulation of snail and shell also metaphorizes the conjuncture at the heart of this book—roughly the moment when *Living in Bondage* came out, in 1992—which calls for forms of analysis stretching out in multiple temporal directions. The part of my analysis that digs back into the shell, as it were, is relatively robust. The part of the analysis that stretches out *after* 1992, however, has only proceeded up to about 2005, the year *Games Women Play* was released. Since then, a lot has changed in southern Nigeria and especially in Nollywood. Indeed, rather than a snail, Nollywood might well be considered a photon, moving at the speed of light.

In recent years, scholars and other industry observers have more or less settled on the term *New Nollywood* to describe the quantum acceleration of changes taking place in the industry.[1] These changes have led to segmentation, such that many means of production, distribution, and reception that have long defined Nollywood may still be thriving, but new means are creating new audience configurations and—most of all—new kinds of films. If a key part of the story of *Indirect Subjects* concerns the ways in which screen media participate in the construction of social relations regarding the state and the global economy, we would be remiss not to mention the ways in which Nigerian screen media segmentation, resulting in the rise of New Nollywood, participates in the construction of new forms of social segmentation, which include something that could be described as *New Nigeria*.

New Nigeria is both physical and conceptual. Connor Ryan's sketch of Nollywood's "metropolitan new style" draws attention to the establishment of alternative exhibition spaces for Nollywood films, which include state-of-the-art shopping malls and internet video-streaming platforms. Many spectators no longer consume Nollywood titles (which are not even "video films" anymore) on television screens in private or semipublic spaces; rather, they sit in the dark, surrounded by Dolby sound, or tap on their phones and tablets. Producing content for these platforms requires access to and mastery of certain technologies that affect the look of the films produced, but those technologies are easier and easier to come by in the New Nigeria. Nevertheless, the spectators who can afford the tickets sold in shopping malls and feel comfortable there, or who have access to the kind of bandwidth necessary to stream video, constitute a small segment of the audience that Old Nollywood cultivated in Old Nigeria. In fact, many of the spectators consuming Nollywood content on streaming services—such as YouTube, IrokoTV, and Netflix—spend a significant amount of time, if not their entire lives, outside of Nigeria, in places where internet connections are relatively strong. Regardless, those who do stream Nollywood movies in Nigeria or watch them on big screens in cities such as Lagos, Abuja, Port Harcourt, Ibadan, and Calabar experience what Ryan describes as "a local iteration of a spatial form that is reproduced around the world, a globalized sensorium providing a unique affective experience and promising to insert spectators, as if seamlessly, into an immersive space of consumption that is shared around the globe."[2] The malls and their promises are therefore not simply islands in a sea of otherwise crumbling infrastructure and informal economic activity, although that does aptly describe the situation. As Karin Barber wrote in 1987 about Nigeria's economy, "The islands of the capital-intensive and bureaucratically rational sector are surrounded by the sea of the informal sector."[3] Little about that geography has changed, but shopping malls and the like are in fact part of an increasingly linked archipelago of formal, commercial institutions linked directly to the global capitalist marketplace. If there is a Nigerian landmass from which this archipelago stretches, it is—ironically—offshore.

Eko Atlantic City is the name of a massive infill project taking shape off the coast of Victoria Island in Lagos. The project is designed to create ten square kilometers of new real estate in the most coveted part of the city.

It will have the best infrastructure that engineers can build. It will prop up several skyscrapers, condominiums, and gleaming retail spaces, accommodating up to a quarter of a million people. The model, as well as the design expertise and much of the capital for the project, comes from the Persian Gulf. Thus, like Palm Islands, Dubai World, and Saadiyat Island, Eko Atlantic represents the kind of wealth that—in the Anthropocene, at least—only oil can produce, especially at the membrane between liberalism and periliberalism. So although sea levels in the physical world are rising, sea levels in some parts of the informal economy seem to be falling, and as the water recedes, landmasses of formal capital like Eko Atlantic look as if they are rising up, revealing submarine connections to things like shopping malls, mobile phone carriers, and other islands in the "archipelago" of formal capitalism increasingly apparent in Nigeria. This is what the popular narrative about "Africa rising" is really all about. However, what it actually means is that some people will find themselves on top of the rising landmass while many others will remain underwater or beached upon its shores.

Each of these developments is having a profound effect on the look and thematic preoccupations of certain Nigerian screen media. As Jonathan Haynes reports, corporate investors—from IrokoTV to MultiChoice and EbonyLife TV—demand that their productions include glamorous settings and beautiful actors who speak clear English.[4] These features suggest that middle-class experiences and aspirations may become reliable images in the New Nigeria: they can be made to be taken for granted. And as Moradewun Adejunmobi notes, New Nollywood stories are thus more likely to have ambiguous conclusions than video films.[5] They can concern themselves with the many ways that people with resources make decisions and, therefore, make themselves, rather than worry about the structural conditions that define subject formation. It is all, of course, very neoliberal.

As I have argued throughout this book, neoliberalism and periliberalism may sometimes overlap, but they are not the same things. The increasingly generic, neoliberal subjectivities that characterize New Nollywood may indicate that the Nigerian film industry is becoming perhaps less periliberal and more like contemporary film culture in other parts of the world. In this vein, Carmela Garritano compares what is happening in Nigeria (and, to a lesser extent, in Ghana) to what happened in India during the 1990s, when the Hindi motion picture industry became Bollywood.[6] Some New Nollywood films are as transnational in their settings and preoccupations as the classics of 1990s Bollywood, whereas other New Nollywood films pursue neoliberal themes entirely within the borders of Nigeria.[7] Rather than index a liberal form of life lived "out there," they seem to be indexing forms of life lived just around the corner, just behind that wall over there topped with razor wire and broken glass, or beyond that traffic barrier flanked by privately funded paramilitary guards.[8] For Haynes, these industry developments do not exactly derive from corporate integration; rather, they demonstrate "eligibility for such integration."[9] Therefore, the lingering question from the point of view of *Indirect Subjects* is whether New Nollywood offers fantasies of integration into the liberal world order, the end of indirect subjection, or something else.

One of the organizing principles common to all the periliberal modes of address I have described in this book is the concept of patience. In colonial cinema, state television, and video film—whether in masculine or feminine melodrama, whether in gothic or comic modes—spectators are imagined and addressed in ways that place them at the very center of the productive processes that have shaped the liberal world order, while also holding them at arm's length, inviting them to experience liberal capitalism not as a past form of exploitation or a present enterprise but as a potential future, one that may arrive if they can tolerantly endure until the conditions for its realization are met. Perhaps, therefore, the arrival of shopping malls and offshore fantasy islands indicates that conditions *are* being met. It may be true, proportionally speaking, that few Nigerians have access to those spaces, but instead of needing to leave Nigeria to experience liberalism, they only need to move up another rung on the social ladder. If they can just land a job in real-estate development, a disruptive start-up, or a multinational corporation (which, to be clear, are jobs that are few and far between), perhaps they too can find themselves sunbathing on an island of capital. Therefore, New Nollywood is much less interested in patience than was Old Nollywood.

Nevertheless, although new sources of capital are central to the rise of New Nollywood and thus appear to be relatively accessible in recent films, profitable businesses and lucrative professions still play complicated roles in film texts. In several recent examples, these indicators of "eligibility for integration" into the liberal world order loom with very little direct attention. In hit comedies like *Phone Swap* (2012), *The Wedding Party* (2016), and *Chief Daddy* (2018), for example, characters to whom sources of wealth are attached work in unspecified corporations, have unexplained relationships with oil and gas, or are described simply as "industrialists." In *Phone Swap*, which was funded in part by a major telecommunications corporation, the utter illegibility of professional wealth and the ways in which it is generated are played for comic effect.[10] In one scene, two tall and barrel-chested brothers from a small village ask a lean and pretentious businessman from Lagos (Wale Ojo) about his "handiwork." He replies that he works for "Mindus Conglomerates, specifically in the areas of product marketing and developmental services, helping to predict strategies for upcoming and future territorial trends for consumer expectations yet to be ascertained." He then asks the brothers about their handiwork, and one (Charles Billion) replies, with a contemptuous look on his face, "Business." Here, corporate wealth seems fatuous, entirely disconnected from the everyday concerns of ordinary people and the real, informal "business" that keeps Nigeria running. Meanwhile, in dramas and thrillers like *Fifty* (2015) and *The CEO* (2016), corporate wealth is given a more nuanced treatment through textured depictions of the lives of high earners in fields like medicine, real-estate development, and telecommunications. Rather than silly, access to capital can be a matter of life and death. In *Fifty* and *Lionheart* (2018), it is also a family matter, where highly competent women manage corporations founded by their fathers, much like Anne Haatrope in *Checkmate* (see chapter 3). However, the business at the center of *Lionheart*, a transport company, serves to index the local economy, exploring tensions between different national sources of capital investment rather than international finance. When international finance does feature in New Nollywood films, often in relation to oil, real estate, and telecommunications, the sources of capital tend to be in Europe and America, but there are lately more and more indications of and even a few important plot points regarding Chinese sources. In *The CEO*, for example, a Chinese "consortium" constitutes the principal threat to African professionals' lives and liberty, although the threat is more widespread than that. At the end of the film, a global company based in Paris has unwittingly fallen under the influence of Chinese business interests. In one very important sense, therefore, New Nollywood, like New Nigeria, is increasingly globalized.

To return to Adejunmobi's argument, New Nollywood films may index globalization, but they tend to be much less moralizing about the accumulation and expenditure of wealth than Old Nollywood video films. She also writes that "if Old Nollywood's melodramas represented individual responses to structural constraints, New Nollywood's alternative palette of stories offers portraits of individuals endowed with initiative in a world without constraints."[11] The globalized landscape of New Nollywood is thus more of a catalyst than a constraint, which actually makes it, to my mind, less global. Indeed, many well-known and widely debunked myths about an increasingly flat world, full of rising boats, are designed to obscure the treacherously jagged terrain of neoliberal capitalism, on which soles, knees, and palms are regularly bloodied. Early video films such as *Living in Bondage, Games Women Play, Billionaires Club,* and *The Master* not only acknowledge that jagged terrain; they also make it palpable. Thus, both Old Nollywood and New Nollywood offer their spectators wild fantasies, but Old Nollywood explores fantasies of survival in a manifestly uneven and iniquitous world, whereas New Nollywood tends to explore fantasies in denial of that world.

In terms of a mode of address, denial isolates spectators from the world as it is. New Nollywood may seem globalized, but it is as local as ever—if not more so. Indeed, although it runs counter to intuition, what Ryan describes as "the metropolitan new style" of New Nollywood should be read not as the increasing globalization of the industry; rather, it should be read as a fantasy of sovereignty constructed in relation to a "combined and uneven" world.[12] If the interconnections that define the modern world have come about only through the transatlantic slave trade, colonialism, and periliberalism—through various forms of extreme exploitation—then a truly globalized cinema is one that looks and feels iniquitous, not one that looks and feels more the same. In other words, Old Nollywood, though addressed to what it imagines as a "local" audience—indeed, because it conceptualizes locality as a construct produced by global forces—is the truly globalized film industry, whereas New Nollywood and its fantasies of sovereignty may constitute a more localized version of screen media.

Denying the world as it is, however, could have its advantages. The future world, if it will be better than the present one, must be imagined in order to be constructed. And if culture is constitutive of reality, not simply representative of it, then I want to resist the urge to categorically condemn New Nollywood's localized style. Part of my argument in this book has been that Nigerian screen media are not simply illustrations of periliberal relations but are constitutive participants that imagine versions of "in here" and "out there," that conceptualize a world held at arm's length from those without whom it would never have been possible in the first place. Nollywood's new fantasies may be localized, but they may also represent a profound break from the history of periliberalism that has characterized Nigerian screen media production since the Greville brothers first set up their tripod in Lagos. Instead of constructing a vision of sovereignty lost, as in Old Nollywood epics, New Nollywood may be laying the groundwork for a form of sovereignty that starts in the present. Of course, pure sovereignty is not possible, and I think that the people whose blood, sweat, and tears have made Nollywood know that. Moreover, although I have signaled that particular paradox, drawing from James Ferguson's work throughout this book, the profundity of the ensuing ironies never wanes. Since at least the implementation of indirect rule in the early twentieth century, Nigeria and many other parts of Africa have been shut out of the liberal world order. Fantasizing about being in it, even though it has never offered much to its indirect subjects, may be less about acquiescing to the demands of liberalism than about imagining a kind of reformation. And if materiality and representation feed upon and constitute each other, then forms of representation can affect the material world. Therefore, Nollywood invites us to consider the possibility that if periliberalism were to end, if indirect subjects were to become direct subjects, then liberalism—which feeds upon its outside—might grow weak. If that happens, perhaps real liberation can begin.

Notes

INTRODUCTION

1. The director of the film is sometimes listed as "Vic Mordi," which is a pseudonym that Obi-Rapu assumed in order to circumvent state television policies against working in the informal sector.

2. This is Rick Altman's term. See "Sound Space."

3. See Pasolini, "The Cinema of Poetry," 558.

4. See Schwartz, "Typewriter," 131.

5. Schwartz, 124.

6. See Barber, *The Anthropology of Texts, Persons and Publics*, 137–74. For a discussion focused on African screen media, see also Carmela Garritano's analysis of a "presentational mode of address" that features in some Ghanaian video films. Garritano, *African Video Movies and Global Desires*, 115, 127.

7. See Agbiboa, "'God's Time Is the Best.'"

8. "Video film" may seem a contradiction in terms, apparently designating the combination of two media technologies. However, "film" in this formulation stands in for "feature-length film," the hegemonic form in global cinema. Therefore, what built Nollywood were feature-length films made with video technology. Many Nigerians also refer to the same objects as "home videos" because they were designed for home viewing, not because they were made in the home.

9. The term *Nollywood* was coined in a *New York Times* article. See Norimitsu Onishi, "Step Aside, L.A. and Bombay, for Nollywood," *New York Times*, September 16, 2002, accessed January 13, 2014, www.nytimes.com/2002/09/16/world/step-aside-la-and-bombay-for-nollywood.html. For more on the politics of the name "Nollywood," see Haynes, "Nollywood: What's in a Name."

10. One study even claims that Nollywood is the second-most-productive film industry on Earth. See "Nollywood Rivals Bollywood in Film/Video Production."

11. For more on "governmentality," or the process by which individuals assume the mentality of government, unofficially managing and regulating themselves and others as officials might, see Foucault, *The Government of Self and Others*.

12. This book's focus on southern Nigeria derives in large part from the meanings associated with the term *Nollywood*. The northern Nigerian film industry, though similarly

based on video filmmaking and contributing to Nigeria's vast production numbers, is organized very differently, both professionally and aesthetically. Its practitioners often refer to their industry as "Kannywood," after the center of production, the massive city of Kano. Many northerners may consume southern Nigerian ("Nollywood") films, but many if not most of the North's filmmakers do not consider themselves part of Nollywood. Nollywood is therefore primarily a southern phenomenon, and a history of northern Nigerian screen media—which I am not capable of producing—would likely tell a slightly different story about Nigeria's relationship to the world.

13. See Rivero, *Broadcasting Modernity*.

14. Shipley, Comaroff, and Mbembe, "Africa in Theory," 658–59.

15. The British case receives more attention in this book, but the French case is equally important. See, for example, Kohn, "Empire's Law."

16. Mehta, *Liberalism and Empire*, 46.

17. Some useful examples of liberal imperialism/imperial liberalism scholarship include a collection of essays edited by Muthu, *Empire and Modern Political Thought*, as well as Bell, *Reordering the World*. See also Fischer, *Modernity Disavowed*; and Losurdo, *Liberalism: A Counter History*.

18. Mantena, *Alibis of Empire*, 38, 2.

19. Mantena, 12.

20. Mamdani, *Citizen and Subject*. In some cases the zones were drawn so that members of one African society oversaw the subjects of other African societies, further complicating the process of indirection. See Ochonu, *Colonialism by Proxy*.

21. Mamdani, *Citizen and Subject*, 3.

22. Mamdani, *Define and Rule*, 27.

23. Lenin, *Imperialism*.

24. Fanon, *The Wretched of the Earth*, 57.

25. Rodney, *How Europe Underdeveloped Africa*.

26. Ince, "Primitive Accumulation," 106.

27. Ince, *Colonial Capitalism*.

28. Brennan, "The Economic Image-Function of the Periphery," 113.

29. Cooper, *Africa since 1940*, 182, 172.

30. Compare Apter, *The Pan-African Nation*.

31. See Hall's masterful evaluation of Gramsci's thought in "Gramsci's Relevance for the Study of Race and Ethnicity," 19.

32. For more on the "world systems" approach to liberalism in world history, see Wallerstein, *The Modern World-System IV*.

33. For a useful overview of Foucault's thought on the subject, see Lemke, "'The Birth of Bio-politics.'"

34. For a particularly generative description of neoliberal subjectivity in relation to television, as well as overarching processes of governmentality that inform even commercial television in the global North, see Weber, *Makeover TV*.

35. W. Brown, *Undoing the Demos*, 94.

36. Ferguson, *Global Shadows*.

37. For insightful reviews of the ideas that Foucault and Butler have contributed to the discussion of subjectivity and agency, see Dews, "Power and Subjectivity in

Foucault"; and Magnus, "The Unaccountable Subject." Bourdieu's ideas on this issue are perhaps best articulated in the chapter "Structures, *Habitus*, Practices" in *The Logic of Practice*, 52–65.

38. Thomas, "Historicizing Agency," 325.

39. de Bruijn, van Dijk, and Gewald, *Strength beyond Structure*.

40. Here, I am self-consciously but derisively invoking Adam Smith's *The Theory of Moral Sentiments*, although it is not central to my argument.

41. Adejunmobi, "Neoliberal Rationalities in Old and New Nollywood," 33–34.

42. Garritano, *African Video Movies and Global Desires*, 15, 11.

43. Garritano, 11.

44. Larkin, *Signal and Noise*, 170–73.

45. I am using the American edition, published in 2000. Haynes, *Nigerian Video Films*, 8.

46. Larkin, "Hausa Dramas and the Rise of Video Culture in Nigeria," 219.

47. See Obaseki, "Nigerian Video as the 'Child of Television.'"

48. McCall, "The Capital Gap," 11.

49. Bud, "The End of Nollywood's Guilded Age?"

50. For more on the changing nature of Nollywood's relationship to formal capitalism, see Haynes, "Neoliberalism, Nollywood, and Lagos."

51. McCall, "The Capital Gap," 11.

CHAPTER ONE: SUBJECTS OF INDIRECT RULE

1. Rice, "Exhibiting Africa," 121.

2. National Archives, Ibadan, Nigeria, Colonial Secretary's Office, 25/1 46, "Proposal for Producing Cinematograph Films," March 25, 1922.

3. Lugard, *The Dual Mandate in British Tropical Africa*, 18.

4. Frankema, Williamson, and Woltjer, "An Economic Rationale for the African Scramble."

5. Barnhart, "Status Competition and Territorial Aggression."

6. See Constantine, *The Making of British Colonial Development Policy 1914-1940*; Mantena, *Alibis of Empire*; and Gächter, "Finance Capital and Peasants in Colonial West Africa."

7. See Mamdani, *Define and Rule*.

8. See Mantena, *Alibis of Empire*, 21–55, for more on the "crisis of liberal imperialism."

9. Maine, *Lectures on the Early History of Institutions*, 392–93, also cited in Mamdani, *Define and Rule*, 131.

10. Lyall, "Life and Speeches of Sir Henry Maine," 290, also cited in Mantena, *Alibis of Empire*, 166, and Mamdani, *Define and Rule*, 21.

11. Mantena, *Alibis of Empire*, 150.

12. Mamdani, *Define and Rule*, 2–3, originally argued in Mamdani, *Citizen and Subject*.

13. Maine, *Village Communities in the East and West*, 215, also cited in Mamdani, *Define and Rule*, 11.

14. Nwabughuogu, "The Role of Propaganda," 86.

15. Nwabughuogu, 91.

16. Olukoju, "The Travails of Migrant and Wage Labour," 60.

17. Stephen, *The Empire of Progress*, 95–96.

18. Detailed descriptions of the footage that was screened prior to the opening of the Wembley exhibition are provided in *West Africa*. See "Nigeria Filmed for the British Empire Exhibition," *West Africa*, June 23, 1923.

19. MacKenzie, *Propaganda and Empire*, 108.

20. Part of that campaign included film. See Grieveson, "The Cinema and the (Common) Wealth of Nations."

21. Simonelli, "'[L]aughing nations of happy children who have never grown up.'"

22. See, for example, Stephen, *The Empire of Progress*.

23. Grieveson and MacCabe, *Empire and Film*.

24. See, for example, MacKenzie, *Propaganda and Empire*, 112.

25. Fry, "Architecture at Wembley," 243.

26. "Pioneers, O! Pioneers," *West Africa*, May 24, 1924.

27. "Two Films That Matter," *West Africa*, April 26, 1924, 393.

28. Mantena, *Alibis of Empire*, 179–88.

29. "The Real African Life," *West Africa*, April 26, 1924, 393–94.

30. Lawrence, *Seven Pillars of Wisdom*.

31. "Nigeria Filmed for the British Empire Exhibition," *West Africa*, June 23, 1923, 670–73.

32. Lugard, "Tropical Africa at Wembley," *West Africa*, May 24, 1924, 3, 5, 7.

33. See Geppert, *Fleeting Cities*, 166–68.

34. Lugard, "Tropical Africa at Wembley," 5.

35. Lugard, 5.

36. Rice, "British Instructional Films."

37. William J. Yerby, "Application of Consul W. J. Yerby for Transfer from West Africa, 1924," W. E. B. Du Bois Papers (MS 312), Special Collections and University Archives, University of Massachusetts Amherst Libraries.

38. Burns, *Cinema and Society in the British Empire*, 71.

39. National Archives, Ibadan, Nigeria, Colonial Secretary's Office, 25/1 47, "Request for names and addresses of motion or moving picture shows in Nigeria," July 13, 1922, 8.

40. *Lagos Weekly Standard*, October 1, 1921, 3. "Fatty" refers to Fatty Arbuckle and "Bunny" to John Bunny, two major comic actors of Hollywood silent cinema.

41. National Archives, Ibadan, Nigeria, Colonial Secretary's Office, 25/1 47, "Request for names and addresses of motion or moving picture shows in Nigeria," July 13, 1922, 8.

42. Trumpbour, *Selling Hollywood to the World*; Jarvie, *Hollywood's Overseas Campaign*.

43. See Trumpbour, *Selling Hollywood to the World*, 64.

44. Grieveson, "The Cinema and the (Common) Wealth of Nations," 87.

45. Quoted in Gott, *The Film in National Life*, 133.

46. See Burns, *Cinema and Society in the British Empire*, 72. Various plans to expand commercial cinema came to naught because of official ambivalence.

47. Ross, *Working Class Hollywood*, 198, 201.

48. "Films of West African Life," *West Africa*, February 19, 1927, 175.

49. Candotti, "Cotton Growing and Textile Production in Northern Nigeria," 1.

50. Lugard, *The Dual Mandate*, 375.

51. Candotti, "Cotton Growing and Textile Production in Northern Nigeria," 7.

52. See Candotti, 10; and Hogendorn, "The Vent-for-Surplus Theory."

53. Grieveson, *Cinema and the Wealth of Nations*, 166–67.

54. Huxley, *Africa View*, 57.

55. Quoted in Huxley, 59.

56. Quoted in Huxley, 295.

57. Youé, "Peasants, Planters and Cotton Capitalists."

58. Beller, *The Cinematic Mode of Production*, 2.

59. Morton-Williams, *Cinema in Rural Nigeria*, 31.

60. Smyth, "Grierson, the British Documentary Movement, and Colonial Cinema in British Colonial Africa."

61. Shaka, *Modernity and the African Cinema*, 210, 211.

62. Shaka, 208.

63. See, in particular, the work of Burns, including his *Cinema and Society in the British Empire*.

64. Larkin, *Signal and Noise*, 32–33.

65. Ferguson, *Global Shadows*, 50–68.

66. For more details about Awolowo's projects, see M. Brown, "The Enchanted History of Nigerian State Television."

CHAPTER TWO: EMERGENCY OF THE STATE

1. Kingsway advertisement, Lagos *Daily Times*, October 1, 1960, 7.

2. See Ferguson, *Global Shadows*, 50–68.

3. Berlant, *Cruel Optimism*, 1, 14.

4. Some of those details are covered in this book, but for more on the subject, see M. Brown, "The Enchanted History of Nigerian State Television."

5. Betiang, "Global Drums and Local Masquerades," 10.

6. See also the foundational early work of Ukadike on the relationship between anglophone African film and television in his seminal book, *Black African Cinema*.

7. M. Brown, "The Enchanted History of Nigerian State Television," 95. The concept of the state as gatekeeper comes from Cooper, *Africa since 1940*.

8. As Cooper writes, even though "we can never distance ourselves entirely from our present . . . we can imperfectly look at different people in their different presents imagining their futures." See "Possibility and Constraint," 169.

9. For detailed descriptions of *Self-Government for Western Nigeria*, see M. Brown, "The Enchanted History of Nigerian State Television," 98–100; and Rice, "Self Government for Western Nigeria: Analysis."

10. Awolowo, *Awo*, 289.

11. In 1953 Awolowo led his party, the Action Group, on a parliamentary walkout during debates over the newest colonial constitution. The governor-general of the colony, John Stuart Macpherson, issued a public condemnation of the Action Group via radio, on the Nigerian Broadcasting Service (NBS). In order to respond, Awolowo requested NBS airtime from the Ministry of Information but was denied. He then realized

that in order to reach the Nigerian public, his party would have to speak louder than the colonial government. For the next six years, he and the Action Group drew up plans for a television station, which they formally launched in Ibadan on October 31, 1959. Versions of this story appear in Egbon, "Western Nigeria Television Service"; Uche, *Mass Media, Peoples and Politics in Nigeria*; and Umeh, "The Advent and Growth of Television Broadcasting in Nigeria."

12. Arms, "Television Comes to Africa," 37.

13. Olubomehin, "Cinema Business in Lagos, Nigeria since 1903," 8.

14. Faleti, "The Origin and Impact of Yoruba Drama."

15. Arms, "Diary from Nigeria: The Second Year," 9.

16. Mazzarella, "'Reality Must Improve.'"

17. See Potter, *Broadcasting Empire*.

18. Mackay, *Broadcasting in Nigeria*, 49.

19. Olusola, *The Village Headmaster*, 9.

20. In 1991 Ukadike referred to *The Village Headmaster* as "the oldest and most highly rated television program to date." See "Anglophone African Media."

21. Olusola, *The Village Headmaster*, 51.

22. This phrase comes from Waterman's study of juju musicians in southwestern Nigeria. See "'Our Tradition Is a Very Modern Tradition.'"

23. Olusola, *The Village Headmaster*, 51.

24. Olusola, 38.

25. Olusola, 51.

26. See Adesokan, "Nollywood and the Idea of the Nigerian Cinema."

27. Gibbs, "'Yapping' and 'Pushing,'" 23.

28. Olusola, *The Village Headmaster*, 52.

29. Olusola, 81.

30. Olusola, 35–36.

31. Olusola, *Tele-scape*, 19, 20.

32. Quayson, *Oxford Street, Accra*, 65.

33. Olusola, *Tele-scape*, 19. Compare with Abu-Lughod's description of the fraught relationship between television content producers and the national elite in Egypt in her book *Dramas of Nationhood*.

34. Olusola, *Tele-scape*, 21.

35. Foucault, *The History of Sexuality*, 140–41.

36. "State of Emergency," 9.

37. See M. Brown, "The Enchanted History of Nigerian State Television," 104–7.

38. Olusola, *Tele-scape*, 111–29.

39. Olusola, 125, 126.

40. Cramer, *Utopian Television*, 11, 12.

41. Olusola, *Tele-scape*, 127.

42. See, in particular, Agamben, *State of Exception*. Chapter 5 of this book provides further analysis of the concept of sovereignty.

43. Cooper, *Africa in the World*, 30, 31.

44. See Daannaa, "The Acephalous Society," 61–85.

45. Olusola, "The Video Shock," 64.

CHAPTER THREE: "NO ROMANCE WITHOUT FINANCE"

1. "*Checkmate* on Screen with Business Zeal," *Guardian* (Lagos), April 19, 1991, 11.

2. Jade Miller, *Nollywood Central*, 13–20.

3. Green-Simms makes a similar argument in "Hustlers, Home-Wreckers and Homoeroticism," 61.

4. For a definition of *osu*, we might turn to intertextuality rather than ethnography. The protagonist of Achebe's *No Longer at Ease*, Obi Okonkwo, derisively describes the taboo, for the benefit of his Christianized father, this way: "Our fathers in their darkness and ignorance called an innocent man *osu*, a thing given to idols, and thereafter he became an outcast, and his children, and his children's children for ever." Achebe, *No Longer at Ease*, 151.

5. Gledhill, "The Melodramatic Field," 33.

6. Gledhill, 33.

7. Brooks, *The Melodramatic Imagination*, 15.

8. Dissanayake, *Melodrama and Asian Cinema*.

9. Adejunmobi, "Charting Nollywood's Appeal Locally and Globally," 114.

10. Zarzosa, "Melodrama and the Modes of the World," 239.

11. L. Williams, "Mega-Melodrama!," 529.

12. For an account of the Sharia "controversy," see Kendhammer, "The Sharia Controversy in Northern Nigeria and the Politics of Islamic Law in New and Uncertain Democracies."

13. Olupona, *African Religions*, 2.

14. Brooks, *The Melodramatic Imagination*, 15.

15. Meyer, "'Praise the Lord.'"

16. Zarzosa, "Melodrama and the Modes of the World," 241.

17. See M. Brown, "Genre as Ideological Impulse."

18. Zarzoza, "Melodrama and the Modes of the World," 245, 244, 243.

19. I draw these claims from L. Williams, "Mega-Melodrama!"; and Weber, *Makeover TV*.

20. Bryce summarizes and responds to some of this literature in "Signs of Femininity, Symptoms of Malaise." See also Green-Simms, "Hustlers, Home-Wreckers and Homoeroticism."

21. Haynes, *Nigerian Video Films*, 29.

22. See Allen, *Speaking of Soap Operas*.

23. For more on this history and its exasperating erasure, see Geraghty and Weissmann, "Women, Soap Opera, and New Generations of Feminists."

24. Levine, "Melodrama and Soap Opera."

25. McClintock, *Imperial Leather*, 223–31.

26. Burke, *Lifebuoy Men, Lux Women*, 178.

27. Quoted in Marty, "Soap Gets in Your Eyes," 1015.

28. See R. Williams, *Modern Tragedy*.

29. Ayakoroma, *Trends in Nollywood*, 41, 43.

30. Clarion Chukwurah, interview by Matthew H. Brown, Lagos, Nigeria, August 21, 2015.

31. Ayakoroma, *Trends in Nollywood*, 42.

32. See Sola Osofisan, "Screenbaiting, Sponsorships," *Guardian* (Lagos), September 16, 1990, B8.

33. Yetunde Adjoto, "Fresh Acts as the Screen Cloud Rains," *Guardian* (Lagos), October 5, 1990, 16.

34. Sola Osofisan, "How the Government Bowed for *Checkmate*," *Guardian* (Lagos), August 9, 1992, B12.

35. See, for example, Chidirim Ndeche, "Relive Your 90s with These Epic Nigerian Films," *Guardian* (Lagos), July 18, 2018, accessed February 2, 2020, https://guardian.ng /life/film/relive-your-90s-with-these-epic-nigerian-films.

36. This phrase, as indicated previously, comes from Ferguson, *Global Shadows*, 50–68.

37. Mann, *From Empires to NGOs in the West African Sahel*.

38. Pereira, "National Council of Women's Societies and the State," 111–12.

39. The theme song for *Checkmate* was also the main title theme of a 1964 British World War II Air Force drama called *633 Squadron*.

40. Garritano, *African Video Movies and Global Desires*, 113.

41. See Afonja, "Changing Modes of Production and the Sexual Division of Labor among the Yoruba."

42. See Griffin, *Bread Winner*.

43. Joan Scott, *The Fantasy of Feminist History*, 21.

44. D. Smith, "Managing Men, Marriage, and Modern Love," 157.

45. The seminal account can be found in Sudarkasa, *Where Women Work: A Study of Yoruba Women in the Marketplace and in the Home*.

46. Lindsay, *Working with Gender*, 203.

47. Lindsay, 203.

48. Lindsay, 78.

49. World Council of Churches, *All-Africa Seminar on the Christian Home and Family Life*, 18.

50. Lindsay, *Working with Gender*, 43.

51. Titus 2:5, NIV.

52. Lindsay, *Working with Gender*, 109.

53. D. Smith, "Managing Men, Marriage, and Modern Love," 164.

54. Lindsay, *Working with Gender*, 211.

55. See Fapohunda, "The Nuclear Household Model in Nigerian Public and Private Sector Policy," 281.

56. Haynes and Okome cite sales of 150,000 copies, as compared to averages of 30,000–50,000 in the same period. See "Evolving Popular Media," 114.

57. Haynes, *Nollywood: The Creation of Nigerian Film Genres*, 81–82.

58. Haynes, 87. He writes that "the film makes the marital issues more important than the maternal ones for the audience."

59. Haynes, 87.

60. Haynes, 94.

61. D. Smith, *AIDS Doesn't Show Its Face*, 3. See also Ferguson, *Global Shadows*, 69–88.

62. Ferguson, 72.

63. Barber, "Popular Reactions to the Petro-Naira."

64. Isama, "The 20 Best Nollywood Movies of All Time."

65. See, for example, Akudinobi, "Nollywood: Prisms and Paradigms"; and Shaka and Uchendu, "Gender Representation in Nollywood Video Film Culture."

66. Haynes, *Nollywood: The Creation of Nigerian Film Genres*, 288.

67. See Novia, *Nollywood till November*, 44–51.

68. Emem Isong, interview by Matthew H. Brown, Lagos, Nigeria, December 9, 2010. See chapter 6 for more on the idea that screen media may function like mirrors.

69. Haynes, *Nollywood: The Creation of Nigerian Film Genres*, 93.

70. Bryce, "Signs of Femininity, Symptoms of Malaise," 84.

71. See Novia, *Nollywood till November*, 46.

72. See McLuhan, *Understanding Media*; and Meyer, "Mediation and Immediacy," 34.

73. McCain, "Video Exposé," 31.

74. Vasudevan, *The Melodramatic Public*, 98–129.

CHAPTER FOUR: BREADLOSERS

1. See Jackson, "End of the Wicked (1999)"; Newman, "Film Review: End of the Wicked"; and Leavold, "End of the Wicked (Nigerian Godsploitation, 1999)."

2. Because of attempts to censor the film, the Nigerian state is implicated in the "powers of darkness."

3. See Marshall, *Political Spiritualities*.

4. Haynes, *Nollywood: The Creation of Nigerian Film Genres*, 77–112.

5. Compare Wendl, "Wicked Villagers and the Mysteries of Reproduction."

6. For the seminal accounts of Africa's "occult economies," see Comaroff and Comaroff, *Modernity and Its Malcontents*; and Geschiere, *The Modernity of Witchcraft*.

7. Green-Simms, *Postcolonial Automobility*, 129.

8. Ugor, *Nollywood: Popular Culture and Narratives of Youth Struggles in Nigeria*, 111, 114.

9. Haynes is perhaps the first on record to note the presence of the *Living in Bondage* motif in *Ashes to Ashes*. See *Nollywood: The Creation of Nigerian Film Genres*, 187.

10. See Haynes, 29–39.

11. Haynes, 18.

12. Consider Hugo's photographic essay *Nollywood* (2009), which is insightfully analyzed by Nomusa Makhubu in "Politics of the Strange."

13. I should add that a scene in *Emotional Crack* involves one of the most painfully and also poignantly memorable moments of first-person subjectivity in Nollywood, when Chudi, while yelling at Crystal, slaps the camera, which moves to the right, then the left, as if inhabiting Crystal's pummeled subjectivity.

14. See Green-Simms, "Hustlers, Home-Wreckers and Homoeroticism."

15. Haynes, *Nollywood: The Creation of Nigerian Film Genres*, 19.

16. For a sociologist's perspective on the intersection of economics, politics, gender, and discourses about marriage, see Chen, *Cut Loose*. On the term *marriage material*, see 123.

17. Haynes, *Nollywood: The Creation of Nigerian Film Genres*, 187.

18. For the first and most thorough account, see McCall, "Juju and Justice at the Movies."

19. McCall, 64.

20. Compare Harnischfeger, "The Bakassi Boys."

21. For more on the production crisis, see Jedlowski, "From Nollywood to Nollyworld."

22. Green-Simms, *Postcolonial Automobility*.

23. For Green-Simms's treatment of cars in Nollywood, see *Postcolonial Automobility*, 123–60.

24. M. Brown, "At the Threshold of New Political Communities."

CHAPTER FIVE: SPECTERS OF SOVEREIGNTY

1. Achebe, *Things Fall Apart*, 205.

2. For more on the political, social, and psychological implications of this moment in the adaptation, see Uwah, "Things Fall Apart on Screen."

3. M. Brown, "At the Threshold of New Political Communities."

4. Comaroff and Comaroff, "Millennial Capitalism."

5. See, for example, Okome's brief discussion of epics in "West African Cinema," 5–6.

6. For a fine overview, see Punter and Byron, *The Gothic*.

7. Haynes, *Nollywood: The Creation of Nigerian Film Genres*, 154.

8. For examples of Igbo kingship institutions and a sense of their exceptionalism, see Opone, "Traditional Socio-political Organization of the Enuani Igbo of South Central Nigeria."

9. Mengara, "Colonial Intrusion and Stages of Colonialism," 33.

10. See Azuonye, "*Igbo enwe eze*."

11. Achebe, *Hopes and Impediments*, 30–39.

12. For an extended and insightful engagement with these kinds of issues, though in a slightly different cultural context, see Meyer, *Sensational Movies*, 252–87.

13. Haynes, *Nollywood: The Creation of Nigerian Film Genres*, 143; and Ayakoroma, *Trends in Nollywood*, 123.

14. Ayakoroma, 123.

15. Makhubu, "Interpreting the Fantastic."

16. Haynes, *Nollywood: The Creation of Nigerian Film Genres*, 155.

17. Achebe, *Things Fall Apart*, 59. Oliver Lovesey identifies this moment as a rare example of free indirect discourse in the novel, but in fact it is slightly more common than Lovesey claims. See "Making Use of the Past in *Things Fall Apart*," 124.

18. Achebe, *Things Fall Apart*, 75, 178, 208–9.

19. Achebe, 68.

20. Olaniyan, *Arrest the Music*, 163.

21. See, for example, Gomba's account in "*Things Fall Apart*: Chinua Achebe's Whetstone."

22. Gomba, 152.

23. Achebe, *Things Fall Apart*, 61.

24. See Ugochukwu, "*Things Fall Apart*—Achebe's Legacy, from Book to Screen"; and Wachuku and Ihentuge, "The Nigerian Film Industry and Literary Adaptation."

25. Ugochukwu suggests they are the ghosts of murdered children. She describes the lace veils they wear as traditional burial garments. See "*Things Fall Apart*—Achebe's Legacy, from Book to Screen," 171.

26. Ugochukwu, 177.

27. Achebe, *A Man of the People*.

28. Haynes, *Nollywood: The Creation of Nigerian Film Genres*, 142–61.

29. Harneit-Sievers, "Igbo 'Traditional Rulers.'"

30. A similar reinvestment in the concept of chiefs, both in real and imaginary terms, is detailed in Meyer's account of Ghanaian video films set in the precolonial past. See Meyer, *Sensational Movies*, 264–73.

31. The popularity of *Igodo* is attested to by the Nollywood filmmaker Charles Novia in his autobiography, *Nollywood till November*, 7–8. *Cultural epic* is the term that Haynes prefers for the genre, although I have often encountered simply *epic* when talking to street vendors in Nigeria.

32. It is the gate to the "diviners' forest" through which a Yoruba *babalawo* would pass. Susanne Wenger was an Austrian artist who settled in Osogbo in 1949 with her husband, Ulli Beier. They later divorced, and Wenger married Ayansola Oniru and became known as Adunni Olorisha. She was initiated into the Yoruba religion, later to become a high priestess, and continued to make art, especially in and near the sacred grove of Osun, a Yoruba deity of water and fertility. I had the privilege of meeting Wenger in 2007, shortly before her death, when she was living a quiet and contemplative life of art and spiritual practice in Osogbo. For a comprehensive and penetrating analysis of the grove and its relationship to African modern art, see Probst, *Osogbo and the Art of Heritage*.

33. Ayakoroma, *Trends in Nollywood*, 128–29.

34. Achebe, *The Trouble with Nigeria*, 1.

35. See, for example, Osaghae, *Crippled Giant*.

36. Mbembe, "Necropolitics," 12.

37. Diala, "Ritual and Mythological Recuperation in the Drama of Esiaba Irobi," 104.

38. Ayakoroma, *Trends in Nollywood*, 130–31. See also Umolu and Onosu, "Nollywood Films as Agents for National Development," 115.

39. See Teju Cole's fictionalized account of a young Nigerian man beholding Muhammed's car, which remains on display in the National Museum in Lagos, in *Everyday Is for the Thief*, 59–66.

40. Roberts, *Gothic Subjects*, 4.

41. Mbembe, "Necropolitics," 38.

42. On the state of exception, see Agamben, *State of Exception*.

43. Olaniyan, *Arrest the Music*, 165.

44. Kortenaar, "Becoming African and the Death of Ikemefuna," 787, 794, 778.

45. Campbell, *The Hero with a Thousand Faces*.

46. Derrida, *Specters of Marx*. Note that Derrida is not the first to use the term *hauntology*. See Davis, "Ét at Présent."

CHAPTER SIX: "WHAT'S WRONG WITH 419?"

1. Okoye, "Looking at Ourselves in Our Mirror."

2. Metz, *The Imaginary Signifier*.

3. Metz, 49.

4. See Lacan, "The Mirror Stage."

5. Mulvey, "Visual Pleasure and Narrative Cinema."

6. See Rosen, *Narrative, Apparatus, Ideology*.

7. Copjec, "The Orthopsychic Subject," 71.

8. Achebe, *Arrow of God*, 46. Citations are from the Penguin edition.

9. In this case I am drawing the language of interregnum from Olaniyan, although he, of course, draws it from Gramsci. See Olaniyan, *Arrest the Music*, 2.

10. See Nixon, *Slow Violence and the Environmentalism of the Poor*, 105.

11. Saro-Wiwa makes the trickster references explicit. Meanwhile, others have re-produced and refined those references. See Saro-Wiwa, "Author's Note." See also King-Aribisala, "*Basi and Company* and WAI," 8; and Hodapp, "A Serious Television Trickster."

12. Saro-Wiwa, *Four Farcical Plays*, 13.

13. See Derrida, "Author's Preface"; and Melchior-Bonnet, *The Mirror*, 85.

14. As is common in television situation comedies, several parts required new actors. In fact, many of the actors from *Basi and Company* also circulated through the Nigerian Television Authority, playing key roles in other influential programs. For example, from the 1989/1990 season on, Basi was played by Zulu Adigwe, who eventually played the role of Professor Edem in the pilot episode of *Checkmate*. Adigwe replaced the original Basi, Albert Egbe, who had played Odunuga in the original run of *The Village Headmaster*. In the episode titled "Lenders and Borrowers," Segi is played by Timi Zuofa, who was the fourth actor to fill that role, following Mildred Iweka, who would later play Ada in *Checkmate*.

15. Jonathan Miller, *On Reflection*, 12. The catalog includes the Velázquez painting *Las Meninas*, discussed at length by Foucault, whose analysis features later in this chapter.

16. Mbembe, *On the Postcolony*, 147.

17. Segi's name, as well as the nickname that others apply to her—"the lady with the beautiful eyeballs"—is a direct reference to the Yoruba-language autobiography of a prostitute, published initially in the *Lagos Herald* in 1929–1930: *Itan Igbesi-Aiye Emi Segilola Eleyinju Ege, Elegherun Oko L'Aiye*, or *The Life History of Me Segilola Endowed with Fascinating Eyes, the Sweetheart of a Thousand and One Men*. For more, see Barber, *Print Culture and the First Yoruba Novel*; and Aderinto, *When Sex Threatened the State*, 51–58.

18. See Lizardo and Mollick, "Oil Price Fluctuations and U.S. Dollar Exchange Rates."

19. See James Scott, *Seeing Like a State*.

20. In the author's note that precedes the novelized version of the series—in which Saro-Wiwa discusses the television program and compares it to tortoise folktales—he claims that he wanted viewers to "learn lessons from the moral of each story and go to bed well-entertained and educated at the end of each session." Saro-Wiwa, "Author's Note."

21. Saro-Wiwa, *Everything about "Basi and Company*," 5.

22. Agbaje and Adisa, "Political Education and Public Policy in Nigeria," 35, 28.

23. Saro-Wiwa, *Everything about "Basi and Company*," 8.

24. Gates Jr., *The Signifying Monkey*.

25. My use of the phrase *moral residue* comes from the undergraduate teaching of Harold E. Scheub, a pioneer scholar of African oral traditions. See M. Brown, *A Customized Version of Harold Scheub's "The African Storyteller*," 94–96.

26. James Brooke, "Enugu: 30 Million Nigerians Are Laughing at Themselves," *New York Times*, July 24, 1987, accessed November 9, 2013, www.nytimes.com/1987/07/24/world/enugu-journal-30-million-nigerians-are-laughing-at-themselves.html.

27. Hodapp, "A Serious Television Trickster," 512.

28. See, for example, M. Brown, "'Osuofia Don Enter Discourse.'"

29. Harrow, *Trash*, 246.

30. Haynes, *Nollywood: The Creation of Nigerian Film Genres*, 226.

31. Haynes, 228.

32. Harrow, *Trash*, 248–65.

33. Elsewhere, I describe this as "performing the unmodern." See M. Brown, "The Long Nollywood Century," 170–90.

34. Once again, see M. Brown, "'Osuofia Don Enter Discourse,'" 57–72.

35. Olaniyan, "African Cultural Studies," 100.

36. *Wahala* is Hausa for "trouble" and is used throughout Nigeria.

37. Harrow, *Trash*, 254–55.

38. Foucault, *The Order of Things*, 3–18.

39. Foucault, 17.

40. Larkin, *Signal and Noise*, 184.

41. See chapter 1.

42. Larkin, *Signal and Noise*, 189.

43. 419 ("four one nine") is the common colloquial term used to refer to all forms of fraud, especially "advanced fee fraud," which is often associated with Nigerian email scams. The number refers to the relevant section of the Nigerian penal code.

44. See, for example, Olu Maintain, "Yahoozee," YouTube video, Reloaded Records, 2007.

45. See, for example, Andrew Smith, "Nigerian Email Scams and the Charms of Capital."

46. "Brian Ross Investigates: Mugus and Masters."

47. "UNICEF Nigeria."

48. Larkin, "State Aesthetics."

49. This formulation of subjectivity obviously paraphrases Marx, *The Eighteenth Brumaire of Louis Bonaparte*.

50. See Comaroff and Comaroff, *Modernity and Its Malcontents*; and Piot, "Border Practices."

51. Ellis, *This Present Darkness*, 21.

52. Copjec, "The Orthopsychic Subject," 64.

CONCLUSION

1. See, for example, Ryan, "New Nollywood"; Adejunmobi, "Neoliberal Rationalities in Old and New Nollywood"; Haynes, "Between the Informal Sector and Transnational Capitalism"; and Jedlowski, "From Nollywood to Nollyworld."

2. Ryan, "New Nollywood," 62.

3. Barber, "Popular Arts in Africa," 32.

4. Haynes, "Neoliberalism, Nollywood, and Lagos," 66.

5. Adejunmobi, "Neoliberal Rationalities in Old and New Nollywood," 35, 38.

6. Garritano, "Introduction: Nollywood—An Archive of African Worldliness." 46.

7. The classic example of an early film in the neoliberal, Bollywood style, featuring transnational locations, is *Dilwale Dulhania Le Jayenge* (1995).

8. For more on these physical features of neoliberal Africa, see Olaniyan, "African Urban Garrison Architecture."

9. Haynes, "Neoliberalism, Nollywood, and Lagos," 70.

10. For more on *Phone Swap* and its funding sources, see Haynes, *Nollywood: The Generation of Nigerian Film Genres*, 298–300.

11. Adejunmobi, "Neoliberal Rationalities in Old and New Nollywood," 39.

12. Ryan, "New Nollywood." The formulation, "combined and uneven," comes from Leon Trotsky and has recently been taken up in world literary studies. See Warwick Research Collective, *Combined and Uneven Development*.

Filmography

Agogo Eewo. 2002. Dir. Tunde Kelani. Yoruba and English. VCD. Nigeria. Mainframe Productions.

Ashes to Ashes 1 and 2. 2001. Dir. Andy Amenechi. English and Pidgin. VCD. Nigeria. OJ Productions.

Basi and Company. Series. 1986–1990. Dir. Uzorma Onungwa. Created by Ken Saro-Wiwa. English. Television broadcast and VHS. Nigeria. Saros International Productions.

The Battle of Musanga 1 and 2. 1996. Dir. Bolaji Dawodu. English. VHS. Nigeria. Gabosky and Chezkay.

Behind the Clouds. Series. 1988–1990. Dir. Matt Dadzie. Created by Paul Emema. English. Television broadcast and VHS. Nigeria. Nigerian Television Authority.

Billionaires Club 1–3. 2003. Dir. Afam Okereke. English. VCD. Nigeria. Great Movies Industries.

Black Cotton. 1927. English. Celluloid. Great Britain. British Instructional Films.

The CEO. 2016. Dir. Kunle Afolayan. English. Digital video. Nigeria. Golden Effects.

Checkmate. Series. 1991–1994. Dir. Bolaji Dawodu. Created by Amaka Igwe. English. Television broadcast, VHS, and digital video. Nigeria. Crystal Gold/Moving Movies.

Chief Daddy. 2018. Dir. Niyi Akinmolayan. English and Yoruba. Digital Video. Nigeria. EbonyLife Films.

Cock Crow at Dawn. Series. 1980–1983. Dir. Matt Dadzie. English. Television broadcast. Nigeria. Nigerian Television Authority.

Cotton Growing in Nigeria. 1927. English. Celluloid. Great Britain. British Instructional Films.

Daybreak in Udi. 1949. Dir. Terry Bishop. English and Igbo. Celluloid. Great Britain. Crown Film Unit.

Dilwale Dulhania Le Jayenge. 1995. Dir. Aditya Chopra. Hindi. Celluloid. India. Yash Raj Films.

Egg of Life 1 and 2. 2003. Dir. Andy Amenechi. English. VCD. Nigeria. OJ Productions.

Emotional Crack. 2003. Dir. Lancelot Imasuen. English. VCD. Nigeria. Remmy Jes.

End of the Wicked. 1999. Dir. Teco Benson. English. VCD. Nigeria. Helen Ukpabio/ Liberty Films.

Fifty. 2015. Dir. Biyi Bandele. English. Digital video. Nigeria. EbonyLife Films.

Fuji House of Commotion. 2001–2013. Dir. Amaka Igwe. English, Pidgin, and Yoruba. Television broadcast and digital video. Nigeria. Amaka Igwe Studios/Crystal Gold.

Games Men Play 1 and 2. 2006. Dir. Lancelot Oduwa Imasuen. English. VCD. Nigeria. Remmy Jes.

Games Women Play 1 and 2. 2005. Dir. Lancelot Oduwa Imasuen. English. VCD. Nigeria. Remmy Jes.

The Gods Must Be Crazy. 1980. Dir. Jamie Uys. English and Khoisan. South Africa. Celluloid. Mimosa Films.

Hot Cash. Series. ca. 1984–1988. Dir. Innocent Ohiri. English and Pidgin. Television broadcast and digital video. Nigeria. Nigerian Television Authority.

Igodo: The Land of the Living Dead. 1999. Dir. Andy Amenechi and Don Pedro Obaseki. English. VHS. OJ Productions.

Ikuku/Hurricane 1 and 2. 1995, 1996. Dir. Nkem Owoh and Zeb Ejiro. Igbo. VHS. Nigeria. Nonks/Andy Best.

Issakaba 1–4. 2000. Dir. Lancelot Oduwa Imasuen. English and Pidgin. VHS. Nigeria. Kas-Vid.

King Jaja of Opobo. 1999. Dir. Harry Agina. English. VCD. Nigeria. Sanctus Okereke/ Stonecold Pictures.

Lionheart. 2018. Dir. Genevieve Nnaji. English and Igbo. Digital video. Nigeria. Entertainment Network.

Living in Bondage 1. 1992. Dir. Chris Obi-Rapu ("Vic Mordi"). Igbo. VHS. Nigeria. NEK Video Links.

Living in Bondage 2. 1993. Dir. Chika Onukwafor ("Christian Onu"). Igbo. VHS. Nigeria. NEK Video Links.

The Master 1 and 2. 2004. Dir. Andy Amenechi. English and Pidgin. VCD. Nigeria. Kas-Vid.

Mind-Bending 1–4. Miniseries. 1990. Created by Lola Fani-Kayode. English. Television broadcast. Nigeria. Cinekraft.

Mirror in the Sun. Series. 1984–1986. Dir. John Ndanusa. Created by Lola Fani-Kayode. English. Television broadcast. Nigeria. Cinekraft.

My Father's Burden. 1960. Dir. Segun Olusola. English. Television broadcast. Western Nigeria Television.

New Masquerade. Series. 1983–ca. 2001. Dir. Charles Ugwu. Created by James Iroha. English and Pidgin. Television broadcast. Nigerian Television Authority.

The New Village Headmaster. Series. 1974–1990. Dir. Dejumo Lewis. Created by Segun Olusola. English. Television broadcast and VHS. Nigeria. Nigerian Television Authority.

Old School. 2002. Dir. Gabriel Moses. English. VCD. Nigeria. Amaco Investments.

Osuofia in London 1 and 2. 2003, 2004. Dir. Kingsley Ogoro. English and Pidgin. VCD. Nigeria. Kingsley Ogoro Productions.

Phone Swap. 2012. Dir. Kunle Afolayan. English, Pidgin, Yoruba, and Igbo. Digital video. Nigeria. Golden Effects.

Red Machet 1 and 2. 2000. Dir. Zeb Ejiro. English. VCD. Nigeria. Hycromax Investments.

Reloaded. 2009. Dir. Lancelot Oduwa Imasuen and Ikechukwu Onyeka. English. VCD. Nigeria. Royal Arts Academy.

Ripples. Series. 1988–1993. Dir. Zeb Ejiro. English. Television broadcast. Nigeria. Zeb Ejiro/Nigerian Television Authority.

Sango. 1997. Dir. Obafemi Lasode. Yoruba. VHS. Nigeria. Afrika'n Vogue/Even-Ezra Studios.

Saving Africa's Witch Children. 2008. Dir. Mags Gavin and Joost van der Valk. English. Digital video. United Kingdom. BBC 4.

Self-Government for Western Nigeria. 1958. Dir. Cedric Williams. English. Celluloid. Nigeria. Western Nigeria Film Unit.

633 Squadron. 1964. Dir. Walter Grauman. English. Celluloid. United Kingdom. Mirisch Films.

Tales by Moonlight. Series. 1984–present. Created by Victoria Ezeokoli. English, Pidgin, Edo, Yoruba, etc. Television broadcast. Nigeria. Nigerian Television Authority.

Things Fall Apart 1–13. Miniseries. 1986. Dir. David Orere. English and Igbo. Television broadcast and VCD. Nigeria. Nigerian Television Authority.

The Village Headmaster. Series. 1968–1974. Dir. Sanya Dosunmu. Created by Segun Olusola. English. Television broadcast. Nigeria. Nigerian Television Authority.

Violated 1 and 2. 1996. Dir. Amaka Igwe. English and Pidgin. VHS. Nigeria. Making Movies/Crystal Gold.

The Wedding Party. 2016. Dir. Kemi Adetiba. English, Yoruba, and Igbo. Digital video. Nigeria. EbonyLife Films.

The White Man's Grave. 1921. Dir. Norman Greville and Vincent Greville. English. Celluloid. United Kingdom. Greville Brothers Company.

Xala. 1975. Dir. Ousmane Sembene. Wolof and French. Celluloid. Senegal. Films Domireew/Société Nationale Cinématographique.

Bibliography

Abu-Lughod, Lila. *Dramas of Nationhood: The Politics of Television in Egypt.* Chicago: University of Chicago Press, 2005.

Achebe, Chinua. *Arrow of God.* New York: Anchor, 1969. Reprint, New York, Penguin, 2016.

Achebe, Chinua. *Hopes and Impediments.* New York: Anchor, 1990.

Achebe, Chinua. *A Man of the People.* Oxford: Heinemann, 1966.

Achebe, Chinua. *No Longer at Ease.* London: Heinemann, 1960. Reprint, New York: Anchor, 1994.

Achebe, Chinua. *Things Fall Apart.* London: Heinemann, 1958. Reprint, New York: Doubleday, 1994.

Achebe, Chinua. *The Trouble with Nigeria.* Oxford: Heinemann, 1983.

Adejunmobi, Moradewun. "Charting Nollywood's Appeal Locally and Globally." In *Film in African Literature Today 28,* edited by Ernest N. Emenyonu, 106–21. London: James Currey, 2010.

Adejunmobi, Moradewun. "Neoliberal Rationalities in Old and New Nollywood." *African Studies Review* 58, no. 3 (2015): 31–53.

Aderinto, Saheed. *When Sex Threatened the State: Illicit Sexuality, Nationalism, and Politics in Colonial Nigeria, 1900–1958.* Urbana: University of Illinois Press, 2015.

Adesokan, Akin. "Nollywood and the Idea of the Nigerian Cinema." *Journal of African Cinema* 4, no. 1 (2012): 81–98.

Afonja, Simi. "Changing Modes of Production and the Sexual Division of Labor among the Yoruba." *Signs* 7, no. 2 (1981): 299–313.

Agamben, Giorgio. *State of Exception.* Translated by Kevin Attell. Chicago: University of Chicago Press, 2005.

Agbaje, Adigun, and Jinmi Adisa. "Political Education and Public Policy in Nigeria: The War against Indiscipline (WAI)." *Journal of Commonwealth and Comparative Politics* 26, no. 1 (1988): 22–37.

Agbiboa, Daniel E. "'God's Time Is the Best': The Fascination with Unknown Time in Urban Transport in Lagos." In *The Fascination with Unknown Time,* edited by Sibylle Baumbach, Lena Henningsen, and Klaus Oschema, 167–88. Cham, Switzerland: Palgrave Macmillan, 2017.

Akudinobi, Jude. "Nollywood: Prisms and Paradigms." *Cinema Journal* 54, no. 2 (2015): 133–40.

Allen, Robert C. *Speaking of Soap Operas*. Chapel Hill: University of North Carolina Press, 1985.

Altman, Rick. "Sound Space." In *Sound Theory, Sound Practice*, edited by Rick Altman, 46–64. London: Routledge, 1992.

Apter, Andrew. *The Pan-African Nation: Oil and the Spectacle of Culture in Nigeria*. Chicago: University of Chicago Press, 2005.

Arms, George. "Diary from Nigeria: The Second Year." *National Association of Educational Broadcasters (NAEB) Journal* 22, no. 1 (1963): 9–14.

Arms, George. "Television Comes to Africa." *National Association of Educational Broadcasters (NAEB) Journal* 20, no. 2 (1961): 35–37.

Awolowo, Obafemi. *Awo: The Autobiography of Chief Obafemi Awolowo*. Cambridge: Cambridge University Press, 1960.

Ayakoroma, Barclays Foubiri. *Trends in Nollywood: A Study of Selected Genres*. Ibadan, Nigeria: Kraft, 2014.

Azuonye, Chukwuma. "*Igbo enwe eze*: Monarchical Power versus Democratic Values in Igbo Oral Narratives." In *Power, Marginality, and African Oral Literature*, edited by Graham Furniss and Liz Gunner, 65–82. Cambridge: Cambridge University Press, 1995.

Barber, Karin. *The Anthropology of Texts, Persons and Publics: Oral and Written Culture in Africa and Beyond*. Cambridge: Cambridge University Press, 2007.

Barber, Karin. "Popular Arts in Africa." *African Studies Review* 30, no. 3 (1987): 1–78.

Barber, Karin. "Popular Reactions to the Petro-Naira." *Journal of Modern African Studies* 20, no. 3 (1982): 431–50.

Barber, Karin. *Print Culture and the First Yoruba Novel: I. B. Thomas's "Life Story of Me, Ṣẹgilọla" and Other Texts*. Boston: Brill, 2012.

Barnhart, Joslyn. "Status Competition and Territorial Aggression: Evidence from the Scramble for Africa." *Security Studies* 25, no. 3 (2016): 385–419.

Bell, Duncan. *Reordering the World: Essays on Liberalism and Empire*. Princeton, NJ: Princeton University Press, 2016.

Beller, Jonathan. *The Cinematic Mode of Production: Attention Economy and the Society of the Spectacle*. Lebanon, NH: Dartmouth College Press, 2006.

Berlant, Lauren. *Cruel Optimism*. Durham, NC: Duke University Press, 2011.

Betiang, Liwhu. "Global Drums and Local Masquerades: Fifty Years of Television Broadcasting in Nigeria: 1959–2009." *SAGE Open* 3, no. 4 (2013): 10.

Bourdieu, Pierre. "Structures, *Habitus*, Practices." In *The Logic of Practice*, translated by Richard Nice, 52–65. Stanford, CA: Stanford University Press, 1990.

Branigan, Edward. *Point of View in the Cinema: A Theory of Narration and Subjectivity in Classical Film*. New York: Mouton, 1984.

Brennan, Timothy. "The Economic Image-Function of the Periphery." In *Postcolonial Studies and Beyond*, edited by Ania Loomba, Suvir Kaul, Matti Bunzl, Antoinette Burton, and Jed Esty, 101–22. Durham, NC: Duke University Press, 2005.

"Brian Ross Investigates: Mugus and Masters." *20/20*, produced by David Sloan, Rhonda Schwartz, Joseph Rhee, and Len Tepper. ABC, 2007.

Brooks, Peter. *The Melodramatic Imagination: Balzac, Henry James, Melodrama, and the Mode of Excess.* New York: Columbia University Press, 1985.

Brown, Matthew H. "At the Threshold of New Political Communities: Some Notes on the History of Nollywood's Epic Genre." *Global South* 7, no. 1 (2013): 55–78.

Brown, Matthew H., ed. *A Customized Version of Harold Scheub's "The African Storyteller."* Dubuque, IA: Kendall-Hunt, 2017.

Brown, Matthew H. "The Enchanted History of Nigerian State Television." In *State and Culture in Postcolonial Africa: Enchantings,* edited by Tejumola Olaniyan, 94–110. Bloomington: Indiana University Press, 2017.

Brown, Matthew H. "Genre as Ideological Impulse: Reflections on Big Data and African Cultural Production." *Cambridge Journal of Postcolonial Literary Inquiry* 4, no. 3 (2017): 1–15.

Brown, Matthew H. "The Long Nollywood Century: Colonial Cinema, Nationalist Literature, State Television, and Video Film." PhD diss., University of Wisconsin–Madison, 2014.

Brown, Matthew H. "'Osuofia Don Enter Discourse': Global Nollywood and African Identity Politics." *IJOTA* 2, no. 4 (2008): 57–72.

Brown, Wendy. *Undoing the Demos: Neoliberalism's Stealth Revolution.* Boston: MIT Press, 2015.

Bryce, Jane. "Signs of Femininity, Symptoms of Malaise: Contextualizing Figurations of 'Woman' in Nollywood." *Research in African Literatures* 43, no. 4 (2012): 71–87.

Bud, Alexander. "The End of Nollywood's Guilded Age? Marketers, the State, and the Struggle for Distribution." *Critical African Studies* 6, no. 1 (2014): 91–121.

Burke, Timothy. *Lifebuoy Men, Lux Women: Commodification, Consumption, and Cleanliness in Modern Zimbabwe.* Durham, NC: Duke University Press, 1996.

Burns, James. *Cinema and Society in the British Empire, 1895-1940.* New York: Palgrave Macmillan, 2013.

Campbell, Joseph. *The Hero with a Thousand Faces.* New York: Pantheon, 1949.

Candotti, Marissa. "Cotton Growing and Textile Production in Northern Nigeria from Caliphate to Protectorate c. 1804-1914: A Preliminary Examination." Paper for the African Economic History Workshop, London School of Economics, May 2009.

Chen, Victor Tan. *Cut Loose: Jobless and Hopeless in an Unfair Economy.* Berkeley: University of California Press, 2015.

Cole, Teju. *Everyday Is for the Thief.* Abuja: Cassava Republic, 2007.

Comaroff, Jean, and John L. Comaroff. "Millennial Capitalism: First Thoughts on a Second Coming." *Public Culture* 12, no. 2 (2000): 291–343.

Comaroff, Jean, and John Comaroff, eds. *Modernity and Its Malcontents: Ritual and Power in Postcolonial Africa.* Chicago: University of Chicago Press, 1993.

Constantine, Stephen. *The Making of British Colonial Development Policy 1914-1940.* London: Frank Cass, 1984.

Cooper, Fredrick. *Africa in the World: Capitalism, Empire, Nation-State.* Cambridge, MA: Harvard University Press, 2014.

Cooper, Fredrick. *Africa since 1940: The Past of the Present.* New York: Cambridge University Press, 2002.

Cooper, Fredrick. "Possibility and Constraint: African Independence in Historical Perspective." *Journal of African History* 49, no. 2 (2008): 167–96.

Copjec, Joan. "The Orthopsychic Subject: Film Theory and the Reception of Lacan." *October* 49 (1989): 53–71.

Cramer, Michael. *Utopian Television: Rossellini, Watkins, and Godard beyond Cinema.* Minneapolis: University of Minnesota Press, 2017.

Daannaa, H. S. "The Acephalous Society and the Indirect Rule System in Africa: British Colonial Administrative Policy in Retrospect." *Journal of Legal Pluralism* 26, no. 34 (1994): 61–85.

Davis, Colin. "Ét at Présent: Hauntology, Spectres, and Phantoms." *French Studies* 59, no. 3 (2005): 373–79.

de Bruijn, Mirjam, Rijk van Dijk, and Jan-Bart Gewald. *Strength beyond Structure: Social and Historical Trajectories of Agency in Africa.* Leiden: Brill, 2007.

Derrida, Jacques. "Author's Preface." In *Psyche: Inventions of the Other.* Vol. 1, translated by Peggy Kamuf, xii–xiv. Stanford, CA: Stanford University Press, 2007.

Derrida, Jacques. *Specters of Marx: The State of the Debt, the Work of Mourning, and the New International.* Translated by Peggy Kamuf. New York: Routledge, 1994.

Derrida, Jacques. *Without Alibi.* Edited and translated by Peggy Kamuf. Stanford, CA: Stanford University Press, 2002.

Dews, Peter. "Power and Subjectivity in Foucault." *New Left Review* 144 (1984): 72–95.

Diala, Isidore. "Ritual and Mythological Recuperation in the Drama of Esiaba Irobi." *Research in African Literatures* 36, no. 4 (2005): 87–114.

Dissanayake, Wimal, ed. *Melodrama and Asian Cinema.* Cambridge: Cambridge University Press, 1993.

Egbon, Mike. "Western Nigeria Television Service: Oldest in Tropical Africa." *Journalism Quarterly* 60, no. 2 (1983): 329–34.

Ellis, Stephen. *This Present Darkness: A History of Nigerian Organized Crime.* New York: Oxford University Press, 2016.

Ekwuazi, Hyginus. *Film in Nigeria.* Ibadan, Nigeria: Moonlight Publishers, 1987.

Ekwuazi, Hyginus, Onookome Okome, Marcellinus Okhakhu, and Elo Ibagere, eds. *Studies in Film and Television.* Jos, Nigeria: Nigerian Film Corporation, 1993.

Faleti, Adebayo. "The Origin and Impact of Yoruba Drama on the Development of the Film Industry in Contemporary Nigeria." Lecture delivered to Bishop Ajayi Crowther University, Oyo, March 27, 2009.

Fanon, Frantz. *The Wretched of the Earth.* Translated by Richard Philcox. New York: Grove, 2004.

Fapohunda, Eleanor R. "The Nuclear Household Model in Nigerian Public and Private Sector Policy: Colonial Legacy and Socio-political Implications." *Development and Change* 18 (1987): 281–94.

Ferguson, James. *Global Shadows: Africa in the Neoliberal World Order.* Durham, NC: Duke University Press, 2006.

Fischer, Sibylle. *Modernity Disavowed: Haiti and the Cultures of Slavery in the Age of Revolution.* Durham, NC: Duke University Press, 2004.

Foucault, Michel. *The Government of Self and Others: Lectures at the Collège de France, 1982–1983.* Edited by Frédéric Gros. Translated by Graham Burchell. New York: Picador, 2010.

Foucault, Michel. *The History of Sexuality: An Introduction*. Translated by Robert Hurley. New York: Pantheon, 1978.

Foucault, Michel. *The Order of Things: An Archaeology of the Human Sciences*. London: Tavistock, 1970. Reprint, New York: Taylor and Francis, 2005.

Frankema, Ewout, Jeffrey Williamson, and Pieter Woltjer. "An Economic Rationale for the African Scramble: The Commercial Transition and the Commodity Price Boom of 1845–1885." National Bureau of Economic Research Working Paper 21213, 2015.

Fry, Roger. "Architecture at Wembley." *The Nation and the Athenaeum*, May 24, 1924.

Gächter, August. "Finance Capital and Peasants in Colonial West Africa: A Comment on Cowen and Shenton." *Journal of Peasant Studies* 20, no. 4 (1993): 669–80.

Garritano, Carmela. *African Video Movies and Global Desires: A Ghanaian History*. Athens: Ohio University Press, 2013.

Garritano, Carmela. "Introduction: Nollywood—An Archive of African Worldliness." *Black Camera* 5, no. 2 (2014): 44–52.

Gates, Henry Louis, Jr. *The Signifying Monkey: A Theory of African-American Literary Criticism*. Oxford: Oxford University Press, 1988.

Geppert, Alexander C. T. *Fleeting Cities: Imperial Expositions in Fin-de-Siècle Europe*. London: Palgrave Macmillan, 2010.

Geraghty, Christine, and Elke Weissmann. "Women, Soap Opera, and New Generations of Feminists." *Critical Studies in Television* 11, no. 3 (2016): 365–84.

Geschiere, Peter. *The Modernity of Witchcraft: Politics and the Occult in Postcolonial Africa*. Charlottesville: University Press of Virginia, 1997.

Gibbs, James. "'Yapping' and 'Pushing': Notes on Wole Soyinka's 'Broke Time Bar' Radio Series of the Early Sixties." *Africa Today* 33, no. 1 (1986): 19–26.

Gledhill, Christine. "The Melodramatic Field: An Investigation." In *Home Is Where the Heart Is: Studies in Melodrama and the Woman's Film*, edited by Christine Gledhill, 5–39. London: British Film Institute, 1987.

Gomba, Obari. "*Things Fall Apart*: Chinua Achebe's Whetstone." *Tydskrif vir Letterkunde* 50, no. 2 (2013): 152–57.

Gott, Benjamin S. *The Film in National Life*. London: G. Allen and Unwin, 1932.

Green-Simms, Lindsey. "Hustlers, Home-Wreckers and Homoeroticism: Nollywood's *Beautiful Faces*." *Journal of African Cinemas* 4, no. 1 (2012): 59–79.

Green-Simms, Lindsey. *Postcolonial Automobility: Car Culture in West Africa*. Minneapolis: University of Minnesota Press, 2017.

Grieveson, Lee. "The Cinema and the (Common) Wealth of Nations." In *Empire and Film*, edited by Lee Grieveson and Colin MacCabe, 73–113. London: British Film Institute, 2011.

Grieveson, Lee. *Cinema and the Wealth of Nations: Media, Capital, and the Liberal World System*. Berkeley: University of California Press, 2018.

Grieveson, Lee, and Colin MacCabe, eds. *Empire and Film*. London: British Film Institute, 2011.

Griffin, Emma. *Bread Winner: An Intimate History of the Victorian Economy*. New Haven, CT: Yale University Press, 2020.

Haggard, H. Rider. *She: A History of Adventure*. London: Longmans, 1887.

Hall, Stuart. "Gramsci's Relevance for the Study of Race and Ethnicity." *Journal of Communication Inquiry* 10, no. 2 (1986): 5–27.

Harneit-Sievers, Axel. "Igbo 'Traditional Rulers': Chieftaincy and the State in Southeastern Nigeria." *Africa Spectrum* 33, no. 1 (1998): 7–79.

Harnischfeger, Johannes. "The Bakassi Boys: Fighting Crime in Nigeria." *Journal of Modern African Studies* 41, no. 1 (2003): 23–49.

Harrow, Kenneth W. *Trash: African Cinema from Below.* Bloomington: Indiana University Press, 2013.

Haynes, Jonathan. "Between the Informal Sector and Transnational Capitalism: Transformations of Nollywood." In *A Companion to African Cinema*, edited by Kenneth W. Harrow and Carmela Garritano, 244–68. Hoboken, NJ: Wiley, 2019.

Haynes, Jonathan. *Nigerian Video Films.* Athens: Ohio University Press, 2000.

Haynes, Jonathan. "Neoliberalism, Nollywood, and Lagos." In *Global Cinematic Cities: New Landscapes of Film and Media*, edited by Johan Andersson and Lawrence Webb, 59–75. New York: Columbia University Press, 2016.

Haynes, Jonathan. *Nollywood: The Creation of Nigerian Film Genres.* Chicago: University of Chicago Press, 2016.

Haynes, Jonathan. "Nollywood: What's in a Name?" *Film International* 5, no. 4 (2007): 106–8.

Haynes, Jonathan, and Onokome Okome. "Evolving Popular Media: Nigerian Video Films." *Research in African Literatures* 29, no. 3 (1998): 106–28.

Hodapp, James. "A Serious Television Trickster: Ken Saro-Wiwa's Political and Artistic Legacy in Basi and Company." *Journal of Postcolonial Writing* 54, no. 4 (2018): 504–14.

Hogendorn, J. "The Vent-for-Surplus Theory: A Reply." *Savanna* 6 no. 2 (1977): 196–99.

Hugo, Pieter. *Nollywood.* New York: Prestel, 2009.

Huxley, Julian. *Africa View.* Santa Barbara, CA: Greenwood, 1968.

Ibagere, Elo. *Social Development, Television and Politics in Nigeria.* Ibadan, Nigeria: Kraft, 2009.

Ince, Onur Ulas. *Colonial Capitalism and the Dilemmas of Liberalism.* New York: Oxford University Press, 2018.

Ince, Onur Ulas. "Primitive Accumulation, New Enclosures, and Global Land Grabs: A Theoretical Intervention." *Rural Sociology* 79, no. 1 (2014): 104–31.

Isama, Antoinette. "The 20 Best Nollywood Movies of All Time." *okayafrica.* Accessed February 1, 2019. www.okayafrica.com/20-best-nollywood-movies-of-all-time-yungnollywood.

Jackson, Dave. "End of the Wicked (1999)." *Mondo Exploito.* Accessed February 10, 2020. https://mondoexploito.com/?p=2525.

Jarvie, Ian. *Hollywood's Overseas Campaign: The North Atlantic Movie Trade, 1920–1950.* Cambridge: Cambridge University Press, 1992.

Jedlowski, Alessandro. "From Nollywood to Nollyworld: Processes of Transnationalization in the Nigerian Video Film Industry." In *Global Nollywood: The Transnational Dimension of an African Video Film Industry*, edited by Mattias Krings and Onookome Okome, 25–45. Bloomington: Indiana University Press, 2013.

Kendhammer, Brandon. "The Sharia Controversy in Northern Nigeria and the Politics of Islamic Law in New and Uncertain Democracies." *Comparative Politics* 45, no. 3 (2013): 291–311.

King-Aribisala, Karin. "*Basi and Company* and WAI." In *Everything about "Basi and Company": The Most Hilarious Comedy on TV!*, edited by Ken Saro-Wiwa, 8. Port Harcourt, Nigeria: Saros International, 1987.

Kohn, Margaret. "Empire's Law: Alexis de Tocqueville on Colonialism and the State of Exception." *Canadian Journal of Political Science/Revue Canadienne de Science Politique* 41, no. 2 (2008): 255–78.

Kortenaar, Neil Ten. "Becoming African and the Death of Ikemefuna." *University of Toronto Quarterly* 73, no. 2 (2004): 773–94.

Krings, Mattias, and Onookome Okome, eds. *Global Nollywood: The Transnational Dimension of an African Video Film Industry.* Bloomington: Indiana University Press, 2013.

Lacan, Jacques. "The Mirror Stage as Formative of the *I* Function as Revealed in Psychoanalytic Experience." In *Écrits: The First Complete Edition in English,* translated by Bruce Fink, 75–81. New York: Norton, 2002.

Larkin, Brian. "Hausa Dramas and the Rise of Video Culture in Nigeria." In *Nigerian Video Films,* edited by Jonathan Haynes, 209–41. Athens: Ohio University Press, 2000.

Larkin, Brian. *Signal and Noise: Media, Infrastructure, and Urban Culture in Nigeria.* Durham, NC: Duke University Press, 2008.

Larkin, Brian. "State Aesthetics: Nollywood, 419, and the Forms of Corruption." Lecture, University of Wisconsin–Madison, Madison, WI, September 25, 2013.

Lawrence, T. E. *Seven Pillars of Wisdom.* Whitefish, MT: Kessinger, 2003.

Leavold, Andrew. "End of the Wicked (Nigerian Godsploitation, 1999)." *Andrew Leavold: Writer, Filmmaker, Film Historian.* Accessed February 10, 2020. http:// andrewleavold.blogspot.com/2017/01/end-of-wicked-nigerian-godsploitation .html.

Lemke, Thomas. "'The Birth of Bio-politics': Michel Foucault's Lecture at the Collège de France on Neo-liberal Governmentality." *Economy and Society* 30, no. 2 (2001): 190–207.

Lenin, Vladimir Il'ich. *Imperialism, the Highest Stage of Capitalism: A Popular Outline.* New York: International, 1933.

Levine, Elana. "Melodrama and Soap Opera." *Feminist Media Histories* 4, no. 2 (2018): 117–22.

Lindsay, Lisa. *Working with Gender: Wage Labor and Social Change in Southwestern Nigeria.* Portsmouth, NH: Heinemann, 2003.

Lizardo, Radhamés A., and André V. Mollick. "Oil Price Fluctuations and U.S. Dollar Exchange Rates." *Energy Economics* 32 (2010): 399–408.

Losurdo, Domenico. *Liberalism: A Counter History.* Translated by Gregory Elliott. New York: Verso, 2011.

Lovesey, Oliver. "Making Use of the Past in *Things Fall Apart.*" In *Bloom's Modern Critical Interpretations: Chinua Achebe's "Things Fall Apart,"* edited by Harold Bloom, 115–39. Philadelphia: Chelsea House, 2002.

Lugard, F. D. *The Dual Mandate in British Tropical Africa.* Edinburgh: Blackwood, 1922.

Lyall, Alfred C. "Life and Speeches of Sir Henry Maine." *Quarterly Review* 176 (1893): 287–316.

Mackay, Ian K. *Broadcasting in Nigeria.* Ibadan, Nigeria: Ibadan University Press, 1964.

MacKenzie, John M. *Propaganda and Empire: The Manipulation of British Public Opinion, 1880–1960.* Manchester: Manchester University Press, 1984.

Magnus, Kathy Dow. "The Unaccountable Subject: Judith Butler and the Social Conditions of Intersubjective Agency." *Hypatia* 21, no. 2 (2006): 81–103.

Maine, Henry Sumner. *Lectures on the Early History of Institutions.* 7th ed. London: John
Murray, 1914.

Maine, Henry Sumner. *Village Communities in the East and West, with Other Lectures,
Addresses and Essays.* 3rd ed. London: John Murray, 1876.

Makhubu, Nomusa. "Interpreting the Fantastic: Video-Film as Intervention." *Journal
of African Cultural Studies* 38, no. 3 (2016): 299–312.

Makhubu, Nomusa. "Politics of the Strange: Revisiting Pieter Hugo's Nollywood."
African Arts 46, no. 1 (2013): 50–61.

Mamdani, Mahmood. *Citizen and Subject: Contemporary Africa and the Legacy of Late
Colonialism.* Princeton, NJ: Princeton University Press, 1996.

Mamdani, Mahmood. *Define and Rule: Native as Political Identity.* Cambridge, MA:
Harvard University Press, 2012.

Mann, Gregory. *From Empires to NGOs in the West African Sahel: The Road to Nongovernmentality.* Cambridge: Cambridge University Press, 2015.

Mantena, Karuna. *Alibis of Empire: Henry Maine and the Ends of Liberal Imperialism.*
Princeton, NJ: Princeton University Press, 2010.

Marshall, Ruth. *Political Spiritualities: The Pentecostal Revolution in Nigeria.* Chicago:
University of Chicago Press, 2009.

Marty, Martin E. "Soap Gets in Your Eyes." *Christian Century* 109, no. 32 (1992): 1015.

Marx, Karl. *The Eighteenth Brumaire of Louis Bonaparte.* Marxists.org. Accessed September 19, 2018. www.marxists.org/archive/marx/works/1852/18th-brumaire/ch01
.htm.

Mazzarella, William. "'Reality Must Improve': The Perversity of Expertise and the
Belatedness of Indian Development Television." *Global Media and Communication* 8,
no. 3 (2012): 215–41.

Mbembe, Achille. "Necropolitics." Translated by Libby Meintjes. *Public Culture* 15, no. 1
(2015): 11–40.

Mbembe, Achille. *On the Postcolony.* Berkeley: University of California Press, 2001.

McCain, Carmen. "Video Exposé: Metafiction and Message in Nigerian Films." *Journal
of African Cinemas* 4, no. 1 (2012): 26–57.

McCall, John C. "The Capital Gap: Nollywood and the Limits of Informal Trade."
Journal of African Cinemas 4, no. 2 (2012): 9–23.

McCall, John C. "Juju and Justice at the Movies: Vigilantes in Nigerian Popular Videos." *African Studies Review* 47, no. 3 (2004): 51–67.

McClintock, Anne. *Imperial Leather: Race, Gender, and Sexuality in the Colonial Contest.*
New York: Routledge, 1995.

McLuhan, Marshall. *Understanding Media: The Expressions of Man.* New York: Signet, 1966.

Mehta, Uday Singh. *Liberalism and Empire: A Study in Nineteenth-Century British Liberal
Thought.* Chicago: University of Chicago Press, 1999.

Melchior-Bonnet, Sabine. *The Mirror: A History.* Translated by Katharine H. Jewett.
New York: Routledge, 2002.

Mengara, Daniel M. "Colonial Intrusion and Stages of Colonialism in Chinua Achebe's
Things Fall Apart." *African Studies Review* 62, no. 4 (2019): 31–56.

Metz, Christian. *The Imaginary Signifier: Psychoanalysis and the Cinema.* Bloomington: Indiana University Press, 1982.

Meyer, Birgit. "Mediation and Immediacy: Sensational Forms, Semiotic Ideologies and the Question of the Medium." *Social Anthropology* 19, no. 1 (2011): 23–39.

Meyer, Birgit. "'Praise the Lord': Popular Cinema and Pentecostalite Style in Ghana's New Public Sphere." *American Ethnologist* 31, no. 1 (2004): 92–110.

Meyer, Birgit. *Sensational Movies: Video, Vision, and Christianity in Ghana.* Berkeley: University of California Press, 2015.

Miller, Jade. *Nollywood Central.* London: British Film Institute, 2016.

Miller, Jonathan. *On Reflection.* London: National Gallery Publications, 1998.

Morton-Williams, P. *Cinema in Rural Nigeria: A Field Study of the Impact of Fundamental-Education Films on Rural Audiences in Nigeria.* Ibadan, Nigeria: West African Institute of Social and Economic Research, 1956.

Mulvey, Laura. "Visual Pleasure and Narrative Cinema." *Screen* 16, no. 3 (1975): 6–18.

Muthu, Sankar, ed. *Empire and Modern Political Thought.* Cambridge: Cambridge University Press, 2012.

Newman, Kim. "Film Review: End of the Wicked." *Kim Newman Blog.* Accessed February 10, 2020. https://johnnyalucard.com/2017/04/09/film-review-end-of-the-wicked.

Nixon, Rob. *Slow Violence and the Environmentalism of the Poor.* Cambridge, MA: Harvard University Press, 2013.

"Nollywood Rivals Bollywood in Film/Video Production." UNESCO. Last modified April 5, 2009. www.unesco.org/new/en/media-services/single-view/news/nollywood_rivals_bollywood_in_filmvideo_production.

Novia, Charles. *Nollywood till November: Memoirs of a Nollywood Insider.* Bloomington, IN: AuthorHouse, 2012.

Nwabughuogu, Anthony. "The Role of Propaganda in the Development of Indirect Rule in Nigeria, 1890–1929." *International Journal of African Historical Studies* 14, no. 1 (1981): 65–92.

Obaseki, Don Pedro. "Nigerian Video as the 'Child of Television.'" In *Nollywood: The Video Phenomenon in Nigeria,* edited by Pierre Barrot, translated by Lynn Taylow, 72–76. Bloomington: Indiana University Press, 2008.

Ochonu, Moses E. *Colonialism by Proxy: Hausa Imperial Agents and Middle Belt Consciousness in Nigeria.* Bloomington: Indiana University Press, 2014.

Odukomaya, Segun. *Television and Film Drama Production and Presentation in Nigeria, 1900–2002.* Abeokuta, Nigeria: Link, 2005.

Ogunleye, Foluke, ed. *Africa through the Eye of the Video Camera.* Swaziland: Academic, 2008.

Ogunleye, Foluke, ed. *African Video Film Today.* Swaziland: Academic, 2003.

Okome, Onookome. "Reversing the Filmic Gaze: Comedy and the Critique of the Postcolony in *Osuofia in London.*" In *Global Nollywood: The Transnational Dimension of an African Video Film Industry,* edited by Mattias Krings and Onookome Okome, 139–57. Bloomington: Indiana University Press, 2013.

Okome, Onookome. "West African Cinema: Africa at the Movies." *Postcolonial Text* 3, no. 2 (2007): 1–17.

Okoye, Chukwuma. "Looking at Ourselves in Our Mirror: Agency, Counter-Discourse, and the Nigerian Video Film." *Film International* 5, no. 4 (2007): 20–29.

Olaniyan, Tejumola. "African Cultural Studies: Of Travels, Accents, and Epistemologies." In *Rethinking African Cultural Production*, edited by Frieda Ekotto and Kenneth W. Harrow, 94–108. Bloomington: Indiana University Press, 2015.

Olaniyan, Tejumola. "African Urban Garrison Architecture: Property, Armed Robbery, Para-capitalism." In *State and Culture in Postcolonial Africa: Enchantings*, edited by Tejumola Olaniyan, 291–308. Bloomington: Indiana University Press, 2017.

Olaniyan, Tejumola. *Arrest the Music: Fela and His Rebel Art and Politics*. Bloomington: Indiana University Press, 2004.

Olu Maintain. "Yahoozee." YouTube video, Reloaded Records, 2007.

Olubomehin, Oladipo O. "Cinema Business in Lagos, Nigeria since 1903." *Historical Research Letter* 3 (2012): 1–10.

Olukoju, Ayodeji. "The Travails of Migrant and Wage Labour in the Lagos Metropolitan Area in the Inter-war Years." *Labour History Review* 61, no. 1 (1996): 49–70.

Olupona, Jacob K. *African Religions: A Very Short Introduction*. Oxford: Oxford University Press, 2014.

Olusola, Segun. *Tele-scape: Some Notes on 20 Years of Television in Nigeria*. Lagos: Ariya Productions, 1979.

Olusola, Segun. "The Video Shock." *Intermedia* 11, no. 4/5 (1983): 64.

Olusola, Segun. *The Village Headmaster*. Lagos: Ariya Productions, 1977.

Onabanjo, Olufemi, and Ritchard M'Bayo, eds. *Emergence, Growth and Challenges of Films and Home Videos in Nigeria*. Bowie, MD: African Renaissance Books, 2009.

Opone, P. O. "Traditional Socio-political Organization of the Enuani Igbo of South Central Nigeria." *Studies of Tribes and Tribals* 10, no. 1 (2012): 57–64.

Osaghae, Eghosa E. *Crippled Giant: Nigeria since Independence*. London: Hurst, 1998.

Oudart, Jean-Pierre. "Cinema and Suture." In *Cahiers du Cinema: The Politics of Representation*, edited by Nick Browne, 45–57. Cambridge, MA: Harvard University Press, 1990.

Pasolini, Pier Paolo. "The Cinema of Poetry." In *Movies and Methods*. Vol. 1, edited by Bill Nichols, 542–58. Berkeley: University of California Press, 1976.

Pereira, Charmaine. "National Council of Women's Societies and the State, 1985–1993: The Use of Discourses of Womanhood." In *Identity Transformation and Identity Politics under Structural Adjustment in Nigeria*, edited by Attahiru Jega, 109–33. Uppsala: Nordiska Afrikainstitutet, 2000.

Piot, Charles. "Border Practices." In *Hard Work, Hard Times: Global Volatility and African Subjectivities*, edited by Anne-Maria Makhulu, Beth A. Buggenhagen, and Stephen Jackson, 150–64. Berkeley: University of California Press, 2010.

Potter, Simon J. *Broadcasting Empire: The BBC and the British World, 1922–1970*. Oxford: Oxford University Press, 2012.

Probst, Peter. *Osogbo and the Art of Heritage: Monuments, Deities, and Money*. Bloomington: Indiana University Press, 2011.

Punter, David, and Glennis Byron, eds. *The Gothic*. Oxford: Blackwell, 2004.

Quayson, Ato. *Oxford Street, Accra*. Durham, NC: Duke University Press, 2014.

Rice, Tom. "British Instructional Films." In *Colonial Film: Moving Images of the British Empire*, edited by Colin MacCabe and Lee Grieveson. 2010. Arts and Humanities Research Council. Last modified November 2009. www.colonialfilm.org.uk /production-company/british-instructional-films.

Rice, Tom. "Exhibiting Africa: British Instructional Films and the Empire Series (1925–8)." In *Empire and Film*, edited by Lee Grieveson and Colin MacCabe, 115–33. London: British Film Institute, 2011.

Rice, Tom. "Self Government for Western Nigeria: Analysis." In *Colonial Film: Moving Images of the British Empire*. Last modified March 2017. www.colonialfilm.org.uk /node/1819.

Rivero, Yeidy M. *Broadcasting Modernity: Cuban Commercial Television, 1950–1960*. Durham, NC: Duke University Press, 2015.

Roberts, Siân Silyn. *Gothic Subjects: The Transformation of Individualism in American Fiction, 1790–1861*. Philadelphia: University of Pennsylvania Press, 2014.

Rodney, Walter. *How Europe Underdeveloped Africa*. London: Bogle-L'Ouverture, 1973.

Rosen, Philip, ed. *Narrative, Apparatus, Ideology: A Film Theory Reader*. New York: Columbia University Press, 1986.

Ross, Steven J. *Working Class Hollywood: Silent Film and the Shaping of Class in America*. Princeton, NJ: Princeton University Press, 1998.

Ryan, Connor. "New Nollywood: A Sketch of Nollywood's Metropolitan New Style." *African Studies Review* 58, no. 3 (2015): 55–76.

Saro-Wiwa, Ken. "Author's Note." In *Basi and Company*. Oxford: African Books Collective, 2005.

Saro-Wiwa, Ken, ed. *Everything about "Basi and Company": The Most Hilarious Comedy on TV!* Port Harcourt, Nigeria: Saros International, 1987.

Saro-Wiwa, Ken. *Four Farcical Plays*. Port Harcourt, Nigeria: Saros International, 1989.

Schwartz, Louis Georges. "Typewriter: Free Indirect Discourse in Deleuze's Cinema." *SubStance* 34, no. 3 (2005): 107–35.

Scott, James C. *Seeing Like a State: How Certain Schemes to Improve the Human Condition Have Failed*. New Haven, CT: Yale University Press, 1999.

Scott, Joan Wallach. *The Fantasy of Feminist History*. Durham, NC: Duke University Press, 2011.

Shaka, Femi Okiremuete. *Modernity and the African Cinema: A Study in Colonialist Discourse, Postcoloniality, and Modern African Identities*. Trenton, NJ: Africa World, 2004.

Shaka, Femi Okiremuette, and Ola Nnennaya Uchendu. "Gender Representation in Nollywood Video Film Culture." *Crab: Journal of Theatre and Media Arts* 7 (2012): 1–30.

Shipley, Jesse Weaver, Jean Comaroff, and Achille Mbembe. "Africa in Theory: A Conversation between Jean Comaroff and Achille Mbembe." *Anthropological Quarterly* 83, no. 3 (2010): 658–59.

Simonelli, David. "'[L]aughing nations of happy children who have never grown up': Race, the Concept of Commonwealth and the 1924–25 British Empire Exhibition." *Journal of Colonialism and Colonial History* 10, no. 1 (2009). doi:10.1353/cch.0.0044.

Smith, Adam. *Adam Smith: The Theory of Moral Sentiments*. Edited by Knud Haakonssen. Cambridge Texts in the History of Philosophy. Cambridge: Cambridge University Press, 2002. doi:10.1017/CBO9780511800153.

Smith, Andrew. "Nigerian Email Scams and the Charms of Capital." *Cultural Studies* 23, no. 1 (2009): 27–47.

Smith, Daniel Jordan. *AIDS Doesn't Show Its Face: Inequality, Morality, and Social Change in Nigeria*. Chicago: University of Chicago Press, 2014.

Smith, Daniel Jordan. "Managing Men, Marriage, and Modern Love: Women's Perspectives on Intimacy and Male Infidelity in Southeastern Nigeria." In *Love in Africa*, edited by Jennifer Cole and Lynn M. Thomas, 157–80. Chicago: University of Chicago Press, 2009.

Smyth, Rosaleen. "Grierson, the British Documentary Movement, and Colonial Cinema in British Colonial Africa." *Film History* 25, no. 4 (2013): 82–113.

"State of Emergency." UNESCO *Courier*. May 9, 1956.

Stephen, Daniel. *The Empire of Progress: West Africans, Indians, and Britons at the British Empire Exhibition, 1924–25*. New York: Palgrave Macmillan, 2013.

Sudarkasa, Niara. *Where Women Work: A Study of Yoruba Women in the Marketplace and in the Home*. Ann Arbor, MI: Museum of Anthropology, 1973.

Thomas, Lynn M. "Historicizing Agency." *Gender and History* 28, no. 2 (2016): 324–39.

Trumpbour, John. *Selling Hollywood to the World: U.S. and European Struggles for Mastery of the Global Film Industry, 1920–1950*. Cambridge: Cambridge University Press, 2002.

Uche, Luke Uka. *Mass Media, Peoples and Politics in Nigeria*. New Delhi: Concept, 1989.

Ugochukwu, Françoise. "*Things Fall Apart*—Achebe's Legacy, from Book to Screen." *Research in African Literatures* 45, no. 2 (2014): 168–83.

Ugor, Paul. *Nollywood: Popular Culture and Narratives of Youth Struggles in Nigeria*. Durham, NC: Carolina Academic Press, 2016.

Ukadike, Nwachukwu Frank. "Anglophone African Media." *Jump Cut* 36 (1991): 74–80.

Ukadike, Nwachukwu Frank. *Black African Cinema*. Berkeley: University of California Press, 1994.

Umeh, Charles C. "The Advent and Growth of Television Broadcasting in Nigeria: Its Political and Educational Overtones." *African Media Review* 3, no. 2 (1989): 54–66.

Umolu, Paul, and James Onosu. "Nollywood Films as Agents for National Development: A Critical Appraisal of *Igodo: Land of the Living Dead*." *Academic Scholarship Journal* 2, no. 2 (2010): 102–19.

"UNICEF Nigeria." UNICEF. Accessed September 19, 2018. www.unicef.org/wcaro /Countries_1320.html.

Uwah, Innocent Ebere. "*Things Fall Apart* on Screen: Re-thinking Closure in Achebe's Narrative." In *Chinua Achebe's Legacy: Illuminations from Africa*, edited by James Ogude, 106–17. Oxford: African Books Collective, 2015.

Vasudevan, Ravi. *The Melodramatic Public: Film Form and Spectatorship in Indian Cinema*. Raniket, India: Permanent Black, 2010.

Wachuku, Ukachi Nnenna, and Chisimdi Udoka Ihentuge. "The Nigerian Film Industry and Literary Adaptation: The Journey of *Things Fall Apart* from Page to Screen." *Creative Artist* 5, no. 1 (2010): 121–41.

Wallerstein, Immanuel. *The Modern World-System IV: Centrist Liberalism Triumphant, 1789–1914*. Berkeley: University of California Press, 2011.

Warwick Research Collective (WReC). *Combined and Uneven Development: Towards a New Theory of World-Literature*. Liverpool: Liverpool University Press, 2015.

Waterman, Christopher A. "'Our Tradition Is a Very Modern Tradition': Popular Music and the Construction of Pan-Yoruba Identity." *Ethnomusicology* 34, no. 3 (1990): 367–79.

Weber, Brenda R. *Makeover TV: Selfhood, Citizenship, and Celebrity*. Durham, NC: Duke University Press, 2009.

Wendl, Tobias. "Wicked Villagers and the Mysteries of Reproduction: An Exploration of Horror Movies from Ghana and Nigeria." *Postcolonial Text* 3, no. 2 (2007): 1–21.

Williams, Linda. "Mega-melodrama! Vertical and Horizontal Suspensions of the 'Classical.'" *Modern Drama* 55, no. 4 (2012): 523–43.

Williams, Raymond. *Modern Tragedy*. London: Chatto and Windus, 1966.

World Council of Churches. *All-Africa Seminar on the Christian Home and Family Life*. New York: World Council of Churches, 1963.

Youé, Christopher P. "Peasants, Planters and Cotton Capitalists: The 'Dual Economy' in Colonial Uganda." *Canadian Journal of African Studies* 12, no. 2 (1978): 163–84.

Zarzosa, Agustin. "Melodrama and the Modes of the World." *Discourse* 32, no. 2 (2010): 236–55.

Index

Page numbers in italics refer to figures and tables.

Mofe-Damijo, Richard, 131
Mohammed, Yusuf, 197
Molobe, Obigeli, 164
money: bride-price and, 161–63; cash, 157, 160, 161, 167–68; with families, marriage and, 161–63; IMF, 233; worth and, 230–31
money-magic cults: in Billionaires Club, 173, 187; in Living in Bondage, 157, 158–59; men and, 153
monogamy, 124–27, 129–30
morality: business ethics and, 99, 100, 165; of corruption, 261; in Games Women Play, 145–47; gothic mode and, 190; Hollywood and, 50–51; melodrama and, 189–90; of modernity, 28; with television censorship, 84; video films and, 22, 282n20
moral residue, 239, 282n25
Morant Bay rebellion (1865), 12–13
Mordi, Vic (Chris Obi-Rapu), 3, 271n1
Morton-Williams, Peter, 60–61, 91
Motion Picture Producers and Distributors of America, 49
Muhammed, Murtala, 212–13
Mukoro, Ted, 79, 84
MultiChoice, 265
Mulvey, Laura, 222
music, 276n22; drumrolls, 89–90, 102; Igbo people and, 198, 201; role of, 188. See also soundtracks
MUSON Center, 132
My Father's Burden (Soyinka), 84
My Headmaster (documentary film), 74–75

narrative perspectives: overlapping, 5–6; primary, 231; secondary, 233, 241
narrative voice, 6, 62, 123, 194–95
Nation, 41
nation, modernity and, 78
National Electoral Commission (NEC), 116
nationalism, anticolonial, 23, 186–87, 201–2
native authorities: indirect rule and, 13–14, 77; in Things Fall Apart, 192, 204. See also indigenous social system

nativism, 12, 13, 79, 87, 214
NBC (Nigerian Broadcasting Corporation), 75–76
NBS (Nigerian Broadcasting Service), 75, 275n11
NEC (National Electoral Commission), 116
necropolitics: defined, 208–9; Igodo: Land of the Living Dead and, 203–15
neoliberalism, 18, 108
Netflix, 264
Newell, Stephanie, 124
New Nigeria, 264, 265, 267
Newsweek (news magazine), 114
New Village Headmaster, The (television series), 79, 94; Adeolu in, 197; Ali in, 88–90, 93; drumrolls in, 89–90, 102; Eleyinmei in, 91–93; Esiri in, 197; "Heroes, Villains, and Others," 87–91; with state and local elites, 86–87
New York Times (newspaper), 239–40, 271n9
Nigeria, 42–43, 53–54, 71, 105, 208, 219; cinema in, 48–52, 74; Independence Day, 66–67, 69; in liberal world order, 11, 29, 63, 70, 86, 183, 269; New, 264, 265, 267; oil and, 16, 26; state power, 48, 226–27; US and cinema in, 48–52, 74
Nigerian Broadcasting Corporation (NBC), 75–76
Nigerian Broadcasting Service (NBS), 75, 275n11
Nigerian Cinema Show Gardens, 49
Nigerian National Archives, 49
Nigerian Television Authority (NTA): actors in repertoire, 282n14; Basi and Company, 28; Checkmate and, 99; as colonial propaganda machine, 82; content, 26, 116; expansion of, 94; Festival of Television Drama, 84; with paternalist mandate, 99; programming, 26, 70, 115–17; role of, 23–24; Things Fall Apart, 185–86, 197, 199–202, 218; viewers influencing, 84; The Village Headmaster, 115, 135
Nigerian Television Network (NTV), 73